# Managing a
# Programming Project

# Managing a Programming Project

## People and Processes

## Third Edition

PHILIP W. METZGER AND JOHN BODDIE

For book and bookstore information

**http://www.prenhall.com**

Prentice Hall PTR
Upper Saddle River, New Jersey 07458

**Library of Congress Cataloging-in-Publication Data**

Metzger, Philip

 Managing a programming project : people and processes / Philip
W. Metzger and John Boddie. — 3rd ed.

  p. cm.

 Rev. ed. of: Managing a programming project / Philip W. Metzger.
2nd ed. © 1981.

 Includes bibliographical references and index.

 ISBN 0–13–554239–1

 1. Electronic digital computers—Programming. 2. Computer
programming management. I. Metzger, Philip W., 1931–
II. Metzger, Philip W., 1931–  Managing a programming project.
III. Title.

QA76.6.B6178  1996

005.1′068—dc20        95–44040

                   CIP

Acquisitions editor: Paul Becker
Cover designer: Defranco Design Inc.
Cover design director: Jerry Votta
Manufacturing buyer: Alexis R. Heydt
Compositor/Production services: Pine Tree Composition, Inc.

© 1996 by Prentice Hall PTR
Prentice-Hall, Inc.
A Simon & Schuster Company
Upper Saddle River, New Jersey 07458

The publisher offers discounts on this book when ordered in
bulk quantities.

For more information contact:

 Corporate Sales Department
 Prentice Hall PTR
 One Lake Street
 Upper Saddle River, New Jersey 07458

 Phone: 800–382–3419
 Fax: 201–236–7141
 email: corpsales@prenhall.com

Printed in the United States of America
10 9 8 7 6 5 4 3 2 1


ISBN: 0-13-554239-1


Prentice Hall International (UK) Limited, *London*
Prentice Hall of Australia Pty. Limited, *Sydney*
Prentice Hall Canada, Inc., *Toronto*
Prentice Hall Hispanoamericana, S.A., *Mexico*
Prentice Hall of India Private Limited, *New Delhi*
Prentice Hall of Japan, Inc., *Tokyo*
Simon & Schuster Asia Pte. Ltd., *Singapore*
Editora Prentice Hall do Brasil, Ltda., *Rio de Janeiro*

*To Scott, Lori, Cindy, and Jeff*
*and*
*To Shirley, my Manager*

Phil Metzger


*To my children,*
*John, Katherine, and Andrew,*
*who are always able to bring a smile to their*
*mother's face, and to mine as well.*

John Boddie

# CONTENTS

# LIST OF FIGURES

# PREFACE TO
# THE THIRD EDITION

The underlying principles of good management have not changed since the first edition of *Managing a Programming Project* was printed. The practical presentation of those principles in the previous editions has helped a generation of managers. The same principles can be found here as well.

What I have done in this edition is to combine them in a different setting, much like a jeweler who designs a new ring using the stones from an older one. The new setting for the management principles reflects several underlying changes in the environment where software is built.

Computing power has become abundant. As a result, programmers spend their time differently than they used to. The amount of programming and design time that I spent in wrestling with the constraints of the first minicomputer I worked on was not spent again when my software was rewritten to run on a new and much more powerful machine. This abundant power has also given rise to tools that make programmers vastly more productive than they were in the past.

The starting point for today's systems is likely to be an older system, not a manual process. This affects the way customers think about requirements and it also affects the work needed to make sure the transition from the old system to the new one goes smoothly.

Integration is a much bigger part of the job than it used to be. A modern system can bring together programs that run on a personal computer, data that lives on a local area network, and industrial-strength number crunching that happens on a mainframe located half a continent away. All these things must work together to give the customer the result he wants and it's the manager's job to see that they do.

The combined effect of these changes (and others) is that the step-by-step approach that worked well in the past is being overtaken by an approach that has many development processes active at the same time. This newer approach is the basis for the management recipe presented in the third edition. So come on in and sit down. There are some new items on the menu, but our dedication to using only the finest ingredients is as strong as ever. Bon appetit!

# PREFACE

As a programmer I knew (as every programmer does) that I could manage as well as my managers did. Early on I got the chance to prove it. I was suddenly in charge of dozens of eager young programmers, most of them fresh out of school. I put them to work on many small, independent programs, none that we would these days call a "system." I shuffled papers, did appraisals, handed out raises, and thought I was managing. All went well until one day I was put in charge of a major software system being developed by IBM for the federal government. Suddenly I was "managing" dozens of people working on a single complex job, and guess what? I was in over my head. I found I knew nothing about developing a system and neither did the managers who worked above and below me.

I was forced, for the first time, to really *think* about the development of a system. Thinking led to some notes. The notes led to the teaching of a series of management classes at IBM begun earlier by a couple of practical eggheads, Joel Aron and Al Pietrasanta. The classes became popular and proved helpful to hundreds of programming managers. My class notes became an internal IBM programming management manual and the manual later became the first edition of this book.

In this book, I have tried to provide exactly the kind of guidance I needed but did not have when I first became a manager. Whatever your particular job in the software development process, I think you'll find these pages helpful. Although the text addresses you as if you are the manager of a programming project, it's intended for managers at all levels who have *anything* to do with programming. It will be helpful to lead technicians as well. These pages describe a practical, human approach to managing, without pretentious theory or confusing gobbledygook—and always with an eye on that most important resource: *people*. Good luck!

# ACKNOWLEDGMENTS

The first editions of this book owed a lot to two people mentioned in the Preface, Joel Aron and Al Pietrasanta. The ideas they taught way back then still run through this book, and I'll always be grateful for the help they gave me.

At Prentice-Hall, the late Karl Karlstrom guided me through the first two editions in his gentle way, and now Paul Becker, a patient and helpful editor if there ever was one, has guided this current edition from a couple of false starts (on my part) into a finished product. I appreciate Paul's help and guidance (and advances!), and I salute the many people, including production editors Patty Sawyer and Beth Sturla who carried out their jobs with excellence.

Most of all, my hat would be off to John Boddie (if I wore a hat) for being the best collaborator an author could wish for. Let's face it: I've been away from the programming mainstream for a while and bringing the book up to date was not something I could have done alone. John filled in the huge gaps in my knowledge and did so with smooth and quiet competence. If I were a programmer, I think I'd like John as my manager. Thanks, John, for a good partnership.

*Philip W. Metzger*

Good projects always seem to have some time for fun. The fun keeps you going and, in the end, it's what you remember best. I've had a lot of fun in this business and I blame it all on the people I've worked with. Sandy DiStefano, Marcos Tomas, Becky Wells, Betty Turner, Tim and Lynda Connolly, Dave Meunch, Mark Harper, Tony Brookfield, Kirsty Farquharson, Gary Andrew, Bill Bracken, Ian Jackson, Al Bongo, Larry Phillips, Doug Feiock, Mary Kwasnik, Paul Holenstein, Dianne Zukusky, Roger Poole and a supporting cast of hundreds have not only done first-class work, but they also supplied needed sanity breaks over the years. It's because of them that I can honestly say that I like my work, and it's because of them that I keep trying to improve.

My list of people who have made work enjoyable would be woefully incomplete without the name of Phil Metzger. There are people who make you feel enthusiastic about working with them from the first minute you talk to them. Phil is one of those people. Thanks, Phil.

I join with Phil in thanking Paul Becker for bringing us together on this project, and in thanking Patty Sawyer and Beth Sturla for their first-class work in turning our manuscript into the book you're now holding in your hands.

*John Boddie*

# PART I

# INTRODUCTION

I like to simplify life and not deal with too many things at once. With that in mind, I've set a single goal for this book: to describe a way of managing the production of a quality software system on time and within budget in a manner that makes the experience pleasurable for the people involved. I have ignored the societal, governmental, and corporate reasons for building a software system—those matters are covered in other books. In these pages we'll concentrate on getting the programming job done once a decision has been made that programs are needed.

I have tried to keep the information presented in this book at a level where it will be most useful to someone who is new to the responsibilities of management. However, if you've already had ten years' experience in managing programming projects, you shouldn't jump to the conclusion that there is nothing here for you.

Since the publication of the first edition of this book many moons ago (1973, actually) a lot has changed in the computer business. The computer on the corner of my desk is more powerful than the first one I programmed, and that one took up an entire floor of a building and required special air conditioning and a team of technicians to keep it running smoothly. It used to be that only the biggest organizations had more than one computer. Today's programmer may have two or more computers in her cubicle and another one at home.

Software has evolved along with the hardware. It has become powerful, sophisticated, complex. I can now write a useful program for my son's soccer league in a single evening by moving boxes around on my computer's display and connecting them with lines. At the company where I'm consulting, almost 20 percent of the programs we use have been "written" by other programs that took definitions of a report layout or entry screen and automatically produced executable code.

Managers, however, have not always kept pace with these changes. The availability of computer power on the desktop has given managers some powerful tools, but the skills required to use them well have been slower in arriving. After nearly a half-century of serious programming, managers still seek to master basic skills that are quite independent of technology.

Management techniques will always trail technology because it's easier to deal with *things* than with *people*. We can explore the moon but we can't fix welfare. I believe, however, that we often make managing more complicated than it ought to be. We can simplify the process. In fact, the more complex technology becomes, the greater the need to simplify management. The aims of this book are to describe a straightforward model for organizing and running a project and to suggest guidelines for selecting and dealing with the most important ingredient in any project, its people.

## MY GROUND RULES

This is not a book about corporate organization or politics or esoteric management theory. Neither is it a textbook on programming. The focus here is narrow and practical: how to successfully and happily manage the production of a software system. I'm addressing you, the reader, as if you were the manager of a medium-sized programming project involving about forty people—programmers, managers, and others. In Part IX we'll discuss larger and smaller projects. If your project is very small, don't assume this book doesn't relate to you. Everything here counts, no matter what the project size. What varies from one job to the next is not the tasks you need to do, but how much horsepower you need to do them.

I have not tried to catalog all the different ways to run a project. What you'll find here is one good recipe, not an entire cookbook. Like any decent recipe, my approach says do this and this and this and expect to end up with a great result. But you can also play with the ingredients and come up with something *you* consider even tastier!

The title "manager" means different things to different organizations. I use it to identify those people responsible for planning and directing work on some job, with direct responsibility for hiring and firing, adjusting salaries, and promotions. A first-level manager supervises the people who actually build the product; a second-level manager supervises first-level managers, and so on.

In this book the terms *program* and *software* are synonymous. *Operational programs* are those written to do the job for which your project exists, such as calculating payroll checks or directing space flights. *Support programs* are those used as aids in producing the operational programs.

## YOUR GROUND RULES

As you read the literature you'll find fuzzy or contradictory definitions of dozens of terms, such as software, module, integration, or system test. I'm not sure we'll ever settle on a clean, universally accepted set of definitions. But you don't have to accept smog on *your* project. Adopt a set of unambiguous definitions and stick with them. What I'm talking about is not trivial. It simply won't do for some members of your project to call something "system testing" while others call that same something "integration." Internal consistency will contribute immensely to a smooth-running, successful project. Here are some ground rules you should establish:

Define your project's *development cycle* and relate all schedules and work processes to that cycle. This book is built around such a cycle and the processes that run through it. When I mention, say, the *Programming Process,* you may be assured I always mean a clearly defined set of activities associated with that process and a clear differentiation between the Programming Process and other processes in the development cycle. Don't call something the "Acceptance Process" in one breath and the "Migration Process" in the next. It doesn't matter what terms you choose—just be consistent.

Define *activities,* such as levels of testing, in a consistent way. Until there is a universally accepted set of definitions, adopt those that make sense to you and stick with them. In this book, for instance, I define "system test" in a certain way. Some people confuse that term with "integration test." Too bad, but at least know what you mean on *your* project and be sure that everybody else does, too.

Define a *system of documents* clearly, consistently, and early. Then hang anyone who operates outside that system (you can tell I'm a forgiving soul). There will be enough paperwork on any project without the headache of random documents that you can't control and whose authority is suspect.

In summary, define the development cycle for your project, use it as the basis for your plans and your actions, believe in it, sell it to your people, and enforce it.

## YOUR CONTRACT

Huh? You don't have anything to do with contracts. This project is being done by the DP department because the shipping department needs it. You're managing programmers, you're not in the middle of all this sales-type stuff. And if you actually believe what you just read, you're in trouble. If you don't actually *have* a contract, you're going to be fighting a long, uphill battle. Half the horror stories about programming involve either bad contracts or no contract at all.

Very seriously, whether you are representing an independent consulting organization or the firm's Data Processing group, the fact that you are going to be managing a programming project means that you will be running a business. You will have suppliers, you will have one or more customers. You will have employees, you will have commitments. You will have financial goals, you will have measured results. Things will go right, things will go wrong. Your responsibility is to manage your business so that everyone—your "investors" (the executives who gave you the assignment), your customers (the people who will use your system for a long time to come), your employees (the good people who gave their nights and weekends to build the system), and you—will look at your operating results and feel a sense of satisfaction.

With this in mind, I'm going to treat you as if you are a project manager for Super Software, Inc. You have responsibility, you have authority, and you'd better start by reading the contract that sets the ground rules for your business.

A contract is an agreement between you and your customer that you will do a certain job within specific constraints for so much money. Don't operate on verbal agreements or casual memos, even if your customer happens to be your buddy down the hall and you both work for the same organization. Within your company you may call your contract a "letter of understanding" or a "Data Processing Service Request"—something that sounds friendlier than "contract." In any case, you need a formal written statement showing clearly what your customer wants and what you agree to provide. Operating without such an agreement is lunacy, as many well-meaning programming managers and irate customers have found out.

If your organization is small, and you have no formal way of dealing with contracts, you can write one yourself to cover these essentials:

1. *Scope of work.* What is the job to be done? If the job definition is too vague, maybe you need two contracts: one to define the job, and a second to write programs.

2. *Schedule and deliverables.* What specific items (programs, documents) are you to deliver to the customer? When? Where? In what form (source code, executable modules, drafts or clean documents)? How many copies?

3. *Key customer people.* Who approves changes? Who accepts the finished product?

4. *Reviews.* When and how shall the customer get reviews and reports of progress? What is required of the customer if he disapproves a report?

5. *Change management procedures.* What will be the mechanism for dealing with items you consider changes to the original scope of work?

6. *Testing constraints.* Who will do the testing? What involvement will the customer have? What systems will be used for testing? Who verifies that the testing covered all areas of concern?

7. *Acceptance criteria.* What are the specific quantitative criteria to be used in judging whether your finished product is acceptable?

8. *Additional constraints.* Are there items peculiar to your working environment? Are you to use customer personnel? If so, what control do you have

over them? Are there special data security problems? Is the customer to supply test data? If so, what kinds of data, in what form, when, and how clean?

**9.** *Price.* What is your price (or budget) for doing the job? Is it fixed or variable? If variable, under what circumstances?

Those are the highlights. We'll address all these items in more detail throughout the book.

## THE NATURE OF THE BEAST

Building a system is not easy, even when things go well. The job of managing a programming project isn't easy either, and projects can spin out of control, overwhelming the abilities of managers who have previously been successful. In the introduction to his classic book, *The Mythical Man-Month* (1975), Dr. Frederick Brooks writes about his desire to answer Thomas J. Watson, Jr.'s questions about why software is hard to build. I'd like to start this book by presenting three reasons why it is hard to manage.

### The System

The thing we're planning to build is a system, a structured combination of interacting parts satisfying a set of objectives. That starchy definition will make better sense if we cite a few examples and examine some characteristics of systems.

There are examples of systems everywhere: the solar system; a power distribution system; the human body; the digestive system; a corporation; a pencil sharpener; a painting; a computer system. They all satisfy the definition. Every system is a subset of another system. This book will frequently mention a software "system," but of course the software system is a subsystem of a data-processing system, which in turn may be a subsystem of a cellular telephone system, which is a subsystem of a telecommunications network system, and on and on it goes.

In order for the system you are trying to build to be useful, it needs to satisfy the needs of other systems. Understanding and defining these needs is not an exact science because there is never (well, almost never) an all-knowing and all-seeing source of information that can tell you what other systems need today and what they will need tomorrow. The problem of understanding and satisfying customer expectations is a recurring one, not only during your project, but throughout the useful life of the system.

### Interactions

By definition, a system contains parts that must interact with each other. In software systems, the parts may be operating systems, application programs, service programs, hardware, human operators, human users, and so on. Controlling the interactions among the parts becomes a major task as the system grows in size and complexity.

Figure I–1 illustrates how the number of potential interactions (I) within a system grows as the number of elements (E) in the system grows. The management energy required to control, minimize, and simplify the interactions within the system is significant. Interactions account for much of the difference between managing the development of a small program having a single function and managing the development of a complex system with many parts, such as an integrated financial management system. Later we'll discuss such ideas as modularity, interface definition, and project organization, which can help reduce the effects of interactions.

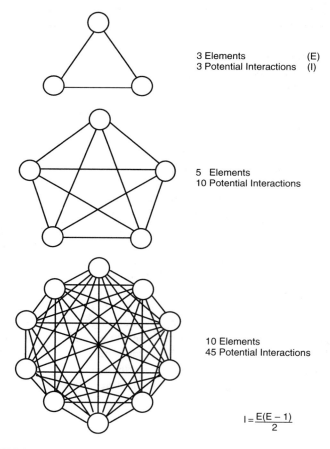

3 Elements                    (E)
3 Potential Interactions    (I)

5  Elements
10 Potential Interactions

10 Elements
45 Potential Interactions

$$I = \frac{E(E-1)}{2}$$

**FIGURE I–1**   Interactions   (Reprinted by permission from *Programming Project Management Guide*, International Business Machines Corporation, 1970.)

## Change

Any job that spans more than a couple of weeks is certain to change. As a manager, you should expect to encounter one or more of the following:

Requirements changes: The problem definition your analysis team labors over at the beginning of the job seldom stands still. The larger the job, the more likely there will be shifts in the requirements.

Design changes: One of the main items we'll look at in Chapter 4 is a baseline design, the foundation for your programming effort. As any homeowner knows, foundations shift and crack and need patching. A software system is no different. Your baseline design is a good start, but expect it to change.

Technological changes: Huge government-sponsored programming jobs (e.g., NASA systems, military command and control systems) are particularly vulnerable to technological change for two reasons. First, they span such long periods that new engineering and scientific developments (for example, in weaponry and data-processing equipment) are inevitable. Second, the nature of these projects is that they push the state-of-the-art and are often directly responsible for technological innovation.

Social changes: Many projects are the unwitting victims of changes in the way our society behaves. For example, programs to handle banking transactions from a terminal at a teller's window change when the bank puts Automatic Teller Machines in supermarkets.

People changes: People leave, die, get sick, change jobs. When you lose a key person from your own staff or when an important member of the customer's organization disappears, you have a potential problem.

Corrections: People make errors—always have and always will. The errors may be major or minor, technical or administrative, outrageous or subtle, but they are errors nonetheless, and must be fixed.

What's important about change is that it be managed, not eliminated. If there is a change in the Problem Specification, so be it, but you'll need to estimate the impact of the change on project costs and delivery dates. If the customer still wants the change, negotiate a contract modification, issue a formal change notice, and get on with the job.

Whenever change comes up, one thing is clear: you can't resolve questions such as the cost of a change if you and your customer don't even agree that what is being discussed *is* a change. You say: "This change, Mr. Customer, will cost ten extra man-months and a two-month slip in the delivery date." He says: "What change? This is only something I expected to get for my money in the first place. Quit gouging me." So you frantically thumb through your Problem Specification, assuming you have one at all, and each of you tries to find a paragraph, statement, clause, or comma to back up your position. This is a common exercise and it often ends in deadlock. That's why throughout this book I emphasize establishing accurate and meaningful baseline documents.

---

### Balancing Act

A project manager is sometimes in the position of trying to run his or her job while nestled somewhere within an organization that is seething with change. A manager in this situation can't hide and pretend the umbrella organization is not changing; neither can she allow those organizational changes to sabotage the current project. It's a tough role, but the project manager must, above all else, complete *this* project successfully. That requires guts. It requires skill in balancing the demands of the changing organization against the needs of the project. It's a matter of putting family (the project) first.

---

## THE LONG RUN

You will look upon your project as something new. Your team will be creating software that has never run on a computer before. However, as new as it seems to you, your project is very likely to be replacing all or part of an existing system, or it may be enhancing or restructuring software that was written earlier.

This is a good time to stop and think about Charles Bachman's observation, "There is no software development. There is only radical maintenance." In time, all good software gets changed. In fact, most of the money, time, and effort spent on software today is spent in "maintenance." You need to think of your management responsibility as stretching beyond the project that is in front of you right now—you need to aim at creating a product that will be understandable and flexible over its entire lifetime. Don't forget that the lifetime starts now. If your project is going to take over six months, you'll probably need to do some maintenance work on some of the first programs you created. If you didn't build your software to be maintainable, you'll find out that paybacks can really be painful.

The emphasis on documentation and standard techniques that you'll find in this book is going to help not only in making your current effort successful, but also in ensuring that the people who work on the system after you do will be able to be successful as well. There are very few things that will do more for your career than creating software that is easy to maintain. As the reputation of your system grows, so will yours.

## CURRENT TECHNIQUES

During the 1960s, '70s, and '80s a lot of progress was made toward bringing order and discipline to the young programming business. There's still plenty to be done, but the accomplishments are impressive, especially if you recall that even in the

1980s some people were coding assembly language and had only the most rudimentary of tools with which to work. Thanks to some truly gifted and hard-working people, programming has undergone a real revolution. There are automated tools now to assist analysts, designers, programmers, and testers (and even managers). Probably more important, though, are the fundamental changes in the way programming people approach their jobs. These days, groups that are consistently successful at building computer software use techniques that incorporate:

A *top-down* approach to analysis and design

Construction of software as sets of *modules*

Extensive *reuse* of proven program templates or libraries

Conventions and tools that support and enforce the construction of *structured* software

These techniques have demonstrated effectiveness that is independent of the specific technology being used. They work as well for object-oriented development using Unix workstations as they do for COBOL life-cycle programming on mainframes. In a nutshell, use of these techniques helps to ensure that (1) analysis, design, coding, and testing are all done by starting at the highest levels of the software system and working downward in a natural, orderly progression, and (2) analysis, design, and coding are done and documented using techniques that insist on order, clarity, and rigor. I'll have much more to say on these topics in the following chapters.

Along with changes to support the technical aspects of software development, there have also been changes in the management approach to systems projects. As the software business was feeling its way toward using a manageable process, it took on some of the characteristics of classic engineering projects, where step one was completed before going on to step two. The system development cycle that was based on the engineering approach became known as the "waterfall model" (Figure I–2).

The "waterfall model" approach works and in some cases it makes very good sense to follow it. However, it takes a long time, particularly for large projects, and the customer often cannot afford the time required to traverse the waterfall. For many projects, the model shown in Figure I–3 is a better description of the development cycle. In this approach, tasks are started before their predecessors are fully complete. A great deal of the work goes on in parallel.

This looks a lot more complicated than the waterfall model, but it contains the same processes. It provides more feedback throughout the cycle, and this can have the salutary effect of improving system quality. The importance of feedback in the development cycle can also be found in other approaches described in books and journal articles, such as the "spiral" and "iterative" development models. On the down side, dynamic flow of information moving both foward and backward between the development processes means that the manager (that's you) is going to have to pay a lot more attention to the documents and communications that hold the project on course.

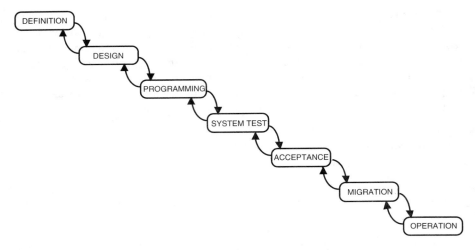

**FIGURE I–2**    "Waterfall Model" Development Cycle

## AN ATYPICAL PROJECT

There are problems on all projects, no matter how well run, and we'll explore lots of them. Our *goal*, however, is a smooth, problem-free project, so let's enter the land of make-believe for a moment and see how your project *ought* to run.

Someone we'll call the "customer" has a problem he thinks can be solved by developing some software to suit his needs. He submits the problem to you and other contractors for bids. You and your competitors jump into feverish activity called proposal writing. Each of you tries to decide how to solve this customer's problem at lower cost and with better quality than the others are likely to propose. Each writes a statement of his understanding of the problem and how he would solve it. Each adds a layer of boilerplate (to impress the customer with his credentials) and submits the proposal for evaluation. Of the contenders considered responsive to his needs, the customer selects one, usually the lowest bidder, to do the job. If none are responsive enough, he redefines the requirements and asks for new proposals.

You win and celebrate your good fortune while the losers gamely applaud, and the project begins. You are now the project manager and you organize a team (partly kept in readiness since the proposal was first submitted) to do the job.

Your team tackles two immediate tasks: one is to define in clear detail the customer's needs, the other is to write a plan for filling those needs. Both tasks were "done" during the proposal stage, but now you refine them. You and your team members work with the customer to write a precise, well-structured Problem Specification to serve as the baseline for subsequent design and programming, and a detailed plan to guide the remaining activities of the project. Your team builds a proto-

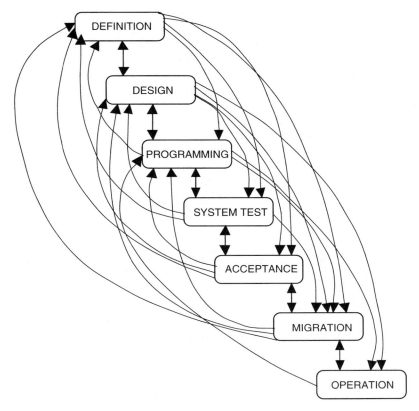

**FIGURE I–3**   "Overlapped" Development Cycle

type to demonstrate their understanding of the problem and to help the customer clearly visualize what he will be getting at the end of the development cycle.

As you work with the customer on the Problem Specification, you recruit and organize the talent needed for the next process: designing the software. You select the best designers you can find and direct them to design a robust yet flexible system to solve the problem defined by your analysis. While design is going on you're busy recruiting people and finding other resources, such as computer test configurations, for the remaining work to be done. You keep an eye on the Project Plan and take steps to meet all the milestones stated in it. Sometimes you see a need to change the plan, and do so.

As the overall system design becomes more detailed, you have it reviewed and approved by your management and the customer. As sections of the design are validated as conforming to the baseline requirements, you turn them over to the programmers.

Programmers further refine the design into smaller pieces until the refinements reach the level of actual code. They code and test the pieces ("modules") and then carefully merge ("integrate") them with one another according to a test plan. As they add modules successfully, the system grows in complexity and usefulness. It reaches several plateaus where it is doing useful and cohesive subsets of its total intended functionality. Because your team sought and achieved design integrity in earlier processes, the system fits together well. As the software grows, you encounter some minor analysis, design, and coding mistakes. Your people make changes, but you strictly control the changes through a simple mechanism earlier planned for.

Finally the software is ready for the customer, along with its set of descriptive documentation and draft user documentation. But the customer does not yet get his hands on the product. First you subject it to another set of tests called "system tests." To assure integrity and objectivity, a group separate from the programmers devises and executes these tests. This group imagines itself the user and tries to raise hell with the system to make it fail.

The defects uncovered by the testers are trifling because you did a good job analyzing the system's requirements and designing the system to meet those requirements. You make changes to correct problems and finally you have a proven system, with clean documentation, ready for delivery.

Now you demonstrate the system to the customer to win his formal acceptance. The terms of acceptance are not subjective; you and the customer agreed on them early in the life of the project. All that's needed now is to show that the programs meet those acceptance criteria.

Once accepted, you deliver the system to the customer. You work with the system's users and provide training to make sure the transition from the customer's previous system goes smoothly. You make changes to the user documentation based on direct feedback from people who are trying to use it. Finally, everything is running smoothly and you take time for some reflection.

You write a history of the project's activities and make a comparison between what was planned and what took place—you'll use this to make better decisions in planning future projects. You promote everybody and go home to get reacquainted with your family.

## THE DEVELOPMENT CYCLE

Unlike the project just described, many projects fail. Some overrun budgets and schedules; some don't deliver systems that do what the customer expected; some don't deliver any software at all. High on the list of reasons for failure is loss of control—managers find themselves unsure of project status and unable to report progress accurately. They don't know "where they are." The first step toward getting control is to define a framework within which all the project's work is to be done. That framework is the *development cycle* for the project. The development cycle is the master road map for the project. It defines the basic, orderly steps necessary to guide the project from start to finish.

The development cycle coordinates the *processes* that must work in concert to deliver the software system. These processes are similar to the "modules" that make up a software system—they're pieces you can get your arms around, pieces that are manageable. Figure I, inside the front cover, illustrates the development cycle I use in this book. I've divided the cycle into seven processes that make sense to me. If you need eight processes, or four, that may be all right. What's important is that each process have a clear set of objectives and definable inputs and outputs. The development cycle provides a single, unambiguous "picture" of your project, a frame of reference everyone can relate to. The development cycle described in this book consists of the following processes:

➤ Definition Process
➤ Design Process
➤ Programming Process
➤ System Test Process
➤ Acceptance Process
➤ Migration Process
➤ Operational Process

Each is the subject of a separate section in the book. Throughout the discussion of the processes, please refer to Figure I, inside the front cover. The processes are depicted there as layers of activity plotted against a time line for the project. Most of the time, there are several processes proceeding concurrently. The coordination of these processes poses one of the primary challenges the software manager must face.

Figure I shows a typical division of total project time and effort among the processes. There may be large departures from this timing for some projects. It's possible for a Definition Process to consume a third of the total resources of time and manpower. On a large defense project, the System Test and Acceptance processes could take half the project's resources. The parts of the development cycle most often shortchanged are the front end and the rear end. On the front end, planning is often haphazard (let's get writing programs), analysis is weak (we all understand the customer's problem), and baseline design is nonexistent. On the rear end, system testing and migration are sometimes not even included in a plan (there's no time left, the programmers' integration test does the same job as system testing, and we can just reload the data from the old system using a standard utility).

There is no reliable industry standard for time allocation among the development processes; experience (both yours and your company's) with similar projects is your best guide. However, most projects will not be far wrong allowing one-third of total calendar time for the Definition and Design Processes, one-third for what I call the Programming Process, and one-third for the rest. But this broad rule of thumb is meaningless unless you understand what's included in those processes.

We'll discuss topics under the processes where they would normally come into prominence. Before considering the processes in detail, a thumbnail sketch of each should help to put things in perspective. Figure II, inside the back cover, summarizes the processes, their functions, the key team members, and important documents associated with each.

**Definition Process.**    During this process, you write a detailed plan for the project and a detailed definition of the customer's problem. During the problem definition activity you'll discuss ideas about solutions, but defer adoption of any specific solution until the Design Process.

**Design Process.**    Now that you and the customer have agreed what the problem is, write a design document describing an acceptable solution to the problem. Usually many solutions are feasible, but you must pick one and stick with it.

**Programming Process.**    You've defined the problem and blueprinted a solution; now build and test a software system according to that blueprint.

**System Test Process.**    After the programmers have built a product they're happy with, hand over the programs to a separate group to perform a new set of tests in as nearly a "live" environment as possible.

**Acceptance Process.**    Demonstrate the finished software system, including its documentation, in order to get the customer's formal agreement that the system satisfies the contract. Acceptance is based on meeting criteria that you and the customer agreed on earlier in the development cycle.

**Migration Process.**    More often than not, your new system will replace an older system. You will need to convert data from the older system and arrange for audits and fallback procedures. If your new system is being introduced as a series of releases over a period of time, migration can be time-consuming and complex.

**Operational Process.**    Once the system has become operational, there will always be a requirement for maintenance and/or performance tuning. The goal of the operational process is to ensure that the system continues to perform at the level required to satisfy the customer.

# PART II

# DEFINITION

Every project manager starts by trying to answer two questions:

- ➤ What is the system I'm supposed to build supposed to do?
- ➤ How should I plan to build it?

The project begins with an attempt to answer those questions. This is the Definition Process, and the people who play a key role are you—the manager—and your analyst(s). At the end of the Definition Process, you will have developed the following responses to those questions:

- ➤ A Problem Specification that accurately reflects the customer's requirements.
- ➤ A Project Plan that identifies all of the activities that are necessary to build and deliver the system described in the Problem Specification.

The Problem Specification and the Project Plan are foundations of the project. You will use them throughout the project to ensure that you are still on course and that you are making progress. Let's get started.

**FIGURE 1–1**   The Analyst at Work   (Hart, "B.C." Creators Syndicate, Inc., *Washington Post,* January 28, 1994.)

# 1

# The Definition Process

It's your first day as project manager and you're savoring the moment. You have a couple of recently promoted programming managers itching to put out some code and a boss above you who's climbing the corporate ladder and expects fast results. You have a customer who loves to play political games. And you have a seventy-three-page contract that begins describing the technical problem on page seventy-two. You have a great opportunity to blow it.

But you've smartened up since that last job—the one that gave new meaning to Murphy's Law. This time you'll do it right. Anyone caught coding will be shot. In fact, anyone caught *designing* will be shot. This time you'll insist on knowing what the problem is before you begin solving it. And this time you're going to write a real plan for the project and rid yourself of the nickname Ad Hoc. *This time* you're going to make the customer a team member early. Yes, this time, by God, it will be different.

## FIRST THINGS FIRST: DEFINING THE PROBLEM

Your first job is to produce an accurate description of the customer's requirements—one that both you and the user agree on. This is usually some form of document, but there are other forms that may work better for you. If a requirements statement has already been written during proposal efforts or studies preceding contract award, your job may be to fill in the details and formalize it. Most often the

---

### Working with the Feds

The federal government often makes use of two-step contracts, especially on very large jobs or when the technical problems are formida-
ble. The government enters into an agreement with two or more contractors simultaneously and funds each to work out a problem
definition and design concept. The government is then free to choose
what it likes from among the various concepts submitted. A single contractor may then be chosen to go ahead with full development according to the approach chosen. The period during which the separate approaches are being worked out is usually called a Contract Definition
Phase. Some software vendors regularly do business this way. The two-
stage approach limits their liability and ensures that the customer understands what he or she is buying. It's an approach that ought to be
more widely used.

---

requirements will have only been sketched, and this first process of your project
will involve plenty of analysis work. It often makes sense to contract for two separate jobs, one to define the problem and one to solve that problem—but it's not always easy to convince a customer of the wisdom of that approach.

*Never* assume that the problem is so obvious that everyone understands it. A
manager I know made that assumption and after almost a year of work the problem
was still changing. This was an in-house job where the work was being done under
"shop order" (a within-the-company contract) to another department. There was no
written definition of the job. After some heated sessions, frustrated managers agreed
to salvage something and complete the job as cheaply as possible, but nobody came
out happy—neither customer, nor programming manager, nor programmers. Because this customer and developer belonged to the same company, no one expected
a problem. Ironically, a more formal arm's-length relationship would have bene-
fited everyone.

### What, Not How

You'll be tempted to design programs immediately, but don't. Concentrate first on
*what* the problem is, not on *how* to solve it. While your analysts are describing the
*what*, they will naturally discuss design ideas, but design is not the job at hand. The
job is to produce a specification describing the problem, not the solution. Begin this
specification by describing the customer's problem from scratch, in nontechnical
language. Identify the customer and the problem environment and explain why the
customer seeks a software solution. Then describe the technical problem in increas-

ing levels of detail. Use diagrams and pictures wherever possible. Be specific about all the capabilities the system will include; if clarity dictates listing items *not* included, then do so. Be precise. Don't leave it to the reader to guess what is included and what is not.

Traditionally, problem analysis starts with a study of the customer's current system. Some sort of paper model of the existing system is usually created. This paper model is an important source of information that will be needed to ensure that introduction of the new system goes smoothly.

Even if the new system will use all new computers and look completely different to the people who actually use it, it is certain to embody some of the business rules and existing data of the system it will replace. As you learn about the old system, questions about why it does what it does will come to mind. When they do, *ask somebody to explain what's going on*. It's the questions that you don't ask that will come back to haunt you.

However, it doesn't pay to put *too much* effort into understanding the system now in place. The fact is that you have been asked to produce a new system because the customer wants to change his business process in ways the current system can't support. You need to spend most of your time concentrating on the customer's new requirements.

## Prototypes

If a picture is worth a thousand words, a prototype is worth a couple of shelves at the library. Very simply, a prototype is a working model of the system that your customer envisions as the end result of the project. In fact, there have been some cases where the prototype worked so well, it was accepted as the final product!

Prototyping allows the customer to clearly define what he wants in a form that will not be clouded by the imprecision of text. When the customer says, "That's what I want!" the technical types (this includes you) should be able to clearly grasp the customer's vision and ask pointed questions about any issues that are still unclear. When this occurs, some very good things happen:

➤ Misunderstandings about what the customer wants and what you think he wants will become immediately obvious and can be corrected with less time and effort than they could be later in the project.

➤ The customer is forced to really concentrate on what he wants and doesn't want. A lot of projects are started for customers who didn't spend enough time considering what was going to happen if they got what they asked for.

➤ The customer gets involved in the system development process as a participant, rather than just as an observer. This will help you communicate more effectively with the customer throughout the project and it will make it easier to get the customer to participate constructively in project reviews and in the testing process.

➤ It allows your project team to produce something that works early in the process.

Building a prototype is a lot more fun than writing a two-volume functional specification and it's good to let your team have some fun early in the development cycle. A key part of your job as a manager is to mold an effective team out of a group of people who may have been strangers to each other only a few weeks ago. Nothing helps the molding process more than shared success in doing something that moves the project forward.

## Simulations

For software that is part of a highly automated business process, prototypes that concentrate on the points of human interface may only apply to a small part of the problem. Simulations that provide a dynamic model of the flow of processing and information can be very effective in presenting "the big picture" when there are many interdependent parts. They allow you to tell a story about what your software is going to do. By telling a story about what happens to Mr. Becker's order for 100 shares of IBM stock as it flows through the portfolio management system you are going to build, you stand a much better chance of getting the customer's active interest than if you just talked about the individual programs your team will write.

It used to be that simulation required a lot of computing power and specialized languages. Today, there are useful simulation products that run on personal computers and use interactive graphics to set up their working models quickly. For example, the "Stella" software that runs on Apple's Macintosh computers allows construction of a network of activities and their interrelationships and then provides an animated display of the flow of work through these activities. If there are bottlenecks in the process that's being simulated, they will be dramatically evident.

Just like prototypes, simulations give the customer the opportunity to use pictures and examples to describe his requirements. It is hard to overemphasize how important this can be. Excellent communications between you and your customer at the start of the project may not be enough to guarantee success absolutely, but poor communications make eventual failure an iron-clad certainty.

## Key Documents

We will discuss many individual documents as we talk about the development processes and under the Documentation Plan in the Appendix. Right now we need to look at a few key documents (Figure 1–2) that help glue the project together. I've chosen short titles that tell you what the document is about. If you choose (or if the customer forces you) to use other titles, use them consistently. Avoid names that are pompous ("On the Characteristics of the Automation of the XYZ Payroll").

| Document Name | When Written | What It Does | Who Writes It | Possible Forms |
|---|---|---|---|---|
| Problem Specification | Definition Process | Defines the problem to be solved | Analysts | Diagrams of data and business functions; narrative text |
| Design Specification | Design Process | Describes how the system will be built to solve the problem | Designers | Diagrams of data and software processes; narrative text |
| Coding Specification | Programming Process | Describes details of design implementation | Progammers | Diagrams of data and software processes; pseudo-code |
| Integration Test Specification | Design Process | Describes test plan to verify interoperability of system modules | Designers and pro-grammers | Checklists; test data; descriptions; pro-cedures |
| System Test Specification | Programming Process | Describes test plan to verify correct functioning of the system | Analysts, designers, and testers | Test scripts; checklists; test data; descriptions |
| Acceptance Test Specification | Design Process | Describes tests and criteria to verify that system satisfies customer requirements | Analysts | Test Scripts; checklists; test data; descriptions; explicit success criteria: site testing plan |
| Migration Specification | Programming Process | Describes schedules and pro-cedures to replace current systems with the new system | Analysts and support staff | Schedules; process flowcharts; audit and fallback procedures |

**FIGURE 1–2** Key Documents

The first three documents in Figure 1–1 are vital to project success. The first, "Problem Specification," is the document your analysis team writes to describe the customer's problem. It defines the *requirements* of the job to be done and it's the foundation for all subsequent work. The second, "Design Specification," is a work product of the next process of the development cycle. It describes the overall solution to the problem. The third, "Coding Specification," is the detailed extension of the Design Specification. It's a *set* of documents describing the software in detail, including code.

These are all "living" documents. They can and should change as you and the customer learn more about the system you're building. We'll talk about the task of managing changes later in the book. As a manager, this is going to be a topic of riveting interest to you.

These documents will keep living even after the system has passed from development to full operational use by the customer. Your customer's information needs are going to change over time and the systems that help satisfy these needs will change as well. Each change to the system needs to build on the requirements, design, and code that went before. As the Problem Specification, Design Specification, and Coding Specification are used and updated with each change, the information needed to maintain the original quality of the system can be passed to each team who works on it in the future. If this seems like some abstract generalization, remember that companies have been known to bring the original developers back to work on major system upgrades—even if years have passed since they last looked at the system!

On larger projects there may be another document defining an overall system (for example, a space-tracking system) of which your programs are only one of several major subsystems. There may be a software subsystem, a radar subsystem, a display subsystem, and so on. Such a document is usually written by the customer or by a special system contractor. If an overall system document exists, make sure your entire analysis team has read it carefully before you start working on the Problem Specification document. The overall system document can give you one of the most valuable pieces of information you need—it defines the *boundary* of your software system.

The document that is most in focus during the Definition Process, the Problem Specification, defines the customer's software requirements in four major categories:

1. Functions or operations to be provided by the system.
2. Performance, including file capacities, timing constraints, input rates, and system loads.
3. Data requirements.
4. Human considerations, such as minimum times for making decisions, maximum times allowable for system responses, and restrictions on program-generated displays.

## Attributes of a Good Problem Specification

There are entire books that focus on the Problem Specification. One of them worth reading is *Software Requirements* (Davis, 1993), which states that a well-written specification should be:

- ➤ Correct
- ➤ Unambiguous
- ➤ Complete
- ➤ Verifiable
- ➤ Consistent
- ➤ Understandable by the customer
- ➤ Modifiable
- ➤ Design independent
- ➤ Annotated
- ➤ Concise
- ➤ Organized
- ➤ Traced (origin of each requirement is clear)
- ➤ Traceable (clear correspondence between software components and specific requirements)

---

### Leaky Foundations

An error in analysis can have a diseaselike effect on everything that follows. Enormous amounts of design, coding, and testing energy may be expended based on some faulty premise resulting from careless analysis. There is ample anecdotal evidence to support this assertion and there are studies (see Boehm, 1981, and Martin, 1984, 1988) that assess the staggering cost of the ripple effect following an analysis error.

I once had a house built in an area where damp basements were a known problem. I asked that measures be taken when the foundation was poured to route ground water away from the foundation. I was ignored and ended up with a wet basement. The contractor made good a year after the house was finished by tearing up the ground all around the foundation, applying extra sealants, and installing drainage pipes. Doing the job after the fact cost him a lot of time and money and cost me the aggravation of having my yard torn up—shrubs, flowers, and all! Can you think of *anything* that doesn't cost more to fix than to do right in the first place?

If you use prototypes or simulations in defining the requirements for the system you're about to build, you should keep the above list in mind and add text documents where necessary to ensure that *all* aspects of the requirements are documented.

## THE ANALYSIS TEAM AND ITS WORK

What kind of people do you need to do the requirements analysis and write the Problem Specification? Your analysis team must represent many disciplines: programming, sales, engineering, psychology, writing. Let's consider what they have to do.

**Meet the Real Customer.**    There are usually many people who are the "customer." Just as you have specialists in your organization, so does your client—and each may make different demands on your analysts. There may be a buyer who has in mind holding down costs, a staff analyst who wants a system with lots of fancy gadgets, a contract administrator who knows little about the technical part of the job, and a user who will eventually operate your system. Your analysis team should not assume the members of the customer's organization talk to each other, let alone agree about what you should deliver. If the members of your team don't talk to the right people at the right time, they will not come away with a clear understanding of what this many-headed customer really expects. Especially important are the end-users. If the analysis team ignores them until it's time to turn over a finished system, the results will certainly be tragic.

---

### Love that customer!

I have this nasty habit. When I'm not treated well by a salesperson I tell the manager. (I also tell the manager when I've been treated particularly *well*.) Customers want, deserve, and ought to get respect! Customers are what any business is there for.

If the people who work for you consider the customer a pain, guess whose fault that is: *yours!* It's up to you to make sure your people treat the customer with courtesy and respect; it's up to you to make your people understand that the customer is the reason they have a job. You do that by training your people and by setting a perfect example. If you speak of the customer in a negative way, your people will certainly do the same.

---

The user who has no part in specifying the system will be reluctant to accept it and may look upon it as a new gimmick being shoved down his throat. Omit no one. Find out diplomatically who controls what, who has the real power, and who will eventually use the product.

**Pick the Customer's Brains.**   Your analysis team must be skilled at finding out what the customer *really* wants, which may be different from what a loosely worded contract implies. Team members need to read both what they're given and what's between the lines. Your team needs to interview people—plunder their brains, so to speak—and understand what's really being said. It's critical that they listen hard, rephrase what the customer has said, feed it back to the customer, and ask, "Is this what you mean?"

Using pictures, prototypes, or simulations can be very helpful at this point because they give both you and the user a common point of reference. All too often when users communicate to analysts, they omit the information that "everybody already knows." Despite what some analysts think, customers aren't being perverse when they do this. They're simply taking for granted that the analysis team knows the background to the problem.

**Ask Good Questions.**   This isn't easy. A good question is one that helps you find the best ways to use a computer to support the customer's business process. All too often, the customer already has a solution in mind when he goes in search of software help. A good question may help the customer to consider another solution that saves both time and money. Some of the best questions are "stupid" questions. Inez Hill, who founded a consulting firm that helps clients create accurate Problem Specifications, once opened a requirements gathering session for a new personnel records system with the question "What's an employee?" It took fourteen people a full day of hard work to agree on the answer, but the resulting system turned out to be far more useful than originally envisioned.

**Watch Out for "Stealth Requirements".**   As your team works at finding out what the system is to do, you may find out that it seems to be growing each time you look at it. While this may simply reflect your success in uncovering additional details, it may be that the requirements really are growing, and *that* can turn into a real management headache. If you can't put some reasonable boundaries on system functionality, you'll never be able to complete your project.

These "stealth requirements" can come from users who look at your project and see it as a vehicle to get the software goodies they've always coveted but could never get budgeted. If your system is going to serve a number of different departments in the company, you can be pretty sure that each one of them will have one or two items that they declare to be "absolutely essential" if they are going to support the project.

Another breeding ground for "stealth requirements" is in the earlier stages of a multipart systems project, such as an enterprise-wide Executive Information System. As these earlier stages get pressed for time, their managers will find creative ways to move some of their requirements to later stages of the project. One of these later stages may be yours. You may even find that some of these unexpected arrivals have higher visibility than the parts of the job that were originally defined for you. After all, those were the functions that were supposed to be available before you started with your efforts. It's difficult to describe the feeling that comes from finding out at the end of your first week on the job that you are already ninety days behind schedule.

There isn't any way to stop these new requirements from appearing. All you can do is try to get them documented before you build your Project Plan. Only when you have the Project Plan in hand will you be able to argue that the expansion of requirements has raised costs and lengthened the schedule to the point where the project as a whole needs to be reconsidered.

**Write It Down.** The analysis team can write the Problem Specification in an infinite number of ways. Some of those ways will be easy for designers to implement, some difficult, some impossible. An analysis team lacking programming experience can kill you. (So can a team with *only* programming experience.) You and your analysts must state the problem in clear and precise language that is acceptable to both the customer and your designers. Beware the techies who "insist on defining the problem in their own terms instead of the customer's terms" (Plauger, 1993). Keep it simple. Don't tolerate any of those programming people Robert Townsend (1970) calls "complicators, not simplifiers."

**Get It Approved—Gradually.** As sections of the Problem Specification are written, you should get tentative customer approval of what has been written. The best way to get approval is to have the customer deeply involved in the analysis process. Users should be part of the analysis team. Never surprise the customer with a finished document. If he doesn't like it, you're in bad shape. One of the ways modern projects involve the customer is through some variation of JAD (Joint Application Design) (Wood and Silver, 1989; Thomsett, 1993). The concept, which can be used in analysis, design, and other facets of the project, promotes customer involvement by including him in small, focused teams that work in a highly structured manner. A team convened during analysis would include, among others, actual end-users of the system—the people who care the most about the system's inputs, screens, messages, and outputs.

Another effective approach is to build a prototype using one of the powerful PC-based tools available. I've seen some excellent client/server prototypes put together using Powerbuilder™. The prototype allows the user to experience directly the "look and feel" of the system you are planning to build. Building a prototype immediately following (or even during) a JAD effort can go a long way toward eliminating misunderstandings and gaining the desired approvals.

As you get customer agreement on elements of the Problem Specification, you can begin the Design Process, which we'll cover in Chapter 4.

## Sanity Check: Can This Problem Be Solved?

It doesn't make much sense to define a problem that can't be solved in a practical manner. As you work your way through the problem definition, your team needs to be doing enough design to convince everyone that there's a way to write software that will do what the user wants. By the time you complete your Problem Specification, your team should be able to clearly identify the key elements of the system design and the way they must work together.

If you get to this point and you don't believe that you can solve the customer's problem, stop the project. You have a duty to your employer, your customer, the people on your team, and yourself to call a halt before you start wasting money and time. But I have to tell you that in practice, this can be a very hard thing to do.

## Analysis Techniques I: Structured Methods

It may be hard to believe, but when data processing was introduced to American business, analysis was an afterthought. Programming was considered an art and individual inspiration was the key to developing good programs. We've learned a lot since then. Smart and dedicated people have brought order and discipline—*structure*—to the programming process. Each proponent of structured techniques offers his or her own slant and inevitably there has been some confusion over conflicting terminology, but the core ideas are now widely accepted. Two of the best known voices among the pioneers are those of Ed Yourdon and Tom DeMarco, some of whose writings are listed in the References. The structured techniques only briefly described here are fully covered in their books.

The structured techniques were not the end of the search for better software development methodologies, but they were a major milestone. Subsequent refinements have complemented the initial focus on process functionality with a recognition of the key role played by data relationships. Modern structured techniques have focused on the importance of the events that initiate processing. Object-oriented analysis and design techniques have further synthesized the roles of function and data. Because modern analysis techniques allow the analyst to work using terminology that is familiar to the customer, the quality of analysis has also improved.

Each approach to analysis has given rise to detailed methodologies, and each methodology can point to successes to which it has contributed. Each methodology also has automated tools available to support you and your analysts as you refine the problem definition. Just remember that there is no methodology or tool set that is absolutely the best for every problem.

As a manager you can't wait for the perfect tool any more than any consumer can wait for the perfect product, and you need to understand that even the most popular and established methodologies and tools may not be the right ones for your project. In *Managing the Structured Techniques* (1989), Yourdon acknowledges that structured analysis and design techniques are not perfect and may not be appropriate in every situation. He goes on to say:

> In general, though, the structured techniques *do* work. They double the productivity of the average programmer/analyst, increase the reliability of the developed system by an order of magnitude, and decrease the cost and effort of maintenance by a factor of two to ten. Finally, they substantially improve the chances that you will deliver a system that your customers will accept—and maybe, just maybe, on time and within budget!

The studies with which I'm familiar don't show improvements at the level that Mr. Yourdon claims. I'd estimate a 15 percent improvement in productivity during development and about a 20 percent reduction in maintenance cost over the life of the system. Even though it's not "an order of magnitude," this is a significant improvement. If your organization isn't using *any* standard methodology, I'd recommend that you move quickly to get your people familiar with the structured methods. There is plenty of literature and training available and the structured methods are supported by a wide variety of tools that will run on PCs. Make sure you allot time to follow all the steps that form the basis for the methodology. What often happens is that some elements of the structured methodologies become widely used while others are neglected because they're too time-consuming or not very much fun. If you fall into this way of doing things, you might get better productivity and quality than if you had no standard practices at all, but don't expect world-class performance.

Traditional analysis documents are long, boring, and difficult to understand because they rely so heavily on narrative descriptions. Structured analysis techniques replace much of the narrative with *pictures* that tend toward less volume and more clarity. Today's analysis tools allow clear definition of *what* the problem is, and many of them provide a straightforward path to the technical design that follows. These tools and the methodologies they support deal with the *logic* of a system, not its physical incarnation.

In order to give you a better feel for the diagrams and their purposes, I'm going to describe the structured analysis scheme used by Yourdon. It's been around for many years, but it's hardly obsolete. It can be used without a big investment in computing power and it doesn't take long to learn or understand. I've used it many times and it's always helped me to understand the problem and find a reasonable solution. It complements a rational process of thinking about the problem and the system, and this is exactly what a useful methodology should do. Structured Analysis uses five tools to define the requirements of the user's system:

➤ Entity Relationship Diagrams
➤ Data flow Diagrams
➤ Data Dictionary

➤ Process Specifications
➤ State Transition Diagrams

**Entity Relationship Diagrams**.   In most cases, if you don't understand the data, you won't understand the problem. After all, the system you're going to build will collect, organize, transform, store, and report data. Items of data are related to each other and you will need to understand these relationships before you can design the system. When structured analysis was in its formative stage, the starting point was most often the data flow diagrams that we'll describe next. These days, the importance of understanding the data relationships has been widely recognized and I recommend that you start by creating a set of Entity Relationship Diagrams. Figure 1–3 gives an example.

The Entity Relationship Diagram shows how different elements of the data are related to each other. It shows whether data elements have a one-to-one, one-to-many, or many-to-many relationship and whether a specific element must be present or is optional. (This is called *cardinality*.) The example in Figure 1–3 uses the Martin notation, named for its originator. There are other notations, but they are all easy to comprehend.

The ease of comprehension is very important at this stage of the project because it helps you to avoid misunderstandings when you are talking to your customer. If both of you are looking at an Entity Relationship Diagram when you are talking about the information that's in an invoice, it will be far easier for both you and your customer to agree on the data that your new system is required to process.

**Data Flow Diagrams (DFD)**.   A Data Flow Diagram is a pictorial representation of the flow of data through a system. This is likely to be your starting point if you are developing a process control system or part of a "software infrastructure," such as a message router that is used by application programs. There are four elements to a Data Flow Diagram: data flows, processes, stores, and terminators.

In Figure 1–4, the system you're looking at is the routing of 911 calls. The flow of data starts from a terminator outside the system, with a citizen making a call to 911. The phone number where the call was made is used to determine the address where the call is being made. This is done by a process that interrogates a database that cross-references phone numbers and addresses. The address is then combined with a description of the emergency and another process dispatches one or more emergency vehicles to the address. As the data moves between the terminators, the processes, and the data store, we can identify its content.

As you sketch Data Flow Diagrams, questions pop up quite naturally. When you're looking at a *picture* (as opposed to narrative) it's usually clear when there's a piece missing. As Tom DeMarco says in *Structured Analysis and System Specification* (1979): "When a Data Flow Diagram is wrong, it is glaringly, demonstrably, indefensibly wrong."

If you look again at Figure 1–4, you'll see that it assumes that the 911 caller is

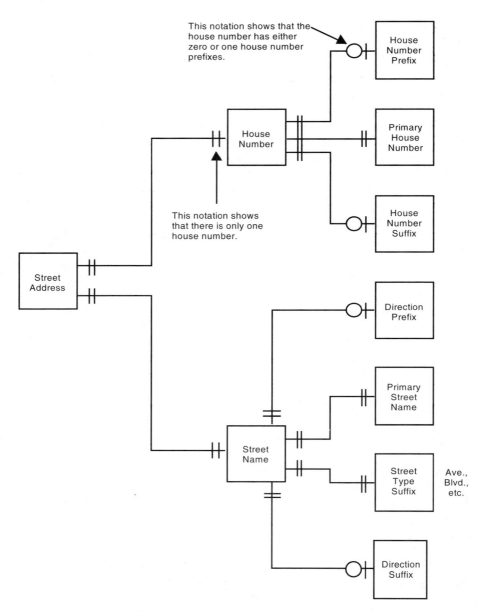

This notation shows that the house number has either zero or one house number prefixes.

This notation shows that there is only one house number.

**FIGURE 1–3**   An Entity Relationship Diagram

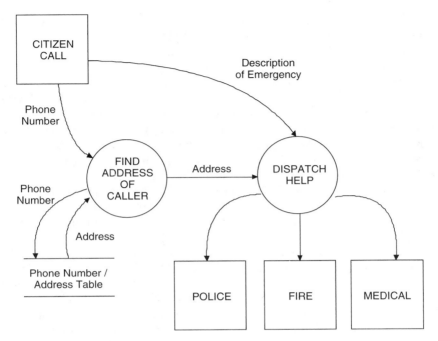

**FIGURE 1–4**   A Data Flow Diagram

at the same location as the emergency. What happens if the caller is calling from a cellular phone? There's no way to correlate the calling number with an address. Something is missing from the diagram.

Attack Data Flow Diagrams from the top down. Your first diagram may show all flows and processes at a gross level. This highest-level diagram is sometimes called a Context Diagram. Diagrams at the next level explode *each process* into more detailed diagrams containing the same four basic types of notation: data flows, processes, stores, and terminators. Continue until a level of detail is reached such that no "what" questions remain. If you number the processes, you can make cross-referencing logical and unambiguous. Process 5, for example, is broken into processes 5.1, 5.2, 5.3, and so on; process 5.2 is broken down into processes 5.2.1, 5.2.2, 5.2.3, and so on. Give all data flows, processes, stores, and terminators unique identifiers, like chapters and paragraphs in a manual, making them easy to find and easy to change. A good CASE tool can help you keep track of all this stuff.

Data Flow Diagrams are also tools for the designers in the next process, so they help provide continuity from one process to the next. In fact, the diagrams produced by the analysts will probably contain some *implied* design.

The best thing about Data Flow Diagrams is that, just like Entity Relationship Diagrams, they are easy for your customer to understand. By their very nature, they use terminology that is familiar to your users and they present it in a way that helps the users to clearly understand your perception of the system. They help you avoid techno-jargon when you talk to your customer and they make it possible for you to find out what "everybody knows" but forgot to tell you about.

**Data Dictionary.**    Define every data element in your system in the Data Dictionary. The Data Dictionary has a hierarchical organization, as do the Data Flow Diagrams. If there is a high-level entry called "telephone number-location," and if one of the items included under the "telephone number-location" entry is "street-address," then another Data Dictionary entry must spell out the makeup of "street-address." In the lowest-level entries, some definitions include quantitative data such as the permissible range of values for an item. Yourdon and others offer a set of simple notations to use in constructing a Data Dictionary. Keep in mind that Data Dictionaries contain *descriptions* of data, not actual data. You should be able to look up the definition of any data item just as you would look up a word in a regular dictionary.

Most CASE (Computer Aided Software Engineering) tools have integrated Data Dictionaries. They make it easy to ensure that the elements in your Entity Relationship Diagrams and the Data Flows in your Data Flow Diagrams are correlated to the definition of the data in the dictionary. It's very easy to lose track of the fact that the Entity Relationship Diagrams and Data Flow Diagrams have gotten slightly out of sync when you have twenty or thirty pages of diagrams on your desk. Although it takes me a little longer to enter the diagrams in a CASE tool, I've found that I wind up saving considerable time when I move from analysis into design if I'm able to make sure that my data and process entities are accurately documented.

**Process Specification.**    Once the Data Flow Diagrams have been broken down to their lowest levels, you must describe exactly what actions are to take place in each bottom-level process. Each of these descriptions, typically written on one page, is called a "mini-specification." The complete set of mini-specs is the Process Specification. Remember, you're doing analysis, not design. These mini-specs describe exactly *what* each small, low-level process is to do, but not how to do it. The mini-specs are the place to state the business rules that the system must support and enforce.

There are several ways of writing mini-specs. In some cases a mini-spec can best be expressed as a decision table or in some other tabular way. It's possible, of course, to write them in English narrative, but such narrative is what we're trying to get away from because it's lengthy and imprecise. Many analysts use some sort of "structured English," organized like a high-level programming language or an outline. For example, a mini-spec might read:

1.  IF caller reports injury THEN:
    a.  dispatch ambulance
    b.  dispatch patrol car
    c.  advise caller

**2.** OTHERWISE
   a. dispatch patrol car
   b. advise caller

Look at 1.a and 1.b. The mini-spec says to dispatch the ambulance first, then the patrol car. It's entirely possible that when you show this mini-spec to your customer (the user), the reaction will be "Hell, no! We always dispatch the patrol car first! Fix that!" Or maybe through some mechanism *both* are to be done at the same time. In either case, the problem shows up clearly on your mini-spec, but it might be buried and overlooked in ordinary narrative.

This has been only the briefest of introductions to the four main components of a structured analysis specification: Entity Relationship Diagrams identify the data elements and the structure of the information; Data Flow Diagrams trace transactions through the system; the Data Dictionary defines all data elements; and Process Specifications spell out exactly what each low-level process is supposed to accomplish. In addition, it is often necessary to include a *state transition diagram,* Figure 1–5, to highlight time dependencies in *real-time* systems.

Real-time systems typically deal with responses to external events, and the sequence of these events affects the processing that is performed by the system. In thinking about real-time systems, analysts often consider the system to be moving between stable "states." The processing of an event that occurs while the system is in state "A" may be different from the processing that would be done if the same event had occured while the system was in state "B." State transition diagrams identify the states and show the transitions between them. These diagrams can be useful in studying many problems where the sequence of events is important, such as text parsing.

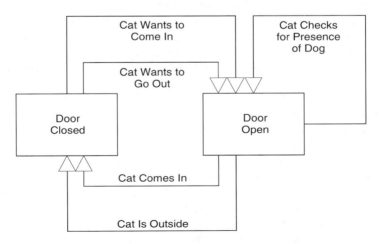

**FIGURE 1–5**   A State Transition Diagram

The door management system reflected in the diagram above shows that the state of the system changes from "door closed" to "door open" when my cat approaches the door either to go outside or to come in. If the door was already open, no state transition would take place until the cat had passed through the door and I had then closed it. Note that while my cat sits in the door checking for the presence of dogs, no state transition takes place. I simply continue to hold the door open, even at six A.M. in the dead of winter.

The classic Yourdon-DeMarco tools have worked well for the analysis of a wide variety of systems, but there have been several improvements on the original methods. The *Event Partitioning* methods developed by McMenamin and Palmer (1984) improve analysis by clearly separating the essential requirements of the system from the characteristics of its implementation. It's very easy for the analyst to slant her thinking about the problem in a way that reflects the desired solution and this bias can affect her ability to really understand what the customer needs.

In fact, many methodologies contain built-in biases. The structured analysis approaches are focused on the processes that make up the system. For many kinds of systems, an understanding of the data is of key importance. There are several methodologies that begin with a concentration on data rather than on process. As a manager, you should invest some time to become familiar with at least one data-centric analysis method. The Jackson System Design methods, named after their founder (Jackson, 1983), are particularly useful because they combine both data analysis and functional analysis to reach a cohesive result.

The Jackson methodology begins by identifying the *entities* that appear in the problem and the *actions* that are associated with the entities. When considering a system for automatic teller machines, a customer is an entity, the bank card is an entity, and the ATM itself is an entity. Actions are associated with the entities— the customer enters a security code that is then matched to the card. The sequence of the actions is also important—the security check must be performed before money can be withdrawn. Customers can talk to analysts about bank cards more easily than they can about normalized data structures, and this can be very valuable when you are trying to understand the way the customer views the information he uses.

If the Jackson methodology is used, the analysts are likely to have a fuller understanding of the problem and its solution than they might if they stuck to the classic structured analysis methods. There is, of course, a cost involved. One of the reasons that your analysts may get more out of the Jackson method is that they are required to put in additional work during the analysis process.

When you have completed your analysis, at the front of your set of analysis documents you should place a brief narrative description that sets the stage by introducing the reader to the customer and his business, with a short narrative overview of the problem this customer has asked you to analyze and solve. Add a fancy cover and all of this constitutes your Problem Specification.

## Analysis Techniques II: Object Methods

Object-oriented analysis (Coad and Yourdon, 1990) extends the consideration of entities, data, and actions as a whole, rather than as a set of distinct parts. It can be worthwhile to perform object-oriented analysis and object-oriented design even if you are not going to use object-oriented programming to implement your system. Object-oriented analysis forces you to concentrate on the ways that data and processes work together and your understanding of this interaction is the key to developing a good Problem Specification. I've used object-oriented analysis and design on several projects over the past two years and I find that it not only helps my understanding of the problem, it makes it very easy to perform "sanity checks" when talking to my clients.

Object-oriented methods seem to be particularly well suited to a variety of systems and/or subsystems and they are currently the focus of both careful evaluation and large volumes of hot air. Object-oriented analysis (OOA) and object-oriented design (OOD) appear to be a natural fit with client/server and other distributed environments where several processes cooperate in order to get specific tasks done. I'll have more to say about evaluations and OO use in Part IX of this book, but a brief introduction to the subject seems appropriate here.

Formal definitions of object-oriented methods may be of limited help in understanding what OO is because most of them refer to concepts that can't be fully understood unless you already know what's being defined. Here's an example from Ed Yourdon (1994): "A system built with object-oriented methods is one whose components are encapsulated chunks of data and function, which can inherit attributes and behavior from other such components, and whose components communicate via messages with one another." Here's a definition from Grady Booch (1994): "Object-oriented analysis is a method of analysis that examines requirements from the perspective of the classes and objects found in the vocabulary of the problem domain."

I think it's easier to get an initial impression of object-oriented programming by looking at an example. The example I'm going to use starts with the invoice I received from Prentice-Hall along with a shipment of books that I ordered. My invoice is an *object*. It is one element (or *instance*) of the set of invoices that Prentice-Hall sent out. Prentice-Hall invoices are a *class* that has common characteristics for each object in the class. The class can be treated as something that contains a definition of the data that can appear on the invoice (items, unit costs, discounts, and so forth) along with the rules (*methods*) that govern the things I can do to an invoice (add an item, apply a late charge, and so on). The class of invoices *inherits* certain characteristics from other classes to which it is related; for example, my invoice carries an ID number and date because it is a customer transaction and the class of Prentice-Hall customer transactions is defined to have ID numbers and dates.

In an object-oriented system, things happen when we send *messages* to objects. If you wanted to add another item to my invoice, an object in your system (maybe the packing list object) would send a message to my invoice object. The message contains data about the book you want to bill me for and instructions to my invoice object to invoke the method to "add a line item." Your packing list object, which told my invoice object to add a line item, can be created without requiring that your programmer know anything about the internal workings of the invoice class.

The differences between the object-oriented methods and the structured methods are fundamental. This is the reason that OO has often been described as "revolutionary." Object-oriented methods are, at their heart, a way to "compose" a system from the objects that are in the problem domain. The structured methods are based on the "decomposition" of a problem into its parts, and these parts are built to conform to the design that emerged from the decomposition activity.

Object-oriented analysis and object-oriented design are highly iterative. You will spend a lot of time, particularly in your early OO efforts, wrestling with the issues of class definition. There is more art than science in this work. As Grady Booch, one of the most experienced OO practitioners, writes: "Frankly, except for the most trivial abstractions, we have never been able to define a class exactly right the first time" (Booch, 1994). If you have sales orders and repair orders and the sales orders can come from distributors or customers and repair orders can come from customers or from the factory, how will you identify your object classes? You'll have orders, of course, but are you going to define customer sales orders as distinct from distributor sales orders, or will you encapsulate all sales orders in one class?

As object-oriented analysis identifies objects and methods, object-oriented design must be started to verify that the objects can be coordinated through messages in a way that yields the desired result for the customer. Don't wait. You are going to need the feedback from the designers to the analysts in order to stay on track.

Although it comes as a surprise to some, the measures used to determine the quality of object-oriented design and analysis are similar to those used to determine the quality of structured analysis and design. As a manager, you must ensure that you and your team continually evaluate their work in the following areas:

➤ *Coupling.* This is a measure of the degree to which modules or classes are linked to one another. A balance must be found between weak coupling, which reduces system complexity, and the OO concept of inheritance, which allows classes to be defined in a way that maximizes reuse.

➤ *Cohesion.* This is a measure of the degree of connectivity between the elements within a class. A class that contains abstractions that are not functionally consistent (such as a class that supports both invoice and payroll abstractions) will be difficult to work with. A class with good functional cohesion (such as a class for company-owned motorized vehicles) will be much more useful because its behavior is bounded in a way that makes the class easy to identify and apply. It's a little like my father's workbench. Dad had a number of jars with items like small brass wood-screws (good functional cohesion).

He also had a coffee can with all sorts of screws and nails that had been dumped in over the years (really lousy cohesion). I might have been able to find a small brass wood-screw in the coffee can, but it was much easier to find the right jar.

➤ *Sufficiency.* A class needs to carry enough of the characteristics of the underlying abstraction to be worth using. If I have a class called *telephone number*, but it doesn't include methods that allow me to check for a valid area code or exchange, then I can say that the class is not sufficient to meet the reasonable expectations of those who might want to use it.

➤ *Completeness.* This is the other side of the sufficiency coin. A class becomes more useful to the extent that it embodies all of the meaningful characteristics of an abstraction. Still, there are limits. There are an enormous number of ways to specify an address—everything from house number and street to global positioning coordinates. If I'm defining the *street address* class so that I can send junk mail more efficiently, I really don't need to include the Federal Emergency Management coordinates.

➤ *Primitiveness.* Think of this as RISC software. RISC, which stands for Reduced Instruction Set Computing, was initially applied to hardware. Instead of containing hundreds of different instructions, RISC chips provided a small number of simple, highly efficient operations that could be combined to implement the more complex operations when they were needed. Primitive operations and classes work the same way. *Get_Selection_List* can be implemented by using *Get_Item*.

If you're mentally saying, "Wait a minute!" at this point, don't worry. The truth is that all these qualities are interdependent and it's probably not possible to maximize all of them in any realistic sense. If the analysis and design effort produces a system with a high degree of completeness and "primitiveness," the coupling may be stronger than desired. As I said, there's more art than science at this stage.

Object-oriented analysis, design, and programming are not inherently mysterious, but they are different from what most programmers, designers, and analysts are used to. I'd compare it to driving a car in England. The driving skills are the same, the cars are very similar, but it sure can feel strange the first few times you do it. For readers in the U.K., it is not the same as driving in France. *Nothing* is the same as driving in France.

## MOVING INTO DESIGN

As you proceed with the analysis work, you will begin to make the passage from analysis to design. It's a good idea to make this move before the analysis and Problem Specification are completed. Here's why.

By taking parts of the system that have already been analyzed and submitting them to the Design Process, you will get early warning of problems related to implementation. Things have a way of looking straightforward at the 50,000-foot level where most analysis takes place. When you get down to the 5,000-foot level during design, you notice that the thing that looked like a meadow during analysis is actually part of a swamp.

You will also get needed feedback on how well your analysis documents will translate into workable designs. It does no good for the analysis material to communicate effectively with the customer if it doesn't also communicate well with the designers and programmers.

Last but hardly least, an early start for the Design Process can help you avoid "analysis paralysis." You can always find a good reason to do a little more analysis, and there are plenty of customers who will let you do so. However, if your designers are pestering you for good quality input for their work, you'll actually have to stop attending meetings and produce something they can use.

As a project manager, you need to keep your ears open for feedback from the designers, even though most of your attention is still focused on analysis and development of the Project Plan. This early feedback can alert you to problems that you have overlooked and that may have a major impact on system complexity and cost. Make sure that you have set aside project time for the designers to talk directly to you and your analysts. If the designers are turning up significant problems, bring the customer in as well. It may be necessary to change the scale of the project.

## DEFINING THE PLAN

A programming manager on a year-long job reported everything "on-schedule" until a month before the deadline. Then he informed the customer that he would be a month late. When the new target date arrived, he nervously offered still another date, two months later. And when that time arrived, his manager took over as programming manager and with a great burst of energy finished the job nine months later. A year late on a one-year job. How come?

Over the years I've had the opportunity to listen to the complaints of managers and programmers from many companies and government agencies. I've seen surveys that attempted to ferret out problem areas. And of course I've pondered the problems I've personally encountered.

The problems all seem to swirl about a central evil: poor planning (Figure 1–6). Let's look at some planning basics, beginning with a brief look at some things that make planning difficult.

### The Project Plan

The Project Plan is outlined in detail in the Appendix. In addition, various elements of the plan are discussed at appropriate places in the following chapters. Here we'll take a brief look at the plan.

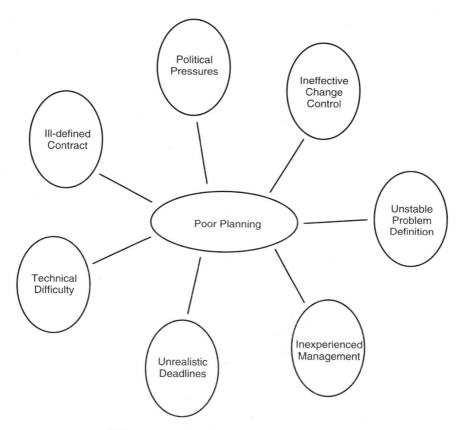

**FIGURE 1–6**   What it all boils down to . . .

*Characteristics of a good plan.* A plan is a road map showing how to get from here to there. Like a road map, it shows alternate routes, landmarks, and distances. Here are some things a good plan is and is not:

➤ It's in writing, not in the manager's head.

➤ It describes what the job is, how it will be attacked, and the resources required to do it.

➤ It's written with care so that it's readable; it's not just an accumulation of papers whose relation to one another is obscure. Pay attention to plan continuity. If you begin with the model plan outlined in this book, you'll have a good start.

➤ It allows for contingencies, actions to be taken in case something does not go as planned. There are two types of contingency planning to consider. The first involves specific, identifiable problems that may arise (for example, if a planned computer is not available on the date specified, where will you get test time, and at what added cost in time and money?). The second is tougher: what actions will you take when you're bushwhacked by unforeseen problems? Obviously, you can't give specific answers because you can't predict specific problems, but you can prepare by being realistic in planning resources. Always assume people will get sick, leave the company, get pregnant, misunderstand a specification, make mistakes. Always assume machines will break down. Always assume misunderstandings with the customer. Plan the best you can to make everything work perfectly, but understand that will never happen. Allow extra resources to cover the unforeseen obstacles.

➤ It's modular. If books were not written in parts, chapters, and paragraphs, reading them would be exhausting. The same applies to any piece of writing, including a plan. Subdivide the document logically so that there is a reasonable flow from one section to the next, but so that each section retains its identity and is useful on a stand-alone basis.

➤ It's brief enough that it won't turn people off. A mountain of paper will not be read. The plan could be as small as one page for each section. More likely, it will require, for our hypothetical project, a notebook of perhaps forty or fifty pages. That's not too much to ask each project member to read. After reading it once, most people will need only refer to specific sections from time to time. How big your plan becomes depends partly on how much tutorial filler you include. You need enough discussion to define terms and to guide the reader through the plan, but remember that too much bulk will cause it to go unread, unused, unloved.

➤ It has an index. It only takes a short time to construct a decent alphabetical index, and its inclusion will greatly enhance the usefulness of the document.

**Writing the Project Plan.**    So far we've considered planning as though it never begins until you have a signed contract and your project is under way. In practice this is rarely the case. Usually a number of planning activities precede your project's Definition Process—your own studies and proposal efforts; customer-funded studies; prior, related contracts; discussions between you and your prospective customer. Thus, you should consider your planning as only one step in an evolutionary process, and this evolution does not end when your Definition Process ends. No matter how good a plan you devise, it will change throughout the life of your project. Even so, the plan you produce during the Definition Process should be as complete and self-contained as you can make it at that time.

The people who contribute to your Project Plan should include analysts, programmers, and managers, all of whom will have continuing responsibility on the project. The user, too, must participate or at least provide input. Leave out any one of these parties and the plan will probably be weakened, perhaps fatally. Although you need to have input from all affected groups, the planning team should be kept as small as possible to reduce interactions and produce a plan that hangs together. It should not read as if written by a dozen different people who never talk to one another.

To get on with the planning job, first write a rough outline. You might start with the model plan outline in the Appendix and then adapt it to suit your own ideas. Next, decide how much calendar time you can afford to spend in the planning activity.

Now consider all the individuals you have available to do the planning—their talents, strengths, weaknesses—and assign them appropriate pieces of the plan along with a schedule of dates when you expect to see completed drafts. The model plan presented in this book is divided into sections, or subplans, which provide a handy basis for doling out the work. For this hypothetical forty-person project, four planners, besides yourself, are probably about right.

When you're ready to make planning assignments, have a kickoff meeting including everyone working for or with you on this project. With everyone (both planners and analysts) together in the same room, define and discuss the project's objectives. Then discuss any constraints under which the project must operate, such as fixed deadlines, customer-imposed milestones, funding, and work location.

Follow up the kickoff meeting with periodic status meetings in which planners (and analysts) can describe their progress and in which you can assess status relative to approaching target dates.

You should allot the Definition Process and the Design Process together about one-fourth to one-half of the total contract time. Planning is a major activity during both those process. You will find it tempting to slight your planning activity because you're anxious to get on with the programming. But if you don't take the time to plan well, you'll pay for it in later processes when things fall apart. Testing will falter, you'll miss schedules, you'll overrun budgets, and the quality of your product will suffer.

**A Project Plan Outline.**   I tried many different structures before settling on the outline presented here and in the Appendix. Modify it to suit your needs, even your temperament—after all, you have to live with it. The Project Plan is divided into eleven sections, which are summarized in succeeding paragraphs:

1. Overview
2. Process Plan
3. Organization Plan
4. Test Plan
5. Change Management Plan
6. Documentation Plan
7. Training Plan
8. Review and Reporting Plan

*Overview.* This section of the plan has two purposes. First, it assumes that the reader knows nothing about the project and it introduces him or her to the job and to the customer. Second, it describes the general organization of the plan.

*Process Plan.* This section defines the development cycle for your project. The Process Plan serves as a foundation for subsequent plan elements. Your Process Plan should contain a chart that relates the project processes (definition, design, programming, system test, acceptance, migration, and operation) by showing time lines and key events. The Process Plan provides you with a base, a point of reference. For example, when you and your people talk about the start of the System Test process, you should all be talking about the same thing. I have often seen breakdowns in communication on fundamental items like this, and that's unforgivable. It leads to confusion and misunderstanding that could easily have been avoided.

*Organization Plan.* This plan element should define the organization during the various processes of the project, and it should define the specific responsibilities of each group within the organization. There are so many reshufflings within a large organization that when the bulletin board announces yet another, the reaction is often, "Here we go again." One might think that if we were smart enough we could organize a project once and be done with it, but there are actually some good reasons for reorganizing from time to time:

➤ As the project moves from one process to another, the emphasis shifts from analysis to design to programming and then to system testing. The organization should shift with the work. For example, there is no need for an installation group as early as the Definition Process, and there may be no need for a requirements analysis group during the Operational Process.

➤ Winning football coaches are good at developing strategies that make the best use of the talent available—they don't try to force-fit the people into a particular preconceived scheme. In the same way, you should organize around the people you have. If a new manager begins working for you midway through the project and expresses strong feelings about how his or her end of the project should be organized, listen and consider reorganizing. There's nothing wrong with that if it enhances his or her effectiveness and does not foul up someone else's.

➤ If the organization you adopted just isn't working smoothly, change it.

*Test Plan.* This section describes the tools, procedures, and responsibilities for conducting all testing levels on the project. The Test Plan should clearly define each separate level of test (for example, "module test," "integration test," "system test," "acceptance test," "site test"), responsibility for executing each level, machine support required for each level, support programs required, and the reporting of test results.

*Change Management Plan.* Dealing with changes in the developing system is one of management's most vital functions. This section defines the kinds of changes to be managed and the mechanism for effecting control over those changes. When you write a change management procedure, you may be tempted to cover every conceivable kind of change no matter how minor. That's a mistake because such procedures quickly become so entangled in details that they collapse of administrative fatigue.

*Documentation Plan.* This key section is usually missing. Its intent is to control the gush of paper that accompanies most projects. One reason we get buried under paper is that we don't take the time to define the documents we want to use on the project. As a result, whenever a project member needs to write something, he or she dreams up a format and suddenly there is a new kind of document to file and keep track of. I'm not averse to a little chaos in the world to keep things lively, but there are better places to allow for it. Keep it out of the documentation system.

The Documentation Plan is a gathering place in the Project Plan for the descriptions of all paper work to be used during the project. (There may also be "documents" that are only viewed on a computer screen and never get committed to paper. Account for these, too, in the plan.) When someone wants to write something there should be an appropriate kind of document outlined in the plan. Keep your document descriptions as uncluttered and as flexible as possible so that writers will have freedom to express themselves. Since pride of authorship is a powerful motivating force in most people, whether they admit it or not, they will ignore documentation guidelines that are too bureaucratic.

Besides serving as an index of document descriptions, the Documentation Plan includes a summary of publication procedures: preparation, approval, reproduction, distribution, and filing, including computer filing.

*Training Plan.* There are two categories of training required on a project: internal (training your own people) and external (training the customer and others). Training is often awarded little or no space in a plan, but this omission can be serious on some jobs. The Training Plan defines all the kinds of internal and external training required, the responsibility for each, and the resources required.

*Review and Reporting Plan.* This plan element defines how project members will communicate status using oral reviews and written reports.

*Installation and Operation Plan.* This describes the procedure for getting your finished, "accepted" software system installed and operating properly in its intended environment, such as a missile defense site or the local computing center. It includes the Migration Plan for replacing systems that are currently being used. Even the simplest of programs can become snarled in such problems as how to convert from an existing system to the new system. These problems are discussed in Chapter 13.

*Resources and Deliverables Plan.* This plan element brings together in one place the critical details associated with your plan: manpower and machine schedules, a summary of project milestones, and a summary of all items you are to deliver under your contract. These data are among the most frequently changed or consulted, so gather them in one place to make them easier to find and easier to change.

*Index.* Not a frill, it's an effective way to make your Project Plan more usable.

**Working with the Outline.**   The toughest part of any writing job is getting started. Once you've decided on a format and a detailed outline, things flow more easily. The Project Plan outlined in the Appendix should get you going quickly. Use it as a starter, modify it to suit your situation, and you're on the way. You might want to enter this outline in your project management software as a starting point and then modify it to match up with the details of the project that you're working on now.

Starting with this outline will pay off in several ways. First, you won't waste time trying to decide how to break up the planning job. Second, this outline has built-in credibility because many experienced programming managers indirectly contributed to it. Third, having *any* outline to use as a starter helps reduce the number of rewrites. I've seen lots of planning exercises (such as proposal writing) in which the manager makes writing assignments according to a sketchy outline or no outline at all. Hundreds of manhours later someone finally firms up an outline and a massive rewriting ensues—not to change technical content, but simply to make all the sections of the document fit together. These early days in planning or proposal writing are hectic enough; there's no point making things worse by guaranteeing false starts.

**Gantt Charts.**   Almost everyone is familiar with Gantt charts in one form or another. They've been around since the early 1900s. They are simple to construct and can be useful in depicting the scheduling or expenditure of resources versus time. Virtually every PC-based project management package can produce them.

Figure 1–7 is an example of a simple Gantt chart that shows people assigned

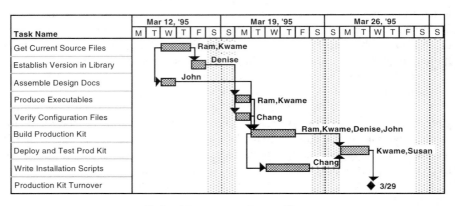

**FIGURE 1–7**   A Gantt Chart

to tasks and relates tasks to the dates when they will be performed. The tasks can be as big or as small as you wish; what's important is that they provide the control you need. As project manager, you need a chart that shows the large tasks, but your first-level managers (those who directly supervise the programmers) will need charts showing the small tasks. For example, if your project is to write a system involving real-time message processing, your chart might show such tasks as "input-message error processing," "input-message error recognition," "input-message error correction," and "input-message routing." These tasks may be of several months' duration. The first-level manager could scarcely exercise control using a chart that broad, so she must break each task into smaller pieces to spot trouble early. Theoretically, her maximum exposure is equal to the longest-duration task.

How finely you break down your tasks depends on the complexity of that part of the job and the experience and competence of your people. You might subdivide a given task into three one-week pieces for one programmer, but you might assign that same task to someone else in one two-week chunk. As a general guideline, the minimum time for any task is a week; a more reasonable time in most cases would be two weeks. If you try to subdivide tasks any finer, your programmers will spend disproportionate amounts of time in progress reporting rather than in progress, and your first-level managers will become bookkeepers, preoccupied with logging and keeping track of all those little tasks.

The maximum time to allot most tasks is about a month—and again, two weeks would be more comfortable. The point is, if a task is in trouble you've got to know it soon enough to take remedial action. It's not helpful to report a week before the project deadline that you're two months late.

You can use Gantt charts in many different ways. Figure 1–7 shows people, tasks, and time. Other charts might simply show tasks versus time, computer-time requirements versus time, or anything versus anything, as long as they help you in planning and controlling. On a separate sheet, you should list and define the tasks shown on the Gantt chart. Every task must require the delivery of a clearly defined product, such as a program module or a document.

**Milestone Charts.**    Webster defines a milestone as a "significant point in development." When you define milestones for your project, don't forget that word *significant*. Don't make the end of each task a milestone. Instead, choose those points in your schedule where something truly significant should have been completed and where some decision must be made—for example, continue, replan, get more resources. Further, base each milestone on something *measurable*; otherwise, you won't know when you get there. Some examples of *poor* milestones:

*Testing 50 percent complete*. Even if "50 percent complete" means something to you, chances are it will mean something different to someone else. It's a poor milestone because there is no sure way of knowing when you get there—it's really not measurable. Even if based on the number of tests to be run, it's fuzzy because tests vary so much in complexity that one "half" may take a week to run and the other "half" may take three months.

*Coding 50 percent complete.* The same objections apply here. Does this mean 50 percent of the anticipated number of lines of code? Or 50 percent of the modules are coded? Maybe 50 percent of the lines are coded, but they're the "easy" 50 percent, with the crunchers yet to come. Again, the number is deceptive because it means different things to different people.

Here are some better milestones. The first three are for the *first-level* manager and the last two are milestones that you'll want to track as well.

*Detailed design on module X approved.* That's important even though that design may later be changed. It means that the program module is laid out on paper and is ready for coding.

*Module testing of module X completed.* This means that the programmer has tested his individual module of code to his satisfaction and it's ready for integration with other tested modules. It's a good milestone because the programmer at this point actually submits his physical program for the next round of testing. It also means, as will be explained later, that the descriptive documentation for that module is completed in draft form, and this is something else that is measurable—something you can hold in your hands. This milestone is much better than "Module X coded."

*Specification Y drafted.* Again, the document is either physically done or it isn't. The manager can look at it and decide whether it's in good enough shape to be considered done, and hence whether the milestone has been met.

*Log-on and Execute Security Check for User.* This shows that your system can now do something it will need to do for as long as it is operational. It also means that the supporting modules to administer user security are working.

*Print Shipping Manifest.* At this milestone, the user can actually hold the system output in her hands and trace it back to ensure it is correct. Both you and your customer can see that you did what your plan said you'd do.

How many milestones should you have? There is no magic number, but consider these guidelines:

Each manager should have his own set of milestones for work done by people reporting to him. This means the first-level manager has milestones for the programmers' work, the programming manager has milestones for the first-level managers' work, and so on. However, one manager's milestones are not simply the sum of all those used by the managers who report to him. Each manager at each higher level must concentrate his energy on broader problems—that's what hierarchical organizations are all about (Figure 1–8).

Don't define the end of every task as a milestone. Allow some flexibility. For example, if a series of four tasks leads to a milestone, this allows those responsible for the four tasks to do some juggling to meet the schedule. Using your PC-based management tool, you can define milestones and clearly relate them to the supporting tasks that must be completed before the milestone occurs. I've gotten into the habit of using my PC-based management tool to create a series of related tasks and then adding a final one-day summary task such as "Demonstrate that the Credit Check Function Meets Requirements" as a milestone. This allows me to see quickly the effect on the milestone date if I run into problems on one of the supporting tasks.

| Milestone | When Does it Occur? |
| --- | --- |
| Problem Specification written<br>Accepted by customer<br>Initial Project Plan completed<br>Preliminary Acceptance Test Specification written<br>Accepted by customer | End of Definition Process |
| Preliminary Design Specification written<br>Accepted by customer | Middle of Design Process |
| Design Specification completed<br>Accepted by customer<br>First distribution of Programmer's Handbook<br>Design Process review completed<br>Integration Test Specification completed | End of Design Process |
| System Test Specification completed<br>Final Acceptance Test Specification and Site Test<br>    Specification written<br>Approved by customer<br>All program documentation completed in clean<br>    draft form | End of Programming Process |
| System Test completed | End of System Test Process |
| Acceptance agreement signed<br>Customer training completed | End of Acceptance Process |
| Installation schedule approved<br>Installation training delivered<br>Data conversion and roll-back procedures<br>    verified | Start of Migration Process |
| Program documentation corrected and delivered<br>System operational<br>Project History completed | Shortly after start of Operational Process |

**FIGURE 1–8**   Major Project Milestones

Milestones should be considered important enough that people will put out extra effort to meet a milestone that is in jeopardy. This means that you should have few enough that you don't have a weekly milestone crisis. After three or four of these crises, your people will hide when you scream for help.

First-level managers should ordinarily space milestones at least two weeks apart. Managers at higher levels should have fewer milestones. All of the managers will need to work together to ensure that they avoid milestone overload.

**PERT Charts and Critical Path Methods.**   Gantt charts are useful, but they don't always show interdependencies among tasks or among people. As a manager, you need to understand the interdependencies in your project and you should create an activity network chart to help you gain this understanding. This is not done to show off by creating yet another chart with lines and boxes. It's something you really need to do to understand the management task that lies before you.

There are two well-known incarnations of activity networks, PERT and CPM, which had their beginnings in the 1950s. Dupont and Remington Rand developed CPM (Critical Path Method) and the U.S. Navy and Lockheed came up with PERT (Program Evaluation and Review Technique). Formal PERT differs from CPM in that it requires three time estimates for tasks: most likely, optimistic, and pessimistic. Normally, when any network chart is finished, there will be a path from beginning to end over which the total time required will be greater than for any other path. This route is the *critical path*. It demands extra monitoring and management attention, since if it slips, the end date slips.

Figure 1–9 is an example of a simple activity network for the job laid out in Figure 1–8. Each of the boxes is a task; the lines show dependencies between them. Estimated units of time for each task and the projected start date are shown in the task boxes. The lines feeding a task from the left represent activities that must be undertaken before that task can be performed. All of the tasks must be completed before reaching the milestone.

In this example the job is so simple that you can easily visualize all inter-

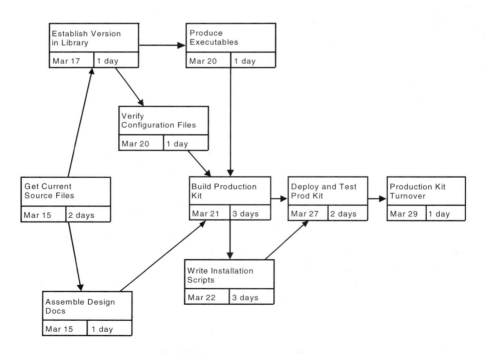

**FIGURE 1–9**   A PERT Chart

dependencies. The times add up nicely, there is no problem, and the network chart tells us nothing we did not already know from the Gantt chart. But suppose that the task "Write Installation Scripts" cannot really begin until the "Build Production Kit" task is finished. (These tasks overlap in the current plan.) Now you have a problem, and something's got to give. You must either start the "Build Production Kit" task earlier, which may be impossible, or slip the milestone date or make some other rearrangement. These interdependencies come to light as you construct an activity chart, because you must constantly answer two questions: "What must be done before I begin the next task?" and "How can I work on tasks concurrently to save overall time?" This exercise is particularly useful on larger projects when it's difficult to visualize all the activities going on.

Before the advent of personal computers, both PERT and CPM calculations were handled either by scarce mainframe computers or manually, so their use was spotty at best. Now, however, there are dozens of software packages for personal computers to help generate and modify activity networks (and Gantt charts). The widely used Microsoft Project© is an example. A manager can plug in new variables such as length of work-week and get an idea how such a change might affect project schedules. In fact, since the project management package I use even shows the activity network dependencies in the Gantt Chart format, I rarely use the PERT notation.

Often, managers on small to medium-sized projects use hand-drawn or PC-created activity networks as a useful *planning* tool—that is, to help lay out initial work schedules—but many of these managers drop it as a *control* tool because of the amount of work required just to keep the charts up to date. There's no point in slogging along with *any* management tool once it's no longer helping you to manage, but remember that a tool doesn't need to be easy to use to be valuable.

**Estimating Guidelines.**   An estimate is *your judgment* of what a job will cost in terms of person-years, calendar time, machine-hours, and other resources. It is a statement of how you plan to expend resources to get the job done. After you translate the estimate into money and calendar time, you call it a *budget*. While there is no industry-standard estimating book like the ones used by contractors or mechanics, there are steps you can take to approach the job with a reasonable degree of sanity.

At the heart of an estimate is the amount of work to be done designing, coding, testing, and documenting. For quite a while, managers tried to figure out the number of lines of code that a job involved and then tried to use that as a basis for their estimates. This didn't work well and I don't recommend that you try it. There are better alternatives.

One tool that I recommend is Function Point Analysis. The principle behind it is pretty straightforward. If you are building a system that has five input screens, four database tables, supports three inquiries, produces a report, and interfaces to a data collection system, the time and cost to build it should be comparable to another system with the same characteristics, even if the two systems are in completely different industries. Function Point Analysis works by counting the inputs, outputs, inquiries, files, and interfaces of a proposed system and then applying a relatively straightforward weighting and adjustment process to yield an estimate of the time and cost to build the system from the design that has just been analyzed.

The usefulness of function points is enhanced by the data collected by IFPUG—the International Function Point User's Group (see References). This group has correlated data about the cost and time associated with systems and the function point values for those systems. IFPUG provides these data for use in developing future estimates. The data collected have industry average adjustments for such things as the program language to be used, so you can figure out if using C will *really* save you time and money over COBOL. These data are the nearest thing available to an industry-standard estimating book. Corporate membership in IFPUG only costs $250 per year and it will repay that the first time it demonstrates that one of your vice-president's blue-sky project estimates is wildly optimistic.

You can use function point analysis without requiring a hyper-thyroid computer and without adding 50 percent overhead to your workload. The method was originally developed for paper and pencil, and studies at IBM and Unisys show an impact to project overhead of less than half a percent (Dreger, 1989).

**Automating the Estimation Process.**   Just as project management tools have become more affordable and widely available, estimation tools are becoming more widespread. Their use is common in sophisticated software development organizations and the accuracy of these automated tools has been shown to be consistently superior to human attempts for the same projects. Capers Jones (1986) has reported on a side-by-side comparison of fifty manual and automated software estimates. Twenty-two of the automated estimates came out to within 5 percent of the actual project results, but only four of the manual estimates did as well.

Many automated estimation tools use function point analysis as a basis for estimation and several have "experience bases" of thousands of previous projects. The logical link between estimation and design has also been incorporated into CASE (Computer Aided Systems Engineering) tools from Texas Instruments and others. By forcing the manager to undertake analysis before making estimates, the use of automated tools can help managers avoid the trap of early "ballpark" estimates that have a way of becoming law.

Despite the growing accuracy and acceptance of automated estimating tools, their use is the exception rather than the rule. If you have access to an automated tool, by all means use it. If you don't have one available, then use function point analysis and apply any additional information you can rely on to temper your estimates.

Keep in mind that the output from any estimating method or tool should be adjusted to reflect productivity in your own organization. This argues for serious efforts at keeping project histories, discussed later. In the absence of good records, you'll need to apply the "rules of thumb" already in place in your organization. If there are none, a good place to look for guidance is a book called *Programming Productivity*, by Capers Jones (1986)—a book I recommend you read in any case. Another source of information is Barry Boehm's *Software Engineering Economics* (1981).

My estimates used to be little more than wild guesses dressed up in planning jargon, but I worked at it and I got better. Here is the way I do my estimates now:

*STEP 0.* I don't make initial guesses! If my customer insists on an estimate, I tell him that I'll have a Project Plan and cost estimates available in three weeks.

*STEP 1.* I design the system. I hear you muttering, "Idiot! What does he mean, *design the system*? That's part of the job I'm trying to estimate!" The truth is, by the time you make your first estimates you *should have already* designed your system to some level of detail just to assure yourself the job can be done. For me, this is typically ten to twenty pages of charts requiring a few days' effort. You have to take the time to consider the size of the problem you're estimating because it's patently impossible to estimate the cost of building something that's completely undefined. In fact, a major key to successful estimating is identifying both what is and what isn't defined.

I carry the design for my first estimates far enough that I have a feel for the major technical problems I face. The more detail, the better. I don't worry that this "design" will probably be changed when the Design Process gets going. Whatever I come up with here is still a better basis for an estimate than if I resorted to the random number method.

*STEP 2.* I go through my "first cut" design and count the function points: Outputs, Inquiries, Inputs, Files, and Interfaces. I assign weights based on level of difficulty and make adjustments for special conditions. I've found it useful to "drill down" on part of the design and develop some complexity metrics (these measure the number of logic paths—the more paths, the higher the complexity). These complexity measures are extremely useful in assigning function point weights.

*STEP 3.* Using my organization's guidelines, I estimate the programming manpower (see Figure 1–10) required to produce the function points I have just derived. I always question the conversion numbers I use. When a guideline says to use

---

## A Word of Caution

Systems that are being built today often follow "layered" architectures where one layer might provide access to the databases while another provides message routing or transaction monitoring. In many cases, the "top layer" is the actual application programs. Although you might be reusing software that exists at lower layers of the system, there are costs involved in identifying it and managing its use. If there is development activity at the lower layers, there can be significant impacts on your estimates if you are concentrating on the application. These "layer management" costs aren't generally accounted for in the function point data now available.

**POTENTIAL COST ITEMS**

[   ] Programming manpower
    [   ] Programmers
    [   ] First-level programming managers
[   ] Support manpower
    [   ] Analysts
    [   ] Designers
    [   ] Testers
    [   ] Managers
    [   ] Engineers
    [   ] Secretaries
    [   ] Typists
    [   ] Instructors
    [   ] Computer operators
    [   ] Administrative assistants
    [   ] Financial assistants
    [   ] Librarians
    [   ] Technical writers
    [   ] Clerical assistants
    [   ] Couriers
    [   ] Consultants

**FIGURE 1–10**    Estimating Checklist: Manpower

$n$ person-hours per function point, I take the time to understand what's included in $n$: Does it cover only the programmer's time? Does it include problem analysis and baseline design? Does it include module test? Integration test? System test? Acceptance test? Documentation? Management time? Support personnel?

*STEP 4.* I estimate the support manpower requirements suggested by the checklist in Figure 1–10. Not all the items listed in this and other checklists are necessarily applicable to every job. In later discussions of organization I'll offer some typical numbers of support personnel, but your own experience may be worth more than my numbers or anyone else's.

*STEP 5.* Estimate equipment costs. Use Figure 1–11 to suggest categories of equipment and users you might need for your job. Later chapters will have more to say on testing and machine resources.

*STEP 6.* I estimate the items in Figure 1–12 that apply to me.

*STEP 7.* Now that I've sized everything in a bare-bones way, I go back and add contingencies appropriate for my organization. For example, I may have shown a requirement for 500 programmer-months of effort, but programmers get sick, take vacations, quit, get fired, go on military duty, attend meetings, and so on. These items may *easily* reduce the average person's effectiveness on my job by 20 percent. If you assume 100 percent use of anybody's time, you'll be in trouble right off the bat. If you decide a task will take one programmer-week of effort, it makes no

**POTENTIAL COST ITEMS**

[  ] Computer time/access
    [  ] Users
    [  ] Operational programmers
    [  ] Support programmers
    [  ] Analysts and designers
    [  ] Management
    [  ] Maintenance people
[  ] Uses
    [  ] Compile and build
    [  ] Module test
    [  ] Integration test
    [  ] System test
    [  ] Acceptance test
    [  ] Site test
    [  ] Project support programs
        [  ] Simulation
        [  ] Report generation
        [  ] Project management
        [  ] Estimation
        [  ] Program maintenance
        [  ] Hardware maintenance
        [  ] Training
        [  ] Contingency reserve
[  ] Configurations needed
    [  ] Target (customer) computers
    [  ] Support computers
[  ] Other equipment costs
    [  ] Office support systems
        [  ] PCs and workstations
        [  ] LAN
        [  ] Copiers
        [  ] FAX
    [  ] Communications (phones, etc.)
    [  ] PCs and workstations
[  ] Special changes to standard equipment
    [  ] Remote devices (notepads, etc.)

**FIGURE 1–11**   Estimating Checklist: Equipment

sense to schedule that task for one programmer over a week of calendar time—that would not make allowance for the "overhead" of lost productive time. Find out what the numbers have historically been for your organization and use them to modify your estimates—either manpower or calendar time, or both. Write down all your contingency factors so that others looking at your estimate will know what you did.

**POTENTIAL COST ITEMS**

[  ] Physical facilities
    [  ] General (office space, furniture, etc.)
    [  ] Special for your project
        [  ] Document storage
        [  ] Tape storage
        [  ] Disk storage
        [  ] Classified storage
        [  ] Program pickup and drop areas
        [  ] Off-site data archive
        [  ] Copier equipment area
[  ] Supplies
    [  ] General (paper, pencils, etc.)
    [  ] Special for your project
        [  ] Computer printer paper
        [  ] Tapes
        [  ] Disk packs/diskettes
        [  ] Carrying cases
[  ] Relocations
    [  ] Moving people
    [  ] Moving equipment and supplies
[  ] Trips
    [  ] Reasons
        [  ] For computer time
        [  ] To customer
        [  ] To other contractors
        [  ] To professional meetings and symposiums
    [  ] Number of trips
    [  ] Number of people per trip
    [  ] Duration
[  ] Special publications costs (work subcontracted to outside publications organizations)
[  ] Other
    [  ] Shuttle service to computer center
        [  ] Cars
        [  ] Drivers
    [  ] Purchased software
    [  ] Leased software
    [  ] Shift premiums
    [  ] Overtime payments
    [  ] Per diem payments
    [  ] Special training aids

**FIGURE 1–12**   Estimating Checklist: Miscellaneous

## FACTORS THAT SHOULD INCREASE YOUR ESTIMATE

[   ] Vague job requirements

[   ] Innovation required—your team will be using a tool or technique for the first time

[   ] System will have more than one user

[   ] System will be installed at more than one location

[   ] System is real-time

[   ] System replaces a system that is used by multiple groups or locations

[   ] System consolidates functionality of multiple existing systems

[   ] Interfaces with other systems are ill-defined or complex

[   ] Your programs are to interface with other programs

[   ] You are to modify someone else's programs

[   ] Your analysts have not worked on a similar application

[   ] Your designers have not worked on a similar application

[   ] Your programmers have not worked on a similar application

[   ] Your managers have not worked on a similar application

[   ] The system is larger than those you have usually worked on

[   ] You must share computer time with other projects

[   ] You do not have complete control of computer resources

[   ] System databases are very large

[   ] The existing data that will be used by your system is of either poor or unknown quality

[   ] You are obliged to follow government Configuration Management standards

[   ] Your background is not in programming

[   ] Customer will supply data base

[   ] Customer will supply test data

[   ] Data base is complex or not yet defined

[   ] Data base is classified for security reasons

[   ] Access to computer is unpredictable

[   ] Your designers are not expert programmers

[   ] Your confidence in personnel continuity is low

[   ] You have little or no choice of personnel who work for you

[   ] The customer must sign off on your design

[   ] Other agencies must sign off on your design

[   ] Customer is inexperienced in data processing

[   ] Customer is very experienced in data processing

[   ] Customer is beset by internal political problems

[   ] Your company is beset by internal political problems

[   ] You expect much change during development (requirements, customer personnel)

[   ] The system has a large number of functions

[   ] The working environment promises many interruptions

**FIGURE 1–13**   Adjustment Factors

*STEP 8.* I consider such adjustment factors as those suggested in Figure 1–13 (Nelson, 1967). I check off each item I think applies to my job. For each item checked, I look to see if I already considered it in my estimate. If not, I decide whether it is of sufficient value to cause an increase in the estimate. In each case there are various parts of the estimate that may be affected, but I (and you) can reasonably limit consideration to the three largest items: manpower, computer resources, and calendar time.

Any item checked would normally suggest an *increase* in your estimates. An item not checked may mean your estimate should be left alone, as far as that point is concerned, or it may suggest that negative weighting is in order—that is, you might *decrease* your original estimate. But go easy—estimates in this business are seldom too high.

Unfortunately, I can't tell you how much of an adjustment to make for each of these items. My recommendation is that you carefully document your assumptions for each adjustment factor you use and then track the impact of that factor as the project moves forward. In many cases, an increase in the time actually spent in dealing with one of your adjustment factors can be an early warning that the job needs to be reestimated.

*STEP 9.* I now convert everything to money by applying average salary, machine time, and other rates for my organization. If people in the controller's office handle this task for you, be sure that they understand what you have included and be sure you know what they may add. For example, they may normally add the contingencies mentioned in Step 7. Since I do the conversion, I discuss the process with the controller's office to ensure I haven't overlooked anything major.

*STEP 10.* My estimate is now the base cost for the job, sometimes called factory cost or direct cost. Now, I add my profit, my overhead expense, and any fees not already included. If I am doing this job for another part of the company, there may be a standard internal charge factor that I can use instead. Once everything is added, I have the completed cost estimate for the job, but I'm not done yet.

*STEP 11.* I write down the assumptions on which I based my estimate. I don't pass my estimate on to anyone without the assumptions—I nail them together. I may have accidentally made some assumptions my executives can't live with or some that conflict with other plans. My carefully crafted estimate may be totally useless if it's based on a bad assumption. A word of advice: if you're tempted to try covering yourself against blame if the project fails by including in the fine print an assumption you know is impossible to meet—don't do it. That's childish and unethical, and I assure you it won't work.

*STEP 12.* As the job progresses through the development cycle, I reestimate all or portions of the job as I get better information. I build in these reestimation points as tasks when I set up my Project Plan. A major point for reestimating is at the end of the Design Process. By then you should have not only a complete system design as the basis for your estimate but a solid Project Plan as well. The process of writing the Project Plan will have greatly sharpened your awareness of all cost items you're likely to face. Make sure that the review and reestimating task is clearly identified in your Project Plan and that you update your estimates at the following points:

➤ Following the analysis of any major subsystem or functional unit
➤ Following the design of any major subsystem or functional unit
➤ Upon approval of the System Test and Acceptance Test Specifications
➤ Following the completion of the unit test for any major subsystem or functional unit
➤ Following any substantial change to the Problem Specification.

Your new estimate may show a need for rejuggling your total resources (for example, using fewer people but more hardware); this is usually within a project manager's purview. If the new estimate shows a need for *additional* resources, you may have a problem. Whether you can get additional resources depends on the kind of contract you have and on the understanding and credibility existing between you and your customer. Often you can show that there has been a change in the work scope, and the customer will amend the contract to reflect the changes. Frequently you can agree to pare program requirements to fit the resources the customer can afford. Sometimes you'll end up doing more work than you are paid for—a fact that underscores the difficulty in estimating accurately enough the first time around.

**Project Histories.**   A hallmark of the data processing business is failure to keep accurate records of *estimates versus expenditures.* The difficulty in doing this industry-wide is that everyone operates differently and it's tough to agree on a standard way of keeping records. However, there is no reason *your* organization cannot and should not compile such data, perhaps with the help of an automated control system. When you choose a project management program to help you keep track of activities and resources (there are many PC-based packages available), be sure you choose one that will provide the kind of summary data you need to help keep a history.

Keep histories for your projects and then *use* them in planning succeeding jobs. Define what records should be kept as part of a history, and designate someone sharp as historian. In the Appendix, under Documentation Plan, I suggest an outline for a Project History. Use it, or devise one of your own, but avoid simply gathering a lot of charts and documents, slapping a cover on them, and labeling the whole mess "Project History."

If project history data are to be helpful on your next job, you must be able to relate the two jobs. Adopt a development cycle and terminology that you stick to from one project to the next. Then when you list manpower or computer costs for items such as "module test," "integration test," and "system test," those terms will mean the same thing on the new job you're estimating as they did on the previous jobs for which you have kept histories.

Decide how you will track program characteristics so that when you estimate the cost per function point on future projects, the costs will reflect experience in *your* organization.

## Selecting Project Tools

During the 1980s and '90s there was an explosion of automated tools designed to assist almost all project activities. This growing library of tools became possible with the introduction of small, powerful, relatively cheap computers that any business can afford. There is a variety of such machines—personal computers, workstations, laptops, and so on. Dozens of companies, some of them tiny startup operations and some the giants in the field, have poured out software to assist you and everyone else on the project in doing your jobs.

There are many books devoted to computer-assisted tools, and computing magazines are full of articles and ads hawking the latest software. The umbrella organization of which your project is a part should maintain a group of people whose function is to recommend tools for the entire organization. These people must stay current with new products and must become so knowledgeable in the use of these products that they can oversee their introduction into the organization and train people in their use. An individual project within a larger organization might also dedicate one or more people to do essentially the same job for that project. Considering the impact a new tool can have on a project's success, don't view such an assignment as wasteful "overhead."

There are some pretty good tools available to the manager to help with the job of developing time and resource estimates. In a few pages, we'll look at what you can expect from them. Unfortunately, some of the really powerful tools probably won't be available to you. They're expensive, several have significant learning curves, and many companies have chosen not to purchase them. Most project managers have to be content with more mundane methods. There are three broad categories of tools to consider: office software and hardware; planning software; and CASE (Computer-Aided Systems Engineering) software.

**Planning Software.**    Planning techniques mentioned earlier—PERT, CPM, milestone charts, Gantt charts (William and Kirby, 1990)—can all be handled manually on smaller projects. Using software to automate their use can be wasteful if the time and energy required to build and update the various documents exceed the usefulness of the documents to you. A three-week project with two or three people may not need such software, but larger projects will almost certainly benefit.

I have found planning and tracking software useful on projects with as few as six person-months. Where there are eighty or a hundred or more people involved and where there are hundreds or thousands of program modules to keep track of, a software package is mandatory. As in the selection of other project software, you need help from people whose business it is to understand what's currently available and who can relate available software to your needs. You need people within your organization to study and recommend software. Don't rely on the sales pitches of software vendors, for they'll be a teeny bit biased. They won't mind selling you a shotgun to get rid of that fly!

**CASE Tools.**   Depending on who is doing the talking, CASE stands for either Computer-Aided Software Engineering or Computer-Aided Systems Engineering. Most discussions of CASE emphasize tools that help primarily in the analysis and design efforts, where much progress has been made. The ultimate goal is to build CASE tools that provide automatic generation of perfect code from a set of specifications. There are some CASE tools that generate code, but so far they seem to do best in specific areas such as database access and user interface design (Fisher, 1991; Martin and McClure, 1988).

Most current CASE tools useful to analysts and designers are based on the methodologies discussed in this and later chapters. Some tools offer support for both structured methods and object-oriented approaches. What these tools provide is a mechanism that both supports and enforces the underlying methodology. That is, instead of adopting a particular notation such as the Gane/Sarson Data Flow Diagrams and writing and revising them manually with pencil and paper, various CASE software allows you to build and modify these diagrams and charts interactively before a computer screen. During the building or modifying processes, CASE tools offer powerful assistance by checking for completeness and consistency. The ability of CASE tools to link process and data elements is an enormous help in moving from higher to more detailed levels of analysis and design. CASE tools can spot holes in analysis or design documents that might easily go unnoticed by the analyst or designer and might otherwise come to light only in later project processes. Modern analysis and design techniques impose rigor, continuity, and completeness on the analysis and design activities; CASE tools make those goals more attainable by reducing human error.

There is one class of CASE tools that is of particular interest during the definition process. This is the set of "reverse-engineering" CASE tools that are designed to help capture information about current systems that can be used to either improve the systems as they are or to assist the people who are developing replacement systems. Most new systems carry over some of the functionality from existing systems, but it is often difficult to find out what the current systems *really* do. It doesn't do much good to study system descriptions that are ten years old when you know the system you're studying has gone through three releases a year since then.

Reverse-engineering and code restructuring tools can help to make the current system intelligible. This, in turn, lets the analysts understand better what the system does and how it might be partitioned for replacement. You may even find buried business rules in the old code.

Introducing a new CASE tool into your project is not as simple as buying a package, loading it, and telling everybody to use it. In the first place, you need plenty of input in selecting the packages to buy—purchasing a new car is a breeze compared to selecting the right CASE package. Second, many CASE tools presuppose you are already comfortable with the paper-and-pencil version of whatever methodology the tool is based on—if not, the tool is of no use to you. Third, your people must be trained in the use of the tool, and that can involve a considerable expenditure of time and money. But before you even think about training you must sell people on the wisdom of using the package at all—don't overlook the power of good old resistance to change!

**Office Software and Hardware**.   The electronic office has arrived and it's here to stay. There are degrees of electronic automation, ranging from shared personal computers to an office where everyone has his or her own PC and is electronically connected to everyone else in the office and to others around the globe. The selection and installation of hardware and software for your company or your project may require the knowledge and assistance of experts.

Here is a brief look at the kinds of services available. I am not listing specific products because by the time you read this, such a list would be out of date. You can get a good idea what's currently available by reading the latest versions of books such as Cheryl Currid's *The Electronic Invasion* (1993).

**E-mail**.   Meaning "electronic mail," E-mail has become an accepted form of office correspondence. In its simplest form, you send an E-mail message by typing it into a personal computer and transmitting it electronically to an "addressee." The message sits in the addressee's "mailbox" until he or she "opens" the mailbox and retrieves it. You can use any of the popular word-processing software, such as WordPerfect, to write the message, and additional, relatively simple software to send the message. Similar software handles the message on the receiving end.

Once you have sent an E-mail message, you may store it for archival purposes or erase it, and the addressee may do the same. An E-mail transmission may comprise a brief memo, a lengthy document, a spreadsheet, graphics—essentially anything you can generate at the sending terminal. You may send E-mail to more than one addressee; send electronic "carbon copies" to others; request a "return receipt" when the addressee opens his or her mail. You can send E-mail to anyone outside your organization whom you can reach via phone line, provided, of course, that your addressee has an electronic mailbox.

The use of E-mail has certain societal ramifications. For instance, it's easy to dash off a quick note and send it within minutes, an action you might sometimes regret! Writing a normal letter or memo has a built-in time delay that allows you a chance to reconsider. Most of E-mail's impact, though, is positive. Communication is nearly immediate; messages tend to be kept short and to the point; paper handling and filing are reduced. I think it's fair to say that E-mail is to regular mail as air mail is to the pony express.

The Software Productivity Consortium is a joint effort by a group of America's leading aerospace and defense systems suppliers that was set up to find ways of reducing cost and increasing quality for the complex software that these companies produce. When a group like this, which is already operating much more effectively than most commercial DP organizations, finds that E-mail makes a substantial difference in team (as well as individual) productivity, I'd say that there's a pretty good reason for you to look into it as well.

***The INTERNET and Other Information Services.***   Most E-mail systems are set up within a company or a building. Information services, such as the INTERNET or CompuServe©, provide you with the ability to send or receive mail from almost everywhere. Beyond this, the services can help you manage more efficiently by providing information on products and services that you can't get any other way. I use CompuServe© whenever I'm evaluating a product or tool that I'm not familiar with. I can ask if anyone out there has experience with a CASE tool or a set of object class libraries and get good, practical information about documentation quality, training, and ease of use. My alternative is to get this information from the advertising brochures, which often overlook details supplied by those who have actually tried to use the product.

***LAN.***   Virtually all large and medium-sized businesses in this information-crazy world have recognized the need for connecting everyone in the organization with everyone else—and with the outside world. They do this through LAN (Local Area Network) technology. LAN technology is a combination of hardware and software used to connect devices such as computers, printers, and storage units. While the term suggests connections only within a limited ("local") area, connections are now made that circle the globe.

There are two basic types of LANs. A client-server LAN consists of a central computer (the server) to which personal computers or workstations (clients) are connected. Both server and client have special software enabling them to communicate. The server typically acts as a central repository for files and is connected directly to printers that clients may access as needed. The second, generally less expensive, type of LAN is called peer-to-peer. It connects all users to each other rather than to a central server. In a client-server LAN, the server must be in operation at all times to be effective. Server down time and file integrity are important considerations. In peer-to-peer LANs, the individual stations rely on the others to be turned on and operable in order for communication to take place. If one network member is responsible for a critical file or if the group's only high-speed printer is attached to his or her computer, there will be hell to pay if that computer is not left up-and-running.

There are many variations to LAN hardware configurations and a slew of competing software packages available to handle network transactions. If you haven't had much experience in setting up or managing LANs, my advice is that you get help from someone who has.

*Fax.*   Facsimile (fax) machines multiplied like rabbits in recent years because they suddenly became relatively cheap. They are devices that can send and receive printed information over phone lines. They are useful when you need to send a document immediately, but as tools such as E-mail become more widely used, there will probably be less need for fax machines as we know them today.

The availability of economical high-performance fax modems for PCs allows you to use fax as a backup or extension to E-mail. Software packages are available that integrate fax and E-mail, and even support voice mail and paging. You may think that a high-end package that does all of this is overkill, but when you consider the number of times that you'll need to be contacted when you're away from your desk—meeting with the customer, attending vendor presentations, and so on—justification of the cost is unlikely to be a problem.

## WRITING ACCEPTANCE CRITERIA

Discussion of acceptance testing is included under the Acceptance Process in Chapter 11, but the actual work of preparing for acceptance begins here, in the Definition Process. Criteria for acceptance must be agreed to now and in writing, and they must be expressed in terms of measurable items. Don't labor through an entire project without knowing exactly what conditions your product must satisfy to be acceptable to the customer.

If you can, try to set up your acceptance criteria so that the customer can approve your work as it progresses. This is a good idea for a couple of reasons. First, it provides an additional incentive for a customer to get actively involved in the project processes. It may sound strange that a customer who is spending half a million dollars on a project needs to be goaded into taking an active role in monitoring its progress, but this is what often happens. If the customer is required to review and accept work as the project goes forward, he will get a better understanding of the end result.

The second reason you want to have your customer accept the system in stages is that it gets the customer into the habit of approving your work. If you wait until the end of the project for the customer to review what you've done, you could be in for some unpleasant surprises. The people that your customer assigns to oversee the acceptance process may be different from the people you worked with when you built the original Problem Specification. They may have their own (and different) ideas about system functionality and user interfaces. You can find yourself back at square one after putting in months of work.

Always remember that you are building the system for a customer and that the customer, not you, will decide if the system is a success. You're going to spend a lot of your time as a manager working with the customer to ensure that her decision is a favorable one.

*The Manager's Bookshelf*

Following each of the "process" chapters in the book, I'll suggest one or more books on the subject that give you additional details related to the material covered. I've used these books myself and I know other managers who share my high opinion of them. Here are some books I recommend that are related to the Definition Process.

Stephen M. McMenamin and John F. Palmer's *Essential Systems Analysis* (1984) is an enormously practical book on the "how to" of conducting an analysis of the system you are about to build.

Peter Coad and Edward Yourdon provide a good introduction to object-oriented analysis methods and techniques in *Object-Oriented Analysis* (1990). If you are really committed to objects, you will want to go considerably deeper, but *Object-Oriented Analysis* will give you enough useful information to apply the method to your system, if only as a sanity check.

Tom DeMarco's *Controlling Software Projects: Management, Measurement and Estimation* (1982) has been around for a while, but it remains the most readable reference for the mechanics of setting up and administering a Project Plan.

**FIGURE 2–1**   The Manager   (Daumier, "The Northern Bear," Howard P. Vincent Collection.)

# 2

# The Manager

It was my first new car in years and I was disturbed about its performance. I called the dealer for my first appointment to get routine service and fix the problems. The service manager was not nearly as sweet as the salesman had been, so it took a while to get an appointment. Finally I left the car with a long list of items needing attention, but on my way out I marked each of the tires.

Four days later I stopped to pick up my car. I paid the bill and walked out to my car. I checked the marked tires to be sure they had been rotated. They had not. I went back to the manager for an explanation. "They *were* rotated," he said. "No, they weren't," I said. "How do you know?" he challenged. "I marked them," I said.

He called the mechanic to join us. The mechanic sheepishly admitted he had not rotated the tires. Didn't think they needed it. "Did you change the oil?" I asked calmly. "Sure," he said. "How about the grease?" I asked. "Of course," he replied. His look said, "Do I look like some kind of crook?"

I finally got the tires rotated and left. By the time I got home I found that a balky seat belt had not been fixed, a muffler rattle was still there, and the engine was bucking and stalling. I wrote a long letter to the owner of the car agency. I sent a copy to the Better Business Bureau, the Consumer Protection Agency, the auto manufacturer's Michigan headquarters, and a local radio consumer-aid service.

Two days later I got a call from the agency owner. He said he wanted to talk over my letter. "Fine," I said. "Call me Bubba," he said. For an hour, long distance, Bubba tried to persuade me that the experience I had was an unfortunate combination of events that rarely happened at his shop. He assured me that if I would give him another chance, he would personally see to it that from now on I would be satisfied. His whining got to me and I agreed I'd try his shop one more time. I said that, in return for his taking the time to call me, I'd remove the big DON'T BUY FROM BUBBA sign from my car's rear window.

We were about to end the conversation when Bubba said he wanted me to know he had reprimanded the mechanic and had docked part of his pay. Now I really got steamed. What was wrong with the place, I told Bubba, was not the mechanic. It was the management. The whole tone of the place was wrong. None of his people cared about a happy customer. They were all busy grousing at one another, slamming down phones, passing the buck, being short and exasperated with customers. While waiting for my car I had witnessed a *shouting match* between a customer and her salesman. I had even been shuffled from one service representative to a second with a message because the two of them were not speaking!

I told Bubba he had docked the wrong person, that he should have begun with his management staff, including himself. I said it was clear the mechanic was only doing what was normal for this outfit.

Let's switch from Bubba the car-guy to you, the programming manager. Bubba failed to set the right tone. If you fail in the same way, you'll have unhappy workers, disgusted customers, and inferior products. Managers make *all* the difference. I'm always startled when I hear someone claim to love his or her job. The norm seems to be that people tolerate their jobs at best, and hate them at worst. Those who like their jobs always work in a well-managed place. The others work for Bubba.

## THE MANAGER AS MODEL

The manager sets the tone for everybody. No matter how strong and independent the individuals in a group, there is a tendency to emulate the manager. That's a heavy burden on you, but nobody expects you to be divine. Your behavior can rub off on those who work for you, sometimes in the strangest ways. I had a visit one time from a young IBM programmer and his wife who had come to my home studio to buy one of my paintings (I was doing a little moonlighting). I had never met them before. After two minutes of conversation, I knew exactly whom this young man worked for. He used the same clichés ("Run it up the flagpole and see if anybody salutes, heh! heh!"), had the same mannerisms, and had even developed a certain facial tic as a certain manager I knew well. I said, "You work for Johnny, don't you?" Surprised, he answered yes and wondered how I knew. I lied my way out and we spent a pleasant evening over coffee and paintings. This young man could have been Johnny's clone.

How you go about setting the tone is sometimes straightforward, occasionally tricky. If you're a decent human being, you'll automatically have a good start. But it takes more than that.

---

### On Love

"Good management is largely a matter of love. Or if you are uncomfortable with that word, call it caring."

from James Autry, *Love and Profit* (1992)

---

## Work a Normal Workday

If the company's hours are eight till five, be there at eight and go home at five. Wait! Don't throw the book across the room. Just think about it. If you make it a habit to stay every evening for an extra hour or two, don't you think your people are going to get the message? It happens every day. Eager young employees see the boss slaving away and figure that's how to become boss and make all that money and get that big office where you can spend your evenings instead of going home and loving your family and mowing the grass. Some pick up the habit out of guilt. It's not fair to go home on time while the boss is still working, is it?

Make your occasional late hours the exception, and make sure you let your people know you expect them to get their work done in a normal workday. Assign work so that people can reasonably be expected to finish their work in a normal workday. If you belong to an organization where twenty hours of unpaid overtime each week is the norm, you'll have difficulty turning things around. Such practices are deeply rooted and rarely questioned aloud. You may have to be the one to go to your manager and begin questioning the practice. He may put you off until there's time for you that evening.

Maybe you feel I'm talking nonsense. No doubt you can hardly get your work done as it is, working a lot of extra hours, so how are you going to get anywhere by cutting out the after-hours toil? It took me a long time to analyze my own work habits and recognize what I was doing. I remember watching others leave when the bell sounded and not only wondering how they managed it, but being resentful of them as well. The shirkers were fellow managers as well as some of the people who worked for me. Finally, years later, I understand some of what I was doing. See if any of this describes you.

First, after years of practice, I found it easy to waste much of my day responding to E-mail and voice messages, discussing company policies with other managers, and spending hours in meetings that only required two minutes of my presence. I knew I could get to my real work that evening. I either stayed to catch up or took home a briefcase full of paper. I simply did not use my time productively during the day. Making it up at night or over the weekend became a habit. At the time I deluded myself into thinking I was working hard both day and night, but I wasn't. I was working dumb and sloppy, and I had plenty of company.

Second, I avoided important decisions by first taking care of the trivia. The important items, usually involving lots of reading, had to wait till evening. Much of my day was devoted to dealing with the junk in my in-basket.

Third, that stuff in my in-basket often *was* junk. I could have ignored it and nothing on the project would be different. When I was new to managing I had the notion I had to read whatever was sent to me. Why else was it sent? There's at least as much junk in your in-basket as there is in a typical day's mail at home. What you need to do is a quick sorting, decide what *really* deserves your precious time, and get rid of the rest. You can throw some away, file some in case you ever *do* need it, and legitimately send some to someone else. I said *legitimately*. Don't send stuff to someone else who shouldn't get it, or you'll put her in the same foundering boat you're trying to escape.

Dealing with junk has become more of a problem than it used to be because there's more of it these days. You still get the morning and afternoon drops in your in-box, but in addition, E-mail and phone messages will come pouring in throughout the day. It has become much easier to create junk and there is no shortage of people who are willing to create it.

Finally, get rid of the notion that if you don't work those extra hours you'll miss something and the project will suffer. Sorry, but you're just not that important. Things will get done, and done well, if you sharpen your work habits, and by example, the work habits of those around you. What this all amounts to is setting priorities for your time and making sure your family life, social life, and personal life are at the top, not the bottom. Can there be any doubt that if your life and your employees' lives away from the job are happier, the job will go better?

## Make Your Workplace More Productive

Hand in hand with the idea of working "normal" hours is the need to make regular working hours productive. Tens of thousands of workers (managers and nonmanagers) spend those early and late weekday hours and those weekend hours at their desks because those are the times they feel really productive. That's a hell of an indictment of somebody.

You know the problem well. You try to get uninterrupted time to do *thinking* work, such as designing or coding or planning, and you're continually rattled by the telephone, the public-address system, meetings, hall-wanderers, and general environmental noise. A manager can do a lot about these things, but not without determination and a willingness to buck the status quo. Decide what environmental problems exist in your area and take them on, one at a time. Some places to start:

*Get rid of the public address system.* Why should everyone on the floor or in the building be interrupted by a page for one individual? One interruption of all forty or so of your people means forty losses of time (the duration of the page and the time afterward that it takes to get back to what you were doing) and forty chances for a bug or loss of continuity in whatever you were doing.

*Muffle the telephones.* DeMarco and Lister (1987) tell of successfully getting people to dampen the sounds of their ringing telephones by stuffing tissue around the bells. The sound left is a purr rather than an unnerving ring. Look into E-mail if you don't already have it. E-mail is quiet and nonintrusive; it can be answered a little later, not *right now* the way a ringing telephone demands.

*Encourage teams of people to organize their work areas to suit them.* Many workplaces have sterile cubicle arrangements and companies restrict what can be done in and around those cubicles, all in the interest of uniformity. Even if you're stuck with cubicles, you can make them *much* more livable. First, have teams arrange the workspace the way they want without regard to some rigid company "policy." (You'll probably have to do battle with the corporate martinets who work for "building management," the folks DeMarco and Lister call "the furniture police.")

*Encourage your people to decorate their spaces to suit them.* Plants, rugs, photographs, knickknacks—even *painting* their walls! Of course, if they're happy with company gray, that's their choice. This will absolutely horrify fascist managers. Visible individuality implies loss of control over the troops. But any manager ought to realize that making the troops' workplace more conducive to work benefits everybody.

*Establish general times for most meetings.* Don't call people together randomly, whenever it suits you. Pick a part of the day when you'll usually call meetings and try to avoid calling them at other times. Make meetings short and to the point (except for those in which project status is being reviewed, when you give everyone a chance to be heard).

*Limit your interruptions of individuals.* Some managers have a habit of "dropping in" and chatting with people. That's warm and chummy, but you should learn to do it at nonintrusive times, such as just before or after lunch.

*Protect your people from the company experts.* You know those actors in TV ads who put on a white coat and pretend to be doctors so they can sell you the newest cure for nose hairs? You've got them in the company, too. They're well-meaning people whose specialty is floor space or color schemes or whatever, but they know nothing about *productivity*. You've got to place yourself between these

---

### The Perfect Workspace

It takes a lot of thought to come up with the ideal workspace for your workers. Here's a way to make the job easier. Give yourself the same workspace they have.

people and your workers. Don't put up with their heckling your people with matters of "company policy" that tend toward uniformity, and don't let them treat your people like identical cards that can be constantly shuffled and rearranged.

## Don't Hog the Credit

Someone smart said, "There is no limit to what can be accomplished if it does not matter who gets the credit." If only politicians subscribed to that thinking! And spouses, parents, and managers.

When a fine new product is released, who gets the glory? Top management, most likely. Managers' names appear on acceptance documents, transmittal letters, thank-you notes, even advertisements. How about exploring ways to attach the names and reputations of product *builders* to their products? A module listing might begin with the name of its programmer, for example. A specification could give its authors a byline. A subsystem could list all those who contributed. Where a number of people have contributed to a product, why not take a page to list them all, including support people. And rather than just list them, how about their signatures—just like the Declaration of Independence! Apple Computer did this when they reproduced the signatures of the Macintosh design team on the inside of the plastic cases of the first Macs.

When you succeed in producing an especially fine product, how about a modest, frameable certificate of thanks and appreciation? When you have a truly happy customer, you might ask him to send a personalized note of thanks to each member of your team—with your help in preparing the notes.

Before a job is even done, why not advertise the names of the people who are to be responsible for specific products? Why let people labor in anonymity, when it can be so much more productive for them and for the project to advertise their jobs?

The idea is to attach people's *names* to their products, allowing them pride of authorship, and *praising* them when a job is particularly well done. From a selfish point of view, associating people with products can only help you as a manager; most people will work harder to build an impressive product if their names are attached to it.

**Be Quick to Praise in Public . . .**   When someone does a good job or comes up with a bright idea, jump on it and praise her. Of course, you say, doesn't everyone do that? A surprising number of managers are niggardly at handing out compliments. Sometimes that's because the manager *expects* the employee to do a good job, and you don't praise somebody for doing what's expected, do you? Why not? Plenty of people take silence as a negative. The only thing you have to lose by passing out praise is a loss of credibility if you overdo it or if you unwittingly hand out praise that's undeserved. In the latter case, you'll lose credibility with the rest of the troops because they'll usually know better. They always know if Jerry is screwing up long before you do.

Another reason some managers are slow to compliment is that they fear the employee will recall the compliment during some discussion of salary. Don't I deserve a raise? You said I did a terrific job! The answer is obvious. Either Joe is already making a salary in line with the good job he's doing, or he's not and you do owe him a raise. Whichever is the honest answer, go with it.

**. . . And Criticize in Private.**   Do so gently, firmly, quickly. Don't let time pass before you tell someone you're displeased. If he or she does not measure up to your expectations, say it now, in private, and be sure you understand each other before you part. Such sessions are no fun, but they need not be tragic if dealt with properly. A trap many young managers fall into is what I call "saving it up." Because it's tough to criticize someone, these managers make notes for future use— when it's time for the employee's yearly appraisal. When unsuspecting Mary asks why she is marked inadequate in such-and-such, the managers says, "Aha! Remember eleven months ago when you were late getting your subroutine in for integration?" Bewildered Mary may have fouled up, but not as badly as the manager who saved up points against her.

The worst offense is a *public* criticism followed by a *private* apology. That's like being vilified on the front page of the newspaper Monday for something you did not do, and having the error corrected Friday in the "beg pardon" section, page eighteen. If you make an error in public, retract it in public.

**Build on Failures.**   A child learning to eat from a spoon might first ram the spinach into his right cheek. Oops! Gotta go to the left. Now he hits his left cheek— but a little closer to his mouth than the first try. Back and forth and pretty soon the spinach finds its mark. Little failures lead to eventual success. Remember that in managing. Both your failures and those of your people help you to do better on the next try. Use a failure as a foundation for success (Hyman, 1993).

---

### Advice from Thomas J. Watson, Jr.

"I believed that the only way for IBM to win was to move, move, move all the time. As the computer industry grew, we had to grow with it, no matter how fast that growth might be. I never varied from the management rule that the worst possible thing we could do would be to lie dead in the water with any problem. Solve it, solve it quickly, solve it right or wrong. If you solved it wrong, it would come back and slap you in the face and then you could solve it right. Lying dead in the water and doing nothing is a comfortable alternative because it is without immediate risk, but it is an absolutely fatal way to manage a business" (Watson and Petre, 1990).

## People Ain't Modules

People are not interchangeable parts. Managers get accustomed to looking at charts that show people as numbers, but if you *treat* people as numbers, well, there's a space in the management graveyard waiting for you. One of the best exercises a manager can practice is this. Each time you talk to anyone working for you, have a background mental program running that's asking: What makes this person tick? Maybe you're considering swapping Joe from group A with Jeanne from group B. Maybe it makes sense to the project on paper. But will it make sense to Joe, Jeanne, and their coworkers? If it does not, the swap may not accomplish what you hoped and it may in fact be harmful.

## Trust Your People

Get to know your people and their talents and capacities so thoroughly that you can let them loose on a task and be confident they'll do well. Nothing is so invigorating and buoying as being given the go-ahead to do something by someone who clearly is confident you can do it. Every now and then I run into a fellow named Jim who worked for me as a programmer. He never fails to refer to me as "the best damned manager I ever had!" What's behind that remark is that I put Jim on a couple of one-person jobs and left him alone. He did the jobs well, I was grateful, and he thinks I'm a hero. The point is, I trusted this young man's ability to do the technical job and to get along perfectly with the customer. *He* was responsible for the trust—all I did was take advantage of it.

One of the easiest and best ways to show trust in those who work for you is to encourage them to manage their own time. Some people don't work well on an eight-to-five schedule. Make it clear that you expect everyone on your team to put in a full week's work over the course of a week, but allow them to choose the days and hours when they will do the work. When a task involves more than one person, let the people involved work out the schedule. If you want several team members to be together for a milestone check or some other project-related activity, make sure you put them all on notice that their presence is expected at a specific place and time and for a specific duration. Most technical people have individual work patterns that are effective for them. Doesn't it make sense to encourage these people to take the steps they need to be at their most productive?

## Stay Technically Competent

All DP managers must make a conscious effort to stay abreast of the technology that they are managing. It's particularly important that first-level managers or supervisors stay technically sharp and totally involved in the work their people are doing. They need to be comfortable and competent in designing or programming or writing test specifications or whatever their people are doing. A first-level manager should be able to take over a piece of the programming if it becomes necessary. Managers must not follow, nod approvingly, and sign time cards; they must *lead*. There must be no doubt that they completely understand their people's output and are competent to judge its quality. They must teach their less experienced people. And while doing all that, they must be learning to appraise, to schedule, to make estimates, to budget funds—all those things that will consume more of their time at the *next* management level.

Doing a good job as a first-level manager is one of the most demanding jobs in the company because you're doing both purely technical work *and* management. But what an opportunity to show your stuff! You have direct control over a product and direct control over people. If you can deliver an excellent product and lead enthusiastic, growing people, you're a hero (or a heroine).

The biggest pothole on the road to managerial success is the perception that "being a manager" is the fastest way to grow in the company (more about this later). Many newly anointed first-level managers immediately distance themselves from the nuts-and-bolts work and begin empire-building. Bad move. You'll have plenty of opportunity to climb that ladder, but don't climb until there's solid ground under it. Do an outstanding job at the first level; build your reputation and that of your group by building a product that is the envy of everyone.

Many promising careers are messed up because a new first-level manager hungrily builds his or her group as big as possible. Big means power. Big means success. These people confuse quality with quantity. A first-level manager, especially in programming, should do everything possible to keep his or her group small, on the order of a half-dozen people. You can't hope to be deeply involved in all your people's work if you allow the group to grow too large. It's tempting, of course. "My, look at me. The boss gave me ten more people today. I must be good!"

If the boss does try to saddle you with too many people, he'll no doubt be flustered when you're not suitably grateful. Work hard to convince the boss that it's the wrong move and not the road to excellence. I once had dozens of people reporting to me as a first-level manager. I was proud of my big box on the organization chart, but I had no idea what all those folks were doing for a living. My manager solved my problem by making me a second-level manager.

One more thing: As a first-level manager you'll no doubt feel a little schizoid trying to be both a technician and a manager, but don't become overzealous. Don't try to become your people's guiding light. Stay the hell out of your employees' private lives. A newly appointed manager in my department, as one of his first official acts, sent his people a memo. (Aren't managers supposed to write memos?) This one said something like, "Hello, I'm your new manager and I want you to know I'm here to help you in every way possible to have a successful career; I want you to feel free to call on me for both technical and spiritual guidance. . . ." Well, we did some fast backtracking and unspiritualizing.

My final word of advice about technical skills at the first level is this: You shouldn't feel that you need to be the *best* programmer or the *best* tester in the group. You need to be competent but you also will need to get comfortable with the idea that you may be managing people whose technical knowledge and abilities are better than yours. As you get more experience, you'll realize that one of the greatest rewards of managing is the ability to recognize talent and arrange things so that those who have it can use it to the fullest.

What about technical competence in *upper*-level managers? Here the story changes. As such a manager you'll find more distance between you and your product. How much distance depends partly on your company and how it operates. Sometimes a second-level manager, for example, is expected to be deeply involved with technical detail. But the further up you go, the more the balance shifts away from technical work and toward planning, setting goals, measuring progress, appraising, reviewing, inspiring, hiring, and firing.

It's a scary time. How do you keep track of what's going on in the trenches? As a first-level manager of six people you knew exactly where you were. Now you have to accept more remote evidence of progress. Stock up on aspirin while you begin to develop a new set of skills.

Start with the understanding that you can't accept too much on faith. You can have the most elaborate reporting and review systems and still not know the status of your project. You must insist on *evidence*. In the case of design specifications or other documents, you have some obvious evidence. But what about programs? A Data Flow Diagram or a listing is *not* a program. How about a disk or a tape alleged to contain a program? No help. You're still not seeing anything to warm your blood. How about a Data Flow Diagram *and* a listing *and* a disk or tape *and* a printed output from the running of the program allegedly on that disk or tape? Now we're getting warmer.

In the Design Process, when your team was structuring the system, they were also designing the *tests* for that system. That's the time to build in tests that can later be relied on to tell you how things are going. They need to include tests at high enough program levels that they'll be meaningful to upper-level managers. Test evidence, with outputs you can read and understand, will help you to manage without undue resort to prayer.

No matter what your level of management, you should fend off technical obsolescence by being unashamed of asking your technicians to explain things to you until you *really understand*. Not only will you and the project benefit, but your technicians will respect you more for wanting to know. Any decent technician is tickled to explain to the boss what he or she is doing if the boss is truly interested. This kind of communication builds a lot of mutual respect.

## Invite Criticism and Comment

As a manager, you're paid to make decisions. You cannot possibly know in advance that each decision will be a good one, but you've got to choose a path and follow it. Sometimes you'll make bad decisions and you'll have to take your lumps, but don't let this paralyze you. No manager of anything, anywhere, is right all the time. You'll make better decisions, though, if you invite discussion. Don't set yourself up as the only one in the department with a brain.

Some managers agonize over every decision, no matter how trivial. You have to sort out the key decisions—those affecting the fate of the project or somebody's career or the reputation of your company—and give them all the time and energy they deserve. Dispatch other matters quickly. Managers are expected to be right on most of the important decisions; they are usually forgiven errors on less important ones.

Push decision-making as low in the management chain as possible so that higher-level managers don't spend time wrestling with problems that could be solved by lower-level managers. Let your subordinates know that you *expect* them to handle some toughies, but make sure they know your general direction and philosophy. When fuzzy questions of ethics arise, for example, your people will waste a lot less time deciding what to do if they know you are unbending in your views about ethical company behavior.

At its heart, management is ethics. As a manager, you will be guiding the people who report to you in an effort to have them adopt a set of values related to the quality of their work, the importance of continuous learning, contribution and interaction within a group of similarly talented people, and a respect for the inherent dignity of a job well done.

## Act Fast to Right a Wrong

Believe it or not, you'll do some pretty stupid things now and then. There's only one way out. Don't lie. Don't fake it. Don't try to nail someone else. Admit it, fix it, and get on with life.

## Reward Technicians the Same as Managers

Many technicians who are good at their jobs make poor managers. They only accept management positions because managing is perceived as *the* way up. Most modern companies try to convince employees that the technical "ladder" is parallel to and equal to the managerial ladder. Pay scales are made the same. Equally silly titles are given each step in both ladders. Equal size offices with equal size windows and comparable wastebaskets are awarded each. Yet the feeling persists that managers are more equal than nonmanagers. The main reason for that is that most decision-making is done by managers. Isn't that what managers are for? Certainly, but most managers are not capable of making decisions involving complex technological matters without help—lots of it. The help comes partly from subordinate managers, but ultimately from the technical experts on the project.

The finest technical people should have a dual role: doing technical work and advising management. It's up to management to make sure the advisory role is understood and honored. It's up to management to promote the best technical people to positions equal in salary and status to corresponding management levels. And it's incumbent on managers that the advisory role be a real one, not window dressing. That means that you, the manager, rely on the technical advisor to help keep you informed; you seek the advisor's advice on decisions; you include her in your management meetings.

Technical advisors in data processing have often been used poorly. Sometimes this is because managers are protective of their exalted positions and resist having their powers eroded by advisors. Many managers tend toward cliquishness and form "clubs" that are hard to penetrate, like some silly fraternity where you need a secret handshake to get in. A manager who does not use the tools available to get the job done is at best misguided, at worst dumb.

Another reason advisors are misused is that we have not learned *how* to use them. I offer two real-life examples:

> Susan was a first-class programmer who had been the technical lead on the Titanic Trophy Company's first successful attempts to move from mainframe to distributed processing. Her opinion was respected within the company and when the company executives decided that they wanted a technical advisor, Susan was an obvious choice.
>
> Unfortunately, Susan never got the chance to advise. As other projects encountered difficulties, the executives assigned Susan to the job of making everything right again. As Susan said, "They didn't want an advisor, they wanted a miracle worker." Susan left the company thirteen months after her promotion and the executives still can't understand why.

> Ram's experience as an advisor took another course. He had done some superb work in optimizing Suncoast Sportcraft's data to provide cost-effective access, and as a result was invited to join the company's technology steering committee. He was told that the company wanted to use technology to "leapfrog" its competition.
>
> Once he joined the steering committee, Ram wasted no time in pushing hard for the introduction of "bleeding edge" technology. When the other members of the group questioned the value of some of the investments he was suggesting, Ram took his arguments directly to the executive vice-president. Disillusioned by the lack of support for his actions, he left the firm shortly afterward. It's hard to blame Ram for what happened. He thought he was doing what he was expected to do. The fact was that Suncoast Sportcraft's executives did not want advice that involved large capital investments and nobody ever bothered to pass that message on to Ram.

## Instill the Idea of Service

No matter how we earn our living, we all provide a service to someone. We can accept that and be happy doing a good job, or we can resist it as beneath us and have a tough life. One of the best things you can do as a manager is to acknowledge that you and your project are serving a customer and love doing it. More of this later.

## Give up Your Perks

Why should managers have special privileges? Sure, you're in a position to invent them for yourself, but does that make it right? Is there a reason a manager should have a closed office and a mahogany desk while a programmer has a cubicle (or worse). What about those reserved management parking spaces that always seem to be empty when the programmers walk past them on their way into the office?

Perks are counterproductive. If you want to build effective teams, you need to look at the people who report to you as associates, not subordinates. If you preach teamwork and then grab perks, your "team" will quite rightly look at you as a hyp-

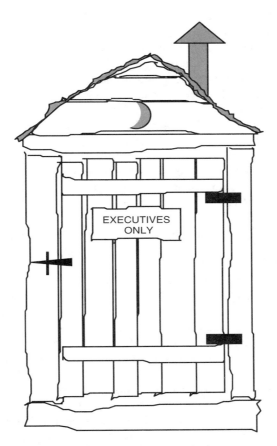

**FIGURE 2–2**    Power Perks

ocrite. By your actions, you are saying (with apologies to George Orwell), "We are all equal, but I'm a little more equal than you are."

## THE MANAGER AS TEACHER

If you're a new manager you should expect your manager to train you for your job. You should *insist* on it. You'll be better off if you can get some classroom training before taking on managing duties, but that's not crucial. There's nothing wrong with learning on the job, but there's plenty wrong with unguided groping.

Consider the case of Walter Secondlevel at Super Software, Inc. He is about to promote Jill Whiz to first-level manager of a group of programmers. Jill has been the best programmer in her group. She's smart and dependable, and gets along with everyone. She enters Walt's office and he graciously motions her to be seated.

"Coffee?" Walt asks. Jill is a little nervous. She has no idea why she has been called in. Walt asks Jill how the job is going, and whether everything is on schedule. Jill shifts a bit in her chair. Finally Walt gets to the point.

"Jill, you're doing such a terrific job, I've decided to make you a manager."

Jill is thunderstruck, but quickly regains her composure.

"That's wonderful, Mr. Secondlevel," she says. "How much?"

"How much what?"

"How much more will I be making?"

Walt is hurt that she is not so elated over the promotion that money is beside the point. He tells her about the new salary and she smiles and nods. They go on to discuss the position and the people who will be reporting to Jill.

Finally Jill asks, "How about training, Walt? I don't know anything about managing, really. When do I go to a management class?"

"Well, we don't have time for that right now. System test is coming up, and nobody can be spared. We'll see about some classes later. Meanwhile, I'll give you all the help you need." Jill leaves the office with serious misgivings. She has a title, but no credentials.

Jill is right to feel concerned. I was given my first management position under circumstances that were very similar to hers. I was hopelessly lost. I still knew all the technical stuff, but I didn't have a clue about how to organize information in order to pass it up to *my* managers. I went through three months of agony before the VP of engineering took me aside for an afternoon and told me about the things I should be doing and about how I could do them without working until midnight every night.

Managers are constantly planning, poring over proposals, giving briefings, meeting with customers, attending classes, reading memos, writing memos, appraising subordinates, listening to gripes, and solving problems. Either positively or by default, they're constantly involved in management training. Aside from specific training required by many contracts, there are three types of training that ought to concern any manager.

## Training Subordinate Managers

Jill Whiz will probably be pretty much on her own. When Walt promoted her, he didn't take the time to consider that his own promotions will hinge on Jill's performance.

Training a new manager is not a generous thing to do; it's in *your own* best interest. Think selfishly for a moment. Your own success depends on meeting your commitments and delivering quality products. You can't do that alone and you can't do it if your people are not good at their jobs. You rely on them absolutely and it is therefore to your advantage to do all you can to sharpen their competence.

First, discuss with a new manager how you see your job and how you see hers. There's no reason to expect someone who has worked for your department as, say, a programmer, to automatically understand your motivations. *Tell* the new manager how you feel about the customer, the schedule, the chances for success. Describe your basic ideas about running the project. Give the new manager an idea of the framework into which you expect her to fit, and at the same time give her a chance to object and question where you're headed. Don't expect the new manager to read your mind.

Second, give her something to read that describes how you plan to manage—not a description of a particular project, but something more generalized, something like the book you're reading now. Have you ever tried sitting down and describing in ten or twenty pages your managing philosophy? Try it. It's an experience that makes you *think through*, possibly for the first time, just what your management ideas and values are. I took the time to do this when I was struggling with a project that was falling apart. It was late, but it was rewarding.

Third, enroll your new, green manager in appropriate classes at the first opportunity. Include both administrative classes that teach the company's general policies, and project management classes. Particularly for first-level managers, see that they keep their technical skills sharp by attending classes and seminars on technical subjects. When anyone in your group attends a class, don't allow the class work to be interrupted. Treat class time as priority time.

Finally, try to ease a new manager into the job. Often you can give someone supervisory tasks before full management responsibility. Sometimes you can team the fledgling with an experienced manager for a while, or make her your assistant for a time. Do what you can to make the transition less traumatic.

Don't, don't, don't tell your new manager, "I'll give you all the help you need." Be honest—you probably don't have that much time. It's better to set a regular schedule to get together and stick to it, with the understanding that your new manager can yell "Help!" if it's a real emergency. It's better to get together for fifteen minutes three times a week that it is to schedule an hour once a week. If something comes up that requires an hour, both you and your new manager will find time for it.

## Training Nonmanagers

I once had a disagreement with a fellow manager over a programmer's reading habits. The manager came into my office all out of joint because one of his programmers spent a lot of time reading magazines. I agreed that that belonged outside of working hours, but then I asked him *which* magazines were the cause of all the fuss. I expected to hear *Rolling Stone* or The *New Yorker.* "Well, technical stuff," was the answer. "*ACM, Dr. Dobbs,* things like that." I wanted to know what was wrong with that. It sounded like a good idea to me. The programmer he was talking about, by the way, was no slouch. My manager-friend said he thought reading ought to be done on the programmer's own time, just as he, the manager, did. I wasn't exactly a flaming liberal in those days, but I thought the manager was surely wrong about this. I guess I convinced him that the reading made sense—at least he didn't go out and make a fool of himself by chewing out the programmer.

There are those who are perpetual students. They are always in classes or reading up on the latest whatnot. However, only if they never got around to doing their jobs would there be any cause to object. In fact, shouldn't you applaud your people's efforts to improve their skills? Their improvement benefits both them and you.

I'm not talking only about programmers, designers, and other technically oriented workers. I have in mind secretaries, typists, administrative assistants, computer operators—everyone who works for you. Keep an eye out for classes or seminars that might help any of them to sharpen their current skills or to add new ones. You can arrange mini-classes within your own project and have your own people teach each other something about their particular jobs. For example, programmers can give secretaries and typists a quickie programming course; computer operators can explain to programmers exactly what happens to computer runs; managers can describe company structure and how decisions get made; customer representatives can describe for you their organizations and how they operate. There is no end to opportunities for such mini-classes. Through them, at little expense, you can have the best-informed project on the planet!

## Training Yourself

Managers are busy. Year after year they fight dragons without time out for their own training. I can't now . . . too busy . . . do it some other time. Pretty soon you pay for not being current. For example, you find you can't communicate well with your programmers. They've gone on to Superlanguage and you're still thinking in FORTRAN. You know, you don't have to go to some high-powered class to learn about a new language your programmers are using. Let *them* teach you! Demeaning? Only if you pompously think you must know more about everything than anybody who works for you. Have Jill Whiz brief you on Super-language. She'll be tickled to do it, and she'll see you as a manager who respects her knowledge.

Aside from what you can do with your own resources, there are endless lists of classes offered by your company or by outside consultants. Attend as many as you can that relate directly to your management work, as well as some that are on the fringes or not directly related at all. Now we're in an area where some of your own time may be involved. The company may not be persuaded to send you to a class on programming a competitor's computer or a seminar on writing better, but get yourself there anyway.

A manager is constantly concerned with how to pay for things. You have a lot to say about budgeting. You must do all you can to get every possible dollar in your budget for training of all kinds. After all, it's not free. Many a company considers training a discretionary expense, fair game for cutting; in any company, but especially one dealing in high technology, that's suicidal.

## SALESMANSHIP

You'll face a lot of inertia as a manager and you'll find you can't always overcome it with management edicts. I overhear in the racquetball locker room every week comments about managers who are trying to impose some new procedure or methodology. It's clear that whatever these managers are pushing may exist on paper but will face tough going and slow-if-ever implementation. The gist of the conversations I hear is (a) what's wrong with the old way we're used to? and (b) the boss never asked *me* what I thought about it. You generally don't dictate what you want done (unless you're in the Marines). You explain it and sell it.

## LET YOUR PEOPLE GROW

Managers are human (usually) and they sometimes tenaciously hang on to their best people, regardless of whether that's good for the employees. An enlightened manager will not only allow the transfer of his or her good people to other departments in the company, but will *encourage* such transfers when they're of real advantage to the employee. Many managers moan and wail and snivel and threaten catastrophe if Mary Magnificent, the best programmer in the shop, is offered a job with a promotion in another department, but manager Bill Goodguy, if he cannot offer Mary as good a position in his own department, will not stand in her way. That's not to say he can ignore his own needs. He'll have to arrange for an orderly transfer so that the work Mary leaves behind does not die when she leaves. But he will not block her promotion, no matter how much it hurts.

It's not just that Bill recognizes that nobody is indispensable; it's his *duty* to watch out for the professional growth of his people. If you think "employee first, my needs second," everybody wins. Mary certainly wins, for she gets a deserved promotion. Bill Goodguy wins because he's made a short-term sacrifice for the good of Mary and the company and has shown himself to be a manager who watches out for his people. Bill is the kind of manager people want to work for.

If you're with me this far, even grudgingly, I'll ask you to take a tiny additional step. Don't just go along cheerfully with Mary's promotion. *Propose* your good people for slots you learn about in other departments. Be on the lookout for opportunities for your people. You say your stomach hurts? Think about it this way: How would *you* like to be treated? How would *you* feel if you were to find out one day your manager had quashed an opportunity for you to move up? We're not talking here about timid, self-serving managers who fear any incursions into their fiefdoms. We're talking about managers who have the courage to let their people grow, even if they grow right out of the department.

Nobody wants to be a martyr. Martyrs are all dead. What I'm advocating will bring some short-term grief, but long-term reward. Why do you think that managers in other departments look forward to working with Bill Goodguy? Why do you think that Bill got those last two promotions? How do you think his ex-workers remember him? And how do you think he feels about himself? As you develop your own managerial lifestyle, you ought to pause from time to time and consider how you feel about yourself. Trust your instincts.

## THE MANAGER AS COMMUNICATOR

Dave was a washout as a first-level manager. He couldn't even *spell* communicate. He underdid it. Another manager, Gabby, overdid it—talked a lot and said little. It was practically impossible to get the gist of what he was saying. Maybe there was no gist. He was the kind of person Talleyrand had in mind when he declared that speech is a cover-up for thought. A manager does not have to be the best administrator, the best technician, the best public speaker, but he or she *must* communicate.

There are many styles of communication. A grizzled old high school teacher, Smitty, would boom out, "All right, Metzger, dammit! Tell us about the Treaty of Ipswich!" She grinned wickedly and waited for my answer. Fear. Intimidation. But Mr. Bailey, in algebra class, would say, "All right, Philip, please put the answer to this week's special problem on the board." He was so nice you felt like a traitor if you were not ready. Soft sell.

You can learn plenty about communicating by reading, attending classes, and watching others at work. In the end, the style you develop is your own, but style aside, let's consider some of the *kinds* of information you must get across, and how you might handle them.

## Job Descriptions

Bees all get very specific jobs. Some clean out the hive, some make war, some bring home the nectar, some live it up with the queen. There's one bee whose sole job is to read off job descriptions to the young bees as they first struggle out of their little hexagonal cells in the honeycomb. She reads off the names and jobs from a computer printout, and when the last name has been read, goes back to her desk, puts her feet up, and snoozes contentedly till the next batch of young bees is ready.

Managers are not so lucky. Bees emerge from their cells, listen, salute, and off they go to do their jobs. Not so with people. They want to know a lot more. How come Edna goes off to visit flowers while we have to stay home and sweep out the hive? They want to know who their cell mates are, what the fringe benefits are, when they're likely to get more nectar. They especially want to know what their jobs are.

I mention job descriptions often. That's because I've seen so many people flop around unsure of their responsibilities. No doubt some of the people who have worked for me had the same problem. If I had only practiced then what I preach now. . . .

A written job description does not have to be a big production. One of the reasons for writing it down is that writing forces you to *think*. There's a huge difference between saying you understand something and actually expressing that understanding on paper. Make a job description fit easily on a single page. Start with a general statement ("write, debug, and document program units assigned by your supervisor and present them, complete and ready for integration test, by the dates shown on the master schedule") followed by something more specific ("using coding guidelines outlined in document X, testing procedures shown in test plan Y"). Or, for an administrative assistant, rather than "assist management in various administrative tasks" you might say "specifically responsible for scheduling all test time each week for the project, collecting biweekly status reports from each first-level manager and compiling a composite progress report." Some people need more detailed job descriptions than others, so tailor the descriptions accordingly. I guarantee that the exercise of writing job descriptions will pay off for you and your employees through sharpened awareness of expectations and fewer misunderstandings (". . . but I thought *Edna* was collecting the nectar!").

There is a little-understood payoff for writing job descriptions for all the people who work for you. It can help to alert you that some of the jobs you have created are either (a) impossible or (b) unpalatable. If you use job descriptions that were written by somebody else, you won't know what you're doing to your people until it's too late.

## Project Meetings

Here I want to concentrate on one specific type of meeting, the kind where you convene your whole group, or the whole project if you are the project manager. You have a *dialogue* about the project. You discuss its mission, schedules, problems, achievements, the customer, the project's relationship to the rest of the company, and anything else that comes up. The purpose of this meeting is to get away from managing from the privacy of your cocoon and to exchange perspectives with your people. You let them know what your view of the project is and, if you do your job right, they tell you theirs. On not-so-well-managed jobs, there is a surprising gulf between the two views. The workers know what they experience in their own relatively insulated portions of the project and what they hear as scuttlebutt; they don't have the advantage of your perspective. Neither do you see things from their positions. An individual programmer, for example, is often privy to information about the project of which you are unaware. She thinks you know all about it because, after all, you're the manager. Sometimes she's scared that you *do* know all about it.

In an article about Project Planning in *Communications of the ACM* (Rettig and Simons, 1993), the authors have this to say about keeping everyone informed of project status:

> We post progress charts publicly, including the ones that show the progress of individual team members. The simple act of posting this information builds morale, helps people feel included, and provides incentive to make progress.

So sit down in a quiet room, all of you together, and talk. You can start things off, if you wish, with a few words about how you see overall progress, but don't make things too structured. Try for freewheeling, uninhibited discussion. Be sure to make clear that's what is intended at this particular meeting, otherwise it will appear to be a bull session and you'll look as if you've "lost control." Have such a meeting regularly, perhaps bimonthly. It does not supplant regular briefings and inspections; it's in addition to them. Its aim is to make the project a family instead of a collection of monks working shut up in their cells.

## Making Meetings Effective

This is not complex. You can do it.

1. Have an objective. Make sure that the people who are asked to attend understand what the meeting is intended to accomplish.
2. Have an agenda. The items on the agenda should relate clearly and directly to the objective.
3. Invite the right people. Everyone attending the meeting either should be con-

tributing to the understanding of the group or should be in a position to do something about the action items that come out of the meeting. Generally, smaller is better.

4. Follow the agenda. Be hard-nosed about this. If you get the reputation for holding short, focused, effective meetings, you will get the attendees you need. If you let your meetings drift, people will find good reasons not to attend. Following the agenda includes starting on time.

5. Care for the details. Make sure that the overhead projector and speaker phone are in working order. Make sure that you have someone who is responsible for taking meeting notes, producing the meeting report, and distributing it to the attendees within eight hours of the meeting. Thank everyone for coming.

6. Clearly identify action items. At the close of the meeting, read off the action items and the individuals who are responsible for taking action.

## The Telephone

Everyone knows how intimidating a telephone can be. When you speak on the phone, you're someone different. Hardly anyone comes across the same on the phone as in person. People hearing you without seeing you are not necessarily overwhelmed by what a warm and loving person you really are. Record yourself sometime and see if you think that's you on the playback.

There may not be a lot you can do about your basic telephone personality, but there are some things you can do about telephone etiquette.

Answer your own phone as much as possible. IBM's T. J. Watson, Jr., made that a practice. He said, "In a service-oriented business like ours, these seemingly minor details of courtesy and style were too important to let slide. If the head man stops taking a proprietary interest in them, pretty soon everybody else stops caring too" (Watson and Petre, 1990).

What about the people who answer your phone other than you? What impression do they make on a caller? It's incredible how many business places you can call and get a rude or unfriendly or dumb reception (or even one where you hear gum-snapping—yech!). When a caller gets anything other than a friendly, businesslike greeting, you've lost stature without even trying. I know it's been suggested by many, but really, have you ever tried calling your own office at random times, just to see what reception you get before the answering person knows it's you? Try it. A courteous, cheerful, civil, educated voice at the other end of the phone line is such a tonic, while a blunt, crabby, who-gives-a-damn tone is such a turnoff.

It's part of your responsibility to help your receptionist or secretary help you. If you don't want to be disturbed, tell your receptionist how long you'll be unavailable. If you're going to be in another location this afternoon, let your receptionist know and tell him how you want your calls handled. If there are high-priority calls that you're expecting, make arrangements to screen the nonessential ones.

Most businesses these days have some form of voice mail. Try to make your voice mail greeting helpful. If you're going to be out of town until next week, let the caller know and give the name and extension of the person who is handling your calls until you get back.

Here's another facet of phone etiquette. You're in your manager's office or you're being interviewed by someone when the phone rings. The manager answers it while you sit and wait. Should you not conclude that you are less important than some random caller? Maybe the proper conclusion is that to get this person's fullest attention you should telephone instead of having a meeting. If you are a manager and you need to talk to someone without being interrupted, make sure your phone is forwarded, either to your voice mail or to the receptionist.

## Memos and Letters

Lawyers write in lawyerese and thus preserve their jobs. If ordinary people could read legal documents, lots of lawyers would be out of business. Programmers often do the same. In love with their jargon, they shun plain English. Managers who write tons of stilted and wordy memos are just as bad. Winston Churchill once said of a document presented at a cabinet meeting, "This paper, by its very length, defends itself against the risk of being read."

Most likely, you don't speak in a stilted way, so why write that way? Make your writing as straightforward as your speech. Instead of a full-page letter saying, "With reference to your invitation to appear before your group to discuss the evolution of the personal computer, let me say that . . . blah, blah . . ." and a couple of paragraphs later, ". . . I therefore am happy to accept your kind offer and . . . blah, blah . . ." why not say, "Thanks for asking. I accept."

A key consideration, even for the most trivial memo, is your concern for the person who will read it. Will this person understand what you have written? If you are asking this person to do something, will he understand clearly what you want done? If this person didn't get this memo, would it make a difference in getting the job done? If your answer to the last question is no, don't write.

There are many courses and books to help with your writing (see Strunk and White, 1979). Think about having someone give your entire group, or at least your managers, a two-hour seminar on clear writing.

## MAPMAKER AND HISTORIAN

When Charles Darwin set out on his travels aboard *H.M.S. Beagle*, he was along for the ride. The real purpose of the trip was for the captain to chart seacoasts for future voyagers. While Darwin was riding turtles in the Galápagos Islands, the ship's captain was seeing to it that future ships would more easily find their way.

Think of your job as similar to that of the *Beagle*'s captain. You've got to get where you're going in decent time so as not to bankrupt those who sent you, and you have to keep your crew happy so they don't throw you to the sharks. And before you leave port you have to figure out how to accomplish all that.

If only the last manager who traveled this route had left you a map!

Do my ramblings seem farfetched? When you're given a programming job to manage, you're told more or less where you're going, but not how to get there. One of your first acts of consequence is to construct a road map (all right, a *plan*!) to guide you. Your first draft won't be your last. It should aim you toward the right continent. Once under way, you take new bearings, find out more about the crew's strengths and weaknesses, and make adjustments to your course. Some months later you usually arrive where intended, although you may have zigzagged your way there.

The *next* time you make that trip, it will certainly be easier. You'll still run into errant winds and new kinds of sea dragons, but your basic direction will be sure. Unless, of course, you kept no log of the first trip, or you decided to leave it at home when you set out on the second.

We're getting a little better at this. We keep better records. We do learn from the last trip, but it's a painfully slow process.

I wailed in Chapter 1 about the need for project historians. Most data processing organizations simply don't keep records of what they have done. Because of this, every project is a voyage of discovery. That's one of the reasons that so many projects wind up "lost at sea." Managers should track their projects in a way that enables them to relate new jobs to those already finished. There is no reason for us to stumble continually over our estimates and develop them out of thin air for each new project. There's all that experience from the last project—why not use it?

The job is conceptually simple. Set up each project in the same way—that is, use the same development cycle, the same testing levels, the same names for activities and documents—so that you can *relate* one project to the next. Do everything you can to make a new project "look" like the previous one. That way you can compare estimates made on one project with those made on another and have the comparisons mean something. The matches won't be perfect. No two projects are that

---

### The Past as Prologue

If your company is making an effort to improve the quality of its work by competing for a Baldridge award or becoming certified as ISO 9000 compliant, you have probably been exposed to the importance that is placed on orderly procedures and record-keeping. The underlying principle is that quality can be improved in the future only if you start out by knowing where you were in the past.

alike. But you can *force* likenesses for the sake of planning and tracking. (See Chapter 1 and the Appendix for more about histories.)

## APPRAISING AND FUND-RAISING

The knock at your office door startles you.

"Yes, come in!"

In walks Harry Hotstuff, his face flushed, blood in his eye.

"Hi, Harry! What's up?" His dander is what's up.

"Boss," he begins through quivering lips, "I'd like to ask you some things about salaries." Omigod, just what you needed. It's been a tough week.

"Sit down, Harry," you say gently, forcing a smile. "Now, what is it you'd like to know?"

"I'd like to know why I do ten times the work that Wally Whiner does and only get paid ten percent more!" Damn, you say to yourself! If only these people would keep their mouths shut about their salaries. You have a sudden flashback, and sure enough, there's Wally whining his way into your heart and the company's treasury and wearing you down until he gets a bigger salary increase than he deserves. While Wally is whining, Harry is at his desk working.

What do you tell Harry? Do you confess that the system is unfair and people are not paid in true proportion to their value? Do you admit that there is a basic lump salary that most people get and that beyond that basic lump there are relatively small adjustments for performance? Will it help to explain to Harry that while his and Wally's salaries right now are not far apart, he should think about the future when he'll be promoted to loftier salary ranges while Wally remains closer to what he is now making? Just what is *fair*, anyway?

You are constantly involved in the question of salaries for your people. You have the obligation to appraise each person's value as objectively as you can and pay him or her accordingly. But there are difficulties, aren't there?

First, you must appraise your people's performance and worth. If you were foreman at an automobile assembly line, the job would be simpler. You'd be dealing with physical products and could easily determine how well they had been assembled. In the programming business, however, products are not so tangible. It's clear, then, you must do your best to *make* them tangible. Start by having a job description for every person who works for you. Write down as explicitly as possible a description of Wally's job. Give him a copy, discuss it, modify it, but make sure he has in his hands a piece of paper saying what is expected of him. As jobs change, rewrite job descriptions (but don't include details that change too frequently). If you've never done this, you'll find it's not always easy to do—and that, I think, proves its value.

The worst part comes next. You must appraise Wally using whatever procedures your company requires. Immediately, you're faced with the problem that *all your people are above average*! The below-average people work for other managers.

It's difficult for some managers to accept that, within a given population, some people are, by definition, "average," some below, some above. (On Public Broadcasting's "Prairie Home Companion," Garrison Keillor talks about Lake Wobegon, where "all the women are strong, all the men are good-looking, and all the children are above average.") Even if you can decide in the quiet of your mind who falls into each category, it's difficult to tell the average and below-average people that that's how you see them. Most people resent being "average" and recoil at being dubbed "below average." They equate both terms to "dud."

Here's what to do. Be a coward. Don't use those terms.

Try instead to rate people against their job descriptions. If Wally completely fulfilled what was expected of him in his job description, that, after all, is average work—but there's no need to use the word. You can say, in category X, Wally is "satisfactory." Now, if he happens to be, in category Y, "unsatisfactory," that's an easier word to say and it's more meaningful than the dreaded "below average" label. Of course, if you rate him "unsatisfactory" in some area, you have to be ready to defend that appraisal. If you are unable to, then he must not be unsatisfactory. Using this sort of rating, Wally is likely to be "satisfactory" in some areas (documentation), "unsatisfactory" in another (using well-structured code), and "outstanding" in others (getting to work on time). Criticize a person's performance, but not the person. It's a lot easier to hear and accept, "Your module had a lot of defects" than "You're a lousy programmer." The messages may be the same, but one is easier to swallow.

In any appraisal, start with strong points. Any employee has *some*. I used to teach watercolor classes and had many sessions during which I critiqued the students' paintings. As they propped up their paintings around the classroom I did a quick, panicky survey to see which ones were going to be the toughest to say something positive about. It was heroically desperate work at first, but I soon learned there is *always* something positive you can say ("I see you got the paint on the canvas, Agnes!"). Having made a supportive and positive start, you can proceed gently, firmly, to talk about areas needing improvement ("Maybe you'd like to try sculpture, Agnes.").

It's extremely helpful to get the employee to talk about his or her own weak points. If you can make that happen, don't lurch across the desk and yell "Gotcha!" Show that you appreciate the candor and try to find a way he or she can improve in that weak area. Make the appraisal a learning experience for both of you. You should both leave the meeting feeling enlightened about each other's expectations. As I mentioned earlier, don't store up negatives with which to bludgeon the employee at appraisal time. Discuss important problems when they first become evident.

What about salary? It's important to appraise your people relative to each other and relative to your company's standards as honestly as you can, and then peg salaries to your appraisals. There is a tendency on the part of weak managers to push the salaries of both the low achievers and the high achievers toward the middle. That's why Harry Hotstuff came boiling into your office. The result of this leveling is that your hotshot makes perhaps ten percent more than your sluggish performer, even though the hotshot does much more and better work. If Harry is worth ten Wallys, why isn't he paid ten times as much?

Maybe you can't change your company's compensation policy overnight, but you should try. Meanwhile, what you *can* do is make sure your top performers are paid at the top of their salary ranges and the poorest performers at the bottom. Crusade to make the difference significant. You may think the salary guidelines in your company are static, but that's not likely. Progressive companies make allowances for the superior performer and provide compensation beyond the normal guidelines. If you are a conscientious and probing manager, you'll learn how to buck the guidelines and better reward your superior workers. Beyond salaries, many companies offer special bonuses or achievement awards. The people who receive those awards usually have a good manager pulling for them.

## GLUE KEEPER

It's not sufficient to deal with individual people. You have to pay attention to the interfaces among your people. You need to be alert to what people are doing versus what they *say* they are doing so that when you see a potential conflict you can get them talking to each other. Suppose, for instance, you have an appraisal session with Pete Programmer and he casually mentions he can't stand Don Designer. Nothing world-shaking, just a little normal human hatred. It seems Don once called red-headed Pete a pumpkin.

While you can't always get folks to like one another, you had better see in this case whether you can bring about a little reconciliation. You may privately agree that Pete looks like a pumpkin, but that pumpkin is writing programs designed by Don. Pumpkin Pete may not do anything to sabotage Don's design, but he's not likely to go to Don to resolve problems either. He'll either work them out his own way, ignore them, or go to Don, chip on shoulder, and tell him what he thinks of his stupid Design Specification.

Take another case: One of your managers responsible for running the computer room writes and circulates a memo telling the various groups needing computer test time that there will be six hours of down time next Tuesday while an equipment change is made. Okay. But one of your other managers has a demonstration for the customer scheduled the morning after. The demonstration manager pays no attention—all he wants is his block of time on Wednesday so he can impress the customer. If his antenna does not vibrate, yours should. A change requiring six hours is probably not minor. The chances your computer operation will be smooth the next day are not 100 percent. Customer demonstrations are important. You may want to alert the two managers to a potential problem and work out different scheduling for one of them. The computer manager did his duty and let everyone know about the change; the demonstration manager had his own concerns and assumed the computer would be ready when needed; but somebody has to take a broader view and head off a problem by getting the two managers together.

As a manager, you have to organize people into neat little groups responsible for specific products or services; then you have to make sure these groups stick together rather than operate in isolation. Norman Augustine (1986) illustrates the sort of thing that can happen when nobody is keeping an eye on the players:

> On another project, two missile electrical boxes manufactured by different contractors were joined together by a pair of wires. Thanks to a particularly thorough pre-flight check, it was discovered that the wires had been reversed. It was left to the post-flight analysis to reveal that the contractors had indeed corrected the reversed wires as instructed. In fact, both of them had.

## CHOOSE YOUR WEAPONS

An important job for management is choosing the tools, procedures, and methodologies for the entire project. By *tools* I mean such things as programming languages and change management systems; *procedures* include change tracking, document control, and organizational chain of command; and by *methodologies* I mean strategies and practices for analysis, design, programming, and testing. You can't make these choices on an ad hoc basis. They will affect the entire project and will determine how smoothly it runs. If you simply divvy up the work and assign it to groups and let them choose their own working methods, you're headed for BIG trouble!

Choosing the tools, procedures, and methodologies and bringing your team to the point where they use them effectively is a big job and most managers wind up only doing part of it—not because they aren't interested in making their teams effective, but because the job typically takes longer than the time available. As a result, the majority of data processing groups cannot repeat their performance from one project to the next. Quality varies widely and cost and schedule overruns are the norm rather than the exception. Most "methodologies" actually in use are homegrown and they lack the rigor that makes most formal methodologies work.

If you want to improve this situation you are going to have to fight the apathy of "that's the way we've always done it here" and get your team genuinely interested in doing better, both individually and as a group. You will need to fight your own management to get money to invest in CASE ("I thought your people were writing programs, not drawing pictures") and the time to invest in inspections ("We don't have the time for meetings. Why aren't your people testing the code?").

Even if you can't change your company, you can change part of it. You should never finish a project feeling that the people on your team aren't better than they were when they started.

## MY COMPANY, RIGHT OR WRONG

Whatever else he did, Stephen Decatur surely did us all a disservice in preaching "Our country, right or wrong." There are managers who similarly embrace such fierce loyalty *to the company* that they will do anything to preserve its "good" name. Their transgressions range from rationalizing company weaknesses to covering up company wrongdoing. There's nothing wrong with feeling and showing loyalty to your company, but don't become blind to its faults. Use your energy to fix faults rather than defend them.

Loyalty is something that needs good managers to help it grow. Programmers start with some loyalty toward other programmers who are their friends. As a manager, you will be doing things that will encourage the growth of loyalty among the project team. Over time, there will be loyalty to the department or the division where all these project teams work. It's only after that that loyalty to the company starts to emerge.

Loyalty grows because the employee sees that her interests and the company's interests are aligned. You, the manager, are the one who is responsible for showing the employee that this alignment exists. You are the one who must push for change when it doesn't.

## SURROUND YOURSELF WITH EXCELLENCE

It's difficult for a good manager to believe this, but it's true: Some managers, afraid and unsure, surround themselves with people who are mediocre. They do this to be perceived as the smartest one in the group. They're afraid of being outshone by their subordinates. What these managers don't understand is that a manager's job is not necessarily to be the best at everything for which the group is responsible, but rather to build a group of people who individually *are* the best at what they do. The manager's claim to fame is in finding and effectively using excellent people.

You don't have to pretend anything to your people. You don't have to be as good a programmer as your best programmer or as good a designer as your best designer. You don't feel you should type as fast as your secretary, do you? Think of yourself as an orchestra conductor. Maybe you were an excellent violinist before becoming conductor, and can still play a mean fiddle, but you can't touch the tuba or the piano or the French horn. As conductor, you surround yourself with the best musicians you can find and afford; you train and plead and cajole and frown and smile and do everything you can to get the musicians to play in harmony; you help negotiate the orchestra's season schedule; you decide what pieces to play and when and how much to rehearse; you assure that what the customers see and hear as they settle back in their seats is a final product that shows none of the agony of its creation.

---

*You know that you're doing a good job as a manager if*

Customer satisfaction is your first priority; and

The professional growth of each member of your team is your first priority; and

The quality of your product is your first priority; and

Keeping your job in perspective is your first priority; and

You can keep your priorities straight.

---

**FIGURE 3–1** The Analyst (Hausner, "Adam and His Judges," Private Collection Vienna, Courtesy of the artist.)

# 3

# The Analyst

The story is told that when Gertrude Stein was dying, a hand-wringing friend sat at her bedside and wailed, "Gertrude, oh Gertrude, what is the answer, what is the *answer*!" After suitable reflection, Gertrude rose shakily on one elbow and said, "Damned if I know! What is the *question*!"

## WHAT THE ANALYST'S JOB ISN'T . . .

Annabelle Analyst works for Fred Freud in the analysis group at Super Software, Inc. She has recently been transferred there from the programming department. They meet Monday afternoon in Fred's office. Fred speaks:

"Annabelle, since you're new here, I wanted to see how your conversion from programmer to analyst is going. Let's see how we're doing on that problem spec for Floorshine Shoes."

"It's a snap, Fred," replies Annabelle brightly. "Here's a configuration diagram showing what they need."

Fred squirms a little. "Mmmmm! I see you've already got a solution down. What I'm more interested in right now, though, is just what their problem is. The proposal that got us this job was pretty fuzzy. We need to be sure we know what Floorshine is expecting. . . ."

"I spent all last week at their headquarters and it looks pretty clear to me. They need a KUMQUAT minicomputer at each retail outlet to keep track of the inventory for that store—how many pairs of shoes of each size and style and color and so on. Instead of fiddling around shelves in the storeroom, the clerk enters what's needed into the computer terminal and right away knows whether the store has that shoe in stock, and where to find it."

"And if it's not in stock?"

"What?"

"What if it's not in stock, Annabelle? Is that a lost sale?"

"Gee, I guess so. . . ." She frowns and bites her lip. Then, brightly: "But Al Sneakers and I—he's my contact at Floorshine—we came up with some stuff they're gonna love!" Annabelle spreads more diagrams on the desk in front of Fred, and continues: "We're going to include KUM-ORGANIZE software to allow each store manager to lay out his store on the video screen to make the best use of his display space—and he'll be able to do the same thing for his storage out back. . . ."

"Good," Fred interrupts, "but I thought they also wanted an inventory control system linking all the stores to the central warehouse so that an item not in stock at the store could be quickly located and sent to the store. . . ."

Annabelle grabs her original diagram and begins scribbling. "Well, if that's what they want, we can easily break in here and . . . let's see, we'll need modems and a system of entry codes into their central computer. . . ."

Fred rubs his forehead and has a fleeting memory of a lake in the Catskills where he has just spent a week's vacation.

"Annabelle," he begins slowly, "you're still programming."

"Sure!" she laughs, "I work for Super Software, don't I?"

"Yes, but . . . tell me, how is it you're talking to this Al Sneakers at Floorshine? Wasn't our contact supposed to be Judy Instep?"

"She was put on another job. They told me to talk to Sneakers."

"I see. . . ."

After some nervous beating-about-the-bush, Fred reaches for Annabelle's charts and rolls them up. He leans back with the rolled charts in his right hand and periodically whacks his left palm with the roll as if to punctuate his speech: "Annabelle, it's clear I haven't helped you make the transition from programmer to analyst. You're still in love with the code!" She stiffens.

"All your career," he goes on, "you've been a problem solver, and a good one, too. But now things are different. You're a problem-definer."

"But the problem seemed so simple . . . I thought I had defined it."

The rest of the afternoon is tough, but by the end of the day Fred and Annabelle reach an understanding about what her job as analyst really is. She understands she must start back at the fuzzy statement of work in the contract; she must find the right people at Floorshine to talk to; she accepts the fact that her job is to write a document precisely defining Floorshine's problem.

"And you need to understand that writing the programs is no longer your job," Fred reminds her firmly at the end of their talk. Weary, but enlightened and ready for a fresh start on Tuesday, Annabelle thanks Fred and leaves his office. Fred sees that she left the rolled-up diagrams behind. He picks them up, leafs through a couple of them and smiles.

"Nice solution," he mutters. "Too bad it solves the wrong problem."

## . . . And What the Job *Is*

The analyst is responsible for getting unanimous agreement from all the people calling themselves the "customer" about a system some of them think they want built. He must also write down a description of what it is they all think they agree they want, get customer management to sign a document saying yes, this is exactly what we want and yes, that's what we contracted for (if there's already a contract) or yes, that's what we'd like to contract for (if there isn't yet a contract). The analyst must write the document in such a way that it is accurate, complete, unambiguous, understandable, implementable, and tells what the system is to do without getting into how to do it.

Conceptually, the job is straightforward. In practice, it's a bugger. The analyst is in a position to plant bad seeds early. If the analyst does a poor job, the result will be poor design based on the poor analysis and poor programs based on the poor design and a poor system containing the poor programs. The ripple effect from bad analysis can be devastating. The overwhelming majority of project disasters start off as breakdowns in analysis.

To understand why analysis is difficult in practice, you need to consider what goes into it. The first thing that goes into it is the customer's perception of what he needs.

## FINDING THE CUSTOMER

You think the customer is someone who walks around wearing a CUSTOMER sign? One of the first hangups on many projects is figuring out just who the "customer" is.

Annabelle thought she was talking to the customer when she discussed Floorshine's needs with Al Sneakers. But Al was not the person originally designated as the customer's spokesperson; Judy Instep was. If you're the project manager or if you're in charge of the analysis team, such a change in customer personnel should instantly alert you. You must immediately talk to your counterpart in the customer's organization and come to an understanding of the meaning of their shift in personnel. Is Sneakers formally replacing Instep on your project? Is Sneakers as qualified as Instep to answer your questions? Was Sneakers in on the project from the start, or must he be brought up to speed? If good old Al isn't qualified for this job, you're in trouble. Satisfy yourself that the people you are dealing with on all levels in the customer's organization really speak for the customer. When there is a question, call on the next higher level in the customer's shop to be sure that the lower-level people you're relying on are the right people. Get things straight now. Otherwise, months from now the head honcho in the customer's house will ask you, "Who said it was okay to do *that*?"

Every customer has people with differing ideas about problems they need solved. Al Sneakers may be concerned with what goes on in an individual store, but his management is looking at a complex of stores and warehouses and how they can all function smoothly to assist one another and boost total Floorshine efficiency. In fact, of course, the customer is generally many people, each responsible for different facets of the business. One person, or group, may be responsible for the formal contract document containing a general statement of work and another group may be responsible for signing off on design specifications and user manuals. There may be separate people who arrange for physical work facilities, hardware selection, transportation, security. With a little luck, there will be someone who pays you periodically. And perhaps separate from all the people in power, but with a special power all their own, are the eventual *users* of the system. All these people may have differing views of what it is you're supposed to be doing for them.

A good analyst will spell out who's responsible for what and will make sure that the roles and people are clearly identified in the contract, but my experience shows me that many contracts don't even address the question. During all project processes you need to be sure you're dealing with the right people, but during the analysis activity, when you're defining the problem that all the rest of the project will be addressing, it's especially critical to sort out who's who. Al Sneakers may be in over his head and although he has the best intentions in the world, he may drive a stake right through the heart of the project.

Once the analyst figures out whom to talk to in the customer's shop, he needs to keep relationships friendly but not *too* friendly. This is particularly important if the customer happens to be another department within your own company. Some analysts get in the habit of making informal agreements with a customer, saying, with a wink, "Don't worry, we don't need to write that down. . . . I'll get the programmers to slip it in." One analyst I knew was an ex-salesman whom the programmers called "Winking Willie." When I met him, I thought he had some sort of physical problem, but it was just that his face had a permanent crinkle from so much winking. He winked one of my projects right to the edge of the cliff, and only executive intervention saved us from going over the edge.

The analyst needs to treat each member of the customer's organization as though she has an important role in the success of the project. Don't ignore administrative people who, like army sergeants, often know more about critical day-to-day operations than the brass. Make sure your analysts treat these people as fellow professionals.

## UNDERSTANDING THE CUSTOMER'S PROBLEM

Remember: you're there to *serve* the customer, not dictate to her. You serve her best by first understanding her problem. You may begin by forming a fuzzy idea of the problem and then correcting your understanding as you learn more and more.

You're like the torpedo described by Maxwell Maltz (1969). It has a target and a steering mechanism that constantly makes course corrections to keep it aimed correctly. If the target shifts, sensors in the torpedo determine the amount of shift and make a course correction based on the sensors' negative feedback. "The torpedo accomplishes its goal by *going forward, making errors,* and continually correcting them."

There are at least three ways of learning about the customer and the proposed system: reading, interviewing, and participating.

## Reading

The first thing to read is the contract, Request for Proposals, or whatever document in your case comes closest to being a statement of the customer's needs. Read the whole thing quickly and then concentrate on that portion describing the customer's technical problem. It's often referred to as the "statement of work." In a perfectly written contract in an orderly world the statement of work would *be* the problem description and there would be nothing much for an analyst to do. Most often, the statement of work is a starting place providing only a rough outline of the job.

After the statement of work there will be all kinds of documents to read. Some will be contract appendices, some will be working papers of various kinds written by customer personnel or your own proposal team. The analyst will need at least to scan such papers, always keeping in mind that the statement of work is (or should be) definitive, and many of the ideas showing up in other documents may express ideas or opinions that have already been discarded. While your analyst cannot afford the time to absorb every historical tidbit leading to the award of the contract, he will gain a lot of insight by becoming at least aware of what's gone before.

## Interviewing

Two weeks after Fred Freud's meeting with Annabelle, he calls her into his office again. She sits down and waits for him to speak.

"Where are your structure charts?" Fred asks with a grin.

"Coding is for programmers!" she shoots back with a look of mock disdain. They both laugh and after some chitchat Fred gets to the point.

"I read the draft report you turned in on Friday. It's looking good." Annabelle smiles her thanks. "I'm curious about the blank section on future loads. Having any trouble getting data? Or is it just that you haven't gotten to that section yet?"

"Well," Annabelle frowns and hesitates. "There's a guy in their forecasting department . . . name's Chuck. . ."

"Mmmmm?"

"It's hard to get anything out of him."

"Is he too busy?"

"No . . . "

"Too shy?"

"No . . ."

"Too dumb?"

"Well, no . . ." She bites her lower lip. "He answers every question the same way."

"How's that?"

" 'How long is a piece of string?' "

"What?"

"He always says, 'How long is a piece of string?' "

Fred rolls his eyes heavenward and leans far back in his chair. "Real deep thinker, huh? I know guys like that—afraid to go on record about anything. Instead of giving you their best estimates, they wear you down until you get so frustrated you make your own."

After a pause, Fred leans forward.

"What we'll do," he grins, "is retitle that section. Call it Section 4.1.1, 'How Long Is a Piece of String?' and leave it blank. We'll soon get some action. . . . Seriously, we need to get that information through Chuck rather than go around him, if that's possible. Don't want to make anybody hostile."

"Maybe he already is hostile. . . ."

"Doubt it. Just another guy trying to cover his butt. Afraid to make a decision. Wonder how he ever got into the *forecasting* department!"

Fred and Annabelle talk over their problem and decide on a course of action to get the information they need. Annabelle will complete her report and, for the forecast numbers, simply fill in the numbers that were used during the proposal phase, even though they had been pulled out of the air by a salesman. Then Annabelle will ask each of her contacts at Floorshine, including Chuck, to read the draft before cleaning it up and sending it on to Floorshine top management as part of the biweekly progress report. They feel reasonably sure Chuck will not allow bad numbers to go to the top—he will have to correct them. Annabelle will get her numbers and Chuck won't lose face. If he decides he is still unsure how long a piece of string is, Fred will get into the act and first meet with Chuck, and that failing, meet with Chuck's manager.

As Annabelle found out, interviewing people to get the information needed is not always simple. Sometimes you end up having to nudge people; in the worst cases you have to threaten, but you need to do everything in your power to avoid getting to the threatening stage.

Interviewing should begin by assuring the customer that your company is there to help solve a problem, but that it cannot be done without the customer's help. Let her know you're completely dependent on her to supply you with information about current operations and ideas about the proposed new operations. As you go along, getting the customer to educate you, you in turn must educate her. She may not know anything about computers outside of how to pick up her E-mail. You can get her on your side and get a lot more help if you trade information rather than just drain her dry. As she learns more about what the new system can do for her, she'll be more enthusiastic about giving you her time. Don't forget, some of the individuals you talk to may be disinterested, or uninterested, or even negative about what it is your company proposes to do. These individuals may view your data-gathering interviews as a big pain.

Make sure you're talking to the right people—maybe Chuck is the wrong contact. Find out who would be better and get to that person. Do it diplomatically; try not to step on toes. One grumbler can do a lot to sabotage your work. One of the "right people" you *must* talk to is the user, that part of the customer's organization who will eventually have to deal intimately with the product you deliver. Insist on talking to the user, even if customer management is reluctant to have you do so. It's easy enough for management to say, "Oh, don't worry, the guys in the parts inventory department are gonna love this system when we get it to them!" But the reality is, people who have no say about new tools often balk at using them. First, people resist changing from the comfortable ways they're used to; second, they resent not being asked their opinions about changes that may vitally affect them.

It's a good idea to use an interview form to aid in your data gathering. The form should state a few obvious items, such as the names of the interviewers and interviewees and the date. It should state the broad subject and then list specific numbered questions for discussion. As soon as possible after the interview, immediately if possible, the answers to the queries should be written out roughly and shown or read back to the interviewee to check on accuracy. Always summarize and play it back. End each interview with "Now, is this what you said?"

## Participating

If you're building something for this customer that replaces an existing system, have your analyst walked through the existing system. It's a lot easier to think about changing something if you first understand the something you are about to change.

Let's say you're building an extension to a system for a company that sells books by mail order. Ordering from small publishers is still done manually and it isn't integrated into the normal back-order processing. Your analyst can profitably spend a couple of days, at least, sitting in at each of the work stations in the current system observing, and where possible, assisting in the operations at that station: receiving and sorting incoming orders, identifying and recording the books from small publishers, matching orders against shipments received, keeping the order status information up to date, and so on. Imagine the benefits of actually experiencing the problems of the users of the old system if you're responsible for specifying the new. If a picture is worth a thousand words, *participation* is worth two floors at the library.

There's a benefit beyond merely learning what goes on: this is a wonderful opportunity to really get to know the users, those people who are at the heart of any system. Participating with them in their various tasks and doing so in a way that plainly says, "I need to learn about your system, please teach me" can do more than anything else to get their cooperation. It's a perfect time to begin planting ideas about what a new, computerized system might do to make their jobs easier. Just be careful not to give the impression you're working on a system that will make their jobs obsolete.

## ANALYSIS AS A TEAM SPORT

Even if your analysts do a great job in reading, interviewing, and participating, your Problem Specification can still be in trouble. Why? Because the information you got from the five people you interviewed, the three documents you reviewed, and the two operations you participated in are more likely to represent ten separate problems than ten facets of the same problem.

Make sure your analysts commit the following true statement to memory: "Users don't communicate among themselves as much as you think they do." This is the reason that it can be twenty-four times easier to develop a Problem Specification for a single user than for four users. Each communication path between users offers two more chances for misunderstandings to be passed to the analyst. The end result is that the analyst eventually produces a Problem Specification that satisfies nobody.

This isn't a new problem. Almost twenty years ago, Chuck Morris of IBM recognized the need to approach customers more effectively during the analysis process. He developed a technique called Joint Application Design, more often referred to as JAD (Wood and Silver, 1989). JAD brings together a group of user representatives in a structured environment that allows all of the key participants to communicate their needs and expectations for the new system directly. JAD sessions typically last two or three days and usually involve between six and ten active participants. In addition, there is a session leader and a person who records the proceedings.

The official work product of a JAD session is a Problem Specification that is agreed to by all the participants. Everyone who participates is expected to contribute to building the final document. As the session proceeds, the users will develop a clearer expectation of what the system will do, and this clearer expectation will be of enormous help when the time comes to specify realistic and unambiguous acceptance criteria.

The analyst is a key participant in the JAD session, but she should never be the session leader. Just like the users, the analyst will bring some preconceptions to the session and, if she is the leader, the other participants are likely to feel that she is manipulating the session in pursuit of her own agenda. This can prevent the free flow of information and opinions.

How important can JAD sessions be? I know of one that was held after the failure of an initial attempt to develop a Problem Specification for a new personnel system. During the first day's meeting, the session leader asked for a formal definition of "part-time." It surprised the session participants to find that a term that all of them had been using on a regular basis meant something different to each of them. No wonder the first attempt at a Problem Specification hadn't worked.

---

### Analysis Paralysis

I think it's useful to compare analysis with mathematics. For many computer scientists and analysts, analysis of systems is treated as an extension of mathematics. Tools and methods have been developed in order to prove that analysis and design are correct.

On the other hand, there are areas of mathematics where exactness cannot be achieved, even in a theoretical sense. This is the mathematics of measurement. We use mathematics of this type to provide reasonable and useful approximations.

On almost every analysis team, there will be someone who will insist on formally defining everything and who will fight against any attempt to start building the system until all of the requirements have been read, reviewed, revised, and countersigned in triplicate. For these folks, there will always be one more unresolved issue.

As a manager, you need to realize that these people are not trying to help you, no matter what they say. Pick a target date; when it arrives, figure out if the analysis is reasonable; and then get on with building the system.

---

## WRITING IT DOWN

Remember that the Problem Specification is the foundation on which you'll build this system. It's not just some reference document that may or may not be used. The project's designers should be able, theoretically, to lay out a system based on the Problem Specification alone. That's the goal, and the fact that the torpedo may zigzag a bit on the way to the goal does not diminish the importance of that goal. A quality Problem Specification does not guarantee project success, but a rotten one guarantees failure.

The writing should be as concise as possible. It must include everything that the designers and programmers need to know but it should not include extraneous details that can cause confusion. Don't think the customer is impressed by tonnage. He'll be impressed by something that answers his needs clearly while straining his brain the least.

The tone of the document should be such that it's comfortable reading for the customer, who should feel as though it's just about what he would have written. But don't forget the designers. Their translation of the Problem Specification into a Design Specification should be smooth. Use analysis tools that minimize the need for translation.

It's alleged that salespeople in this business sometimes paint a picture with a very broad brush and leave it to others to handle the details. ("Here, I caught this tiger, now you skin 'em—heh! heh!") That won't do for the analyst. The analyst must write documents describing the customer's problem in descending levels of detail. In the Floorshine case, the Problem Specification ought to include these topics:

- ➤ What business is Floorshine in?
- ➤ What is Floorshine's organization? Name names and describe responsibilities.
- ➤ How big is Floorshine?
- ➤ How does Floorshine operate now? Trace the product from initial conception through design and manufacture to distribution and sales.
- ➤ What is the impact of Floorshine's current systems? What use will be made of Floorshine's current data?
- ➤ How does Floorshine want to operate in the future? What parts of its operations are to be changed? What parts are *not* to be changed?

The last topic is the heart of the document, of course, but it will only be effective if the preceding topics are done first. Don't jump into a document and say "here are the changes" without first establishing what it is that's being changed.

Watch out for loss of consistency from one section to the next. This can happen if more than one analyst is writing the document (and that's most often the case). Don't allow one section to be developed using structured analysis, and another, some other method. Make sure the items in your document hang together (unlike a sign I saw in a Louisiana store window: SNAKE-BITE KITS AND FRIED CHICKEN).

Make sure no assumptions are left unwritten. The specification needs to cover everything that *is* to be included in the system; it also needs to state certain constraints, or items *not* to be included. In the latter category may be items that have been contested by the customer. You'll need to decide whether to include those negatives in order to head off future misunderstandings.

I remember a newspaper article that said, "This is clearly a gray area." Avoid clearly gray areas in a Problem Specification. If you come to a section where you find yourself fudging or unable to write what that section promises, recognize that your analysis is not finished. If you can't write it clearly now, what are the designers going to do with that section when it's their turn? Sometimes we reach an impasse because we have a big sack of information and it doesn't seem to make sense. Organizing it may bring clarity. Kepner and Tregoe (1965) make the point that organizing your information (into grids, decision tables, charts) may be the only way of arriving at valid conclusions.

## AND IN YOUR SPARE TIME

I wrote the first version of this using a popular personal computer and a popular word-processing program. They're like my new car—nice when they work. But it's clear that two documents were shortchanged by the people who developed both the computer and the software.

First, the user manuals. When I began using my new system I made many long-distance calls to some pleasant folks in Utah and lots of calls to my local computer salesman. Some things in the manuals were stated obliquely, and some were flat-out wrong. The manual for the operating system, in particular, had obviously gone through many revisions and in the haste to get to the market a lot of slop got through. The trouble with many manuals is that no one ever defines their audiences. People try to make a manual all things to all people.

An analyst should either write or have direct influence over the writing of user manuals. While toiling over the Problem Specification, he should always have the user's interests in mind and should approach each piece of analysis with the question: Now, how would I explain this to a user? The analyst is in the right frame of mind to explain to a user *what* the system does. The user also needs to know *how* the system can be made to do what it does, but not the *internal how* that a designer or programmer might offer. The user wants to know how to manipulate the system without getting involved in the jargon of the system's builders. My manuals read as though written by programmers whose primary concern was to get the damn job done and get back to writing programs.

The second document critical to the success of your system is one that defines acceptance criteria. The initial phase of the project, when analysts are defining what the system is supposed to do, is the time for writing these criteria that will be used later to determine whether your system satisfies the contract. Acceptance criteria should be defined in the contract—they do, after all, constitute the first real test of the proposed system—but they're often expressed there so broadly as to be useless. Had meaningful acceptance criteria been written and met for my computer's software, it's likely that I would not have paid long-distance phone charges to find out that if the printer isn't connected when you start the program, the program will assume that you never want to print.

## KEEPING SOLUTIONS IN MIND

The analyst's job is to concentrate on *what* the system is to do, not *how* it is to be built, and the resulting document must stick to that premise. But let's be realistic. Not only is it impossible to compartmentalize your brain so thoroughly as to keep out design ideas, but it would be foolish to do so. One of the attributes of a good analyst is that she knows enough about designing and writing programs to understand what's reasonable and practicable. The analyst must understand the problems of converting the analysis document into software. It's entirely possible to write the *what* in such a way as to make the *how* difficult, if not impossible.

What should you expect your analysts to do? They need to concentrate on the problem and consider design issues without bending the analysis document to favor the programmers. It's almost always better if the analysts go the other way and favor the user. Always keep in mind the customer's business objectives, because if the elegant system you deliver does not satisfy those objectives, it's of no use to anyone. When you meet with your analysts, keep the focus on the user's needs.

The analyst may be destined to go on to the next phase, change hats, and become a designer. That's common and often practical, especially on smaller projects. But she must wear the analyst's hat *first*. The urge to get into the solution is often irresistible, but understand what DeBono (1967) says about this: "Precise statement of a problem is a long step toward solving the problem."

## GETTING APPROVAL

Some of us like to work in isolation and only emerge from our caves after we've got a finished product. For an analyst that won't do. You cannot expect your analyst to spend time gathering data, disappear into an office for a couple of months, and then emerge with a product that has much chance of approval. Unless you're using JAD or a similar group specification method, the Problem Specification must be approved the same way as the system itself is approved—incrementally. Aim to make final approval a formality. When the customer sits down to read your final document, there should be no surprises. Try to bore him.

Get approval of each new chunk by having the customer sign a simple approval form, but make sure the form makes clear the importance of the approval. Use blood, not ink.

When you finish analysis and have a document cleaned up and ready for final approval, conduct an oral review for both the customer and your managers and key technical people. Once the final fixes have been made, you have the first important *baseline* for the project, an agreed-upon point of departure for everything that follows. Hallelujah! It's something you'll constantly look back to in later phases for guidance. And it's something subject to change only under clear change management procedures. We often speak of "freezing" a baseline, but that term is misleading. It's frozen in the sense that no changes are allowed without both you and your customer invoking a predetermined set of procedures (see Chapter 6). Never, *never, NEVER* allow changes to a baseline on a casual basis. As soon as that happens, you lose control of the project!

## SO, WHAT IS AN ANALYST?

I recall a session with a customer that almost lost us a job. There were a half-dozen or so of us from IBM and a like number from the customer's organization. We were discussing the customer's role in staffing a project. The customer in this case was supposed to program part of the job, and we were doing the rest. One of our bunch, an analyst we'll call Neander, had a high opinion of himself. I didn't share in the opinion, but Neander had our leader convinced he was indispensable.

We sat around a table and discussed who was to work on what; one of our people would do this, one of theirs would do that. Then the leader of the customer delegation asked, "How do you feel about going to Des Moines and spending a month with our order entry group?"

"I don't think that the folks in Des Moines will be able to understand what we're trying to do," Neander offered.

The question posed by the customer might just as well have been, "What do you think of customers?" and Neander might just as well have answered, "I don't think much of them."

Now, you might argue that there is a place for Neander somewhere on a project, and you might try to justify it by citing his technical skills. Just keep him out of sight and don't put him in the same office with a customer. I would argue that there is *no* place for him, out of sight or not. If you encourage your staff to respect the customer and you also continue to keep Neander on the staff, your entire team (and the customer as well) will see that you are not committed to practicing what you preach.

An analyst does not have to be Secretary of State. I don't think it takes special training or a rare talent to produce an analyst who can relate well to people. It simply takes a decent human being who likes other human beings and does not carry around a lot of baggage in the form of angers and prejudices. Part of the analyst's job is to get busy people to give information. As a manager, you need to choose analysts who can be friendly and businesslike at the same time.

An analyst must enjoy providing a service to a customer. Other project people, such as programmers, are more removed from the customer and they provide service indirectly. But the analyst, like a clerk in a store, actually faces the customer and tries to answer his needs—and to be a good analyst, she must *like* the idea of being of service. No matter how good the analyst's technical and writing skills are, she needs the cooperation of the customer to do her job. That cooperation will not be forthcoming if the customer gets the impression that the analyst isn't giving him any respect.

As a manager, you need to monitor the tenor of your own dealings with the customer. It's easy for a manager to set the wrong tone by referring to the customer in derogatory or condescending terms, and it would be the rare analyst who did not carry that negativism into meetings with the customer. I'm not suggesting, of course, that all customers are equally lovable, but they *are* your customers and they deserve your best efforts to help them get the systems they need.

Your analyst must be technically competent. In the computer business, people end up in jobs for a lot of reasons, not all of them sane. I've known "analysts" who were very poor technicians, appointed because they had been good salespeople or simply because they were available and, what the heck, anyone can be an analyst! Earlier I talked about the idea of keeping solutions in mind even while formulating the problem. Analysts need a good technical background if they are to avoid committing the project to the unattainable.

There are lots of things an analyst ought to be, but nobody is born an analyst. One of management's most important functions is to train people for their jobs.

Fred Freud seems to be training Annabelle by throwing her at a job and fixing problems as they arise. That's not good enough. There ought to be formal training within the company for analysts, just as there normally is for programmers and security guards. Training topics should include:

➤ Current analysis methods
➤ Interviewing
➤ Effective listening (very important)
➤ Effective writing
➤ Effective presentation
➤ Software engineering economics
➤ Estimating techniques

I have not included data processing training in this list because I think it should be a prerequisite for becoming an analyst in the first place. Training in programming does not mean, however, that the analyst must have been an ace programmer before becoming an analyst—only that he understand, through direct experience, the problems faced by working programmers. Some managers feel strongly, in fact, that programmers and designers make poor analysts because they are incapable of separating problem solutions from problem descriptions. If you don't retrain your programmers so that they can succeed as analysts, you shouldn't be surprised if they continue to approach problems the way they always did.

## WHEN IT CAN GO WRONG

Fred Freud wearily plops himself in a chair across the desk from his boss, Peter Projectmanager.

"Cripes!" he sighs, "What a day!"

Peter Projectmanager smiles wanly and nods in agreement. Yes, it *had* been a tough day. He looks across at his analysis manager and laughs: "Take off your Floorshines, Fred, and relax."

Fred glances at his feet and grimaces. "Peter," he begins, "I learned a lot today. Old Bootfoot was really ticked off. . . ." Bootfoot is the boss at Floorshine. "I'm sorry you had to witness that. . . ."

"Me, too, Fred. But we can pick up the pieces and still do a good job here. I've got some thoughts, but I'd like to hear yours."

Fred studies his hands and practices making his thumbs circle one another. Then he sits up straighter and leans forward.

"Well, to start off with, I made the mistake of assuming this was a pretty straightforward job and I felt safe enough putting Annabelle on it. Sometimes you figure somebody really bright can handle anything that comes up. . . ."

"Mmmmm. No way. A talented salesman can make a rotten programmer."

After a moment of reflection, Peter continues: "Our immediate problem—the thing we have to deal with right now—is their rejection of our problem spec."

"Yeah," Fred says, "their list of objections is pretty long, but we should be able to satisfy them with a couple of weeks of rework. I knew we should have by-passed that damned Chuck . . . the forecast data we finally got out of him were so fattened up they threw all the rest of our thinking out of whack."

"True, but just think how bad off we'd be if their management hadn't finally caught the bad info. If we'd gotten into design still working with those fat numbers we'd have ended up specifying a system big enough to run the Pentagon, let alone Floorshine!"

"Mmmmm! Chuck was really trying to cover his butt! Couple weeks back I should have seen that coming. Instead of being afraid of hurting his feelings or alienating him, I should have gone straight to his management."

"In hindsight, that's true. We all need to be a little firmer in dealing with the customer. I think, Fred, we need to be firmer in dealing with our own people, too."

Fred feels his neck and face warming.

"As far as the problem spec is concerned, it's you and me and Annabelle we need to concentrate on."

"Well," Fred breaks in, "I think I understand my mistakes there. I was too busy to stay close to what she was doing. She was new to this job and I left her too much on her own. Didn't train her . . . I should at least have worked with her for a few days till I could be sure she was on track. But what I really should have done was team her up with somebody experienced. I don't think, after this, I'd ever make one person alone responsible for analysis, no matter what the job."

"We keep learning, don't we?" Peter interrupts. He likes what he hears Fred saying. "It wasn't too many years ago we might have skipped analysis altogether and gone right into design!"

"Or programming!" Fred adds.

The two talk about how to repair the damage already done and how to avoid more of the same. They consider how to revise the project schedule, since the Problem Specification will now be a month late. They part late in the afternoon. Fred seeks out Annabelle to get her restarted with another analyst to assist her. With some queasiness, Peter ponders the new schedule they had roughed out.

It's five o'clock and time to go home. Peter Projectmanager puts on his jacket, picks up his briefcase and starts for the door. He literally bumps into a somber Fred Freud.

"Hi, Fred! Talk to Annabelle about the rework?"

"Yup."

"And about teaming up with someone?"

"Yup."

"Go okay?"

"Nope."

Peter sighs. "What's the problem?"

"Annabelle told me that she just talked to Sam Seattle and that she'll be moving out to the Northwest Division at the end of the month to fill his lead developer slot."

## SOME PRACTICAL ADVICE ABOUT MANAGING ANALYSTS

There's an old saying in the painting racket, generally attributed to Rembrandt: If you would paint an apple, first *be* an apple. In the good old days, anyone could manage anything. If you need someone to manage an analysis group, well, there's Fred over by the water cooler. He's not real busy—he's our man. Hey, Fred!

But the good old days are littered with failed projects, and we're trying to do better. We cannot be satisfied with a project landscape resembling a scene from *The Road Warrior.*

If you're going to manage analysts, there are some things you need to do about your own credentials. Get yourself trained in the current thinking about doing analysis. Just as programmers are breaking free from the old days of ragged flowcharts and sloppy coding and wasteful debugging techniques, analysts, too, are seeing new tools and methods. Structured and object-oriented approaches are replacing the old chaos. If you came to manage the analysis group straight from managing, say, programmers, you're in the same boat as Annabelle. You have a new discipline to learn, and some other things to unlearn. Is there a modern course for analysts in your company? If yes, take it; if no, get one started. If you're in charge of analysts you're in the business of building foundations; everything that follows you in the project will rest on your work.

If your first duty is to get yourself trained, certainly next in importance is to get your analysts trained. Fred Freud got Annabelle off to a shaky start because he failed to *re*train her as an analyst. Her whole inclination was to do what she was comfortable doing, solving problems. Freud gets an "F" in training. (In fairness, though, he at least recognized she was doing the wrong job and he attempted to redirect her.)

He also flubbed in sending Annabelle off as the sole analyst on the job. Even had she received proper training, it was not a good idea to let her handle her first assignment alone. In fact, I don't believe any job of any size should be staffed by a single analyst. There should be at least two people, so that one can always ask the other: Is this what you understood the customer to say? This is a case where it's better to use two people for one month than one person for two months. Where the job is so small there is no way to justify more than one person doing the analysis, the manager can at least spend the first couple of days on the project with the analyst to help assure a sound start.

When it's necessary to circumvent an ineffective customer contact and find someone who really is in charge, it's normally the analyst's job to do the circumventing. But given someone as inexperienced as Annabelle, the manager should step in. Fred could have called on his counterpart at Floorshine and established who else, besides Chuck, was in a position to get Annabelle the information she needed.

Always remember that the Problem Specification is as important to you, the manager, as it is to your analyst. The two of you need to make a conscious effort to stay coordinated during the analysis period. The analyst is going to encounter information that affects the business side of the contract, and you are going to encounter information that changes the technical side. If you and your analyst don't stay connected, you're already lost. It's just that you won't recognize your situation until later. By then it could be too late to save the project.

---

*You know your analysts are doing a good job if*

> They want to spend more time with the users.
>
> They use more than one analysis method to provide a sanity check.
>
> They look for ways to simplify, not complicate.
>
> They look at both data and processes.
>
> They keep their focus on the problem.

# PART III

# DESIGN

Design is where the magic is. Given a Problem Specification and supporting analysis documents, there will be several ways to structure and implement the software that will eventually do what the customer wants. The translation from *what is to be done* to *how is it to be done* remains the area where creativity can deliver its biggest benefits. During the Design Process, the manager needs to be conscious of the quality of the design and the implications of the design for eventual programming and maintenance.

Because design can be so volatile, the manager will spend a lot of time matching up the Design Specification and the Problem Specification, using the design documents as a source of changes to the Problem Specification and using the Problem Specification as a control on the design process.

In every project I've worked on, this is the part that is remembered as the most fun and the most rewarding.

**FIGURE 4–1** An Almost Complete Design (The Leaning Tower of Pisa, Courtesy Bob Sparks.)

# 4

# The Design Process

As you go through the work of creating your Problem Specification, you have already started the design process in order to convince yourself that the system can be built. Even before you know all the details, the nature of the problem suggests the form that the system will take. In addition, some specific design requirements will be clear very early in the Definition Process, such as the need for user log-on and security checking or the need to process messages received from Automated Teller Machines.

As soon as you and your customer have agreed on a specific part of the Problem Specification, you can officially begin the process of design. The Problem Specification doesn't have to be complete. If your customer wants to have the new system provide an audio response when an invoice number is entered through a telephone keypad so that suppliers can check on payments, once you've agreed on the information in the response *and* you and the customer have documented this agreement in the Problem Specification, you can tell your designers to figure out how to make this part of the system work.

## DESIGNING THE SYSTEM

A key output of the Definition Process was the Problem Specification, which defines the job to be done. The next important document to write is the Design Specification, the blueprint for the system. It will become the starting point for the programmers. This is the time to ensure a quality product. It's impossible to overemphasize the importance of constructing this document before coding begins. Don't play the game Larry Constantine calls WISCA (Why Isn't Sam Coding Anything?), a ruinous game played by managers who confuse motion with progress.

The Design Specification states a solution to the customer's problem. It's a solution chosen by project management and designers from among alternatives offered by the design team. The design you choose must be the "best" one for the project. It may not be the best in terms of elegance, nor the one you would choose if unlimited resources were available, but it must be the best you can implement, given the constraints on available time, talent, equipment, and money. Whatever design you choose must completely satisfy the requirements stated in the Problem Specification.

## The Designers

Your designers must be expert programmers, and at least some of them should have been heavily involved in the problem analysis activity. Ideally, you should earmark some of the designers as lead programmers or managers during the upcoming Programming Process to provide project continuity.

Like analysts, good designers are people who can go quickly to the heart of a problem and not get trapped into wandering down all the dark alleys. They must be practical; they must know what can reasonably be expected of the various components of the overall system—the machines, the programs, the people. Above all, they must communicate. We all know some superb programmers worth ten run-of-the-mill programmers as far as technical ability is concerned, but they can't communicate. They are content and productive if you carve out a big chunk of the system, define its interfaces with the rest of the system, and turn them loose. These people are usually more helpful in the Programming Process than in the Design Process.

The manager must know the technical leanings of the designers. Strong biases could easily prevent sound design tradeoffs from being evaluated. Designers are human, and they will often start by using approaches that worked well for them on other projects. Biases are inevitable, but if you know they're there, you can probably keep them from killing you. We'll explore the qualifications of designers much further in the next chapter.

## The Design Environment

People are exploring new approaches to all facets of software development, with particular emphasis on the design process. To get a feel for some of the creative ideas being tried, read the diverse articles in the October 1993 issue of *Communications of the ACM*. The issue is devoted to project organization and management, but the articles concentrate heavily on software design. The articles come at the design process from many different directions, but they have some important common threads.

The design process is an intellectual pursuit not easily tamed by rigid rules and procedures—please note that I'm talking about the *process*, the *activity*, not the tools used during the activity. Tools can be very procedure-oriented, but the human activity that somehow fabricates a design must be allowed a lot of mental elbow room. If there is a place for some "controlled chaos" (this used to be an oxymoron) on your project, it's here. You need to feel comfortable letting your designers battle out a design without excessive management control. What's excessive? For starters, the team should be spared constant interruptions, unnecessary meetings, and chores not related to designing the system. You don't need to treat the designers as prima donnas, but you have to let them know you understand that their job is not quite as orderly as laying bricks! Be as sure as you can be that the design team leader is someone who has the spine and the recognized technical competence to resolve conflicts.

## The Role of Architectures

Very few systems live their lives in isolation. The information they produce as output becomes input for some other system. Recognizing that systems must work together, many data processing organizations have established architectures to provide orderly development, communications, and transition for all of the company's systems.

Software architectures describe the ways in which the various systems allocate the work that needs to be done by the company and the means they use to work in concert. The architecture may require that all field edits be done on a workstation and all context edits be done in an application server. (The workstation can detect that 000–000–0000 is not a valid phone number, but the application server needs to interrogate the databases to determine if a valid phone number such as 610–994–0377 is already being used by somebody.) The designer needs to take the architectural rules into consideration when designing your system.

## THE DESIGN SPECIFICATION

The Design Specification describes an acceptable programming solution for the requirements stated in the Problem Specification. The Design Specification is the *baseline* for detailed design and coding.

Management and the designers must select the appropriate tools to use in writing the specification (see next section). The design documentation vehicles you use should be the result of investigation and reasoned decisions—don't just let something happen because of inaction. Don't let one designer use one method, another a different method. Think about how your baseline documents will interface with what preceded them (the Problem Specification) and what will follow them (the Coding Specifications) and choose the most compatible tools you can find.

The Design Specification consists of overall design concept, standards and conventions, program design, and database design.

**Overall Design Concept.**   The overall design concept is a brief combination of narrative and diagrams providing an overview of the entire system design at a high level. It should be suitable for communicating with members of your organization and the customer's organization who are not programmers. The overall design concept must clearly show the way in which your system will conform to the data processing architecture. You probably developed the overall design concept while you were doing the problem analysis.

**Standards and Conventions.**   This section states the rules for describing both the baseline design and the detailed design to be done later by the programmers. It identifies the *design* tools, naming standards, interfacing conventions, and message formats you'll use. It also includes *coding* standards and conventions for the Programming Process, including prohibited, required, and recommended coding practices. If such standards already exist for your organization, refer to those standards here. Any manager has to watch out for overdone standards. Heaven knows we need standards to guide us in most things, but people who devise standards sometimes go a little crazy and begin heaving long lists of commandments from the mountaintop. Remember this algorithm:

```
IF ( STANDARDS=TOO RIGID )
   THEN BYPASS STANDARDS
OR IF ( STANDARDS=TOO MANY )
   THEN IGNORE STANDARDS
ELSE FOLLOW STANDARDS
```

**Program Design.**   Program design is the core of the document. Through a combination of diagrams, narrative, and tabular information, it describes the architecture of your system. It begins with the overall program architecture and then breaks the system into smaller chunks for a closer look. The level of detail must be such that you leave *no major design problems* to the Programming Process, but don't carry this baseline design to the ultimate level of detail. There are two reasons for this. First, detailed design would make this too large a document for applying effective Change Management. Change Management must focus on the structure of the system at a relatively high level or it will be overwhelmed by the number of changes. Second, don't make the programmer a robot who codes someone else's design. The individual programmer should be your expert at coming up with a solution (detailed design and code) that best handles a specific problem. Build a solid framework for both your programs and databases and let the individual programmer concentrate on devising the best possible code to fit within that framework.

**Database Design.**    Database design is the companion to the program design section. It defines in detail all system databases—tables or files accessed by more than one program module. Thorough database definition minimizes the danger that individual programmers will independently design tables "on the fly"—tables that later prove incompatible. In one real-life example, two teams developed major program subsystems based on different ideas of what the system tables were to be like. After more than a year's work the teams discovered that the two subsystems were miserably incompatible because the tables each assumed were worlds apart. One subsystem was scrapped, along with its manager. Let's face it: the project manager should be held responsible in a situation like this. Avoiding such incredibly bad communication is one of management's prime responsibilities.

## DESIGN THE WHOLE SYSTEM FIRST

This does not mean that you must completely develop and document all details of your design before you do anything else. What it means is that you must start with a clear description of a framework that will carry all the details as requirements become clear and as the actual work of designing the system proceeds.

Modern analysis tools that you use in the Definition Process help you by identifying events or objects. If you were going to design an interactive information system that would be placed in a kiosk and used by visitors in a shopping mall, you would know that your system would need to process user requests, that it would need the capability to enter and change store information, and that it would need to have the ability to display advertising, current headlines, and weather information. There is probably a lot of stuff that you don't know yet, but your team can put together a high-level design for the whole system that shows the major functions and how they relate to each other. Now, when you have agreement from your customer that only certain administrative users will be able to change store information, your designers can see clearly where the system elements required to perform user validation will fit in the design.

We'll talk more about top-down design later in this chapter. What you need to keep in mind is that virtually every successful methodology uses the top-down approach and relies on successive refinement of the design as the project moves forward. This is critical not only from the standpoint of having a good design, but also from the standpoint of making the Design Process manageable.

### Designing Improves Definition—and Vice Versa

Starting the Design Process while the Definition Process is still active is a good idea for two reasons. The first reason is to convince yourself that you are defining a system that can, in fact, be built. We talked about this earlier.

The second reason is that the work of designing can strengthen the analytical activities within the Definition Process itself. A lot of systems look straightforward if you think about them at a high enough level. You don't realize that you're being asked to cut through the rain forest with a pocket knife until you get down to the real details. By getting an early start on design, your team will encounter problems and they will start generating questions. The answers to these questions should be incorporated into your Problem Specification. The end result will be a Problem Specification that may be considerably more complete than it would have been if you hadn't tested it to see if there was a designable system that could satisfy the problem.

The Design Process brings a different point of view to the problem. In the Definition Process we asked, "*What* is to be done?" In the Design Process, when we ask ourselves, "*How* are we going to solve this problem?" we are forced to take another look at the problem from a different perspective. Sometimes we see different features.

Just as the Design Process can strengthen the Definition Process, the Definition Process strengthens the Design Process by providing a standard for judging the quality and completeness of the design. A high-quality design should clearly correlate to the requirements put forward in the Problem Specification. It should be possible to identify specific system elements in the design that will satisfy specific requirements in the Problem Specification.

---

### Oh! Didn't We Tell You about *That*?

Several years ago, I worked with a group that wanted to build a system to scan the Chicago Board of Trade ticker and identify specific transactions, such as a buy order for a September wheat contract at a certain price. When one of these transactions was found, the system would set off an automatic, computer-generated order to buy or sell. This didn't sound very complex.

It wasn't until I started designing that I realized that the Board of Trade occasionally issued "correction" transactions for items erroneously placed on the ticker. The presence of these transactions meant that on-line scanning could only be reliable if the correction immediately followed the erroneous original. When this was brought to the attention of the customer, he told me that the correction could be delayed by five minutes or more. In that time, we could have automatically liquidated a client's holdings based on a reporting error from the Board of Trade. My design work had exposed a problem that would have come back to haunt us.

## DESIGNING FOR INTEGRATION WITH OTHER SYSTEMS

Driven by the accelerating growth of client/server architectures and distribution of data to departmental and desktop computers, integration with other systems is now a major part of many programming projects. The actual amount of work required often comes as a surprise to project managers and their customers.

At first glance, putting system components together doesn't look like it should be too difficult. Your system produces database entries that are queried by other systems or it exchanges messages with other systems. No big deal, right?

Well, not exactly. Wait until you run into the fact that the system you're communicating with expects your message fields to be null-terminated, but that isn't the way you're formatting them. Or maybe you need to respond to another system's message within 300 milliseconds so that they can complete their transactions, but you didn't know this when you designed your system to make twelve database accesses before it responds. These are the kinds of issues that drive you crazy when you try to put the parts together.

You should plan to spend about 20 percent of your design effort dealing with integration issues if your new system will be exchanging data with other systems. As the number of interfaces goes up, the amount of design time spent on them should rise as well. One of the reasons that the time spent on interface design rises rapidly is that your designers must work out the interfaces in greater detail than is required for other parts of the design. Another reason that time requirements grow is that your designers need to work with people on other teams in order to validate the design.

Some managers believe that the detailed design required for integration should be deferred until the programmers are available to work out the details. My experience shows me the opposite. The nature and number of the interfaces is determined in large part by the architecture of the system and the state of the systems that your system will communicate with. If you are going to be communicating with other systems that are being designed or developed at the same time your design process is underway, the earlier that your designers and the other system's designers can come to agreement on the nature and mechanisms, the easier it becomes for the programmers to move ahead smoothly.

Some organizations develop Interface Specifications as a "detachable" part of the Design Specification and you should consider doing this as well. The Interface Specification documents can provide a means of both communication and control for the project manager. They establish a "contract" between two teams whose work needs to mesh for either system to satisfy its objectives. It will often be true that systems projects will develop "simulators" for the other systems they will eventually communicate with. These "simulators" are useful in both unit testing and systems testing because they bypass problems of scheduling system access between the two groups. In addition, the "simulators" can be programmed so that they can create error conditions that will be difficult to reproduce once the real systems are put in place.

When designing for integration with other systems, pay attention to:

➤ Response or performance requirements
➤ Data compatibility
➤ Middleware characteristics (middleware includes data routers and transaction monitors that provide necessary housekeeping services in a network of inter-dependent systems)
➤ The degree to which the systems you are interfacing with are defined
➤ The introduction of new hardware or software products that affect inter-process communications

In a few pages, we'll start dealing with change management. The interfaces with other systems need to be subject to stringent change management procedures as early in the development cycle as possible. If you don't make plans to manage changes to the interfaces, the changes that are made (and there *will* be changes) will come as a big surprise when you try to put the pieces of the overall system together. You really do not want this type of surprise. Trust me.

## DESIGN GUIDELINES

Designing a system is not the black art some programmers would have you believe. There are some reasonable guidelines for the design process. Good designers observe these guidelines almost automatically.

**Conceptual Integrity.**   When good designers begin to structure a new system they'll be full of novel ideas and clever techniques and will have an almost irresistible urge to incorporate them into the system. But if they are *really* good, they will resist that urge. A good system design does not begin with lovely branches and leaves; it begins with a sturdy trunk. It's up to the chief designer to assure the integrity of the system by ruling out niceties that belong in somebody else's system. He or she must keep the design aimed at the eventual user. Brooks (1975) argues that "conceptual integrity is *the* most important consideration in system design. It is better to have a system omit certain anomalous features and improvements, but to reflect one set of design ideas, than to have one that contains many good but independent and uncoordinated ideas." A well-designed system best starts with a small number of people so that a single philosophy prevails.

**Modularity.**   When I was a boy, I dug a lot of ditches. I went about that inspiring job methodically. First I outlined the ditch, broke loose a neat two or three cubic feet of earth with the pickaxe, and then shoveled away the loose earth cleanly so I could see and attack the next chunk of ditch. I always felt I could see my progress better that way, and that little game probably kept me from going nuts. The alternative was to whack away with the pickaxe for a longer time, piling up a strip of loosened earth, and then shovel for a long time—but that way there would be fewer chances to look back and see progress clearly.

A programming job is like a ditch. It has a beginning and (sometimes) an end. You can attack it methodically, always having a good feel for where you are, or you can lurch forward with no intermediate goal in mind except to bull your way to the end. Either way, you'll strike rocks. Mr. Neat, however, can clean around the rock, see it, pry it loose, or bypass it. Mr. Bull's rock is obscured by all that loosened earth.

Your designers should lay out the system in chunks, or modules, not only to aid in the design process itself, but to give a big assist to the rest of the project. Modularity—that is, subdividing a job into compartments—has many advantages. I'll list them at the risk of stating the obvious:

➤ Modularity provides visibility. A system can quickly get so big and complicated that it's difficult to see what's going on unless you can look at it and deal with it one piece at a time.

➤ Modules encourage simplicity, and as a result, fewer errors.

➤ Modules are often reusable. The more restricted the function assigned to a module, the higher the probability it can be used elsewhere in this or some other system.

➤ Modules are a convenient basis for assigning work to the programmers, making projects more manageable.

➤ Modules are handy building blocks that can be put together in a deliberate, controlled manner during testing, whether you are working top-down or bottom-up.

➤ Modules provide a convenient basis for reporting progress and keeping statistics.

➤ Modularity makes later changes easier to effect.

➤ Modularity makes program maintenance easier.

Module, as used in this book, is a general term meaning a clearly identified portion of the system at any level in the hierarchy. Figure 4–2 shows a general hierarchy of modules making up a system. For purposes of discussion in this and later chapters, I have named the modules at each level as follows: unit, component, package, subsystem, system. The diagram simply says units make up components, components make up packages, packages make up subsystems, and subsystems make up the system. Each box in the diagram represents a program module. You may choose to call your modules at the various levels by other names—whatever names you choose, use them consistently throughout the project. You may also need more or fewer levels, depend-

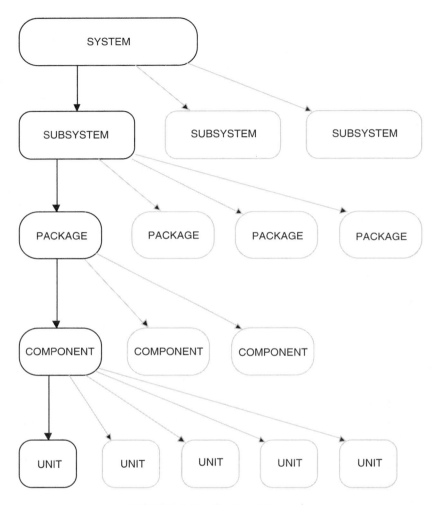

**FIGURE 4–2**   System Hierarchy

ing on the nature of your system. (The neat arrangement in the figure does not imply anything about the actual structure or arrangement of modules in a given system—it's simply a point of departure for discussion purposes. It's entirely possible and reasonable, for instance, for a module in some high level of the hierarchy to directly call a module more than one layer down in the hierarchy.)

The module called "unit" is the lowest level module independently documented and controlled in the system. It's assigned to an individual programmer. The programmer, in coding the unit, may break it into smaller pieces, such as routines, subroutines, and macros, but when the work is documented it is all contained in a single tidy bundle called a unit.

**Interface Definition.**    While the designers expend much energy in defining the system in terms of modules, they must pay equal attention to defining and documenting the interfaces among modules. The Design Specification should spell out exactly how modules communicate. Do not give programmers writing individual units the "freedom" to combine their units however they wish. Ten program units would be a small system, yet if they were all hooked together in different ways there could be as many as forty-five different interfaces. Imagine the difficulty in isolating a problem in all that mess during testing (or later during operation, when the programming team is no longer around). This is not the place to give the programmer artistic license.

Part of the designers' job, then, is to include in the Design Specification explicit, detailed explanations of the following:

➤ How do modules communicate with other modules?

➤ How do modules communicate with databases?

➤ How do databases relate to other databases, including the use of "foreign keys" linking one table to another?

➤ How do human operators interface with the programs? For example, how shall the operator manually enter a message to select a system option? What are the conventions and formats for interactive video screen use?

➤ How do the programs pass data, such as error messages, to an operator?

➤ How does the system pass information to other systems or to equipment such as display devices?

Many data processing organizations today have rich libraries of "middleware" to handle much of the housekeeping associated with interfaces. This makes the designer's job easier, but it does not provide an alibi for sloppy thinking. The design must specifically identify the Application Programming Interfaces that are being used, even when they are being provided by a standard commercial product.

**Simplicity.**    Robert Townsend (1971) has this to say about what he calls "computers and their priests":

> First get it through your head that computers are big, expensive, fast, dumb adding-machine-typewriters. Then realize that most of the computer technicians that you're likely to meet or hire are complicators, not simplifiers. They're trying to make it look tough. Not easy. They're building a mystique, a priesthood, their own mumbojumbo ritual to keep you from knowing what they—and you—are doing.

Sounds like he's run across some of our brethren who insist on giving their work a "professional" look by throwing in hieroglyphics and fancy symbols. This tendency is often apparent in professional journals. Perfectly normal people who speak clearly and communicate well succumb to some sort of seizure when

---

## Ode to Simplicity

Everybody believes in simplicity, but it's tough keeping goodies out of a system. Norman Augustine (1986) tells of the foreman in an automotive plant commenting on auto reliability: "The part you engineers don't put on the machine ain't going to cause no trouble." The foreman is only a little less poetic than Tennyson:

> Foremost captain of his time,
> Rich in saving common-sense,
> And, as the greatest only are,
> In his simplicity sublime.

---

they write an article for a journal. The subject could be dog food, but there in the middle of the article is a set of equations describing how to optimize the size of the can. If you can find a designer who can discard such nonsense and express design in simple, understandable language, you've got yourself a *real* professional. "It is never unprofessional . . . to make oneself clear," says Robert Gunning (1968).

Although we ask systems to satisfy increasingly complex requirements, computer scientists insist that program designs become simpler. IBM's Harlan Mills, a leader in the search for better programming and management techniques, urges us to look for the "deep simplicities" in program design. Strive for modules so simple and explicit in their function and structure that you can reuse them in other systems.

**Simplified Module Coupling.**   We've all seen programs in which modules are strongly *inter*dependent because the operation of one module depends on its "knowledge" of what's happening in the other. In extreme cases, one module might alter the contents (sometimes instructions—aaarrgh!) within the other. We say that such modules possess strong coupling, and their effect is to complicate the system. Designers should aim for the *weakest possible coupling*—that is, the greatest independence—between modules. Weak coupling makes each module easier to treat as an entity, easier to design without considering its effect on other modules, and easier to alter or replace later (Stevens, Meyers, and Constantine, 1974). Yes, later. Let's not forget the people who will have to maintain the system.

People who use object-oriented techniques point to the fact that their approach minimizes the coupling problem by "hiding" the information and processes that are "inside" an object. These people are absolutely right. The tools they use enforce a discipline that you and your designers need to be conscious of when you use other techniques.

**Minimum Commitment.**   In his course on program design at the Information and Systems Institute in Cambridge, Massachusetts, Larry Constantine has stressed the idea of "minimum commitment"—the idea that a designer should solve detailed problems at the "lowest level" of the system as possible. In practice, this is a useful guideline as the design becomes clearer, but you shouldn't insist on it too early in the process. Let your designers have the freedom to approach the problem from several directions (sometimes simultaneously!).

**Rule of Black Boxes.**   As a corollary to "minimum commitment," Constantine advises the designer to state a required function as a "black box," defining its inputs and outputs with little regard for internal structure until a later pass through the design. Joseph Orlicky (1969) describes the black box as a device "we simply postulate by defining its inputs and outputs." A black box, he says, "does everything we want it to do." Again, avoid getting so deeply involved with details that a sound basic design never shows through.

**Top-Down Design.**   If you were designing a building, probably you'd start by considering the building's total environment (for example, where will it sit, on how big a piece of land, of what shape). Then you might try to decide what style of building would fit both its intended use and its surroundings, not to mention the customer's budget and tastes (and *your* tastes). After that you might be ready to sketch out the main structure, without details. Given tentative agreement about building height, number of floors, general shape and style, and so on, you could proceed to designing the major parts of the structure—main entries, office areas, shop areas. Then you'd design specifics such as offices, meeting rooms, rest rooms, shops, connecting hallways, stairwells, elevator shafts. Finally, you would need to address the placement of doors, windows, lights, outlets, plumbing, decor, and a thousand other details without which the building would not function. All through the process you would find that decisions about lower-level items would affect decisions already made at higher levels. The very tools and materials to be used in doing the job (for example, concrete or glass) might affect, and be affected by, decisions you made earlier. Many iterations later, you solidify decisions (sometimes arbitrarily, in order to get on with the job) and finally the design is ready for the workmen.

The building design does not begin by concentrating on the size of the toilets, and program designs do not begin with the layout of a housekeeping module. Start with the highest, grossest, most inclusive level of functions, and refine it in ever smaller steps ("stepwise refinement") until you have accounted for all functions in a coherent and systematic manner. This is top-down design.

Top-down design is not new. Competent programmers have been doing it since programming began, although the "top-down" label came later. The more the techniques of top-down design are used, of course, the more natural they become, and the less likely that a manager will allow his programmers to proceed in shotgun fashion. Yet, senseless as it may seem, some managers still hack a job into a number of chunks that sound sensible and then throw the chunks to people or groups like meat to the lions. ("We'll worry about tying them together later; right now let's get something cycling. The customer is breathing down my neck!") That's like having people build windows, doors, closets, rooms, and so on, hoping later to make them fit together.

Let's remember that right now we're talking about the writing of a baseline design, a point of departure for the entire detailed design. The designers must decide where to stop the baseline design; this document must establish the framework for the system, establish all the communication conventions, and solve all the flow and control problems. The design of the individual modules is left to the programmers. There is no way to state exactly where to stop baseline design; that will be different for each project, and will reflect the experience, even the personalities, of the designers, managers, and programmers. When the baseline design shows a complete and viable solution to the problem stated in the Problem Specification, it's finished.

**Existing Programs.**   I know very few programmers who wouldn't rather rewrite from scratch than use existing programs. Making use of existing code can be a headache because of poor supporting documentation or because the code is not exactly what you need and must be modified. Besides, using someone else's code is unexciting. Nevertheless, your designers are derelict if they do not consider what exists and how they may adapt it to your system. Stevens, Meyers, and Constantine (1974) make a strong case for building (at least within a given organization) program modules so simple and independent that they can be used for later needs, not just to satisfy the requirements of one system or contract. The more we use structured design and code, and the more we treat modules as "black boxes," the closer we'll come to realizing that goal. There are, in fact, reports of organizations that are doing an excellent job of reusing code. As *object-oriented development* (see Chapter 6) gathers momentum, code reuse promises to expand significantly (Yourdon, 1994).

**Pity the User.**   Designers must constantly think and act with the total system in mind. That system includes people and machines, not just programs. You're not designing something to show how clever you are. You're building something humans are to use, and they are not necessarily computer-oriented. If the computer makes their jobs easier, they may accept it. Otherwise they'll ignore it and continue to work in their old, comfortable ways. If you shove the computer and its complicated manuals down their throats, they may even sabotage your efforts.

Rarely should you trade off ease of use in favor of ease of programming. I like what Orlicky (1969) says on the subject: "Coddle the user, not the computer, and remember that the primary goal is not the efficiency of the computer system but the efficiency of the business."

**Iteration.**   The designers are not finished the first time they have a set of charts that seem to include modules to cover all the required functions. Good design is usually the result of many iterations. Things learned while designing at the component level are bound to give the designer second thoughts about what he or she did at the package level.

## DESIGN DOCUMENTATION TOOLS

In Chapter 1 we discussed the introduction of *structured techniques* in the analysis area. These concepts carry over into design—in fact, some of the tools of structured analysis were originally introduced as design tools. The idea of *structured design* is to combine effective, graphical documentation with design guidelines (including those discussed earlier in this chapter) to produce more rigorous, logical, understandable designs. Before the 1970s most design documents took the form of narrative plus flow charts, with an occasional decision table or graph or other chart thrown in. During the 1970s and '80s more rigorous tools were developed by Constantine, DeMarco, Yourdon, Gane and Sarson, Booch, and many others. Detailed technical discussions of the different aspects and merits of each are outside the scope of this book (see References for more information), but we can cover some basics. Keep in mind that no design tool does the designing for you. The act of designing is still an intellectual process. Improved tools and procedures are a tremendous help, but they don't replace that process.

As will be apparent, some of the design documentation tools currently in use require a lot of work to keep them updated. One reason Data Flow Diagrams, for example, are often unreliable as true mirrors of the code they supposedly represent is that programmers rarely keep them in step with the code. That's tedious, boring work, compared to the excitement of writing code! The availability of PC-based CASE tools makes updating much easier, but the sad fact is that most development staffs never go back to update the design documents once the actual coding has begun.

As a manager, you need to constantly teach and demonstrate the value of treating the design document as the standard that governs the code that will be created. Explain to your staff that if they work hard and keep the design up to date, you will work hard and keep their paychecks up to date as well.

**Entity Relationship Diagrams.**   A change in a process usually affects only the processes with which it directly communicates. A change in the data structures can cause ripple effects throughout the system. Your designers need to start their work by understanding what the data are and identifying the ways they are transformed in the system. Only when they have done this will it be possible to identify the processes that will be required to do the work.

---

## The Endless Search

In seeking out project tools, you may become frustrated by the constant stream of ideas offered in books and articles—each with its own proponents (some promising to change the world), each with its own political spin. As a manager, you have to understand that the search for better tools will never end. You must make choices *now* from what's available and not worry that next month someone will come up with a better tool. Choosing a set of tools for your project and sticking to your choice is far superior to making no choice at all and allowing individual project members to go their own ways.

---

**Data Flow Diagrams (DFD).**   These are the same diagrams discussed in Chapter 1 as an analysis documentation tool. A high-level data flow diagram (probably already produced by the analysts) is the starting point for process design. It shows the functions the system is required to perform, but it shows them in an abstract way, without laying out actual program modules. A good set of Data Flow Diagrams, supported by Entity Relationship Diagrams and a Data Dictionary serves as the primary vehicle for tying together analysts, designers, and programmers (and users!).

**Structure Charts.**   Entity Relationship Diagrams and Data Flow Diagrams are very useful in bridging the gap between the Definition Process and the Design Process. They give you a feel for the way the system functions as a whole, but they don't do a very good job of showing the modules and interfaces that bring the system to life. Since you need to understand the physical parts of the system as well as the logical parts, you will help the project by requiring structure charts. Figure 4–3 is a fragment of a structure chart. Module 1.0 invokes module 3.0 asking it to calculate the amount of interest on the principal at the current rate. Module 3.0 invokes module 7.0 to get the rate schedule, and invokes module 8.0 to extract the rate. And so it goes. The notations alongside the short arrows represent the interfaces between the modules, indicating what is passed and in which directions. Notice that data flows and control flows are differentiated.

It doesn't matter which methodology you're using to guide the Design Process, you will need to identify the parts that must be built in order to deliver your system. Object diagrams produced using Grady Booch's notation have the same role in the design process as the structure charts used by Yourdon and Constantine when structured analysis was first introduced. As Booch writes in *Object-Oriented Analysis and Design* (1994), "Object-oriented design is a method of design encompassing the process of object-oriented decomposition and a notation for depicting both logical and physical as well as static and dynamic models of the system under design."

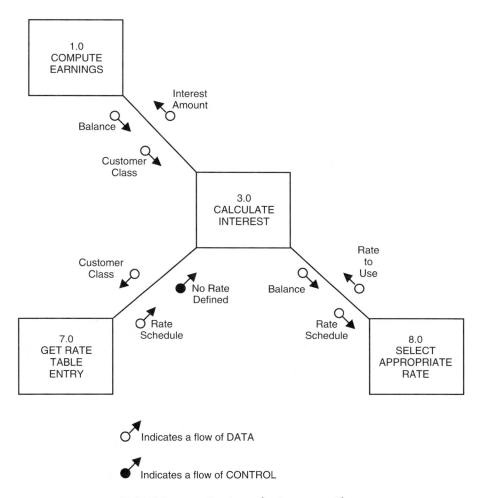

**FIGURE 4–3**   Portion of a Structure Chart

**Structured English, or Pseudocode.**   The same type of language mentioned in Chapter 1 for writing process mini-specifications can be used effectively for documenting program design. There is no single system of structured
English. Instead, there are a number of schemes used in different organizations,
tailored to both the needs of that organization and the coding language(s) used.
In fact, structured English *could* take whatever form an individual designer or
programmer wishes—but you should avoid that like the plague. Structured English should be standardized at least throughout a project, if not throughout an installation or company. If not standardized it loses its value as a crisp means of
communication.

Structured English has the advantage of "looking like" a high-level procedural coding language, so it's a comfortable form of documentation for many programmers to use. It's easier to update than charts that require artwork, so chances are better that it will be kept in step with the code than might some of the chart-type documents. If the structured English used to design programs is close to the structure of the coding language to be used, it would seem but a smallish step to use the actual coding language instead. In fact, the gap is extremely narrow if you are using one of the fourth-generation database languages to build your applications.

**Decision Tables.**   A decision table is a simple, convenient way of summarizing "if-then" situations. It shows at a glance what action to take if a given condition or set of conditions exists.

If you are developing systems for process control or other real-time applications, you are very likely to encounter decision tables in the form of *state tables*. In these, the responses to external or internal events are shown as entries in a matrix that defines changes in the "state" of the system. For example, my system may be in the "idle" state waiting for either an operator action or a signal that somebody has dialed my modem. Depending on the actual event, the system will change to be in either an "operator" state or a "communications" state. Each of these has limits on the functions that will be performed while the system is in that state and each has a set of events and subsequent state changes required when they occur. To continue the example, when my system gets to the "end" of the communications state, it may return to the idle state, but when it reaches the end of the operator state, it may enter the communications state in order to transmit the data entered by the operator.

Figure 4-4 shows a simple decision table. Here programs decide what kind of ticket to issue to an airline passenger. In the table, Y means yes, N means no, and X means action. Again the example is simple, but consider expanding this table to cover a more complex set of circumstances. Add a line entitled "Is alternate acceptable?" Then, if first class is requested but unavailable, and tourist is available, the action is to issue a tourist ticket rather than put the passenger on a waiting list. The example is simple, but it shows some vital information at a glance. The greater the number of choices and the greater the number of actions, the more useful the table becomes.

There are many practical uses for such tables because you can design them to show in one place all possible decisions for a given set of conditions. Using flow charts to show the same logic would cover a lot of paper and would be much more difficult to read. In addition, decision tables are easy to check for completeness by inspecting rows versus columns. It's more difficult to look at a flow chart, for example, and see whether you have accounted for all required combinations of conditions. (My use of the term "decision table," by the way, is loose, and possibly offensive to mathematicians. True decision tables are structured much more rigorously. The examples I have shown might more accurately be called "incidence tables.")

| | Rule 1 | Rule 2 | Rule 3 | Rule 4 |
|---|---|---|---|---|
| Request is for 1st Class | Y | Y | | |
| Request is for Tourist | | | Y | Y |
| 1st Class is Available | Y | N | | |
| Tourist is Available | | | Y | N |
| Issue 1st Class | X | | | |
| Issue Tourist | | | X | |
| Place on Wait List | | X | | X |

**FIGURE 4–4**    Decision Table Example  (Metzger, 1970, IBM Corp.)

**Coverage Matrices.**    A coverage matrix is a means of showing the relationship between two kinds of information. An index in a book is a coverage matrix showing what pages in the book cover what subjects. A coverage matrix in a program design document might show system functions versus program names; that is, for a given capability stated in the Problem Specification, what program module(s) in the Design Specification provides that capability? Such a matrix is even more useful in testing, where you can use it to list functions to be tested versus identifications of the tests that cover those functions. One manager I worked for used a coverage matrix in another way. He listed down one axis all the items of work specifically called out in the contract and along the other, the names of the people responsible for those tasks. The first time he used this matrix he found tasks not covered by anyone. When the coverage matrix was passed among the workers, it also showed that the boss thought person A was responsible for a particular task and A thought that task was being handled by person B.

**Flow Charts.**    These should be used as private design tools if they are used at all. The danger of using them in the design process is that they are completely process-focused and ignore the data relationships. Design decisions made solely on the basis of flowchart information will come back to haunt you almost every time.

**Other Tools.**    The literature describes a number of other tools, most of them some variation on those already discussed. Each has its champions and professional designers should make an effort to become familiar with several of them, including Gane and Sarson Data Flow Diagrams (1977); Booch diagrams (1994); and Jackson structured design (1975, 1983).

## ASSESSING DESIGN QUALITY

It's hopeless to try "adding" quality after a product has been built. Your only shot at assuring quality is now. If you design poorly, your product will plague the customer and the maintenance programmers who stand by with first-aid kits. Formal inspections (discussed later) should give you a good feel for design quality. There's reasonable agreement about what constitutes good design, and we've already touched on some of that. There are questions you can pose that help get at the "goodness" of a piece of design (Musa, Iannino, and Okumoto, 1987; Nelson, 1967).

1. Are all functions listed in the Problem Specification fully accounted for in the Design Specification? A coverage matrix helps to answer this.
2. Have the interfaces between the system and human operators been designed with *ease of use* in mind, even at the sacrifice of some programming simplicity?
3. Is the system broken into modules small enough to fit on a single computer printout sheet (say, 40 to 60 lines of code)?
4. Is each module designed to do a single specific function? Such modules are said to possess "functional strength."
5. Is each module designed with maximum independence in mind? The best means of communication between modules is data coupling: module A calls module B, passing to B needed data and receiving data back from B. Modules should never alter the contents of other modules.
6. Does each module have complete predictability? Modules whose behavior is dependent on self-contained status indicators are less predictable and more difficult to test than others.
7. Are the rules of module-to-module communication and access to all data clearly and completely stated? *Leave no room for private agreements among programmers* concerning intermodule communication.
8. Is this system maintainable? Will future designers and programmers find these programs easy to modify? One of the key issues here is *complexity*. Software with many modules and many control paths that relate those modules will be difficult to build, test, and maintain.
9. Are the documents representing the design clear, complete, and ready for refinement and coding by the programmers? Have any important design problems been left hanging?

## Complexity

Good design minimizes complexity. That's easy to say, harder to do. Some business problems are complex, and the systems used to deal with them will inherit some of that complexity. An example of a complex job is building intelligent browsers for data warehouses. The data varieties that are present each have their own set of relationships that must be managed and this may lead to thousands of control paths that could be taken during the course of an extended transaction.

Complexity gets in the way of understanding and that, in turn, has an impact on the number of defects and the lifetime cost of the system. Complex design will always lead to complicated code, so it's very important that you measure the complexity of the design that is proposed for your system and keep up the pressure on your designers to simplify, simplify, simplify.

The industry standard measurement for complexity is the McCabe complexity metric, named after its developer, Tom McCabe. Many current CASE tools incorporate the McCabe metrics as a standard feature, making it quick and easy for your designers to obtain feedback about their designs. The McCabe metric is based on counting decision points in the design (it can also be applied to code—and you should make a note to see that it is). The more decision points, the greater the number of control flows through the system, and the more opportunities for designers and programmers to lose track of the details. Even if the total number of decision points for the system is high, your designers need to structure it so that the complexity at any point is manageable.

## PROJECT PLANNING

In parallel with the baseline design effort, you need to do further planning and preparation during the Design Process. Most of this work falls into these areas: change management, preparation for testing, resource estimating, documentation, and training.

### Change Management

The design process does not end when you have produced the Design Specification. Throughout the life of the project, and especially during the Programming Process, people will propose changes to either the Problem Specification or the Design Specification, or both. I'll describe a mechanism for dealing with and controlling change in Chapter 6, but *now* is the time to set up the apparatus. When change proposals come in, you should be ready to dispose of them quickly.

### Preparation for Testing

Testing begins during the Programming Process, but you get ready for it during the Design Process. Detailed discussion of testing is left to later chapters, but here's what concerns you now.

**Defining a Test Hierarchy.**   Define the types, or levels, of testing to be done on your project. Define them, publish them, and stick with them. When terms such as "integration test" and "system test" are used, their meanings often depend

on who is using them—this is an area where we have never agreed on clear definitions. You need to be sure that *for your project* you have unambiguous definitions
understood by all the project members, management outside the project, and the
customer. I offer the following definitions of test levels in a test hierarchy (they are
further discussed in succeeding chapters):

> ➤ *Module test.* In Figure 4–2 there are four levels of modules shown making up
>   the system. Module test is the testing done on any individual module before
>   combining (integrating) it with the rest of the system. Module test is usually
>   done by individual programmers.
> ➤ *Integration test.* Also simply called "integration," this is the process of adding
>   a new module to the evolving system, testing this new combination, and re-
>   peating the process until finally you have brought the entire system together
>   and thoroughly tested it, either top-down or bottom-up.
> ➤ *System test.* You run the integrated system (that the programmers consider
>   clean) through a new series of tests, not prepared or executed by the program-
>   mers. These new tests are run in as nearly a "live" final environment as possi-
>   ble, and their main objective is to test the programs against the original Prob-
>   lem Specification to determine whether the system does the job intended.
> ➤ *Acceptance test.* The system is tested under conditions agreed to by the cus-
>   tomer. Your objective is to demonstrate to him that the system satisfies the
>   contract requirements. Sometimes acceptance testing is controlled by the cus-
>   tomer.
> ➤ *Site test.* After installation in its ultimate operating environment, the program
>   is tested once again to assure complete readiness for operation under field
>   conditions. (This is not required on every project.)

**Top-down vs. Bottom-up Integration Testing.**   Like many aspects of the
programming business, the theories and practices concerning testing have undergone a good deal of change, both philosophical and practical. Traditionally, a
system made up of several levels of modules has been tested "bottom-up." Lowest-
level modules (in Figure 4–2, "units") were coded and tested first on a "stand-
alone" basis. When the units making up a higher-level module ("component") were
ready, they were combined and the combination tested until that component ran
successfully. Meanwhile, in parallel, other components were readied in a similar
manner, and eventually appropriate groupings of components were tested. And so
on up the hierarchy, until finally the system was tested.

Top-down testing is just the reverse, at least philosophically. Testing begins
with the top-level modules and proceeds down through the hierarchy. The lowest-
level modules are the last to be added to the system and tested.

You can choose either method of testing and either will work, given adequate
planning and control. But you need to understand what's involved in each method
and what's at stake in making your choice.

The choice between top-down and bottom-up testing is a choice between two philosophies, or basic approaches. They are not necessarily mutually exclusive testing methods; each involves some of the other. For example, in using the *bottom-up* method, it's normally necessary to provide a framework into which the modules can be inserted for test purposes. This framework is often a bare-bones version of the system's control program (a high-level module in the eventual system). In *top-down* testing, it's often necessary to code and test early some modules (such as an output module) that have been shown at a low level in the hierarchy. So neither approach is completely sanitary; there will generally be some mixing of the two. There's nothing wrong with that—what counts, after all, is that the system be well tested and done on time. But it *is* important that one basic approach or the other be selected for your project. You have to know where you're going.

The approach most experts recommend today is top-down. Following is a summary of the reasons for making this choice. (For detailed discussions of top-down versus bottom-up testing, see Hughes and Michton, 1977; Mills, 1976; McGowan and Kelly, 1975; Yourdon, 1989; and Baker, 1975.)

➤ Top-down is a "natural" method; it involves building a framework before adding details. It fits comfortably with the ideas of top-down design and top-down coding. The whole idea of top-down development is that of a natural progression.

➤ As new modules in the hierarchy are added to the system and tested with the already tested higher-level modules, the system evolves as a living, growing entity, "complete" at any given stage. Bottom-up is a more piecemeal approach, involving more finger-crossing and more surprises when you throw groups of modules together for the first time.

➤ It's easier to produce *intermediate* versions of the final system; effectively you have an intermediate version right from the beginning—something is cycling and showing results. This makes it easier (1) to show the customer results faster, thus avoiding end-of-project shocks; (2) to deliver interim (incomplete) versions of the system; and (3) to show management that you really are producing something. Upper management and the customer have always been in the untenable position of having to accept too much on faith; it's so hard to *see* those darned programs!

➤ In top-down development you need less throwaway scaffolding (specially written test support code, such as dummy driver programs).

**Writing Test Specifications.**   The individual programmer does module testing without a formal test document The other four levels—integration, system, acceptance, and site testing—are done according to previously defined test specifications. There is a separate set of test specifications for each level. Many individual tests will serve more than one test category. For example, many (perhaps all) of the acceptance demonstration tests can be taken from the set of system tests.

Figure I (inside front cover) shows at what point in the development cycle each specification should be ready. It's evident that if the Integration Test Specification is to be ready for use when integration testing begins, it must be prepared during the Design Process; similarly the System Test Specification must be written during the Programming Process, and so on.

Test specifications are described later. Here it's sufficient to mention that each specification contains general test objectives and success criteria, and a number of specific test cases. A test case contains all the background information, test data, and detailed procedures required to execute one specific set of tests.

**Defining Test Procedures.**   The time for creativity in testing is when you're devising the tests, not when you're executing them. There will always be nail-biting moments during testing (especially during acceptance testing) no matter how well you prepare; don't add to the tension by flying blind. Write your test specifications spelling out procedures, responsibilities, and predicted results ahead of time.

**Providing an Accessible Test Environment.**   As manager, you can have significant impact on the testing process by providing the best possible access to a test system that is as similar as possible to the production environment where your system will eventually run. If the testing must be performed in batch mode, streamline the logistics of getting programs and results of program runs to and from the computer. Arrange for pickup and drop stations to be close to the programmers' work areas. If necessary, supply courier service to speed program materials to and from the computer. Make submission procedures simple. Provide ample storage for disks, tapes, and listings.

If you're working on a project requiring the use of classified data, keep it out of the computer for as long as possible. Work with simulated, unclassified data. Introduce classified material late in the development cycle, preferably not before system test. Once introduced, confine the data to as few tables as possible and make sure that access security is tight. I've worked on several projects that required a classified (usually SECRET) database. The complications that arise as soon as you introduce classified material can be horrible. Any printed output is now suspect. You may argue in vain with a security officer over whether or not a given output needs to be classified, stamped, logged, and kept under lock. You can count on long meetings, outrageous procedures, and slowdown in your operation once the stamp-wielders get in the door.

Another area deserving management attention is that of contingency reserve computer time, or planned idle time. In a paper on resource analysis, A. M. Pietrasanta (1968) makes this comment:

Queuing theory indicates that, as idle time approaches zero, wait time between jobs will approach infinity. The manifestation of this theory is very common to harassed programmers: turnaround time gets longer as the computing center load builds up. . . . Whatever the proper percentage of spare computer time, it is certainly unfair to demand that the computing center get rid of all idle time and still maintain tolerable job turnaround time.

Churchman, Ackoff, and Arnoff (1957) describe an experiment at Boeing Aircraft that bears on reserve time. The problem at Boeing was to determine the optimum number of toolroom clerks required to service a fixed number of mechanics in the factory. Since the mechanics came to the toolroom at an uneven rate, one clerk could not service them immediately and lines formed. At other times the clerk was idle.

The investigators applied measurements and queuing theory. They showed that it would be economical to increase the number of clerks, even though they would sometimes be idle, to provide faster service to the higher-priced mechanics. Every time a mechanic had to wait in line, he represented lost time and lost production. They also showed that, for a given set of mechanics' and clerks' salaries, there was some optimal number of clerks. Further increasing the number of clerks would begin to show a net loss when the cost of idle clerks became larger than the cost of idle mechanics.

The computer serves the programmers as the clerks served the mechanics. Plan some idle time to improve turnaround, prevent long waiting lines, and improve the efficiency of all those high-priced programmers being serviced. At some point the cost of the planned reserve is balanced by the improvement in programmer efficiency.

How much reserve time should you plan for? There is no way of knowing without experimenting, but studies in other fields indicate that a contingency reserve of about 30 percent might be a reasonable start. Start with *something* and adjust the amount of reserve as you go along. Don't plan 100 percent use of the computer resource.

**Plotting Test Results.**   It's useful to keep track of testing progress, especially during integration testing, by drawing simple graphs. Graphs are useful for showing trends. Suppose, for example, that you plot "test cases executed" along the horizontal axis and "test cases executed successfully" along the vertical axis. If the curve suddenly flattens out and does not rise significantly during a long period of time, that's a warning that something is rotten in Programland.

## Resource Estimating

As the Design Process provides more detail about the system you are building, you need to reestimate the resources needed to finish the job. You can make your early guesses about manpower and computer time more realistic because you've learned so much more about the job to be done. If your new estimate is higher than the original, that's a problem you and the customer must somehow resolve. Better now than at the end of the project.

## Documentation

The Documentation Plan should be followed throughout the Design Process, with documents defined and fully outlined. The first version of the Programmer's Handbook should be ready and the project library should be set up as one of the earliest Design Process activities.

The Programmer's Handbook, outlined in the Appendix, contains information vital to the programmer in doing his job. It includes a description of the technical requirements, the baseline design, support software, test procedures, and hardware information. The handbook should be ready when programming begins. Entrust its preparation and upkeep to a technician, not an administrator. Don't let it become too broad, with a section for filing every conceivable kind of document, and don't include such items as the detailed program descriptions. Handbooks often die of bloat.

When I wrote the first edition of this book, I assumed the Programmer's Handbook would be a loose-leaf binder. Now that personal computers and terminals of various kinds are practically everywhere, the "handbook," like much other information, can be computer-stored and available on a video screen, with a hard copy available as backup. If you don't have such an office setup and still rely on hard copy, then you probably need one copy of the notebook for each programming manager. Wider distribution is usually not necessary, and it's an expense you can do without. Besides, the more copies of *anything* that float around, the tougher it is to keep them updated.

The project library should be organized and operating at the time that the first formal output is generated by the Design Process. Figure 4–5 shows a way of functionally organizing the library. Every item (document or program module) should be given a unique identifier. Nobody but the librarian should ever lay hands on the master copy of a document or a module. This is a convenient control point for the project, but it will lose much of its value if project members are allowed free access to it. The use of the library will be discussed further in the next chapters.

## Training

During the Design Process you should be training the programmers for their jobs during the Programming Process. By the time the Programming Process begins, they should all know the equipment, the programming language, the test facilities, the problem definition, and the baseline design.

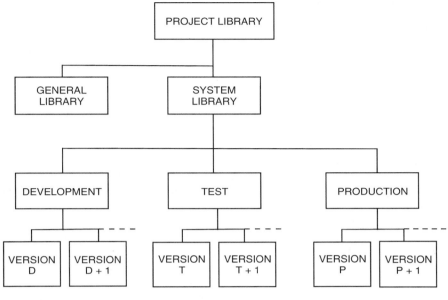

**FIGURE 4–5**    Project Library

## DESIGN PROCESS REVIEW

You should have a status review *at least* at the end of every process in the development cycle (see Review and Reporting Plan in the Appendix). Because the review held at the end of the Design Process is so critical, we'll look at it here in some detail.

At the end of the Design Process you're almost at a point of no return. You have already committed major resources (programming manpower, testing manpower, and computer time) and you'd better have a warm feeling that the system can be built to satisfy the requirements. Once you begin implementing the baseline design, it's exhausting, expensive, and morale-busting to have to stop for a major overhaul. The objectives of this review are (1) to assess the completeness and adequacy of the baseline design and the Project Plan, and (2) to provide management with sufficient information to decide whether to go to the next process, do further analysis or design work, or kill the project. All are real options.

### Preparation

Don't be ambivalent about this review. You really need it! State the objectives of the review and give someone complete responsibility for making all arrangements—that may be a full-time job for several days or more.

**Scheduling People.**    Include as reviewers a cross section of your own project members and representatives of management above you. In addition, be sure to invite disinterested outside reviewers or consultants who are competent technicians and managers. Don't invite your buddy, hoping for good marks. Give this review a chance to uncover problems. If problems are there, they will surface sooner or later, and the later they are found, the more difficulty you'll have fixing them. For instance, a design problem might be solved in a day or two during the Design Process. That same problem, not caught until programming is well under way, may cause a great deal of reprogramming and retesting.

Don't invite the customer. You may get into internal problems during this review, and the customer's presence would be inhibiting. It's better to solve as many problems as possible and *then* brief the customer. This isn't double work at all, for you can treat your internal review as a warm-up for a customer review. The intent is not to hide anything but to present the customer with solutions and alternatives, not problems.

Choose as speakers project members who are most competent in the areas to be discussed, but avoid starring someone who may be so glib that he or she glosses over problems and lulls the listeners into thinking things are in better shape than they are. I'll never forget a review session that began with a "the-project-is-in-good-shape" attitude and ended in grief. Once the pretty speeches were out of the way, a reviewer began asking probing questions. Shortly, one of the frustrated first-level managers, in response to a question, hung his head and mumbled that there wasn't a chance in hell of making the schedule. Shocked silence. What he had voiced was not really news to the workers on the project, but this was the first time a manager publicly vented his feelings. Some rapid changes followed.

How much time you need for the review depends on the size and nature of your project, the complexity of the technical problem, and the difficulties you see in future processes. On a one-year project you can plan to spend three to five days profitably in this review. You should anticipate some prolonged discussions of problems and schedule people accordingly.

**Scheduling Meeting Rooms.**    Hold the meetings as far away from your office (and telephone) as possible. That may mean renting a hotel conference room for a week. Arrange for frequent coffee breaks and, if necessary, for luncheons. Find a place that's air conditioned and quiet; it's tough to compete with jackhammers next door.

Sometimes you may decide to break people away from a main meeting to form smaller "task forces" to look in depth at a specific problem. If so, you'll need to arrange for space for them. But resist breaking up the group, at least until all main presentations are complete. Since the object of this review is to show whether the whole project hangs together, all reviewers should hear all presentations, both technical and nontechnical.

**Preparing Presentation Aids.**   Decide what presentation media (for example, videos, slides, flip charts, chalkboards) to use and make sure the appropriate equipment is available for each presenter. If a support group is to help you prepare materials such as charts, find out how much time they need.

**Preparing Handout Materials.**   Be selective about what you give the reviewers if you expect them to read it. The two documents they should surely get are the Design Specification and the Project Plan. Beyond that, it's up to you. Whatever you hand out, make sure it's clean and readable. Send the documents to the reviewers a couple of days before the actual meeting.

## What to Cover

The objectives are to review plans and the baseline design. Figure 4–6 suggests an outline of topics you might use. The section on Background should give the reviewers a feel for the environment in which you are working and a general idea of the technical problem as well as your proposed solution. Under the Project Plan heading, present at least a capsule description of each plan section and a more detailed look at the Process Plan, Organization Plan, Test Plan, and Resources and Deliverables Plan. The Baseline Design section should describe in increasing levels of detail the design you have produced. It may be a good idea to break for a while, once a first level of detail has been presented. This will give the reviewers a chance to absorb what they've heard, look through the design document, and return better able to absorb more detail. The Summary presentation should paint an honest picture of where you think you stand and what major problems you face. Distinguish between problems you feel you can solve and problems requiring your management's help.

## Results

What you want from the review is the go-ahead to continue with the job. Usually it will be clear when the review ends what kind of shape you're in. In some cases, you or your management will insist that certain problems be resolved before programming can proceed.

---

### Pay Now or Pay More Later

"So *pay* the two dollars!" That's the punch line in a joke about a man who refuses to settle a parking ticket and ends up in front of a firing squad (Garment, 1994).

Managers, take heed. If a project review exposes serious problems, take your lumps and solve the problems *now*. Solving them later will be ever so much more costly!

---

**I. BACKGROUND**
   **A.** The Customer
      1. His experience
      2. Your prior experience with him
      3. His organization
   **B.** The Job
      1. Reason for this project
      2. Job environment
      3. Overview of requirements
      4. Overview of design
   **C.** The Contract
      1. Overall schedule
      2. Costs
      3. Major constraints

**II. THE PROJECT PLAN**
   **A.** Overview
   **B.** Process Plan
   **C.** Organization Plan
   **D.** Test Plan
   **E.** Change Management Plan
   **F.** Documentation Plan
   **G.** Training Plan
   **H.** Review and Reporting Plan
   **I.** Installation and Operation Plan
   **J.** Resources and Deliverables Plan

**III. THE BASELINE DESIGN**
   **A.** Program design
   **B.** Table design

**IV. SUMMARY**
   **A.** Current status
      1. End items delivered
      2. End items remaining
      3. Confidence
      4. Assessment of risk
   **B.** Problems
      1. Technical
      2. Managerial
      3. Financial
      4. Contractual
      5. Legal
      6. Personnel
      7. Political
      8. Customer
      9. Other

**FIGURE 4–6**   Design Process Review Outline

When you set up the review, ask certain participants to be prepared to put in writing their opinions of your project's status, their listing of your outstanding problems, and any suggestions for dealing with those problems. Encourage reviewers to state what they see as problems even if they have no suggested solutions. You should solicit written comments from each outside reviewer and from selected project members. Give their comments to your management along with your own recommendations. Every review should end with a formal written report from you.

At the conclusion of a successful review, or after making changes because of the review, the green light is on and the Programming Process takes center stage.

---

### The Manager's Bookshelf

Books on analysis and design that have more to say about design than analysis are in short supply. In my opinion, Michael Jackson's book *System Development* (1983) provides a good and comprehensive treatment about design and how it flows from the underlying analysis. The book is focused on the author's proprietary methodology, but most of what he says translates easily to other methods as well. Another good reference for design is James Martin's series of books on Information Engineering. If you're going to use object-oriented programming, your best choice is *Object-Oriented Analysis and Design* by Grady Booch (1994).

---

# THE FAR SIDE

## By GARY LARSON

**Professor E. F. Gizmo and some of his many inventions**

**FIGURE 5–1**  A Well-Known Designer

# 5

# The Designer

One day I found I had a possum in my attic. I had a typical ranch house whose roof overhung the outside walls. The possum had settled himself snugly in part of the overhang where I could see him in the flashlight beam but couldn't crawl close enough in the restricted attic space to get hold of him. I analyzed the problem: The job requirements were to get the critter out without hurting him and without getting bitten.

I had other things to do, so I jumped on the first solution that came into my head. I began removing plywood panels outside the house that formed the underside of the overhang near where the brute was settled. Off came the first panel, not without plenty of sweat and not without messing up the panel where the nails pulled through. Naturally, when the panel came off Mr. Possum was nowhere to be seen. Considerably smarter than his antagonist, he simply moved to an adjacent panel. I had not designed a good solution to my problem. I could have removed all the panels from the overhang around the entire house and still been no closer to my prey. He only needed to keep moving about the attic and I'd never catch him. Even if I did, I'd have to rebuild half my house.

I looked at my young kids watching me and decided I'd better find a simpler solution or all my credibility as a parent would be shot. I came down from the ladder and announced that I would now do my Tarzan bit and capture this beast with a snare. I rigged a loop in a rope at the end of a long bamboo pole and crawled back into the attic. In the flashlight beam, I found Mr. Possum in the overhang a few feet from where I had torn loose the first piece of panel. He sat calmly looking at me and probably wondering what in hell I would tear apart next. But this time I had him. My superior intellect (superior to the possum's, that is), knowing that possums really do "play possum," told me he would stay still while I poked the long pole toward him, slipped the noose around his neck and pulled it snug. He did and I did and pretty soon I gently tugged him out of the overhang and near enough to me that I could steer him into a bucket. I put a lid on the bucket and crawled down from the attic to display my catch. We took a ride into some woods where we set the possum free.

Two minutes' thinking about the problem would have produced the better solution without the silliness of tearing the house apart. That better solution would have saved me the work of repairing the overhang. It would also have allowed me to save face with my kids. I'm sure they were smart enough to see that my house-wrecking was dumb (although they were also smart enough not to point it out to me).

I'm not the only impatient fellow around. People are always coming up with half-baked solutions to problems. Programming types are notorious for this. Lots of programming managers and plenty of customers are so anxious to see something abuilding that they allow, or even promote, coding before developing a solid design. That's *always* wrong.

Can you imagine pouring concrete and laying bricks and erecting girders for a building that has not yet been blueprinted, and then later tearing out girders and chopping away bricks to fix things? If it's wrong to build physical objects before designing them, why isn't it wrong to build programs before designing them? Because program instructions are "soft" and easily changed? No way! It's as expensive to toss out badly conceived program bricks as it is to chop out building bricks. If you are managing designers, get the job done right. Don't have programmers yelling at you for passing on bad design.

## BRIDGING THE MUCK

A designer's job is to build a solid bridge between the analysts and the programmers. The analyst's output is the designer's input. The designer's output is the programmer's input. The designer must translate the analyst's *what* document (the Problem Specification) into a *how* document (the Design Specification). The Design Specification should be a natural extension of the Problem Specification. If you have chosen your documenting tools well, a reader will make the transition from one document to the next without trauma.

Since a well-written Problem Specification will always reflect some implied design and may even look like a design document, and since folks are always anxious to get on with the coding, you may be tempted to skip design as a formal phase and begin writing code, designing as you go. There may come a time when no book need talk ever again about this problem, because everyone finally understands it's necessary to design before coding. But not yet. People still jump from a fuzzy understanding of the problem right into coding a solution. The design bridge never gets built and lots of programmers and managers fall into the dark slime below.

Whatever the cost of designing well, the cost of *not* designing well is many times greater. Here's a common scenario: On a typical project a design is rushed through and an impressive list of modules is identified and strung together neatly enough to convince uneducated management that the design is complete and programming should now begin. The designers know they have not thoroughly worked out the interface mechanisms and they know that one black-box module is going to be tricky, but Tricky Dick Programmer, who was one of the designers, knows pretty much how he's going to handle it. Two months go by and tons of code pile up in the master listings, enough to make any programming manager proud. Integration test begins. Programmers devise interfaces as they go along. Intermodule communication becomes confused, integration attempts fail, ROLAIDS stock becomes a good buy. Tricky Dick leaves the project.

You lose a lot of time trying to resolve communication problems. Private arrangements have produced a hopeless mishmash of interdependent modules. There is poor module coupling and a load of pathological connections. Tricky Dick's modules, especially the one that was a question mark even to him, are indecipherable. It's finally clear to management that all motion is in reverse.

You shuffle managers, make speeches, authorize overtime, and make unlimited computer time available. You do everything *except* stop and redesign. I've seen it happen, and you probably have, too, unless you're new to this business. By rushing through design, you saved *n* weeks. Then you lost many times *n* weeks trying to fix things. However, calendar time is the least of the problems. People exhaust themselves physically trying to make things work; they exhaust themselves emotionally knowing they're producing garbage; costs go through the roof; the customer becomes a harsh, demanding enemy rather than an understanding partner; morale sinks out of sight. Any product finally delivered is a patchwork bound to fail when it meets real conditions not envisioned during the frantic testing.

You can measure the cost of not designing properly according to a sort of Richter scale. There is no simple one-to-one relationship between a design flaw and its consequences. If the building is partly up and you have to move an elevator shaft six feet to the left, the cost of moving it will dwarf the cost of having designed it right in the first place. Design errors ripple through everything that follows.

To manage the design process effectively, you've got to understand the difference between good and poor design and you've got to subject the products of your designers to scrutiny by other designers, by programmers, by analysts, and by the customer. Before you even *begin* to design, you must understand and choose the tools you'll use. So . . .

## FIRST THINGS FIRST

It's the kickoff meeting for the Design Process on Project SOB. The manager of the design group, Marty Martinet, has gathered his designers in the conference room.

"Good morning!" he bellows as he comes bounding into the room. His ruddy face practically glows with good cheer.

"Good morning," mumble the five designers sitting about the table.

"Dennis, glad you could join us," says Marty to one of the group. Dennis is a senior designer on loan from another project here at Super Software, Inc. It seems the Floorshine Project has been delayed and Dennis is available.

Marty cracks his knuckles loudly. Still standing before the seated designers, he takes a stack of papers from his briefcase and passes them around the table.

"Here's the problem spec for the job," he says. "Copy for each of you. I looked at it over the weekend . . . looks pretty good. And on time, too! That's a first!" The five designers begin leafing through their copies of the Problem Specification.

After a few minutes, Marty goes on: "I'd like you to take today to read the spec. Then first thing tomorrow morning we'll meet again right here and talk about the schedule and who'll do what. Okay?"

Dennis speaks up: "What tools are we going to be using to capture the design?"

Marty looks at him quizzically. "The dataflows are already done. They're attached to the problem spec. All you need to do is identify the modules. I don't think you need a $5000 CASE tool to do that."

The other four designers shuffle their feet under the table and glance toward Marty, whose face has taken on the benevolent look of a kindly dictator. He walks around the table and stands alongside Dennis. With a hand on Dennis's shoulder, he says, "We've found that we wind up spending a lot of time with the programmers to help them understand the design anyway, so what we do is rough out the module boundaries and identify the interfaces. Then we sit down with the programmers and work out the implementation details." Marty glances at his four designers who sit looking on impassively. He pats Dennis on the shoulder and marches around to the front of the table and leans forward, knuckles on the table. Slowly his voice rises in pitch. "Back when I worked on SAGE"—his four designers stiffen and try not to make eye contact with one another—"we had nothing to use but flow charts and they worked great. You take practically any programmer and start talking about a programming problem and what's the first thing he does? Scribbles his own diagrams on whatever's handy, that's what!" Dennis is beginning to slump in his chair as Marty leans farther forward and his knuckles whiten as they sustain his weight against the conference table.

"Trouble is, all these CASE vendors are just out selling overpriced drawing packages. Most of the stuff turns into shelfware." Marty's face is three shades redder than normal. He takes a deep breath, pulls back, and composes himself. His voice lowers to a more paternalistic tone and he smiles down at Dennis. "No, Dennis, none of that for us. We just keep it simple. If we messed around trying to follow a bunch of rules that someone else thought up, we'd never make the schedule."

Somewhere in the past Marty Martinet stopped growing. It happens to lots of people. They run out of steam and let advancing technology pass them by. As a manager, the demands on your time may frustrate you, but you've got to make room for your continuing education. As a popular TV spot in the mid-'90s pleaded: Never

Stop Learning. An educated manager understands that designers and their managers need to choose thoughtfully their design methodology—the rules, procedures, and tools they will use during the design process.

There once was little choice. Designers drew up flowcharts and threw in some narrative and a few supporting tables and that was it. Now you get to choose from a menu of methodologies. You may protest that such choices should have been made long before the Design Phase arrived, and you'd be right. The designers should already know how they're going to go about designing before it's time to design. If no conscious decisions have been made to use this methodology or that, management has been asleep. Don't expect to retrain your designers in a day to get them using object-oriented design if all their careers they've used nothing but Gane and Sarson tools and methods. It may be better in that case to go along with whatever methods your designers are used to and swear to change things before the next project.

## GETTING AT THE POSSUM

Armed with a proper set of design tools, your next concern is to understand the problem and the constraints the analysts have passed on to the designers. But then what? Is there some reliable, automatic means of arriving at a decent design?

There is not. Tools and an understanding of the problem can take you to the edge of battle, but then you're on your own. The guidelines suggested by structured or OO design techniques will help steer you, but the real work of design is a mental process that relies on experience and ingenuity. Fortunately, you can seek out designers who possess both those qualities, especially experience. There are few systems that are really new. Try to name a type of program that has not been written before. If just one of Marty Martinet's designers have had previous experience in a project similar to SOB, that's a huge advantage. Perversely, if *all* his designers have had similar experience on a related system, that might not be so hot. While it's obviously helpful to draw on experience, it's dangerous for everyone to have the *same* background. If SOB is a payroll system and all five of Marty's people are payroll experts, where will fresh ideas and new approaches come from? Who will act as devil's advocate? Who will come up with a fresh, new approach because he or she doesn't know any better? Look at Marty . . . he's so hidebound, he can't see any advantage in using CASE. You need people with *related* experience as your designers, but you also need people with *unrelated* experience to keep the others from plodding along the same old potholed road.

Allow for detours and dead ends during design. Each approach thrown out narrows the choices so that you home in on an acceptable answer. Notice I said acceptable; don't worry about finding that ultimate, perfect solution. You usually can't afford the time for such a search. This is where a manager, even if not deeply involved in the day-to-day design process, must exercise leadership. If you're the design manager, you need to keep one eye on the design scheme your people are proposing and the other on your schedule. You need to be able to say *this* design is what you'll go with. Your designers may object that it's not elegant enough, but you need to make the determination that the design is sound and satisfies the requirements of the job, and that you cannot justify further iteration. That last mouthful is what excellence in managing designers is all about: Is the design sound? Does it satisfy the job requirements? Is further expenditure of resources justified? Tearing the house down to get the possum out would clearly not be sound; shooting him would violate the humaneness clause in the job requirements spec; and training a lady possum to woo him down from the attic would involve unjustifiable time and expense.

## WHAT IS GOOD DESIGN?

How do you know your designers have come up with a good design? There is some decent guidance in the literature, but one of your best assurances that a design is good is when good designers *say* it is. Formal inspections are an excellent means of assessing design quality. Among those who participate in such reviews should be the people who will inherit the Design Specification—the lead programmers and managers who are to produce the programs based on your design. If you're a small operation and the same people who design also do the programming, it's imperative to find experienced, competent reviewers from outside your immediate group who have no stake in the outcome. Having a design inspected by competent people who did not produce the design may be your best way of knowing the quality of the work.

You can do much more. You can provide training for yourself and your designers. Since the late '70s, people on the trail of better design methods and tools have done much excellent work. Books and articles written by these researchers (see References) are a good place to start. Many authors offer seminars and courses on design and you can reach them through their publishers. I nag you to look for ways to educate yourself and understand the newest methodologies because I know how easy it is to fall behind. In my early years as a manager, I did not take advantage of what instruction was available (always too busy with today's problems) and I paid for that. Catching up is always tougher than keeping up.

## A BRIDGE TOO FAR?

"This is all very well, Mr. Nickleby, and very proper, so far as it goes . . . but it doesn't go far enough." So says a Dickens character in *Nicholas Nickleby*.

"This design stinks, Boss! It makes me nothing but a coder! It goes too far!" So says Perry Programmer of the Design Specification just handed over by the design group.

Somewhere between those extremes is the limit to which you should carry the Design Specification. The programmers who inherit the design need latitude to in-

---

## Details

The story is told of an artist who worked in San Francisco during the late 1960s and became renowned for his psychedelic concert posters. The famous promoter Bill Graham commissioned a poster for an upcoming concert and a week later, the artist came by with his work. What Graham saw amazed him. Colors, letters, and figures swirled in wild abandon on the paper. It looked like the poster was vibrating and Graham felt himself getting dizzy just looking at it.

"Unbelievable, man!" he told the artist, "This is the most incredible thing you've ever done!"

"Yeah," said the artist, "I really took off on this one."

Graham looked at the poster again and then asked, "Where's the concert date?"

The artist then scanned his poster for several minutes before turning and saying, "Well, I can't tell you exactly, but I know I put it in there."

---

vent solutions; they don't want to supply code like so many robots. Give them a chance to contribute something of excellence. Don't have architects putting bricks in place, even if they're good at it. Let the bricklayers do it—they're even better at it.

Another reason for stopping overall design short of a mass of detail: You need a concise document for communicating with the customer and with your own management. I had a manager whose eyes not only glazed over, but actually nearly closed whenever I got beyond a certain level of detail. At about the third level of structure chart he looked like a lizard in a coma.

Finally, remember that this design document is a baseline, and it must be kept manageable in size and content if it is to be a useful reference point for change proposals.

## THE CART BEFORE THE HORSE PUTTING

Project SOB is well along in the design phase. There are lots of charts, Data Flow Diagrams done by Marty Martinet's four designers, and structure charts done by Dennis. Marty is content to see the pile of charts growing and is sufficiently lulled by the briefings he gets from his designers that he is not too worried that they're not all using the same tools.

Friday he and his designers give a briefing to Paula Projectmistress and her staff. Paula is putting together the rest of the organization she will need to program, test, and install the system Marty is designing.

The first twenty minutes of the review go smoothly enough, as the analysis manager discusses the SOB problem and Marty begins presenting the design. He plasters a wall with charts, leads the group through the context diagram, then turns to his chief designer, Dicky, to go through the more detailed charts. Paula Project-mistress soon interrupts:

"Dicky, so far, so good. But I've been glancing ahead at your other charts, and all I see are programs. . . ."

Dicky cocks his head questioningly.

"What I mean is," Paula continues, "I don't see anything representing the data base. Do you have separate charts showing how you're handling that?"

"Well . . ." Dicky flushes a little and glances toward Marty. "We're working out the data base as we go along. As we see the need for the next item of data, we add it on. We keep a chart showing all the tags and field lengths, but we didn't clean it up for the briefing."

Paula abruptly turns her questions toward Marty. "Isn't this pretty much a data base–driven system? My understanding has always been—and I think our problem spec bears this out—that we're dealing with a large assemblage of fairly complex data with plenty of cross-referencing."

"That's true," answers Marty, not sure of what Paula is getting at.

"Then doesn't the structure of the data base become pretty critical?"

"Well, data's data!" exclaims Marty reassuringly, with a shrug and a smile.

"Seems to me," continues Paula, getting a little restless, "that if you're dealing with a mess of calculations with only small amounts of data in and out, your data base problems are not huge. But in SOB, where three-quarters of the programs manipulate the data, the structure of the data base becomes at least as important as the structure of the programs, hmmmm?"

Dicky looks toward Marty for help, while Dennis inspects his shoes. Dennis had argued for structuring the data base early in the design effort, but had been brushed aside by Marty. Marty belches softly and looks for a way out:

"Paula, I think we have what you're looking for . . . we just don't have it ready for the briefing. Didn't think we'd bore you with a lot of details about the data."

Paula glances at her watch. "Suppose we continue the briefing Monday morning. I'd like to see the data diagrams right along with the program charts."

The meeting ends. Marty and his group make tracks for his office, while Paula takes the elevator to the next floor. She stops at Peter Projectmanager's door and sticks her head inside.

"Peter! Got a minute?"

Peter looks up from the papers on his desk and smiles: "Hi, Paula! C'mon in!"

She settles in a chair across from Peter.

"How'd your briefing go?" Peter asks cheerfully. Then, glancing at his watch, he adds: "Hmmmm! Pretty short briefing. Good or bad?" He is pretty sure he knows the answer.

"Listen . . ." Paula begins, "I've only been here a short time . . . you've been around longer. What do you think of Marty Martinet? Can he hack it?" Without waiting for an answer she relates her misgivings about the handling of SOB's data base.

"I'm afraid what I'm going to see Monday is a collection of data fancied up to look like an honest-to-God structured data base. Worse yet, I didn't see any real attempt at designing the overall system first, before either the programs or the data base. . . . What I'm really concerned about is, do I have the right person as design manager?"

A week later, Marty Martinet has been reassigned to address a pressing problem in New Jersey. Dennis Designer is the new design manager. He is meeting with the four SOB designers.

"This is all pretty brain-rattling," he begins. "An awful lot has happened this week. I hope you'll all bear with me while I get used to this job."

They chat until all five feel more comfortable, and then Dennis makes some announcements.

"Paula has arranged to reschedule the project by a few weeks," he says. "Here's what the new schedule looks like. It gives us a chance to get a fresh start, and since we already know plenty about the job, this time it'll go a lot faster. I'm getting Jerry Junioranalyst in to make sure all the design is captured in MegaCASE. We can't stop and train each of you to use the tool and still hope to make the schedule. I'll be concentrating on the data design and we'll meet regularly to make sure the processes and data match up correctly. Right after this project I have Paula's promise we can all attend an object-oriented design course in New York."

There are appreciative nods from the four designers.

"The main thing I want to stress right now," continues Dennis, "is that we'll be designing the data base from scratch and we need to get its overall structure pretty solid before we get very far into the programs. But even before that, we need to really go back to the beginning and look at the basic system design. Now here's what I think we need to do. . . ."

## MANAGING CHANGE

You manage designers pretty much like you manage anyone else, but certain areas need special care. Working together, designers and customers can change the system in ways that can make it unrecognizeable.

It's late in the day and Dicky comes barging into your office.

"They've changed the damned specs again!" he cries.

"Who?"

"The customer!"

"What makes you think so?"

"Alfie said so. He just came back from there."

"Ask Alfie to come in, will you?"

It happens regularly on any job. No matter how careful you are about writing specifications and getting them signed off, people will propose changes. You'll accept some and reject others. Deal with changes by having clear change management procedures. Once you set up procedures and sell them to the customer, you need to make sure your designers understand and abide by them. They need to understand that the Problem Specification they are designing from never changes until they hear it from you (management). No matter how many informal discussions there may be about *possible* changes, your people never agree to changes, but only pass them on through the official change management channels. If there is any place on a project where you need formal procedures, this is it.

Designers want to be helpful. That's good. If your salesman tells one of your designers that the customer has asked if a feature could be added and the designer doesn't see much technical difficulty in doing so, the new feature will be designed in with all the other features. That's not so good. The salesman might have misunderstood the customer (this happens occasionally), or the designer might have misunderstood the salesman (this also happens occasionally), or the designer's first appraisal of the difficulty might be off-target (even this happens from time to time). If any of these things happen, you are going to find that your Project Plan doesn't match the work that's being done and you will have no credible response to complaints that your project is out of control. The time to put an end to undocumented design changes is before they start.

Alfie comes in.

"Dicky says the customer wants something changed. What's it all about, Alfie?"

"They need the ident field expanded. They've just had a corporate directive to expand their product identifiers to ten characters."

"Have they written us a change request yet? I haven't seen one."

"Gee, I don't know."

"Okay, no problem. I'll call over there and make sure they put the thing in as a formal change request. If they do, and if it gets approved, it may have to wait for version two of the system."

Alfie relaxes a little. "Do you want us to see what it would cost to make the change?"

"Nope! Business as usual until we get it in writing . . . or if it's something earthshaking, I'll be around to let you know. In any case, always listen to their requests, but tell them to get them in the change proposal mill."

Alfie leaves happy and you do your management duty and get on the phone to make sure the change proposal, if it really is one, is handled according to the procedures you and the customer agreed to. No fuss. No panic. Some things on a project ought to be routine.

I've known some managers, one in particular I'll call Don, who insulate their subordinates *too* completely from the real world of change. Don was an excellent programmer and designer. As a manager of programmers and designers, though, he became much like a rooster protecting its flock. That's probably better than the other extreme, the manager who filters out nothing and causes his people lost time and energy, yet Don does some real damage. The people who work for him are in for some shock when they finally waddle out of the warm nest and face the big, bad world! People who are too protected by their managers may be temporarily more efficient than others, but they pay a price eventually, like overprotected kids leaving Iowa and heading for New York.

## Avoiding Wanderlust

Dicky is going to get the urge eventually to depart from the Problem Specification. He'll want to add some frills not called for in the spec. What he might not appreciate, and what you should, is that an addition that may cost the designer nothing more than a box on a chart is likely to cost more later, in programming and testing the goody. It will often be reasonable to make such changes, but don't let that be Dicky's prerogative. Whether changes are dreamed up by your people or by the customer, treat them all the same: control them.

## How Much Design?

Constantly review the evolving Design Specification to be sure everything in the Problem Specification is being satisfied, of course—but satisfied to an appropriate level. Your Design Specification should (a) explicitly satisfy each requirement in the Problem Specification; (b) stop as far short of coding as possible; (c) explicitly define the rules for all communication among program modules, between programs and data, and between people and programs; and (d) not leave problems to be resolved during programming whose solutions might cause changes in the baseline design. I probably should add (e) aim for a perfect, change-free design, but don't be surprised when you don't get it.

## Keeping the Customer Tuned In

Choose designers who can work well with the customer; don't hire anybody who thinks customers are a pain. Although the analysts were in closest touch with the customer, your designers cannot ignore him. Your people, and you, must keep appropriate customer people informed of your progress and your approaches. As design proceeds you need to answer questions and maintain customer confidence. Set the tone so that your people have a healthy attitude and don't consider the customer a bother. Obviously, you must also keep the customer from interfering with design progress—there's such a thing as too much togetherness, and it's up to you to establish what too much is.

## Training (Again)

It makes sense to push your designers to try new design approaches and tools. Left to their own devices, designers are liable to get into a rut, just like programmers who get comfortable with one computer language and don't want to learn another one. Don't forget that the choice of a design method or tool is going to limit your designers' ability to think about the problem that's in front of them. I don't just mean that it will affect the *way* they think about the problem, I really mean that it will affect their *ability* to think about the problem! It might never occur to a designer who approaches problems using process decomposition that the problem might be approached from an object perspective that provides additional insights.

If you let your designers get too comfortable, you will be sacrificing opportunities to improve the quality of design in your organization. Why would you want to do that? Get serious about training your designers, and make sure they get the message. A designer who goes through a year without learning more about the practice and techniques of design should not be given a raise—and the manager who let her slide should be treated the same way.

---

*You know your designers are doing a good job if*

> They want to spend more time with the analysts.
> They consider more than one design.
> They understand the need for architectures.
> They're always looking for ways to *not* build code.
> They try to create a good design rather than a perfect design.
> They want the programmers present at design inspections.

# PART IV

# PROGRAMMING

This is where the system stops being a set of ideas and becomes something tangible. Dr. Frederick Brooks, who managed the development of IBM's OS/360 Operating System software, has described the task of constructing software as "the most complex ever undertaken by humanity" (1987). In programming, we entrust people to translate designs that may be unclear into a series of precise instructions to be executed by a unforgiving computer that will do exactly what the instructions tell it to do without any concern for whether they make sense. It's your job to make sure that this difficult work is done correctly.

For years, programmers were regarded as "artists" who had a "gift" for writing code. Some of that legacy is still with us. There are studies that show that some programmers perform up to twenty times as effectively as their less efficient co-workers, but we are not sure why this disparity exists. We know that some programmers must meticulously extend the design to lower and lower levels before they make the translation to code while others dive in and create a "first cut" at a program that they successively refine. We know that both methods, in the appropriate hands, can produce excellent programs.

For managers, particularly those who are guiding one of their first projects, the Programming Process is a wrenching experience since it's necessary to let go of the one area that is probably most familiar—writing the programs themselves. Nevertheless, letting go is exactly what is required. If you insist on "contributing" to the code that is written by people who work for you, the project may come crashing down around your ears.

If you were a programmer and are now a manager, remind yourself that it is time to pass the torch. But keep your eye on the flame.

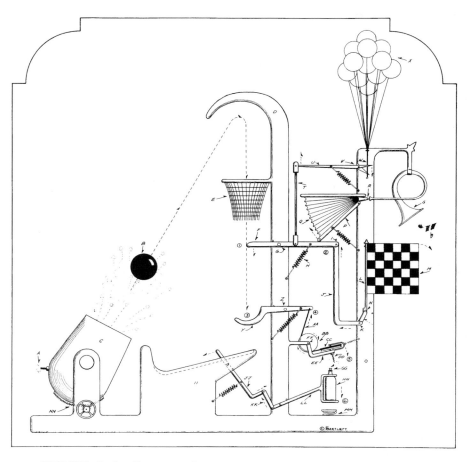

**FIGURE 6–1** Programming (Nearly Instantaneous Victory/Celebration Gadget" F. W. Bartlett II, Wapwallopen, PA.)

# 6

# The Programming Process

At last you're ready to write programs, and all hell breaks loose. You have more people to manage; the paper pile keeps growing; programmers scream for more terminals and computer time; flaws show up in the baseline design; the customer leans on your programmers to bootleg changes; Jack programmer is a dud; Jill programmer leaves to pursue her Masters degree; and your spouse is bugging you about being married to that stupid computer. These are normal snags that no amount of planning can prevent, so not to worry! If you've planned well up till now, you'll be able to deal with day-to-day glitches while you get on with the job of writing and testing programs and continuing preparations for later processes.

## THE NATURE OF PROGRAMMING

It's the programmer's job to comprehend thoroughly the baseline design, extend its level of detail, and translate it into a set of detailed orders that are given to what is, in most cases, a fairly limited but very fast device that interprets and changes patterns of ones and zeroes. Back in the dark ages of programming, when they wrote their programs, programmers actually used numeric codes that reflected the ones and zeroes used by the processor. It used to be standard practice to give programmers the hardware manual for the computer so that they could find out which instructions were available to write their programs.

> "Our understanding of the forces that motivate programmers and of the cognitive processes in programming is shallow."
>
> Ben Schneiderman, *Software Psychology* (1980)

For most programmers, times have changed considerably. Your team will probably work with languages and tools that allow them to concentrate on the nature of the problem without being constantly mindful of the constraints of the machine. In some cases, part or all of the program code may be generated automatically by another program.

In spite of these advances in the craft of programming, the essential nature of the work requires concentration and discipline. It's up to you, the manager, to make sure your team applies both of them.

## Coding as a Last Resort

If you want to make your programming process as efficient as possible (and what manager doesn't?), your best bet for increasing productivity is to use programs or pieces of programs that are already available. It takes time to enter lines of code and compile them and test them and correct them and document them. Why spend all this time if you don't have to?

In the early stages of the Programming Process, your programmers must be encouraged to work closely with the designers to look in existing systems and libraries for code that can track users, report errors, and set up screens. In some companies, the whole backbone of the program will be available as a "shell" that can be modified to do the job at hand. Make sure that your designers and programmers understand that you regard reuse of existing code as a *very good thing*.

If you are developing your system using object-oriented programming, there are class libraries of useful objects that you can purchase. In addition, there may be objects used by other projects that can be either used directly or adapted to suit your needs.

## STRUCTURED PROGRAMMING

Even with an emphasis on reusing code, the chances are that your team will need to create some new programs. There are a lot of ways to do this badly, and there are a few ways to do it well. Most of the good ways build on the principles of structured programming.

Structured programming is a formal approach to coding that aims at order, clarity, and readability, with the goal of error-free code. Structured code can be more easily tested and it can be readily understood by people other than the program's author. It's a philosophy that banishes "spaghetti" code. The days of intricate secret code written by snobs or messy code written by poorly trained programmers are, we may hope, ending. There is such a strong drive to bring order to the business that the entire complexion of the programming activity is changing for the better. Most of your programmers will know about structured programming; your problem is to ensure that they maintain the discipline to practice it.

## Goals of Structured Programming

The goals of structured programming go right to the heart of the programming job.

**Correctness.**   Nobody wants to structure programs simply to make them pretty, although that is certainly a benefit of structuring. What *really* counts is that programs be correct—that they do their prescribed functions flawlessly. Using structured programming and related ideas, people are writing complex programs that run correctly the first time. A book you and your programmers should read (Linger, Mills, and Witt, 1979) begins:

> There is an old myth about programming today and there is a new reality. The old myth is that programming must be an error prone, cut-and-try process of frustration and anxiety. The new reality is that you can learn to consistently design and write programs that are correct from the beginning and that prove to be error free in their testing and subsequent use. By practicing principles of structured programming and its mathematics, you should be able to write correct programs and convince yourself and others that they are correct by logic and reason rather than by trial and error. Your programs should ordinarily execute properly the first time you try them, and from then on. If you are a professional programmer, errors in program logic should be extremely rare, because you can prevent them from entering your programs by positive action on your part. Programs do not acquire bugs as people do germs—just by being around other buggy programs. They acquire bugs only from their authors.

Expert programmers do not slap together some code, ram it into the computer, and pray. Instead, they program with discipline and with confidence that their code will execute correctly. This doesn't always happen, but it happens often enough to make error-free programming a realistic goal.

**Readability.**   There is no place in today's computer business for programs that cannot be read by other than the original authors. In the past we tended to excuse such code as the work of either a genius or a dud. If that of a genius, many managers felt technically incapable of challenging such practices, or afraid of losing their "star" performers by presuming to question their programming practices. If a dud, the programmer might be nudged into "fixing up" the programs after the fact. Programs must be readable from the start so that they can be inspected by managers, supervisors, and other programmers who are checking logic or tracking down problems; they must be readable at the finish so that maintenance programmers can understand them.

**Testability.**   It's far easier to track down a bug in a program that's readable and clearly structured than in one full of Byzantine logic paths. In practice, readable programs are also easier to write, but they do demand some preliminary thought.

**Increased Productivity.**   Improvements in the first three goals (correctness, readability, testability) automatically lead to the goal of getting a correct program in less time and at lower cost.

## Techniques of Structured Programming

Detailed structured programming techniques are beyond the scope of this book but an introduction to them is in order. I urge you to study full treatments of the subject, even if you're going to use object-oriented approaches, fourth-generation languages, or program generators. Some excellent sources, which in turn refer to many additional readings, are Yourdon (1989), Hughes and Michton (1977), McGowan and Kelly (1975), Baker (1972, 1975), and Linger, Mills, and Witt (1979).

The essence of structured programming is this: It has been proven in a formal, mathematical sense that only three structures are needed to write a correct program and that any solvable programming problem can be solved using these three structures. The first is sequence: Do A, then B. The second is decision: If A is true, then do B, otherwise do C. The third is iteration: While A is true, do B.

In a paper that became the basis for much current work in structured programming, Bohm and Jacopini (1966) proposed that a program, any program, can be written using combinations of these three program structures (Figure 6–2). Two extensions of these three structures commonly accepted are DO_UNTIL, a variation of DO_WHILE where the exit condition, rather than the entry condition, is checked; and CASE, a variation of IF_THEN_ELSE that describes decision points with more than two outcomes.

If your programs are constructed using these structures, all unconditional branches (and the program complications they cause) will be eliminated. The result is a program readable from top to bottom, from beginning to end. The code (including supporting comments) is self-descriptive. How is this accomplished?

First, the consistent use of structured programming principles eliminates most of the need for unconditional (GO_TO) branching in source code. There will always be some controversy over whether it is possible to eliminate all such branching. The answer is partly dependent on the languages you use—some lend themselves more readily to the elimination of such branches, some make it difficult or impossible. Nonetheless, there is general agreement that programmers can and should eliminate most of this kind of branching. Where there are recognized needs for exceptions—a common example is module exits—individual organizations set up strict rules governing those exceptions.

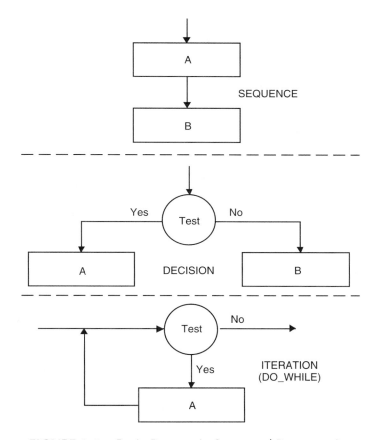

**FIGURE 6–2**    Basic Patterns in Structured Programming

Elimination of unconditional branching means that, as you read down a program source code listing, continuity is not destroyed by a branch that forces you to flip to other pages in the listing. I remember trying to investigate a problem in a COBOL program that was swarming with GO TO statements rather than PER-FORMs. When I asked the programmer about this, he told me, "GO TOs save time." Well, they certainly don't save time for anyone who has to figure out how the program works.

There are variations in how to depict the structured operations, and they may be implemented with differing syntax within the various procedural programming languages. But the impact is the same: any program can be constructed using combinations of these structures, and the program listing reads from start to finish telling a straightforward story without disruptive branches. In addition to the rigorous use of these structures, good programmers write structured code according to sensible rules of indentation and alignment. The effect is similar to that of a table of contents, where indentation and alignment show logical groupings of chapter titles and subheadings.

## Is Structured Programming Obsolete?

With every new way of writing programs, there will be an accompanying claim that all the old ways are obsolete and that it is time to rethink the ways in which we construct our systems. It's time to sound the trumpets—the new paradigm is at hand!

Bah, humbug! No matter what language or methodology you are using, you need to ensure that the execution of the program proceeds in an orderly manner. You need to design the program to execute logically and you need to write the program to execute as it was designed. This is sometimes called the "control flow" of a program. Structured programming relates directly to the control flow of programs and it is the only proven approach that can be relied upon to yield programs that execute as they were designed to do.

If you are writing your programs using the C++ language, you will need to ensure correct control flows. If you are using a fourth-generation language such as ADABAS, you will need to ensure correct control flows. If you are programming in Visual Basic, you will need to ensure correct control flows. Unless your programmers understand and apply the principles of structured programming, their program control flows will probably be defective.

Structured programming principles are no more obsolete than arithmetic.

## OOP

Object-oriented programming must be preceded by object-oriented analysis (OOA) and object-oriented design (OOD). While you can use OOA and OOD as the basis for a non-OO implementation, it doesn't work in the opposite direction. Structure analysis and design methods do not provide a good foundation for OO programs.

Object-oriented programming is less of a break from previous technologies than OOA and OOD are from the structured methods. To a significant extent, the actual work performed at the programming level is evolutionary—programmers are using many of the same skills and making many of the same mistakes using C++ that they previously did in C.

However, from the standpoint of managing object-oriented programming, there are a couple of things to remember:

➤ Communication within the programming group becomes more complex. The inherent distribution of objects will be reflected in the way that programmers work independently on their classes. In order to develop a program or test environment, a programmer may now have to talk to many other programmers

---

### The Twisted Path

Most object-oriented modules are relatively small, but this doesn't mean that OO-based software is always easy to understand. An update to an invoice may wind its way through dozens—even hundreds—of classes as it moves from the initial order to the final bill. If you're trying to verify that all of the work required to complete the transaction is reflected in the programs that were written, you can easily lose your way.

There really is some truth to the analyst's lament "We finally got rid of spaghetti code. We replaced it with lasagna code."

---

to understand the methods that are available. You'll need to make sure that your programmers document their objects clearly and in a timely manner so that other programmers can use them.

➤ The probability that object-oriented programming will initiate changes to the design is higher than it is with procedural programming, particularly in projects that are pioneering the use of object-oriented methods. The definition of classes and their boundaries may shift many times as programming moves forward, just as it does when using OOA and OOD. As programmers discover commonality in the classes they are programming, new classes can emerge. In turn, the emergence of these new classes can affect the ways that methods are implemented in other classes.

➤ Object-Oriented programming is not a declaration of independence from the established principles of structured programming. Use formal inspections to ensure that the C++ code that your programmers build into the object classes that make up your system is well structured and error-free.

## WHEN SHOULD PROGRAMMING START?

Many books and articles about software project management (including earlier editions of this book) have advised managers not to proceed with programming until the design has been completed. There are a lot of arguments in favor of this approach. The most important are as follows:

➤ The act of programming introduces a strong bias in the way the programmer looks at the problem to be solved. Since the programmer is being asked to decompose the design to its lowest level, each programmer will wind up making design decisions based on his own paradigms of how to build software.

➤ Programming that occurs before the overall design is complete may contain design implications that constrain the remainder of the higher-level design.

➤ Because code is considered to be more tangible than design, and since programmers generally have strong pride of ownership in their creations, the code will start determining the design, rather than the design determining the code. This can lead to disaster.

This is all true, but I now believe that it is outweighed by the need of the manager to determine how well the Design and Programming Processes work together. Also, from a practical standpoint, the risks associated with an early start to programming are outweighed by the benefit of producing a tangible product early in the project.

You should get your programmers started once a section of the project has been designed that can stand alone from both a programming and unit testing standpoint. Several times I have used the "LOGIN and SECURITY CHECK" functions of a new system as the first piece of the system to be coded. In order to make this work, the programming team must first get the development environment set up. This includes arranging the work space, setting up links to the development system, configuring the database and operating system, and obtaining necessary terminals and printers.

Then the programmers must work with the compilers, debuggers, libraries, and documents they will use to actually create the code. Even more important, they must learn to work with each other. By starting early on a *well-defined part* of the system, both the programmers and the manager have a chance to iron out any problems that could become real stumbling blocks when the team finally tackles the larger and more complex areas of the system.

Finally, and by no means the least important, you will get a chance to have some first-hand feedback about the quality of the design. It is not too difficult to create a design that is almost impossible to turn into a program. Sometimes it's difficult to recognize this condition when the design is reviewed. However, if your programmers can take the design and turn it into working programs without questioning the mental capacity of the designers, you ought to conclude that the design process is proceeding effectively.

## A Word of Caution

On smaller projects, it's not unusual to have people first work as designers and then take responsibility for turning their designs into programs. If this is the case, the manager needs to be very hard-nosed in refusing to let them start programming before their designs have been reviewed. *In no case and at no time should you allow programming to proceed without having a reviewed design to serve as a guide.* It does not have to be the whole design for the system, it simply needs to be complete for the functionality that the new program will deliver.

## ORGANIZATION

There are several ways of organizing the project team. One is functional organization, wherein you "borrow" people from groups of specialists within your company. Specialists are on loan to you to do their part of the job, and then they are gone—on loan to the next manager who needs their skills. Ineptly managed, this is BAAAAD NEWS! This arrangement gives you, the project manager, little control because the person you borrow is likely to be more concerned with the home organization than with your project. Typically, you have little or no say about whom you get, and there may be frustrating substitutions before your job is finished. There may be little or no continuity of people on your job. There is little opportunity to develop team spirit.

This so-called "matrix management" can work, but it depends on agreements between the affected managers and their abilities to work well as a team. A lot of companies and government agencies have tried it and many of them have moved on to trying something else.

Despite the difficulties, some form of matrix management is going to be present in most systems development projects. The importance of specialists in database administration, network and system optimization, training development, and other disciplines cannot be ignored. Only very large projects will have the budget and workload to incorporate these skills on a full-time basis. As a manager, you will either need to find these specialists in other parts of your organization or be prepared to obtain them through consulting agreements. I'll have more to say about this a little later in the chapter.

A second kind of organization is the "job-shop." To use it, simply break the system into several major subsystems and assign a manager and group total responsibility for developing that subsystem—analysis, design, programming, the works. I attacked a job that way many years ago and regretted it long afterward. Here the problem is that nobody has an eye on the *system* because the managers are concerned only with the subsystems. A job-shop arrangement works best if you are doing small, unrelated jobs (in other words, not a system). If you're a manager accustomed to a job-shop organization and are about to manage the development of a system, remember that what worked before may not work now.

Neither functional nor job-shop organization is entirely appropriate for producing a system. What you need is project organization, in which the people involved devote their efforts to a single project and they all work for a single project manager.

Project organization can take many forms. Every company has its rules about lines of authority, degree of autonomy, reporting to outside management, and so on.

Putting such considerations aside for the moment, we need to consider project organization in terms of two approaches: conventional and team organizations.

## THE FIRST APPROACH: CONVENTIONAL ORGANIZATION

Figure 6–3 illustrates two conventional ways to organize your forty-person project. The only real difference between (a) and (b) is the number of management levels between you, the project manager, and the people who do the work. The choice of (a) or (b) depends on your strengths and weaknesses and those of the managers available to you. If you are technically strong, able to absorb detail, and can handle as many as seven managers reporting to you (a hefty number), then (a) might be your choice. The danger is that you may become swamped in details, lose sight of broader project objectives, and lose control. If you prefer to delegate more responsibility so you can concentrate on the important problems that arise, (b) should be your choice, with second-level managers reporting to you. Either way your project has many managers (seven besides you), and that may horrify your boss ("Where are the workers!?"). As I hope to show, these managers are not papershufflers. Since they are very much involved in technical decisions, the ratio of managers to workers is not as bad as it looks.

In most situations I would choose (b) over (a). What's important, however, is neither the number of boxes on the organization chart nor their titles but that you account for all jobs to be done. Then be sure all members of the organization know both their own and other people's objectives. Given that, you're off to a good start. The remainder of this section describes the functions of the various groups shown in Figure 6–3b and ends by considering some typical numbers of people in the various roles.

### Analysis and Design Group

Although you've now entered the Programming Process and programmers are at center stage, you can't put the analysts and designers out to pasture. In addition to continuing their work in the Definition and Design Processes, the original analysts and designers also need to perform the following critical jobs:

**Managing Change.**    The most important function of this group is to carry out the Change Management procedures described later in this chapter. This means investigating proposed changes, recommending adoption or rejection, and documenting results. The group acts as a filter. It relieves other project members, particularly the programmers, of much of the burden of digging into a proposed change and tracking down the consequences of making the change. On many projects the investigation of a change proposal falls on the programmers and this sidetracks them from their main job. To a person doing something as logic-oriented as programming, every interruption means a loss of efficiency. When the interruption

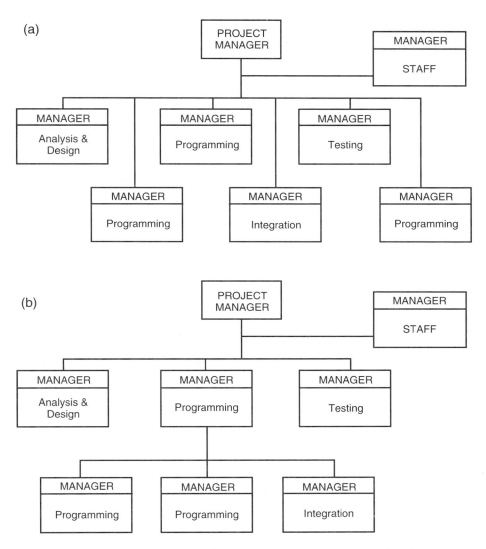

**FIGURE 6–3**   Conventional Work Organization: (a) two levels of management; (b) three levels of management.

ends, the programmer must say, "Now, where was I?" Besides the wasted time backtracking, he or she may end up with a bug at the point of interruption. Often the frustration of constant interruption causes programmers to give hasty answers and to agree to the change just to get the problem off their backs. Let's get on with the coding! Those hasty answers will return to haunt you.

Having analysts and designers handle change proposals concentrates a vital function in one place instead of spreading it thinly over the project. Furthermore, it concentrates the function of Change Management at the *right* place and the *right* time! When a change is proposed, the first thing you need to do is answer the questions "How does this change affect the definition?" and "How does this change affect the design?"

If the definition or design changes, your analysts and designers can take the time to evaluate the impact of the change. They can make changes to the Problem Specification and the Design Specification before discussing the changes with the programmers. They can show the effects on cost and schedule to the customer.

**Data Control.**   This is really part of the Change Management function. Data control means insuring that nobody makes unauthorized changes to system databases. By "system databases" I mean those organized collections of data accessed (either stored into or retrieved from) by more than a single program module. System database structures, a dictionary defining each data item, and all the rules for using system data should have been defined as part of the baseline design. Just as it is necessary to control changes to *program* design after you have established the baseline, you must control changes to the data bases. Don't leave it to the programmers to reach informal (and undocumented) agreements about data base structure as they go along.

**Writing User Documentation.**   User documentation includes anything you are responsible for writing that will help the customer to use the system. (The other major category of documentation is *descriptive*, something telling how the system is built. That's the programmers' job.) User documentation may include the following topics:

➤ Installing the system
➤ Periodic testing of the system after installation
➤ Start-up and shut-down procedures
➤ Operating procedures, options, and error correction
➤ Preparing inputs for the system
➤ Analyzing outputs from the system

Providing user documentation requires assistance from the programmers, but it should be the responsibility of analysts and designers, who have a better understanding of the customer viewpoint. On some projects, the *user* writes these documents with the assistance of the project members.

## Programming Groups

The programmers are the focus of this organization. Their job is a series of five steps: detailed design, coding, module test, documentation, and integration. Individual programmers are responsible for the first four and they assist in the fifth.

**Detailed Design.**   The programmers inherit from the designers the document called the Design Specification. This is the baseline for all their work. The programs they write must mesh perfectly with the baseline design; otherwise, either the programs or the baseline design must change. The manager or supervisor assigns a piece of the baseline design to an individual programmer. Let's assume this is a single module. The programmer's first job is to design the module in detail, living within all the rules laid down in the Design Specification. That detailed design is what I call the Coding Specification for that module. The detailed design is expressed using some combination of the design documentation tools discussed in Chapter 2. The programmer devises the best detailed design possible, *consistent with the baseline design.* No one violates the baseline design!

A problem managers have always faced is that some programmers have no use for detailed design documents. They would rather code directly from the baseline design (assuming there is one) and skip the detailed design. Other programmers would rather code first and design later. What to do?

The answer is simple: all programmers will produce detailed documentation before they code! Programmers opposed to this way of working should signify their opposition by saying, "I resign." Without detailed design, how can your programmers know if a piece of existing code can do the job? How can they know *as they write their code* that it will do the job it is supposed to? How will they help other members of the team, including you, understand and review the code they have written?

I call the detailed design document a Coding Specification to indicate its primary purpose. The Coding Specification allows you to:

➤ Review the programmer's work before it gets too far into coding and testing.

➤ Establish a base for continuing design review and eventual code review.

➤ Improve the final product by providing better support for reviews and inspections.

➤ Keep going if the programmer must leave the project for any reason.

Despite these arguments, you may *very occasionally* allow coding to be done directly from the baseline design. Some portions of the baseline design may have been done in sufficient detail to allow this. Like everything else on the project, if you go that way, make it the result of a reasoned decision. Don't just shrug and let it happen.

**Coding.**   Coding is the translation of the detailed design into computer instructions. (It's what most people think of as "programming.") As coding proceeds, changes in the detailed design will occasionally be found advisable or necessary. Making these changes is the responsibility of the programmer, except when the baseline design is also affected. Make sure the programmer understands the requirement to update the Coding Specification whenever it changes in response to coding issues.

Managers should watch for programmers who have a penchant for writing unnecessarily tight, complex code. Although at times it's necessary to save every possible bit and microsecond, there are usually more important considerations. For example, code must be readable by another competent programmer. I can cite more than one instance when a pseudo-professional programmer left behind a batch of code that worked (sort of) but was unintelligible to anyone but its originator. In one case, a programmer left a marvelously efficient program, but one day of course it became necessary to modify that program. The unsuspecting manager promised the customer that the modifications would be done and delivered in four weeks. Six months later, the job was not done, and the embarrassed manager finally had to have the program rewritten from scratch. An extreme example? Nope! Watch out for it. Here simplicity pays off. If you want to challenge your programmers, challenge them to write efficient code that even *you* can understand.

First-level managers should work as a team in setting up and enforcing reasonable coding standards. There is plenty of room for any programmer to show creativity in coding a module without violating sensible coding standards. Decent standards will give you reasonable assurance that others will be able to understand and maintain your code. CASE tools can help alert you to potential problems by signaling possible breaches of "rules" governing such areas as module size and levels of nesting.

**Module Test.**    This is the testing of an individual module in an isolated environment before adding it to the evolving system. The objective is to assure that this module, when inserted into the system, will do its job as a black box. It should accept its specified inputs and produce exactly the right outputs. I've chosen not to call this "unit test" because the module being tested may appear at any level in the hierarchy. If you are doing top-down testing, early modules to be tested will belong

---

### The First Bug

In the 1940s mathematicians used a computer called the Harvard Mark II to calculate ballistics firing tables for the U.S. Navy. On a hot summer day in 1945 the computer was shut down by a malfunction. Mathematician and pioneer programmer Grace Murray Hopper recorded in the computer's log the cause of the malfunction. A moth was found lodged in one of the Mark II's thousands of electromechanical relays. Thus was born the term "bug" for the cause of a computer program malfunction (*Understanding Computers*, 1990).

to the "subsystem" level, followed by the "package" level, and so on. Should you choose bottom-up testing, many early modules will be "units," those lowest in the pecking order, followed by "components" and then "packages," and so on up the chain.

Although the project may supply test aids, module testing is primarily the individual programmer's job. I don't suggest imposing any rigid, formal module test scheme—only good general guidelines. The programmer should put on paper, in his own words and own format, the steps he proposes to execute to test the module. The programmer should include the test plan as an integral part of his Coding Specification; he should subject it to an inspection, modify it if necessary, and execute it.

Module testing usually involves these steps: (1) Desk-checking by the author; (2) clean compilation; (3) a formal inspection of the Coding Specification, the code and the module test plan; (4) fixes and recompilation, if necessary, resulting from the inspection; and (5) execution of the tests. Depending on test results, of course, there may be one or more repetitions of any or all these steps.

Some programmers will read the above paragraph and grouse: "Leave me alone! I know what I'm doing!" So did Jack The Ripper. The truth is, most professionals go through these steps routinely. The problem for you, as a manager, is that they also overlook things routinely.

Decisions concerning the nature and extent of module test will be influenced by whether you are testing top-down or bottom-up. If you are testing *bottom-up*, you normally use drivers of various kinds to represent the "top" of the system—that is, the part of the system above the module in the hierarchy and responsible for invoking the module. In *top-down* testing, the "top" of the system already exists. The module can be added to the existing system. What you need to simulate here is any relevant module *below* the one being tested. In this case, the programmer writes code called "stubs" to stand in for the missing lower module(s). Stubs, generally simpler than drivers, may simply record that they have been called and return control to the invoking module. Stubs may go further and simulate the actions that will eventually be taken by the real modules for which they are temporarily substituting.

One way to provide stubs is to build an entire set in advance, rather than have them introduced by individual programmers as needed. As new modules are completed and inserted into the system, corresponding stubs are deleted.

Remember that stubs may be reusable. When they are called by upper-level modules, they not only receive data from the originating module, but they actually use the same interface as the real module that will replace them.

**Documentation.**    "Document unto others as you would have them document unto you"—so sayeth Kreitzberg and Schneiderman (1971). Good advice. Here is where an otherwise good product may be poorly represented. The programmers are responsible for the documents that describe in detail how the system is constructed. The vehicle they use is the Coding Specification, a combination of the documentation tools discussed in Chapter 2 and the code listing. The Coding Specification (before code is done) shows detailed design intent. The final document contains both design and code. The logic and the code described in the Coding Specification should, of course, be completely accurate and consistent. What ties all the individual Coding Specifications together is the Design Specification.

DESIGN SPECIFICATION + ALL CODING SPECIFICATIONS
= SYSTEM DESCRIPTION

**Integration: Top-down.**    Integration, or integration testing, is the process of gradually adding new modules to the evolving system and testing to assure that the new module and the system perform properly. Let's assume you've chosen top-down integration testing as your project's approach, consistent with your use of top-down design and top-down structured programming. How to proceed? There are several avenues:

1. All integration testing could be done by a separate group (see Figure 6–3) whose sole function is integration testing. The members of the group do not write any of the programs. Programmers turn over individually tested modules to this integration test team. The team adds each module to the developing system and tests it according to a predetermined integration test plan.

2. All integration testing could be done by individual programmers (eliminate the "Integration" group in Figure 6–3). Each programmer is responsible for adding his or her modules and running tests according to the integration test plan.

3. Integration testing could be handled by a group that also has programming responsibility. Logically, this would be the group charged with writing the higher-level modules in the program hierarchy—the "executive" program, "control" program, or whatever you name the set of code that serves as the system's framework.

The third alternative is generally best. This choice guarantees that the people responsible for integration have the most intimate knowledge of the system. Choice 1 is workable, perhaps even best, for large projects, where there are so many programs involved that integration is a huge task. But keep in mind that a separate group with no part in the actual programming may be too far removed from the system. They would be in a less favorable position to spot problems and devise solutions; and they might be less motivated, since they have no code of their own at stake. A strong counter argument, of course, is that such a separate group could be more objective, for the very reason that their own code is not under question.

Whether you decide on Choice 1 or Choice 3, the integration effort will be smoother when the original analysts and designers participate. With these people participating in the testing, any problems can be immediately correlated with the original definition and design and required changes can be made in an orderly manner.

Choice 2 invites chaos.

**Integration: Bottom-up.**   As tested modules become available from the programmers, the process of integration begins. Theoretically, this means that units are combined and tested together to form components; components are grouped and tested to form packages; and so on up the pyramid until the complete system has been put together and progressively, exhaustively tested. In practice, you will usually find that no matter how neatly you lay things out on paper, the process is not quite that orderly. One reason is that some "components" will be ready while other "units" are still being coded; another is that when bugs show up at each level of test, buggy units have to be reworked.

There are at least two ways to proceed with bottom-up integration. One is to have programmers produce the lowest-level modules and turn them over to a separate group for integration. Another is to have the programming groups integrate their portions of the system and turn their work over in larger chunks to a separate group. The first way may be theoretically more attractive, but the second way is more practical and more satisfying to the programmers because it gives them more responsibility than to produce parts for someone else to assemble.

As in top-down testing, the group responsible for integration also could be responsible for writing the basic control program for the system, the top-level module or modules. You'll need to decide during earlier test planning at what level the Programming Groups turn work over to the Integration Group. For example, you might give your Programming Groups responsibility for detailed design, coding, module test, documentation, and integration up through the program package level. When integration of an individual package has been completed, the Integration Group accepts the package for final merging of packages into subsystems and subsystems into a system. You may, of course, choose any level at which to submit modules to the Integration Group. In fact, it may make sense to define groups of modules to be submitted without regard to levels in the hierarchy.

**Integration: The Test Specification.**   Since the Integration Test Specification is key to the formal testing process, let's look at it in some detail. (An outline is suggested in the Appendix.)

The Integration Test Specification must be ready to use early in the Programming Process, when integration begins. It must, therefore, be finished during the Design Process and it should be treated as a key deliverable product of that process. It describes test objectives, general procedures and tools, and success criteria, and it includes a coverage matrix showing which specific tests (or "test cases") cover which functional areas of the system. You need it whether you test top-down or bottom-up.

The Integration Test Specification calls for test cases. A test case contains the detailed objectives, data, and procedures required for one test. A look at the coverage matrix mentioned earlier shows which test case or cases apply to a given functional area. The key items in a test case are the data required for the test and a script. The script (often called a scenario) for each test case is a set of step-by-step procedures telling what is to be done, who is to do it, when it is to be done, what to look for, and what to record. Similar scripts are described in the next chapter for system testing.

Tacking test cases onto a basic test specification, rather than writing one huge testing document, is another example of modularity. It's so much easier to see where you are when things are done in clean, finite chunks. Going back to repeat a test is simple when you can point to a single test case and say, "Do it again."

Figure 6–4 illustrates four formal test specifications that I'm advocating here and in the next two chapters. Each has the same conceptual organization. In fact, as the figure shows, some test cases may serve equally well during integration, system, acceptance, and site testing. Good planning early in the project will enable you to maximize the multiple use of test cases.

If you ask integration test programmers what they wished they had done differently after the job was all over, you often hear: *If only we had laid out tests in advance!* When integration time arrives you should concentrate on running the tests, evaluating results, and making fixes. It's too late to begin test planning when testing begins. All you can do then is fumble and pray that baseline designing and module testing have been done extraordinarily well and that things fall into place easily.

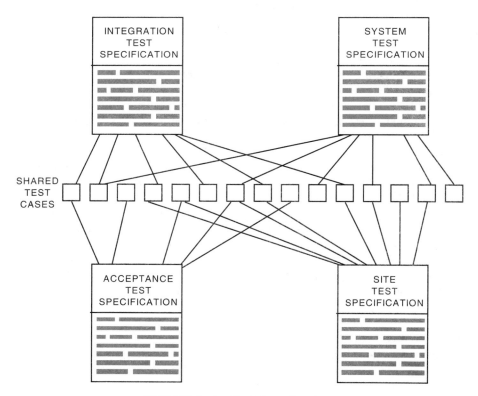

**FIGURE 6–4**  Test Specifications

## Test Group

During the Programming Process, the job of the Test Group is to get ready for *system test*, *acceptance test*, and *site test*. This is *not* the same group responsible for integration test. Its orientation is quite different. While the integration testers were concerned with putting program modules together, testing interfaces, and testing both system logic and function, the system and acceptance testers are almost solely concerned with testing function. They are not directly concerned with the structure of the system. They focus on how the system does its job and satisfies the requirements stated in the Problem Specification. The Test Group comes into prominence in the next two chapters, but they must prepare now, during the Programming Process. During this process their job includes writing test specifications, building specific test cases, predicting results, getting test data ready, arranging for computer time, setting up test schedules, organizing test libraries, and choosing and securing test tools.

## Testing from a Management Perspective

Managers who are trying to control Definition, Design, and Programming Processes will often find plausible excuses to let test definition slide a little. After all, testing comes later. This is industrial-strength stupidity and I'll tell you why.

The quality and performance of a manager is not the easiest thing in the world to measure. One of the only means available to judge how well the management job has been performed is to see if the system works. If you are the manager and you can point to a series of stringent tests that your system (or your part of the system) has completed successfully, your superiors and your staff will both conclude that you have been managing effectively.

Guess what these people will think if you turn over an inadequately tested product that blows up when the customer tries to use it. Okay, now do you still want to let test definition slide?

## Staff Group

Some technicians look at staff groups as hangers-on, paper-pilers, drains on the overhead, and general pains in the neck. Sometimes that view is justified. Some managers surround themselves with so many assistants that it's hard to find the manager. This happens in big organizations because rules, regulations, and associated paperwork get out of hand and staff people are hired to control them. Some staff people create more rules, regulations, and paperwork, and the disease spreads rapidly. It's like hiring a virus to cure a virus. This occurs even in smaller organizations, particularly when the *customer* happens to be big. For example, if you deal with the federal government, the amount of paperwork needed to conform to government regulations can be daunting. An RFP (Request for Proposals) issued by the

Department of the Army is a case in point. (An RFP describes a job the customer, in this case the Army, wants done. Prospective contractors study the document, find out whatever else they can about the job, and bid on it.) This RFP was three inches thick: one inch described the job to be done, the second inch was appendices, and the third contained descriptions and lists of government regulations to which the proposals had to conform. That last inch was a killer, and the immediate reaction to it was dismay. The next reaction was, "Well, we can't change the government and we can't ignore these regulations or we'll lose the job." Result: All kinds of staff people were hired to handle all the requirements of those regulations, and before we knew it we had an organization in which a handful of people did the technical job, with an army of support.

A manager often hires a staff member to do a specific job. An ambitious staffer will define his or her own work scope and will soon generate requirements for more staff help. A less ambitious person will do a specific job that consumes 20 percent of his or her time and spend the rest wandering the halls. There's only one way I know to avoid amoebalike growth of staff functions: you have to define the staff member's job as clearly as you would define a programmer's job. Surely you wouldn't hire a programmer and tell him or her to find a piece of programming work to do. You'd say, "Here's the overall job, here's the piece I'd like you to do, here's the schedule, and this is how I want you to report progress." Do the same with a staff member. Don't hire one and say, "Okay, go do staff stuff!" Be ready to assign him or her specific responsibilities.

The two kinds of staff functions you're likely to need on your forty-member project are technical and administrative.

**Technical Staff Functions.**   The people supplying technical support must themselves be technically competent. Their function is to focus on tasks that help all the other technical people on the project, and their work can be important to ensuring consistency among all of the projects that are undertaken by your organization. Their specific jobs cover quite a range:

*Data Base Administration.*   Data Base Administrators (DBAs) play a key role in the areas of system performance, intersystem communications, standards enforcement, and requirements development. That's a lot of key roles and the people who can handle them all well aren't easy to find. It's a good idea to keep the DBAs regularly informed about the progress of your project, even when it isn't the main focus of their work. The DBAs are the people who are going to be intimately involved if you need to partition or optimize your databases. The more they know about your system and the earlier they know it, the better prepared they will be to provide you with the support you need.

*Controlling Computer Time.*   Even with multiprogramming systems, this becomes an issue during module testing and system testing. For the development of real-time systems, particularly process control systems, the allocation of dedicated computer time is a recurring issue. My experience has convinced me that one person should collect all computer time requests, secure the time each week, schedule it as equitably as possible among those who request it, resolve conflicts, observe priorities, keep accurate records of time requested and used, plan for time needed weeks and months ahead, and dispense the aspirin when time is canceled. I had this job on one project. Since everyone on the project knew there was one person to go to for computer time, we avoided many potential conflicts. On a specific day each week, I collected requests for computer time for the following week. I juggled requests against the amount of time available for that week (always too little) and made up a tentative schedule in grease pencil on a big plastic wall chart. Everyone had a day or so to look at the charts and squawk. (I tried not to clobber anyone two weeks in a row.) Then I put the schedules on paper, passed them out, and that was it for the week.

Part of this job is to coordinate testing schedules with owners of other systems. If you are developing an application on a server that communicates with processes running in the mainframe, somebody needs to make sure that there is a time when both of them will be available.

*Housekeeping.*    Another part of the technical support job is to free the programmers from the burdens of the "housekeeping" functions that surround programming activity. The staffer should arrange for pickup and delivery of test runs and computer outputs, and provide for such physical facilities as bins and cabinets and for courier service if necessary. In short, this person should be the interface between the computer installation and its users.

*System Administration.*    Today's development environment can include Local Area Networks, multiple processors, a mix of terminals, PCs and workstations, and several software packages, such as relational data base systems and transaction monitors, purchased to provide functionality for the system. I'd advise you to find a person whose primary responsibility is systems administration. Once you find her, make sure she gets all of the training necessary to support your project. In today's client/server environments, the system administrator's job can be very complex and you cannot afford the slip-ups that come with the trial-and-error approach.

*Maintaining the Programmer's Handbook.*    The technical staff should organize the handbook and keep it updated. The handbook is discussed in Chapter 2 and is outlined in the Appendix.

*Training.*    Unless training is such a large function for your project that it requires a separate group, the Staff Group should be responsible for both internal and external training and should provide for instructors, training facilities, written training materials, schedules, and training cost estimates. Remember that a bunch of staff people who are otherwise underemployed is not the same thing as a training group.

*Investigating Productivity Tools and Techniques.*   There should be an ongoing search for the best available tools and techniques for use on the project. Although there will be suggestions from all over the project about various CASE packages, methodologies, code generators, or commercially available class libraries, your organization should see if it can find a specialist with the job of investigating and making recommendations about improving the software development environment, not just for your project, but for all of the other projects your organization is responsible for.

*Special Technical Assignments.*   Sometimes there are specific, short-range technical jobs to be done, but there is no specific place to assign them. For example, you may need to track down a troublesome problem that cuts across several of your groups. You may need someone who has experience in using a new debugger or source code administration tool. With the increase in multivendor, multiplatform systems, the availability of specialists has become a critical planning issue for many managers. On the project I'm managing now, we just lost two days because the person who was to show us what we had to do to assemble our software modules for automatic distribution was attending a seminar about the next version of the distribution system. I suggest that you include room in your staff estimates to allow for specialized help and that you put some effort into finding alternative sources for that help.

**Administrative Staff Functions.**   I began this section grumbling about staff groups getting out of hand. The group that generally runs amok is the administrative staff. Before I list its functions, here is what an administrative staff is *not*. It's not project management; it's an aid to project management. It's not a quality control department; quality control is a management function, and you will not assure quality by having a thousand administrators looking over the programmer's shoulder and filling out forms and reports. It's neither a personnel management group nor a salary administration group; those are management jobs. The functions of the administrative staff *are* as follows:

*Document Control.*   The administrative staff handles documentation as laid out in the Documentation Plan. The job includes setting up and operating the project general library, handling interfacing between the project and outside technical publications organizations, keeping track of document numbers and issuing new ones, publishing a periodic index of all project documents, and providing for reproduction services and equipment. A specific document controlled by the technical rather than the administrative staff is the Programmer's Handbook.

*Report Control.*   The staff helps you by gathering status data and drafting status reports from you to your management and from you to the customer. It also obtains and distributes to you and all managers on the project periodic financial status reports. There are many PC-based project management programs on the market. Selection of an appropriate package for your project will make it easier to keep track of and report status—there should be little need for hand-drawn charts and graphs. The staff prepares inputs to such programs (from data obtained from line managers) and distributes their outputs. The staff prepares a final report, the Project History described earlier.

***Contract Change Management.***    When you have accepted a contract change on the technical level, the staff handles the job of completing the paperwork showing that the customer formally agrees to the change. Part of this job is assessing the cost of the change. In handling this, the staff coordinates among four parties—the technical people who make the first estimate of cost, you, your company's financial and legal services, and the customer.

***Secretarial and Typing Support for the Project.***    You may be building the paperless office, but you're going to kill a lot of trees getting there.

**Outside Help.**    It may be hard to find staff with the skills you need, either on the technical or administrative side. If the people who are available to you inside your company don't have the skills you need, you'll have to go outside the company to find them. There is no shortage of firms who will tell you that they have the expertise you need. Many of them don't. There isn't any universally reliable guidance I can give you about consultants and professional services firms, but my experience leads me to use the following rules of thumb:

➤ *Don't look for the lowest price.* Firms that have held on to their employees by investing in education and decent benefits can't offer rock-bottom prices. Besides, you ought to be looking for the best people you can find, whether you're getting them from inside your company or from outside.

➤ *Ask around.* Word of mouth in your industry is usually pretty reliable. You may not get a good lead out of asking, but you will avoid getting stuck with a bunch of turkeys.

➤ *Interview consultants as if they were going to become employees.* Have your staff talk to potential consultants—not the consulting firm's marketing types, but the people who will be working with you. Get a feel for what they know and how helpful they will be.

## Numbers

Figure 6–5 shows a three-level hierarchical organization with a summary of the jobs of each group and numbers of people in each group. The numbers will vary from one project to another, but I'll briefly give my rationale for choosing these numbers.

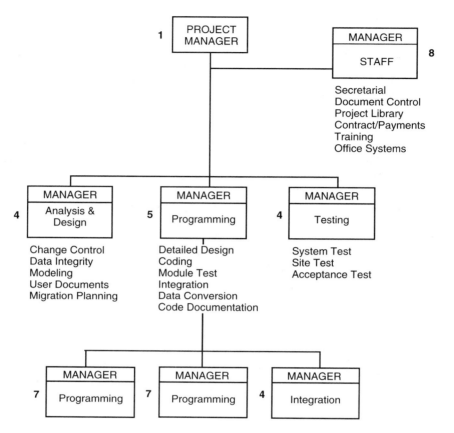

**FIGURE 6–5**    Staff Size (During the Programming Process)

**Project Manager.**    Of course there is a "1" in this box—what else? Unfortunately, there are sometimes two people. The second has a vague title such as "assistant project manager." Avoid this because it's difficult to know who's responsible for what. After all, the managers who work for you are all "assistants," and one of them should be capable of standing in for you when you're sick or on vacation. (If you're not grooming people for your job, you're not doing your job.)

**Staff.**    One manager and seven workers. The seven are three technical staff members and four administrative workers. Among the administrative members are three secretaries or typists. The remaining administrative member, along with the group's manager, handles contract matters, documentation control, and report preparation.

**Analysis and Design.**   Three workers plus the manager should be sufficient to handle the functions I've described. Toward the end of the Programming Process, you may reduce the number or the group may merge with the Test Group to help with system test and acceptance test.

**Test.**   During this process, the Test Group gets ready for system test, acceptance test, and site test. Four people should suffice.

**Programming.**   I've shown small groups—small compared to the group sizes often seen on projects. Indeed, all the groups in this organization are intentionally small. The job of a first-level manager is tough. You shouldn't give him or her ten or twelve or twenty people to manage and expect a first-rate job. Keep groups small enough that managers can be intimately involved with the details of the work. If you give a manager a cast of thousands, you will surely create a paper-shuffler.

Although I've shown one team as "Integration," the integration work might be incorporated into each of the programming groups, raising the size of each group and leaving a smaller "integration" group to handle the details of common interface definition and implementation or reuse management.

## THE SECOND APPROACH: PROGRAMMING TEAMS

The team approach is a way of organizing around a group of specialists. One of the first and most widely known embodiments of the team approach in programming is called the Chief Programmer Team. A lot of projects have tried to emulate the original successes of this type of organization.

IBM's Harlan Mills, originator of the concept, compares the Chief Programmer Team to a surgical team, where a chief surgeon plans and performs an operation with vital help and backup from highly skilled assistants, both surgeons and nonsurgeons. Dr. Mills, a prime mover in this and many other modern programming innovations and improvements, played the role of chief programmer in a well-known experimental project (Aron, 1970) to write a system called Definitive Orbit Determination. The goal was for a single expert programmer, Mills, to produce the DOD system in six months with the aid of a supporting team; the task had been estimated as a thirty person-year job for a conventional programming group. The task finally took about six person-years to complete, more than the stated goal, but far less than the conventional estimate.

### How It Works

The core of a Chief Programmer Team is normally three people: a chief programmer, a backup programmer, and a technical librarian.

The chief programmer is the technical manager responsible for the development of the system. She normally writes at least the critical "system" modules—that is, the portion of the system exercising control over, and interfacing with, all the lower-level "working" modules. Depending on the total size and complexity of the job, the chief programmer and the backup might write the entire system. Where others are involved, the chief programmer assigns work to them and integrates all their modules with her own. The chief programmer is the main interface with the customer, at least in technical matters (there may be a managerial counterpart who handles nontechnical tasks).

The backup programmer assists in any way assigned by the chief programmer, but his primary function is to understand all facets of the system as well as the chief programmer does and to be ready to take over as chief programmer. The backup programmer normally designs, codes, and tests specific portions of the system and handles other duties, such as preparation of a test plan.

The technical librarian is responsible for running the Development Support Library. This person is a full and vital member of the team, not on part-time loan. The librarian's duties include preparing machine inputs as directed by the programmers, submitting and picking up computer runs, and filing all outputs.

The important thing to consider about the Chief Programmer Team is that it achieves excellent results by identifying technical staff members with superior talent and organizes the rest of the staff to support the superior technicians in a manner that adds to their productivity. The Chief Programmer Team approach is the antithesis of a management approach that tries to "spread the work out evenly" in the hope that nobody gets overloaded.

So why not try to set up a Chief Programmer Team for your project?

It's time for a reality check: If the Chief Programmer Team structure is so great, we should see it everywhere. The main reason we don't is that *real* chief programmers don't grow on trees. We don't find the combination of requisite talents in every good programmer who comes along. Not only must a chief programmer be an excellent programmer, but a top-notch analyst, designer, tester, and communicator as well. How rare are chief programmers? I've been in this business for over thirty years and I've only met six people I would put in that class. I'm not one of them.

## Informal Teams

No matter what formal organizational structure you adopt, there is abundant evidence throughout industry that a team approach (small "t") is the way to go. The Japanese seem to be good at it. Big American companies, including General Motors' Saturn Division, are getting the idea. On a smaller scale, little-noticed groups all over the workplace achieve good results because of a hard-to-define yet effective team spirit. A good team effort accomplishes the two most important goals of management: success in reaching the project's goals *and* a happy, satisfying work experience for the team members. In some cases, the small team approach is used to create "software factories" where these teams move from one task to another in the organization. By using a derivative of this approach, one software development organization in DuPont has achieved productivity gains in excess of sixty percent for the majority of the projects they take on. By this I mean that they complete their projects in a third of the time that they used to and that their quality has similarly improved. It's also important to note that this organization was pretty good before it made those gains.

There's no formula for creating a good team environment, but there are things you can do to clear the path. You can minimize distractions for the team; you can give them all the tools they need; you can show your trust in them by turning them loose on a job and not checking every hour on how they're doing. You can get them started and get out of the way. You can accept the fact that corporate goals are at the bottom of most people's care-list. At the top of their lists are personal goals, followed closely by team goals. Managers with any foresight at all understand that when their troops attain their private, high-priority goals, the company automatically attains *its* goals. One of the things a manager can do, as suggested by De-Marco and Lister in *Peopleware* (1987), is to provide "frequent opportunities for the team to succeed together." At the least, this means not imposing the stupid, unachievable deadlines that have been endemic to the software business.

No matter what you do, though, there won't be success without good chemistry among the team members. If someone does not fit in, the other team members will know it, but you may not. You can hope the others will either set the errant member straight or somehow let you know he or she isn't working out and should be replaced. Keep an ear wide open for warning signals.

## BUILDING QUALITY IN

Quality is not something you add to a program once it's been written. It starts with good design and continues with good coding that follows the design. The programmer must consciously build programs in a way that considers software quality with every line of code and comment that is produced. Every shortcoming found in testing, production, or maintenance was put there by a programmer whose attention to quality wavered.

If you only heard the music of Bach when it was played by eight-year-olds at their first piano recitals, you probably wouldn't understand how people could speak of its complexity and grace. If you then heard it played by a professional orchestra, you might then say to yourself, "So *that's* what they've been talking about." The same holds true for programming. It's not enough to talk about good programming, you need to see that your programmers have the opportunity to actually see and read and study good programs.

If you treat quality as an abstraction, it will wind up meaning something different to each programmer (and designer) on your team. Make it concrete. Provide examples. Show your programmers what's good and what's not. If you're not an excellent programmer, borrow code from someone who is. Talk about the features of the code that add quality to the product.

## KEEPING DEFECTS OUT

Once a nontrivial program has been written, it is virtually impossible to prove that it has no defects. Testing isn't sufficient (although I recommend that you *do* continue to test). Even an excellent software producer like Microsoft gets hundreds of calls about its products because some user tried to do something that wasn't tested. When you hear about software malfunctions in a space satellite, doesn't it make you wonder why the problem wasn't caught during testing?

Your best approach to ensuring that the programs that make up your system are as error-free as possible is to do things that keep errors from getting into the code in the first place. This leads us to inspections and walkthroughs.

### Inspections

One of the most important things that the team does is to act together in order to improve the quality of the final product. The tool that they use is the inspection, which is an organized review of a project member's work by other project members.

The practices of formal design and code inspections were developed by Michael Fagan of IBM almost twenty years ago. Many studies have been done to determine the effectiveness of inspections and the studies show that a combination of design and code inspections usually removes between 60 percent and 90 percent of the defects in a system. Since inspections typically take up less than 20 percent of the project cost, they are one of the last great bargains in software development.

Inspections get their effectiveness through several mechanisms:

➤ Checklists are used to focus the reviewer's attention on defects that have been observed in previous programs or designs.

➤ Inspections emphasize the detection of defects; they aren't a forum for fixing them.

➤ Reviewers prepare for inspections before they are held and arrive with lists of defects that they have already identified.

➤ Every person in an inspection has an assigned role: moderator, author, reviewer, scribe. The moderator is never the author. Management is not invited.

➤ Moderators are trained in moderating inspections before they actually do it.

➤ Data is collected in each inspection and is used to improve future inspections.

The people who are selected as reviewers in an inspection should have a direct interest in improving the quality of the design or program being inspected. Programmers might be selected to review designs. Testers or designers might be selected to review code. The job of the reviewer is the same in all cases. Reviewers must identify specific items in the design or code that are missing, confusing, or incorrect. When reviewers work together, the inspection process is strengthened. Details that concern one reviewer lead to closer focus on the problem area and may uncover related defects.

There are important benefits that result from formal inspections of all the project's design and programming products:

1.  Where the product is actual design or code, there is a demonstrable and significant saving when errors are found early. The later in a project's life an error is found, the greater the cost of fixing the error. In some cases, the cost curve can be exponential! Expensive, time-consuming regression testing might have to be done to ensure that making a change to fix an error embedded deep in the system does not adversely affect other code already tested and presumed clean.

2.  There can be great benefit in promoting what is called "egoless programming" (or egoless anything, for that matter). In an excellent book all programming managers should read, *The Psychology of Computer Programming* (1971), Gerald Weinberg makes a strong case for taking steps to make the programmer less defensive about errors in his or her work. He promotes the idea of programmers reading each other's code to find problems and cites evidence that code reading prevents many bugs from ever seeing the computer. The advantages go beyond that, however. Extensive and regular reading of code provides a beautiful opportunity for helping to train newer people, and the process fosters a feeling of openness on the project.

3.  Inspections, once they become an accepted way of project life, lead to better software in the first place, because developers will not knowingly submit sloppy work for such scrutiny. It's common for a programmer under time pressure to throw together a "quick-and-dirty" program or document, intending to "clean it up" later. But all too often, later never comes. Inspections can go a long way toward eliminating such costly habits.

4.  There is a powerful educational benefit as a result of inspections: it becomes impossible for individuals to work for long periods in isolation from other project members, with their work hidden from scrutiny. Everybody knows what everybody else is doing (which may be a mixed blessing!).

5.  When you summarize and publish the results of inspections, your programmers are kept focused on preventing defects when they create the code. The inspection checklists should change as the programming process proceeds because errors that happen frequently will become well known to programmers, who, in turn, will check for these errors as they create the code. If the first group of programs inspected had problems with uninitialized pointers, the second group will probably have far fewer instances of this particular defect.

## Walkthroughs

Walkthroughs have the same goals as inspections, but in practice they are less structured and significantly less effective at identifying defects. Many organizations
have decided that they aren't worth the effort it takes to perform them. I strongly
suggest that you ignore walkthroughs and direct your group's efforts into making
their inspections more effective.

## CHANGE MANAGEMENT

Changes occur every day, but you should not attempt to bring all of them under formal control. Too much control will strangle you and too little will lead you straight
to hell! Think about the critical items over which you *really* need control, and leave
the rest for day-to-day management action.

### Baseline Documents

First, decide what to use as foundations, or baselines. I suggest two baseline documents: the Problem Specification and the Design Specification. If you set up procedures to control changes to them, you're off to a good start.

There is a third kind of baseline to consider. The two mentioned above are established early in the development cycle and they govern production of the system.
If you are responsible for maintenance or for versions of the system beyond the initial delivery, then the *delivered software system* becomes a new baseline. In other
words, in working on a second or third or nth version of the software system, you
may use the last delivery (and its design and specification documents) as the baseline. Here we'll concentrate on a single-delivery development cycle.

### Management Procedures

If we agree to manage change using the Problem Specification and the Design
Specification, we can now consider a simple control mechanism. Whenever anyone
sees a need for a change that may affect a baseline, he proposes a formal change.
The Analysis and Design Group analyzes the proposed change and recommends
adoption or rejection to the Change Management Board. The board makes its decision, subject to override by either you or the customer. The Analysis and Design
Group documents the decision, and the change, if adopted, is implemented. Now
let's take a closer look at how this procedure might work.

**Proposing a Change.**    Anyone in your organization or the customer's may
propose a change. To do so, he fills out a simple Change Proposal form describing
the need for the change, and, if possible, the way to make the change. As a rule, a

programmer proposes a change *only if he thinks a baseline might be affected*. Programmers do not submit a Change Proposal every time they alter a detailed design for a module.

**Investigation.**    A member of the Analysis and Design Group handles each change proposed. He scans the proposal to get an idea of its importance and impact, and schedules it for a decision at a future meeting (usually the next scheduled meeting) of the Change Management Board. If the change is urgent, the investigator calls a special meeting of the board as soon as there is enough information to make a recommendation.

The investigator looks into all pertinent aspects of the change, writes a recommendation, and gives a copy to each member of the board within a reasonable time (say, two working days) before the board is to meet. An investigator's report includes:

➤ The originator's name and organization
➤ Classification of the change, Type 1 or 2 (see below)
➤ The impact of the change on costs, schedules, or other programs
➤ A summary of the proposed change
➤ A recommendation for or against adoption

**Kinds of Changes.**    The investigator may put the change into either of two categories: Type 1 if the change affects either of the baseline documents *or* would cause a cost, schedule, or other impact; Type 2 if the change affects no baseline and has negligible cost, schedule, or other impact. Be sure that changes don't too easily become categorized as Type 2, when they really *do* cost something and ought to be Type 1. Type 2 changes can nibble you to death.

You can make things a lot more complicated, but don't. There is no sense inventing a dozen different change categories to cover combinations of situations. Either the change will cause some problems (Type 1) or it's no sweat (Type 2). Even the ponderous machinery of the federal government's Configuration Management gets by with only two categories of change. Surely you don't want to be shamed by the world's biggest bureaucracy!

**Change Management Board.**    The board includes representatives from various project groups. At periodic meetings (say, once a week) the board considers all scheduled change proposals. When there are no proposals pending, the board does not meet. The board discusses each change and decides how to dispose of it. You'll have to decide whether your board will operate democratically by voting on each issue or will allow the chairperson to make the decision after hearing the arguments. Democracy is great, but you may find things move faster if you give the chairperson the power to decide what the board's recommendation should be. You can always overrule if one of the board members convinces you that a decision was a bad one. (Don't overrule too often or you'll destroy the chairperson.)

The Change Management Board should consist of the following:

➤ Chairperson: usually the manager of the Analysis and Design Group
➤ Permanent members: the manager of the Programming Group, the manager of the Test Group, and the manager of the Staff Group
➤ Others: the investigator for the proposal being considered; technical personnel invited by any of the permanent members

At any board meeting, then, there will be at least five participants—four regular members and one investigator. It's important not to let these meetings get too big by inviting many extra people, but obviously you need to invite anyone who can really shed light on the problem. Often this will mean that the person who proposed the change will be there.

Should you invite the customer to board meetings? Generally, yes, although there may be times when you choose not to have him around. For example, exclude the customer whenever company proprietary data are to be exposed or discussed. The best way to handle this question is simple honesty: Mr. Customer, we're discussing dark secrets this week, so please get lost!

**Types of Recommendations.**    If the board agrees with the investigator that a change is Type 2, the change is automatically accepted and no further board action is necessary. If it is a Type 1, it must recommend how to dispose of the change. There are two possibilities:

➤ Acceptance of the change and a recommendation about when the change should be made (immediately or in some future version of the program)
➤ Rejection of the change

**Customer-Directed Changes.**    The customer will insist on some changes. They must still be investigated, considered by the board, estimated, and formally approved by the customer. The customer has the right to override any decision by the board, provided you negotiate appropriate contract changes to cover costs and schedule changes.

**Implementing a Change.**    Depending on the board's recommendation for a Type 1 change, two concluding actions are possible. If the board recommends rejection, log the proposal as closed. If the board recommends adoption, the investigator writes up a summary of the change, its cost, and the schedule for making the change. If there is a cost or schedule impact, you send the package to the customer for approval. When the customer approves it in writing, the investigator finally

---

### Accepting Change

You've got to keep an open mind about change—it's not a four-letter word. Try as you may to do things perfectly the first time, you won't succeed, so some change is both inevitable and desirable!

In *Lila* (1991), Robert Pirsig has this to say: "Just as the biological immune system will destroy a life-saving skin graft with the same vigor with which it fights pneumonia, so will a cultural immune system fight off a beneficial new kind of understanding . . . with the same vigor it uses to destroy crime. It can't distinguish between them."

Be ready to recognize and accept beneficial change.

---

gives to all concerned a written description of the change, and now the change can be made.

The Analysis and Design Group keeps track of the schedule for all approved changes. On many projects changes come thick and fast. Some are designated for immediate action, some are deferred to specific later versions of the software system. It's important that everyone—you and the customer—know exactly when accepted changes will be made.

The foregoing is the *formal* procedure. There will be times when you cannot delay a change for days or weeks. Here you speed up the process by investigating immediately, calling a quick special board meeting, writing out the recommendation in longhand, approving it verbally, getting the customer's agreement verbally, and telling the designers or programmers to go ahead (see Figure 6–6). Make sure the formal paperwork follows—customer's approval, change notice, and so on—otherwise, you'll lose track of things.

## A Few VERY IMPORTANT Words about Change Management

Consider where the project is at this point. You are fully engaged in both the Design Process and the Programming Process. The Definition Process has been largely completed, but the Problem Specification is still subject to change.

As a manager, most of your time is being spent dealing with changes. As I've already pointed out (and I'm sure you remember), you can discover things in the Design Process that affect the Definition Process and you can discover things in the Programming Process that can affect the Design Process. The only way that you are going to be able to deal with all the changes that occur is to establish effective points of control. If you're not sure how to do this, I recommend that you start by taking direct responsibility for the Problem Specification and the Design Specification baseline documents. Whenever something happens that causes a change in these documents, you can be sure that it will also affect costs, time lines, and work

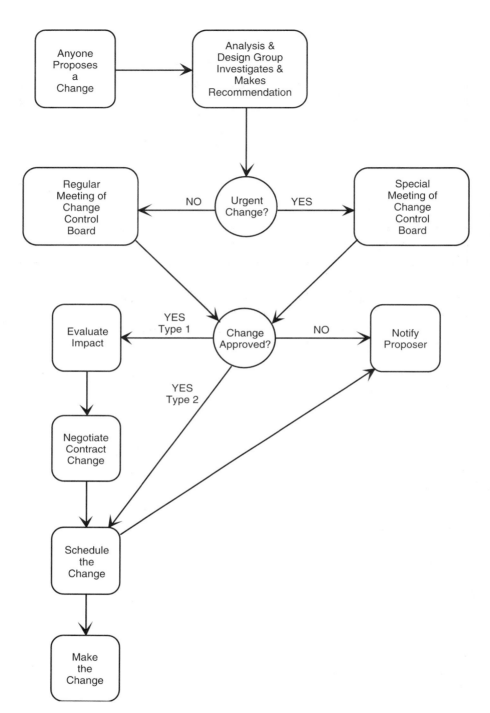

**FIGURE 6–6** Change Management

assignments. By using these common points of reference as your points of control, you will be able to understand the impacts of proposed changes and explain them more effectively to the customer.

These two baseline documents have the additional advantage of direct correlation with your milestone events. Each milestone that is tied to the programming and testing processes should reflect completion of significant activity for a part of the design. You'll be able to look at the cost and time involved in reaching a milestone and make adjustments to your schedule and budget estimates based on actual team performance.

Although there's a lot more to managing a project than providing progress reports to your customer, it's your customer who is eventually going to decide whether or not the project was successful. When you provide accurate reports of project progress and can tie them back not only to the original requirements and design but also to the changes that have been made, you are ensuring that the customer will not be surprised by the system you deliver.

## PROGRAMMING TOOLS

Select tools for doing the programming job long before the Programming Process begins. Some analysis and design tools, such as the data dictionaries, should carry over to the Programming Process to serve as a foundation for detailed design. For coding, the choice of language(s) is as important as any decision on the project, and you must make it early. Your choice may be dictated by the nature of the problem (scientific, business, and so on) or by customer mandate (you'll use C++ or else!). Language choice may also be most influenced by the experience and biases your programmers and designers have developed through other job experience.

An important consideration is the quality of support offered by the candidate languages—how sophisticated are their compilers, how extensive are their built-in debugging features, and do they support the hardware you'll be using. In many cases, this level of support can differ depending on who supplies your compilers and utilities. Careful. I know of a job in which the contract specified the use of COBOL, but the project manager learned when the actual programming started that the version of COBOL he was told to use couldn't access the corporate standard relational data base system. For over two months the customer insisted on adherence to the contract, saying that the required libraries were due to be delivered "any day now." He agreed to use another compiler only after the project manager threatened to pull everyone off the job until the updated version of the mandated compiler was delivered. You can say that the contractor should have caught the error before the contract was signed and that the customer shouldn't have been so pig-headed, but the point is, it happened.

When you choose a language, don't forget that your system will spend most of its life being maintained. Think about the customer's potential problem of finding people who are familiar with the language so that changes can be made to the system in the future. This isn't much of a concern if you're planning to use COBOL or C, but if you're planning to use Eiffel or FORTH make sure that the customer understands the implications.

## Written Specifications

Figure 1–2 in Chapter 1 lists some key documents. Four of them are so important they deserve repeated emphasis here.

*Problem Specification.* The analysts write this during the Definition Process to describe the problem that your project is all about. It's a baseline document.

*Design Specification.* The designers write this during the Design Process to describe the overall software system architecture, the solution to the problem. It's also a baseline and it sets the stage for all detailed design.

*Coding Specification.* The programmers write these specifications during the Programming Process. Each specification describes in detail the design and code for a small part of the system that is laid out in the Design Specification.

*Integration Test Specification.* Written during the Design Process, this specification defines the objectives for integration testing, and spells out specific test procedures and test data for reaching those objectives.

## Test Executives

Most software systems include some form of top-level control program, or executive. In *bottom-up* testing, a test executive is a modified version of the eventual full executive program. It begins as a simplified form of the ultimate program. It's written early to provide a framework for integration testing. Some test executives contain "dummy" modules or "stubs" that are gradually replaced as their "real" counterparts emerge from module test. The stubs may do little more than record and print an indication that they have been invoked. Or they may do some simple operation in imitation of what the real module will do when eventually inserted into the system. As you replace stubs with real modules, the software system begins to take shape. In *top-down* testing, your test executive is essentially the code for the higher-level modules.

Some test executives contain special test aids that you remove during the final stage of integration test. One such test aid may be a trace program to keep track of sequences of events within the system for later analysis. Another is a program to provide displays, or "snapshots," of key software variables or to record contents at strategic times.

An example of a test executive used in the early stages of development of "real-time" systems is a *non*-real-time version of the system's control program. Similarly, a single-processor control program is often written before development of a full multiprocessing capability.

Although a test executive can be complex, you should aim to keep it simple for two reasons. First, part of its value lies in having it ready early, before the "real" executive program is finished. If you put too much into the test executive, it won't be ready much sooner than the real one. Second, the more complex you make the executive, the tougher it will be to separate *its* defects from those of the modules you're trying to test.

## Environment Simulators

An environment simulator is a program that temporarily, for testing purposes, re-places some part of the world with which your software system will eventually communicate. For example, suppose you are writing a software system for directing air traffic. A piece of equipment with which your programs must eventually com-municate is a radar set. But because the radar is still being developed, or because it's not yet feasible to hook up to it, you may need to develop programs that "look" like a radar. These special programs might simulate both the radar's inputs to your operational software system and the radar's responses to your outputs.

Other simulation programs might replace special display consoles not yet available. Still others might feed your system sets of data representing real-world operational conditions—in our example, traffic loads or weather information. To be most effective, an environment simulator must be transparent to the using pro-grams—that is, your programs should require little or no special modification to communicate with the simulators. Your programs should think they are dealing with the real world. Any change you make to allow your software system to run with the simulator lessens your confidence that the system will run properly when you finally substitute the real thing for the simulator. Depending on the size and na-ture of your job, your environment simulation programs may operate in the same computer as your operational programs, or the simulators may run in a separate computer connected to yours.

The cost of developing environment simulators can be huge. In the air traffic control job suggested above, the cost of the simulators could easily be greater than that of the operational programs. You must address the need for these tools in the Definition and Design Processes. Simulators require the same care in design and programming as do the operational programs, and their development may require an organization separate from yours.

Environment simulators and test executives are strategic investments for your project and you should assign one or more senior people to work on them full time. These tools will be used by each of your programmers as they go through the process of testing their modules. When programmers are forced to write their own testing support frameworks, they're likely to cut corners and wind up doing an inad-equate job of testing. Alternatively, they may find themselves spending as much time getting their testing tools working as they spent writing the module they are trying to test.

By investing in a quality test environment, you can ensure that your pro-grammers' productivity will improve over the life of the project. The quality and quantity of your programmers' module testing will also improve because they can plan good tests with the knowledge that the tools they need will be there to support them.

## CASE Tools

As mentioned in Chapter 1, CASE (Computer-Aided Software Engineering) tools can provide substantial assistance in all processes of the project.

CASE tools can check for both high-level (Design Specification) and low-level (Coding Specification) logical errors. Although CASE tools are unlikely to increase productivity during initial design activity, they can make a positive contribution to improving the quality of the design and they can deliver a huge jump in productivity when changes need to be made. Some CASE tools, called "Integrated CASE" products include code generators that will produce logically correct programs directly from the design charts that you have created. The Texas Instruments IEF tool uses the Information Engineering methodology defined by James Martin and can produce code that is both correct and fairly efficient for a wide variety of business applications.

Unless your customer tells you, "I don't really care about the quality, just deliver some sort of system by December first!" you should be using a CASE package to help you design and code your system.

## Power to the People

There was a time (also known as "the dark ages" or "the good old days") when programmers did all their assembly, compilation, and debug work right at the computer console. I remember some long sieges back in medieval times when I was working on the SAGE air-defense programs. My buddy and I sometimes hogged an entire computer site (and there were two computers at each site) for a whole shift. We sat at consoles tracking down bugs by single-instruction-stepping through the program, occasionally stopping to insert new instructions into the machine by flipping banks of external switches. Those were the days when you briskly kicked a card reader to cure an unexpected halt in the system. It was all great fun then, but a colossal waste! Times really have changed. Now there is less "block time" and more sharing of computers through multiprocessing operating systems.

Programmers today may go through an entire project without setting foot in the computer room. In fact, there's very little reason to do so. The programmer of today often has more power on his or her desktop than I had when I sat at the SAGE console. Powerful PCs and workstations can be connected to Local Area Networks that may themselves communicate over high-speed links to large-scale servers or mainframes.

Some of the compilers and debuggers that were once only available on the main computer are now available on the desktop. MicroFocus COBOL© runs on the desktop and has become the accepted programming tool for the vast majority of my clients who use COBOL. PCs also support sophisticated development environments for the C, C++, and Pascal languages. Using a PC-based compiler, the members of your programming team can code, compile, and test without leaving the comfort(?) of their cubicles. When they are done, they can submit their completed modules electronically for integration into the final system.

There are conditions where it will pay off to provide an individual programmer with *two* PCs or workstations instead of just one. If the modules she is developing have direct interaction with a terminal or a client process running on a PC, the programmer can use one PC as the target environment and the other to monitor testing and debugging progress. I have seen groups where the programmers use screen windows to achieve the same result as having multiple workstations. You can do this, but make sure that you get PCs with plenty of power and large displays.

If there is a downside to having all this power on the desktop, it's that it's easy for an individual programmer to be sloppy and to waste this resource just because it's so handy and easy to use. You'll need to see that the good habits of careful analysis and attention to detail are encouraged and reinforced. The regular practice of holding inspections is one way to ensure that your team isn't content to let the computer find the errors. The computer will *never* find all the errors.

## Debuggers and Run-Time Monitors

There are many good debuggers and run-time monitors in the marketplace today and there's no reason why your programmers shouldn't have access to them. The ability to set symbolic breakpoints and initiate traces can cut days from your development schedule by helping your programmers isolate and fix problems in their code. Using a good debugger is a lot cleaner than having your programmers insert their own trace messages in the modules they're coding. It can be much more selective as well.

The project I'm managing now gave me my first opportunity to see a run-time monitor in action and I wish I had one years ago. Using it, we were able to detect that one of our modules was requesting increasing amounts of memory for a queue that should have been relatively static in size. Further analysis showed that a pointer had not been reinitialized properly. This would have been a terrible problem to identify without the monitor.

## The Project Library

A library is an organized collection of information. Your project's library should consist of two sections: the general library and the system library (see Figure 4–5).

**General Library.**   Keep master copies of all project documents in this section, other than those in the System Library. A basic list of documents to include:

➤ Project Plan
➤ Problem Specification
➤ Design Specification
➤ Test Specifications
➤ Technical Notes
➤ Administrative Notes
➤ Change Documents
➤ Test Reports
➤ Status Reports
➤ Project History
➤ Forms
➤ Documentation Index

In addition, keep a copy of the modules and documentation for any previous version of the system you have completed and delivered. The librarian should give every document in the library a unique identification. The librarian should have quick access to reproduction equipment and be able to run a copy of a master document (or print it directly from computer storage) when requested. He may keep copies of often-requested documents rather than run them off only on request. The librarian should keep a log of document numbers so that when any project member is ready to issue a new document in some category—for instance, a Design Change Notice—he need only call the library to get a unique document number. Periodically, the librarian should send out a new Documentation Index, a printed listing of all documents currently in the library. The listing should show document titles, authors, dates of issue, and identifiers.

The librarian should periodically gather vital records and store them in a place physically separate from your facility. Vital records are whatever materials you decide are necessary to reconstruct your system if a fire or other catastrophe were to wipe you out. Vital records might include a tape or disk copy of your software system, along with a copy of the specifications describing the system at that time. It costs little to do this job, and it can save you a lot. One project during the 1960s had made no such provisions. The programs were being developed in a "fireproof" building at an Air Force base in Florida. The system was nearly completed when one night fire gutted the building and destroyed practically everything—punch cards (anybody remember those?), tapes, listings, the works. And, of course, no other copy of the system existed. The story has a happy ending because the programmers had enough bootlegged listings in their homes to piece the system together again. Contract saved, payment made.

**System Library.**   The system library is the project's central storage place for the *official versions of the developing software system.* It usually consists of three sections: the version of the system being developed, the version undergoing integration and test, and the system that is currently in production.

The system library contains, on disk, tape, or other computer storage, the programs you are developing and data relating to their development. Exactly what you store depends on the nature of the project and the computer system being used, but typically the system library includes the most current source code and object code for all modules in the developing system, test data, and so on.

The production library is often kept in a part of the system library that is carefully locked away from the programmers. It consists of the current source, executable, and environmental files and run notebooks showing the output results of test runs. The production library also contains archival documents—older versions of listings kept for historical and backup purposes.

Your system library is likely to contain more than one software system at a time because:

➤ There may be versions of a system at different levels of completion at any time, especially on larger projects (see Part IX).

➤ The library may serve a larger community than just your project. There is no reason a number of projects may not make use of the same library facility. In this case, you may need more than one technical librarian.

Every set of data, whether program code, file data, or test data, is uniquely identified within the library. Unique identifiers distinguish different versions of a program from one another and different projects from one another.

It's important that the technical librarian be well trained and capable, for the job is an important one. It's important, too, that he be thick-skinned and not easily bribed. Do not allow programmers to skirt library procedures; if that happens, the library immediately loses its value as a project control point. Programmers are infamous for putting in those little last-minute changes. There are no little changes. Each change is potential dynamite, especially if you're nearing system or acceptance test. Guard against midnight patches by making internal library storage virtually inaccessible. Your programmers may be irked, but that's better than having an acceptance test blow up in your face while the customer looks on.

The librarian's job is so important that I have taken responsibility for it on smaller projects. It plays a pivotal role in change management and it allows a clear assessment of the state of the project. On larger projects where you have a full-time librarian, make sure that he is included in your inner circle. The librarian can do a better job when he is aware of what is changing and why.

When you rise to an executive position and are faced with handling promotions, you'll find it a good idea to insist that anyone being considered for promotion to a project management position must have served as a librarian on a previous project.

---

*The Manager's Bookshelf*

Steven C. McConnell's *Code Complete: A Practical Handbook of Software Construction* (1993) is an excellent book that concentrates on showing programmers how to write better programs. It's written for "C" programmers, but its lessons can be understood by any programmer who uses a procedural language. Get a copy of this book for yourself and also get a copy for each of your programmers.

---

**FIGURE 7–1**  The Missed Deadline  (Goya, "The Third of May," Museum del Prado, Madrid.)

# 7

# The Programmer

In 1955 I got my first real job. I was through with college, through with the Air Force, and not really prepared for anything. IBM had built a new plant in Kingston, in upstate New York, near where I was raised. I applied and was hired as a programmer. I had no idea what a programmer was or what computers were all about, but I was about to find out.

After a few weeks' training I went to work on the SAGE project. SAGE was an air-defense system whose computers were to be dotted around the country. Each SAGE site boasted two computers, one for active air defense, the other a standby, ready to go active if the other crapped out. I was assigned to work on the control program for the standby computers. The two computers occupied a huge concrete building spread over an acre. There were large consoles, rows of tape drives, thousands of vacuum tubes, miles of cabling and air-conditioning ducts, and an array of blinking lights and manual switches.

I feel sorry for those programmers today who never get their hands on the heart of the hardware. When my friends and I got computer time, it was in Ann Arbor or Kansas City and we got the whole building, often both computers, for an entire shift. The only walls between us and the computer were an assembly program and a card reader. No batch submissions, no operating system, no job control files, no operator. The computer was ours.

More recently, the people who wrote some of the first applications for PCs have done programming in much the same way as I did almost forty years ago. It's a game of one-on-one; the programmer versus the box. When I talk to these PC pioneers, I find that they experienced the same feelings of power and excitement that I felt. But even with PCs, the work of software development has changed. A programmer today can work on a complex application and not know much about the hardware architecture that will execute her code.

Those "good old days" *were* good in some ways. The programmer was not a slave to operating systems and language constraints and programming standards—those things were still in the future. We worked hard, if not smart, and nobody screamed too much when things were late or when we exceeded budgets. In fact, from our lowly vantage point, it seemed there were few budget constraints.

A few decades later it's clear that the romance of the old days is not only gone for good, but ought to be.

Programmers of the first generation of computers often had sloppy habits. There was little discipline, few tools with which to work, very little guidance. My manager, as new to the business as I, was happy if I got results; forget program structure, forget sophisticated techniques—does the thing *work*? But before long, thoughtful people in the field began to look at what programming really was. The search began for better ways of doing things and for a handle on just what programmers and programming really are. The search continues.

## THE PROFESSIONAL(?) PROGRAMMER

One constant over the past three decades is that the demand for programmers has continued to be strong. The field pays well, it promises exciting and fulfilling careers, and lots of people can become programmers. I've worked with programmers who came from such disparate beginnings as mathematics, history, psychological testing, grocery clerking, engineering of all stripes, the U.S. Navy, and chicken farming. What's more, getting into the programming business is easy. Almost anyone can take a few courses at the community college, pass a short test when they apply for the job, and become professional programmer.

So what level of performance can we expect from this less than auspicious start? We can expect to find a lot of people who represent themselves as programmers who aren't very good at programming. One author and teacher whose work puts him in touch with thousands of programmers wonders whether we don't have a lot of clerks holding down programming positions, people for whom programming is just another job and not a profession.

Despite the modest abilities of many programmers, managers over and over have continued to treat programming as something done by skilled artists and have caved in to programmers' reluctance or refusal to learn a new language or to do the "dirty work" of programming—documenting, for instance, or keeping detailed testing logs. Managers (sometimes including this one) have been guilty of allowing and even promoting an aura of specialness that exempted programmers from doing chores that a truly professional programmer regards as an integral part of the job.

> "Programming a computer does require intelligence. Indeed, it requires so much intelligence that nobody does it very well. Sure, some programmers are better than others, but we all bump and crash around like overgrown infants. Why? Because programming computers is *by far* the hardest intellectual task that human beings have ever tried to do. Ever."
>
> Gerald M. Weinberg, *Understanding the Professional Programmer* (1982)

Programmers have come to believe that their work is special and that they are, too. The truth is that a few programmers *are* special, but most aren't. Some of the early studies of programming ability showed some programmers are *twenty times better* than others when they are measured in the time required to write a program and the quality of the code. Similar results have been seen in exercises such as the "Programmer's War Games" put on by the Atlantic Systems Guild. It's interesting that the contestants in the "War Games" are their employers' best programmers and not a random sample.

As a manager, you may get lucky and find a truly excellent programmer for your team. If this happens, you need to be flexible and organize the development team's activities to support that programmer's work so that the project will have the full benefits of her skill. The bad news is that you probably won't be able to find one of these rare people. Don't be disappointed. And don't try to take a programmer who is simply the "best of the bunch" and treat him as if he were really brilliant.

The good news is that most successful programming projects have been completed by teams of programmers who fall in the "better than average" category. If the team is well managed, team members can use their individual strengths in a complementary manner, making the team stronger than any individual member. As a manager, you will have a good chance of completing your project successfully if you can find some of these "better than average" programmers and provide an atmosphere where they can be highly productive.

## FINDING GOOD PROGRAMMERS

When you start to assemble your programming team, you can be sure that you will be offered a mixed bag of talent to choose from. Start by eliminating the prospective programmers who can't help you. Here are two steps that I recommend.

First, start by talking to each prospective programmer about the project. Try to generate some enthusiasm or convey a sense of challenge. Watch carefully for recip-

> "Unfortunately no one hires programmers because they want to see in-
> teresting technical problems solved or so that they can marvel at ele-
> gant code. No, businesses bring people in to solve what they see as
> business problems."
>
> Janet Ruhl, *The Programmer's Survival Guide* (1969)

rocated interest. Listen to the questions that the programmer asks. Is he really trying
to find out more about the job or simply being polite? No matter how good their
technical qualifications are, you shouldn't bring programmers on to your team who
aren't interested in your project. They don't do anything to help the people they work
with and they're prone to leave for other projects at inopportune moments.

Second, have the programmer write a program. I am absolutely amazed at the
number of programmers who get hired without first demonstrating that they have a
command of the basic skills needed to do the job. What is the difficulty with giving
the prospective programmer a problem and seeing what kind of code he writes and
how he goes about writing it?

There are several simple programming problems that can be presented as exercises—for instance the "eight queens" problem where the program must calculate
the positions for eight queens to be placed on a regulation chessboard so that no
queen can be captured by another.

Watch how the programmer attacks the problem. Does he design a solution or
just jump into writing code? Does the programmer document as he goes? Is the final
code understandable? Does it work? How long did it take him to write the code?
Are there any errors and, if so, what kind of errors?

Your DP department may have other standard tests that you'll have to administer, but I advise you to pay more attention to the way the prospective programmer
performs in doing the work he'll be expected to do on your project.

## COMPENSATING THE ACHIEVERS

Wouldn't you like to hire one professional and get rid of ten slugs? I discussed earlier the imbalance in compensation for achievers versus drones. I bring it up again
here because the problem seems so much more prevalent among programmers than
within other disciplines. People in sports who excel command those absurd salaries
we all know about. Why not in programming? I believe a company can make enormous differences in productivity and quality of output by breaking the usual hiring
and compensation habits and, like the U.S. Marines, looking for a few good people
(and paying them *very* well).

## PROGRAMMING VERSUS CODING

The programmer is a translator. He or she translates a blueprint into a product, a Design Specification into a system.

To varying degrees, almost every programmer does at least some designing, coding, testing, and documenting. The proportion of effort spent in each facet of the job depends greatly on where he works. Some companies look on programmers as coders and attempt to limit the amount of design programmers do—design is for designers. Some companies also limit the testing an individual programmer does, preferring to leave that to a test team. Such severe circumscribing of the programmer's job is self-defeating. Individuals not encouraged to see beyond their little cubicles are not going to add much pizzazz to their company. They'll tend to be clerks putting in their time and not caring much about the company's goals or about a product of excellence. Conduct your project so that programmers are never considered simply coders. Here are some practical ways to make this happen.

### Stop Design Soon Enough

I talked about this earlier. If you carry the system design so far that the programs are practically written when design is finished, you will have robbed the programmers of the chance to be more than coders. That, in turn, means that you limit the chances for a programmer to learn how to design well and move out of programming into other positions, such as analysis. Don't smother creative people. If your programmers resent your boxing them in, they'll go somewhere they can breathe. If they *don't* resent being boxed in, they may not be worth keeping around.

Programmers must assume both design and coding responsibilities if they are going to improve their skills as programmers. Good code is the reflection of good design. You need to encourage your programmers to work carefully at the detailed design level before they start creating code. If you can get them to do this, they will have a much better chance of creating code that does what it is supposed to without any errors. They will feel better about their jobs, and more confident in their own abilities. As a manager, don't you want your programmers to feel this way?

### Move People Around

Programmers go on to design; analysts later become system testers; designers take on the role of lead programmers or programming managers. Assigning people different jobs on the project during different phases provides needed continuity and it gives people a chance to grow (which is to say, it keeps people from being pigeonholed in jobs too narrowly defined). As you shift a person from one role to another, however, make sure you do so with clear definition of each job. When the Design

Specification is finished and Calvin Designer is about to become Calvin Programmer, take away his designer badge and give him a programming button.

Not everyone *can* be moved around successfully. Some programmers would make rotten analysts, for example, and vice versa. Don't plug people into places they obviously don't fit.

## DOCUMENTATION

I was either lucky or blind—few programmers who worked for me whined and sniveled about doing documentation. Most of them actually did a decent job of documenting. (My own first manager was not so lucky. My first programs were classic examples of rats' nests and the documentation proved it.)

But there *are* a lot of shirkers out there, and plenty of systems get delivered for which the program descriptions miss by a mile matching the program code. Where that becomes a problem, of course, is in program maintenance. The first time a maintenance programmer tries to track down a bug that crawls to the surface after system delivery, he or she stands a good chance of finding programs and documentation that don't match. Even if programs and their text descriptions *do* match, the maintenance programmer is likely to develop a heart murmur simply trying to make sense of the program's detailed logic.

For both problems—inaccurate documentation of well-constructed programs and accurate documentation of poorly constructed programs—managers have some solutions. The most obvious, but least effective, is to write standards and directives for what you expect in the documentation, and make compliance a requirement for continuing employment. More humane, however, and more sensible in every way, is to start with programming practices that make it difficult to write really rotten code.

One time-proven practice that can be used with almost any procedural language (FORTRAN, C, COBOL, and the like) is *structured programming*. Structured programming eases the documentation problem in two ways:

1. The programmer sticks to a small number of powerful coding conventions that nearly eliminate branching from the current page of code to another. In a well-structured program, the reader can follow the code from top to bottom of a page, and from one page to the next, in much the same way as you read this book.
2. The programmer formats code according to simple rules of indentation intended to lead the reader easily down the page as he follows the logic; both the original programmer and the maintenance programmer can more easily follow the code.

Structured programming by itself will not solve the maintenance documentation problem. Whatever documentation methods are adopted, it's still up to management to *insist* that people follow the guidelines. There's no mechanical substitute for good old *management control*.

## CHICKENEGGCHICKENEGGCHICKEN . . .

The Design Specification is coming to life and it's time to turn loose the programmers. How do you organize them? Do you choose the programming organization at the beginning of the project? That's the way it's often done. The result is that you divvy up the finished design so that it fits your organization. Charlie's group gets these pieces, Jill's gets these. . . . In fact, the projected programming organization might affect the design process itself. Let's see, we'll have three programming groups, so we'll start by splitting the design into three major subsystems—the control program, the collection subsystem, the output subsystem. The resultant division of labor might fit the organization chart very nicely, but it might not be the best way to organize the programs. A better approach would be to wait until the design comes together, and then organize your programming talent to fit that design.

## INTRODUCING NEW IDEAS

Jill Whiz has been managing programmers for six months. Unsure about managing at first, she now feels comfortable and enthusiastic about her new job. She calls a meeting of her six programmers.

"Things are going so well I wanted to let you all know how I appreciate your work. We finished integration test with a few days to spare, and so far, system test has been a breeze."

"Yeah," volunteers Cagney, "and I guarantee those guys in system test won't find much to report. We really wrung the system out before they got it!"

"That's what I think, too," Jill smiles. "That's why I've scheduled the whole crew for a three-day seminar starting Monday."

"Great!" cries Lacey. "Where? Is it out of town? Do we get expenses? What's the subject?"

They all laugh at Lacey's priorities. Lacey loves to eat on the company expense account.

"No," Jill answers, "it's right here in Washington, and the subject is object-oriented programming. Ed Burden is conducting it and the timing is perfect for us."

"Why OO programming?" asks Lacey, with a frown.

"Well, Super Software is beginning a push to get everybody trained in the newest techniques—analysts, programmers, the whole bit. Management thinks object-oriented programming is the place to start."

"Why?" asks Lacey.

"Why what?"

"Why OO programming? What's wrong with what we're doing now?"

Harvey pipes up: "I think our programs are well structured and modular as is. Look how we breezed through integration."

"They are well structured," Jill smiles. "That's why we're good candidates for this class. We already think in terms of good program structuring and modular construction, so whatever Burden has to offer that's new, we'll be able to appreciate it and evaluate it better than . . . well, than certain other groups in this company. Everybody in this room is a professional and as professionals we should always be looking for better ways to do our jobs."

"Suppose we listen and decide it's the pits?" asks Lacey.

"Fair enough," replies Jill. "It may be that OO has nothing to offer us, but we're the ones elected to find out. If we like what we hear, we get to spread the word to the other groups. If we don't like it, we squash it."

"Why us?" asks Cagney.

"Because we're the best damn group in the company, and management figures we're the ones to take a look. Peter and Paula and the other project managers agreed we should be the ones to go."

"Sounds good," says Cagney quietly.

A week later Jill sees Winslow Wimp in the cafeteria and settles at his table. Nobody else is there because people generally avoid Winslow at lunchtime. He's something of a hypochondriac and loves to discuss his current maladies. He's happy to see someone join him.

"Hi, Jill! How ya doin'?"

"Good, Winslow, how about you?"

"Not bad, except for a little bout with labyrinthitis over the weekend. . . ."

"Mmmmm! Too bad! Listen . . ." she continues quickly. Damned if she's going to hear a half-hour medical history of his labyrinthitis. "Is your group going to volunteer for the next object-oriented programming seminar?"

"Uh-uh! Nope! Waste of time."

"My group really got a lot out of it. They were skeptics going in, but converts coming out."

"What's the big deal? Everybody structures programs. Everybody knows how to do modular development."

"But there's more to it than that. . . ."

"Like what? Damn! Ear's still buggin' me some!"

"Look, I'd be glad to talk to your group and give them a sort of introduction. Kind of pave the way for a real class."

"No, thanks. Listen, you know what the labyrinth is?"

People resist change in any number of ways and for lots of reasons, especially lethargy and fear. The ways of selling a new idea are as varied as the number of sellers.

➤ Mild threat ("Your progress in the company depends on your ability to learn and to grow, blah, blah. . . .")

➤ Serious threat ("The people who don't get with this program had better be polishing their resumes!")

➤ Appeal to self esteem ("You don't want Jill's people to make us look like monkeys, do you?")

➤ Opportunity ("We finally have a break and we can take a few days to look into this new technique.")

➤ More opportunity ("Here's our chance to blaze a new trail for the company!")

➤ Bribery ("Do this and I'll remember it when salary reviews come up.")

And so on. Although you might think that it would be unnecessary to have to sell anyone on improving his or her credentials, people do resist. As a manager, you're in a position to apply the more humane of the techniques listed above and work your will with your subordinates. But how about convincing *management*? Often the technical people are eager to try new methodologies, but management is slow to go along because:

1. If the group spends time going to this class, the project will fall behind. (There should always be time planned for training.)

2. It'll cost too much—there's nothing in the budget. (There should be money budgeted for training.)

3. How do we know it'll do any good? (You don't. Some classes will be a waste of time, some ideas deserve to be discarded, but most deserve a hearing.)

4. That's way over the heads of my programmers; better not rock the boat. (The organization needs new programmers or, more likely, new managers.)

Some companies are bold enough to conduct experiments with new ideas: separate groups work the same problem using two different methodologies, holding constant everything except the methodology, as far as that is possible. Jill's group can be pitted against Winslow's, both programming the same problem. Such experiments are difficult to conduct because there are so many variables, but the payoff can be great. It takes enlightened management to pay the bill. Complex government systems development projects sometimes take this approach, where the cost of making the wrong choice might be measured in lives as well as dollars. In the corporate world, I've seen an increase in the number of "proof of concept" projects that are performed to investigate whether an approach that sounds good on paper is actually workable.

## THE CORPORATE COCOON

There is a burnout problem among programmers just as there is in any group. You can't expect a programmer to sit for weeks, months, *years*, doing the same type of

programming, and not slack off. If all he does is write payroll programs in
COBOL, you're going to have on your hands one stale programmer. He will pretty
soon be doing nothing more than dusting off the last program and applying it to the
not-so-new next job—no fresh thinking, no innovation. Who cares? Columnist
Hugh Sidey speaks of a "cocoon" in corporate life, where "a group of talented people gather their ideas from the same information base and debate them with one
another day after day." Result:   stagnation and ignorance of what the rest of the
world is doing.

Preventing stagnation is the manager's job. A manager should constantly be
training, supporting, coaxing, helping a subordinate to be successful. Don't let your
programmers settle for long in cozy nooks, even if they seem to like it. *Get them totally away from their current jobs.* Push them to learn new languages, new methodologies, not only in programming, but in design, analysis, testing, writing. Don't
wait until there is a specific job that will require them to retrain. Maybe nobody in
your company uses C++; maybe they should. Maybe you think ACM conferences
and Datamation and language seminars are for eggheads. Do you realize that most
modern programming practices are first broached in such forums? Get your people
to attend and to read and to question. Encourage them to share what they find out
with other members of the group. They can only grow from the experience, and you
and your project and your company can only benefit.

## MANAGING PERRY PROGRAMMER

Jill Whiz works for Walt Secondlevel. They are in Walt's office greeting a new hire
who has just joined Jill's group.

"Walt," smiles Jill, "I'd like you to meet Perry."

Walt smiles and shakes hands with Perry and motions Perry and Jill to have a
seat. He buzzes his secretary for coffee.

"So, today's your first day at Super Software!"

"Yes, Sir," says Perry quietly, a little nervous.

"Sir!" Walt slaps this thigh and guffaws. "You hear that Jill? 'Bout time
somebody around here called me 'Sir'!" He enjoys himself while Jill squirms a little
and Perry smiles bleakly.

"Let's see, now," continues Walt on a more serious level, "you went to school
at . . . Northeastern?"

"Northwestern."

"Right! Well, listen, I want to welcome you to our little company. I hope you
enjoy working here. We're pretty new, but growing fast and that means there's a lot
of opportunity for anyone who works hard."

"I like what I've seen so far, Mr. . . . Walt . . . I chose this company *because*
it's young and growing. I'm anxious to get my first assignment."

"Jill will be taking care of that this morning, right, Jill?" Jill nods, and Walt continues, "You'll probably find the real world a bit different from what you got at school. . . ."

Walt leans back, hands clasped behind his head, and puts his feet on his desk. He spends the next twenty minutes recalling his first job in programming.

A little later, Jill and Perry are finally alone in her office. They sit comfortably facing each other with neither desk nor Walt's feet between them.

"Perry, I know you're anxious to get at your first program, but there are some more important items first." She smiles, sits back, and sips her coffee thoughtfully for a moment, then continues. "When I first got into programming, I thought I knew what programming was because, like you, I had taken some courses in college. I found out real fast that I didn't know much of anything about writing a program in an actual business environment. It's a lot more complicated than doing a problem in school . . . but it's a lot more exciting, too!"

For the next hour, Jill scribbles on her chalkboard and describes to Perry Super Software's business, its organization, how its projects work. She talks about a project development cycle and how Perry's work fits into the cycle.

"It's about time for lunch, so let's go and meet the rest of our crew in the cafeteria. After lunch we'll all come back here and just chat a while. Then, the rest of the afternoon I'd like to go over some things with you . . . some more introduction to our project. Tomorrow morning, the group will meet here for our biweekly project review. The timing works out well . . . it'll be a good chance for you to hear just what we're doing."

"Sounds super!" says Perry. "After that will you be giving me an assignment?"

"Sure will!" says Jill.

At the end of the day Walt Secondlevel saunters into Jill's office as she is clearing her desk to go home. Floyd Hotshot, another first-level manager, is with her.

"Hi, Jill, Floyd! How'd it go with Perry, Jill?" he asks cheerfully.

"Fine, Walt. He seems smart and eager. I think he's gonna work out fine."

"Great! What assignment did you give him?"

"The EDIT module," Jill lies.

They chat another minute or so and Walt leaves. Floyd looks at Jill quizzically. "I didn't think you had told Perry yet what his assignment is."

"Right," she grins, "but don't tell Walt that. Listen, when I first came here somebody threw a manual at me, showed me where to sit and said, here, program a thingamajig."

"That's about it," says Floyd, shaking his head in wonderment. "The first time I get somebody new on board I'll sure as hell break him in better. Guess that's what you're up to, huh?"

"Yup! I've even written myself a little checklist. . . ." She opens a desk drawer and takes out a sheet of paper. "This is it—want to see?"

"Yes." Floyd takes the paper from Jill and quickly skims over it. "Hey, good stuff, Jill! How's chances of borrowing it?"

"Sure. Run a copy and leave the original back on my desk. I've gotta run."

Floyd thanks her and heads for the copier. He decides to stay a few minutes late to look over Jill's checklist. He settles back in his chair and reads:

*NEW EMPLOYEE CHECKLIST*

FIRST DAY:

1. Meet Walt Secondlevel and Peter Projectmanager.
2. Meet the group.
3. Assign a work space.
4. Describe company and its goals.
5. Describe project organization and how it works.
6. Describe how our group fits in.
7. Discuss generally where employee's work fits in.
8. Give employee copy of company handbook.

SECOND DAY:

1. Have group briefing on project to give technical overview and status. Each member speaks briefly.
2. Assign first task and schedule; group still present.
3. Assign a "teammate" from the group to assist new employee in first assignment.
4. Turn them loose.

ABOUT FIFTH DAY:

1. Meet with new employee and teammate; assess how things are going; work out snags.
2. Meet alone with new employee;
3. Now that employee has an idea what we're all about, spend couple of hours going over list of programmer's guidelines. Give him copy.

ONE MONTH:

Meet with employee and discuss:

1. His progress.
2. His education. Explain what I can do to help. Discuss seminars, classes, trade magazines, submitting papers.

3.  His career. Free-ranging discussion; where does he plan to go from here; what's available within the company; what about outside the company. Discuss how promotions and transfers are handled; emphasize he is not limited to advancement only within my group, that I'll always look for good openings even if I have to lose an employee.

Next day, Floyd stops at Jill's office.

"Hey, Jill! Got a minute?"

"Sure, c'mon in."

"Here's your checklist . . . I made a copy. Listen, I want to tell you, I'm impressed. You go through all that stuff the first few days—the first month—and the new guy's bound to get off to a good start, unless he's a complete nerd!"

Jill is flattered. "Glad you like it, Floyd. I started it when I brought Lacey into the group, and now Perry. Helps a lot. It was easy to write down—I just listed all the things I wished somebody had done for me when I started. . . ."

". . . and didn't! I know. Same with me when I joined the company. When I got into managing, though, Bill Goodguy did a pretty good job of getting me up to speed. Still, I don't think even he is this thorough. Mind if I pass this on to him?"

"No, I'd like you to . . . " she bites her lip and adds, "But wait an hour or

---

### Jill's Programmer Guidelines

The design specs: stick to them exactly until and unless changed formally.

Change control procedures: how specs get changed.

Working with the customer: he's our partner, not the enemy; discuss who's who; will meet customer people soon.

Coding: no tricky, obscure code; define coding standards and conventions and set up class if necessary.

Coding: detailed design first, then code.

Documenting: how we do it, what tools to use; importance of documentation to a quality product; clean documentation before going on to next module; importance to employee's appraisal.

Your program modules vs. the system: not enough to program brilliantly—it must fit into the system perfectly and must satisfy the specs perfectly.

Code reviews and inspections: what they are; their frequency; your responsibility.

so. Let me throw a copy at Walt first. Wouldn't want to wound his pride, you know."

Floyd laughs knowingly. "You bet! And thanks . . . see you later!"

---

*You know your programmers are doing a good job if*

They want to spend more time with the designers.
They produce pictures before they code.
They don't try to postpone inspections.
They want to show you their detailed designs.
They concentrate on minimizing code complexity.
They take programming errors personally.

**FIGURE 8–1**    It Only Seems Like This    (From Harper's Weekly, 1869.)

# 8

# Day-to-Day Management

Your job as manager is the promotion of excellence. That means excellence in career satisfaction for your people as well as an excellent product. Satisfied people and product excellence go hand-in-hand. This chapter will touch on some of the elements of managing programmers and programming.

## TECHNICAL LEADERSHIP

Technical leadership does *not* necessarily mean being the best technician in your organization. It *does* mean knowing enough that you understand technical advice when you get it. It means being sufficiently up to date that you can choose from among the alternatives you'll face. If you never coded in anything but COBOL, you'll find it difficult to make decisions about adopting competing object-oriented languages for your project. There is a theory that a good manager can handle any job, whether running a programming project or a MacDonald's, equally well. That's true for a handful of gifted people, but for most there's no easy transition from hamburgers to programs.

Throughout this book I've mentioned programming approaches such as structured design, object-oriented analysis, top-down development, and formal inspections. These are tools conceived by computer scientists, programmers, managers—people interested in improving the quality of the programming process and product. All these methodologies are both technicians' tools and managers' tools. They help technical people in the execution of their jobs, from analysis through designing, coding, and testing their products. At the same time they help technical leaders and managers to control the development process. What this says to managers is:

1. The traditional manager's manual is not enough; understand these technical-managerial tools and use them to communicate with your technical people. There is no reason the project manager should not understand prototyping or information hiding. Given detailed design expressed in combinations of diagrams and pseudo code, there is no excuse for a first-level manager not to understand what the programmers are doing. Harlan Mills, a leader in the development of programming and management methods, said in a paper on software productivity (1976): "If management doesn't review design (and suggest valid improvements now and then) and doesn't read code (and recognize excellence), programmers are not likely to care either."

2. Make sure you always allow time and money in your budget—insist on it— for *all* project members to continue their career education. Don't just send managers to management classes and technical people to technical classes; send some of each to the other. And don't rely on the traditional classes offered by your company or by a vendor or user; set up your own classes for your project. If some of your people are unfamiliar with visual programming, configuration management, or whatever, organize classes and seminars for them. Encourage them to take time to learn about their business without having to feel guilty because they're not "producing. "

You may feel no longer competent to dig into technical matters once you become a manager. But the tools are there for you to understand and contribute if you will (1) learn the tools, and (2) let your technical people know that you *want* to understand and that you expect them to talk to you in language you *can* understand.

Lead by example. If you want your team to be concerned about learning and improving their skills, make sure they see that *you* are putting time and effort into doing the same things you are asking them to do.

## PLANNING AND CONTROLLING

Planning means laying out what you want to happen; controlling means making sure it does happen. Planning and controlling are what this entire book is about. The opposite philosophy is drift, a notion voiced by Dwayne Andreas (quoted in Will, 1992) of Archer Daniels Midland this way: "If you don't change your direction, you'll end up where you're headed."

## COMMUNICATING

You must make sure everyone on the project is tuned to the same station. Consider this conversation:

"Where does your job stand, Dick?"

"Pretty good. I think we're in system test."

"Oh, you mean integration?"

"Yeah, I guess so. . . ."

That was an actual conversation. How can people work together on a project unless there are basic agreements about who's doing what? Dick "thinks" he's in "system test," whatever that means, but he readily substitutes the word "integration." No doubt he would agree to anything to be left alone to return to whatever it is he's doing. It's your job to establish and enforce basic definitions and core understandings for your project.

## BUILDING CREDIBILITY

Try to establish an environment in which people speak out and tell you when things are not right. One way to do this is to be on the alert for the first comment that sounds like a valid complaint or criticism, pounce on it, fix whatever was being criticized, and make sure that everyone knows you acted positively because of someone's criticism. Conversely, if you turn off the first criticism, you may never hear another, constructive or otherwise. Some time ago I attended a project meeting in which the boss discussed status, levied a few new ground rules, asked for questions, and adjourned the meeting when there were none. Immediately afterward, a small knot of programmers gathered near my office and hanged management in absentia. I listened in and then asked the most vocal member of the group why he had not spoken up at the meeting. He said management never listens, so why bother. How many times this happens every day is anybody's guess, but there is only one person who can prevent it: you, the manager. You set the tone. You've got to destroy the us-versus-them attitude that so often exists between managers and "workers."

## CARRYING THE WATER

Whatever product you build, it's your people who put it together. Part of your job is to provide them with the environment and the tools they need to do their job. You must maximize their chances of success. Robert Townsend (1970) says a good manager "carries the water for his people so they can get on with the job."

One thing you can do is set up the best physical facilities you can afford. Maybe programmers don't need carpeted offices, but they need quiet and privacy. The Programming Process can tolerate neither a noisy factory environment nor constant interruptions. If you hang a dollar sign on each distraction or disruption a programmer experiences during a day, you'll quickly invest in some remedies. When a programmer is interrupted in the middle of a complex piece of code, she has to backtrack to pick up the thread and may easily forget some part of what she originally had in mind. The result is a bug. The bug means a loss of the programmer's time during module test; it consumes extra computer time; it may show up during higher-level tests when it will cause a disproportionate loss of people time and computer time.

Another way you can help is by providing the best possible test environment. You can raise hell with the computer center to provide adequate and predictable computer services. You can arrange for pickup and drop areas for printouts and listings. You need to demand powerful workstations and reliable, high-speed communication links.

Act as a buffer. Get needed information to your people and screen the "administrivia." Any large organization is plagued by too much paper going to too many people. This often happens because a manager circulates everything with a "read and pass on" note. No matter how safe it may make you feel, you simply cannot have everyone read everything.

Finally, be sure that in your project planning you search out the best tools for both management and programming. It takes enlightened management to encourage people to read the literature, snoop around, and do the digging required to come up with new tools and new ways of doing a job.


## ASSIGNING THE WORK

I once worked on a proposal effort whose objective was to win a huge programming job under contract to the federal government. The proposal involved more than fifty people. A high-level manager was appointed to run the proposal job in his spare time. He assigned people loosely to jobs. Some areas of work were covered by three or four people, each of whom thought that he or she alone should be doing that job. Other areas were not covered at all. (The manager who had the power to correct all this had a reputation for not making specific assignments. He preferred that people step forth and volunteer.) The idea that a busy executive can be acting manager of a major project in his spare time is ridiculous. Better to appoint a slightly less qualified person to the job full time than to assign the job to an acting manager who can't devote enough time to do the job right. (P.S. We lost the job.)

Suppose you're the manager of a project or proposal effort. First gain a rough understanding of the job. Then break up the job and assign pieces to individuals. But that's not enough. You must write down a description of each person's job. I can't say it too strongly. *Write it down!* Give a copy of all assignments to everyone. The first thing that will happen is that half your crew will come storming in to complain that someone else's job assignment bites into their territory. If you're lucky, someone will come in and point out that nobody's assignment covers area X. After you've had a day or two of complaints and people have had a chance to chew on the assignments, set up a meeting to talk over the problems. Then rewrite the assignments and pass them out again. It may take a couple of iterations, and some meetings may be uncomfortable, but soon you'll have job descriptions that don't overlap and do cover what needs to be done.

## WORKING HOURS

If you're new to the computer programming business, maybe you have not yet taken part in panic projects where everything was late and management had to resort to that ultimate remedy: scheduled overtime.

I doubt there is a much worse waste of resources than this. We're tempted to think that by working people 25 percent more hours a week, 25 percent more work will get done; some managers even think crash overtime helps to bring the troops together and that a strong feeling of camaraderie develops—something like having a buddy in the foxhole with you. Experience proves otherwise.

First, 25 percent more hours can easily produce 10 percent less work, or at least less usable work. Given more hours to work each day for an extended period of weeks or months, most people will simply settle into a new routine, pacing themselves more slowly. Their work may get sloppier.

Some extra work may get done the first week, of course, and perhaps even the second and the third, but after that, forget it! People unconsciously slow their efforts to fill the scheduled time. And even extra work accomplished during that first week or two will not be nearly in proportion to its cost—either the dollar cost or the cost in morale as private and family lives are affected. As for that feeling of camaraderie, it soon devolves into negativism: damn the customer for insisting on that delivery deadline; damn management for agreeing to it; damn the computer time; damn everything!

Note that we're discussing *scheduled* overtime. It simply does not work well. The only real chance for overtime to work well is when it's done voluntarily and over short time spans. Mills (1976) says this about overtime:

> It is almost impossible to imagine a situation where directed overtime would not reduce total productivity. If the motivation is not present for voluntary overtime to increase productivity, it surely will not be generated by involuntary overtime. . . . If high motivation brings voluntary (unpaid) overtime, increased productivity may result in the short run—a few weeks, say. But in the long run, even a voluntary overtime activity may be counterproductive. Enthusiasm may wear off, and be replaced by resentment at being expected to put in overtime by precedent, if not by direction. Overtime may become a habit and an excuse for not working smarter.

There is something else to consider about working hours. Various companies have experimented with the idea of "flextime," letting employees set their own hours. Generally, companies set the total time to be worked each day, but allow starting and ending times to float. You can go further by setting a number of hours for, say, an entire week, and leaving the specific days or hours up to the individual. Carried a *big* step further, you might eliminate hours as a measure of work altogether; the means of measurement or control might be completion of a given task by some predetermined date! Perhaps those latter notions are too liberal for now, but the idea of the floating workday is not. It's been tried and it's been shown it can work. According to an Administrative Management Society survey in 1986, 28 percent of U.S. employers offered flexible time scheduling to most of their workers (*USA Today*, 1986). As long ago as 1971, Germany's Lufthansa instituted *gleitende arbeitzeitz* (gliding work-time), allowing most employees to choose a block of work time between 7:00 A.M. and 7:00 P.M., Because of this arrangement, Lufthansa claimed it had practically done away with one-day sickness (Fellows, 1971).

Flextime has the obvious advantage of catering to the individual needs, inclinations, and body clocks of each employee, which should lead to improved job satisfaction. There are also disadvantages—for example, how can you call a department meeting when you never know who will be around at any given hour? And how about the frustrations of programmer A who needs to talk to programmer B, but A's chosen hours are early in the day and B's are late?

You can experiment with the set-your-own-hours idea by starting small, seeing how well it works, and adjusting as you go along. Begin by limiting the range over which individuals' hours might float. Set aside a part of each day, say 1:00 P.M. to 4:00 P.M., when you expect everyone to be on the job. That will allow some to work from 7:00 A.M. to 4:00 P.M., others from noon to 9:00 P.M., still others from 10:00 A.M. to 7:00 P.M. Sound like a management headache? All right then, back to your cave!

## ADDING MORE PEOPLE

Just as resorting to overtime is usually wasteful, neither is it helpful to load the project with more people to bail out of problems that are the result of poor planning. Don't hold to impossible deadlines in the mistaken belief that what you lack in calendar time you can make up with bodies. It just does not work. Frederick Brooks (1975) claims to be oversimplifying outrageously when he postulates Brooks' Law: *Adding manpower to a late software project makes it later.* But having witnessed and participated in exactly such sad rescue activities, I think his law makes terribly good sense. "The bearing of a child," he says, "takes nine months, no matter how many women are assigned."

There are two reasonable alternatives to adding more people when the project falls behind:

1. Reschedule. This, of course, will make the customer scream; and that in turn will make your management scream.

**2.** Arrange to deliver interim, incomplete versions of your system. If you can make the first delivery at the time you were *supposed* to deliver the final product, that timing should help; then you'll only have to reschedule the final version.

If you get involved in rescheduling and delivering interim versions of the system, be as sure as you can that *this* time you can make the deliveries as promised. There will be a terribly compelling urge to deliver as soon as possible, and it's probable that you'll offer new dates that are again too optimistic. The manager who keeps coming back to his management with a series of two-week schedule slippages is not going to manage for very long. Make your stand now, admit to any bad planning or execution you've been responsible for so far, but don't repeat those mistakes. Screaming customers are a nightmare, as are screaming bosses. Don't let their screams wear you down when you feel you're right; otherwise, you'll hear it all again in a few months, only louder.

## REPORTING TECHNICAL STATUS

Anyone doing a job for anyone else must somehow communicate how things are going. Usually, there is a need for both written reports and oral reviews. Let's consider each.

## Written Reports

Reporting the status of anything presupposes there is some baseline plan to report against. It's of little use to report that program module ABC has been tested if there never was a plan showing when ABC *should* have been tested. Therefore, the first requirement for effective status reporting is that there be a plan including milestones against which to measure progress (see Chapter 1).

A second requirement is that reports be tailored to fit the management level for which they are intended. Tailor both content and frequency. A reasonable scheme for your project might work like this. Individuals—for example, programmers—report biweekly to their first-level managers on the status of all tasks, or work packages, to which they have been assigned. First-level managers, after receiving inputs from their people, report to the second-level manager the status of *selected* tasks; that is, those tasks shown as milestones on their work assignment Gantt charts. A first-level manager responsible for, say, fifteen tasks, might report to a second-level manager only four or five. In turn, the second-level manager reports to you the status of milestone tasks on his or her charts. What you receive is a net summation of all the individual pieces of work on the project. Rather than pass on all possible status data, each manager acts as a filter and lets through only what's important. In turn, you pass on a condensed report to your management and to the

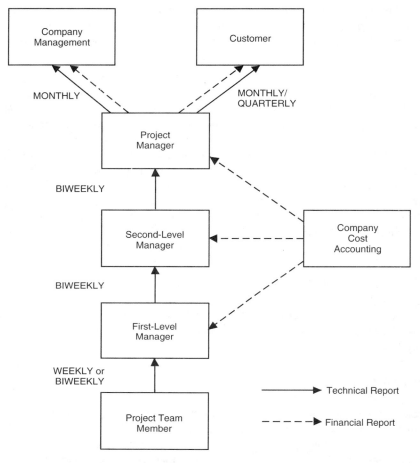

**FIGURE 8–2**   Status Reporting

customer (see Figure 8–2). All the reports in this chain should follow similar, compatible formats.

Some of today's PC-based project management systems can help you in setting up the reporting hierarchy. They allow summary tasks to be defined at different levels so that the list of all the tasks in the project looks like a large, neatly indented outline. Managers at each level can report on the summary tasks at that level and every manager, at every level, can see not only his or her place in the overall scheme of things, but can also be aware of activities that will impact the work under his or her control.

In the problem section of a report include problems appropriate to the level of the reader. Don't whine to a high mucky-muck manager about your problem getting a new file cabinet. If you can't solve that one, the manager is going to wonder about you just a little. State your problems according to their priorities; that is, make sure the reader of the report knows which problems you consider most important. Always describe the status of attempts at finding solutions. Give the reader the warm feeling that you're working on the problem (if you are). Earlier I emphasized laying out work in discrete chunks. Report on those chunks in your status reports. Don't let anyone get by with qualitative mealy-mouthing or meaningless "percent complete" reports. Insist that your people report to you in quantitative terms. I recall a project in which we reported partly by filling in a bar chart. When a bar became entirely black, that job was theoretically done. Unfortunately, we ran out of bar early. We found that filling in the bars told us nothing. They simply made depressing wall decorations in a status-control room.

## Oral Reviews

I discussed these in Chapter 2, but here I'd like to emphasize their usefulness. They are a good excuse for getting people together, whether or not they succeed in exposing problems. Oral reviews help give people a sense of belonging to something besides their two-by-four cubicles. They help people to understand the part their work plays in the total job. They provide a break from routine. And, of course, they provide a forum for uncovering problems and broaching better solutions.

## REPORTING FINANCIAL STATUS

Financial reports are often generated by some cost-accounting function separate from the management of the project. These reports may be sent only to you, the project manager, or to your subordinate managers as well. You should insure during planning that the tasks, or work packages, used as the basis for financial reporting are the same tasks used for technical reporting. You should always be able to compare technical and financial reports without need for a conversion exercise to find out how the two reports relate. A good PC-based management package can help you here.

## TRAINING

Every manager is responsible for career training for his or her people, totally apart from training required by the contract. A manager must try to raise the level of competence and understanding of every individual in the organization—otherwise, the organization stagnates. When times are tough and an organization's overhead costs must be trimmed, education is one of the first expenses cut. It's considered a luxury. Classes are canceled because they add to overhead, and yet the same people who would have attended those classes now sit around, still charging their time to some form of overhead, doing little or nothing. There are many reasons for this, mostly concerning internal company bookkeeping. But books be damned. Get those idle people into education programs and let the bookkeepers worry about the books. (Of course, if you work for a company that gets rid of people when they become idle, the argument is academic.)

There are several kinds of training to provide, and a number of ways of providing it. Let's start with your technical people—for example, the programmers. You should train them in, or at least expose them to, programming languages and computers other than those on their current jobs. How else will they grow? How can they offer you alternative technical solutions if all they know is machine x and language y? Give them the time and encouragement to attend formal classes, subscribe to and read technical literature, and hobnob with their counterparts on other projects. Some of this is hard for a manager to swallow—it's like encouraging coffee breaks. But what a payoff! Your people will never approach their potential if all they ever study is the current job.

Your newer programmers need special attention until you have a feel for the competence of each. Managers, especially green ones, often accept their new recruits as experienced, professional people without demanding any proof. I could write a whole chapter on incidents involving programmers fresh out of school (and a few who were more experienced and should have known better). For example, consider Greg, whose way of unit testing a certain math routine was quietly to increase a hidden counter (posing as a "constant" in his program) by "1" until the answer to a given test case came out right! I'm not kidding! And there was Bill, who didn't trust data structure libraries and never used them. Or Ned, who, instead of simply setting a variable to zero, always put two identical initialization instructions in a row in case the first one didn't work. Luckily, he trusted most of the other instructions. Another winner was Don, whose solution to a problem was always to branch around the offending code.

How do you recognize Greg, Bill, Ned, and Don and set them straight? By making code inspections routine procedures for every programmer on the project. The documented experience of hundreds of companies across many industries has shown this approach to be extremely valuable, both as a quality control technique and as a training mechanism.

An important kind of training for all your people (and you) is rotation through jobs other than their normal ones. This can be done without an enormous investment in time, and the payoff is handsome. Programmers who bitch about machine room operations can learn and contribute plenty just by becoming computer operators for a few days; operators will become better operators by taking some basic programming courses; programmers will become better documenters (and designers) if they spend some time maintaining other people's programs.

Rotation, or cross-training, is helpful to your nontechnical people, too. How about a basic course in the fundamentals of programming for your secretaries and typists? They would enjoy knowing what all those scribbles are about, and would do a better job of transcribing them. There is no one on the project who would not benefit from at least some exposure to what goes on outside his or her own job, and this will in turn benefit the project.

A word of caution: Some federal and state labor laws restrict the types and duration of rotations you may legally use. You may not, for example, freely interchange "professional" and "clerical" people. Ask your company's lawyers what's allowable in your area. (Don't ask them if you *can* do it; lawyers love to say no. Tell them you're going to, and ask how to do it legally.)

Then there are the managers and supervisors who report to you. They need day-to-day assistance from you; they also need to attend management classes and seminars. They need technical updating classes to help stave off obsolescence. The managers working for you need to see in you a good example of how to manage. If you plan your activity poorly (and rely on excessive overtime to get your own work done), you're providing, by example, excellent training in sloppy management.

Perhaps most important of all—and I've said this before—you must bring together the entire project often enough to update everyone on status and plans. There's tremendous benefit to the project when everyone understands what is going on and where he or she fits in.

## APPRAISING AND COUNSELING

As a manager you can have a whopping influence on the lives of your people. How well you pay a person is important, of course, but just as important is your ability to help each person on your project to find a fulfilling job. Many things about the project may be bad, but if you can just carve out a piece of work that appeals to an individual and is within his or her capabilities, other problems fade. Nietzsche said, "He who has a why to live for can bear almost any how."

You and your employee must agree on a suitable task and a schedule for doing it. Again, the simple act of writing down a description of people's assignments and getting their agreement to it can be extremely helpful. Give people as much say as possible in setting deadlines. Deadlines imposed from above are not good motivators.

When one of your people goes off course or does a bad job, you've got to let him or her know it the best way you can. This can be so difficult that some managers avoid doing it until forced to. By then things are usually at crisis stage. A way of avoiding big problems is to subdivide the job and have enough checkpoints so that missing one is a signal, not a catastrophe. When people do go off course, try to work with them to see what needs to be done to correct the problem. Be helpful, not critical. Everyone can have a few bad days—even you.

Any manager's success should be gauged by how well he or she encourages growth and by how fairly he or she rewards hard work and deals with incompetence. A good manager will not hesitate to promote a subordinate to the manager's own level. A good manager will not selfishly hide a key employee within the organization; instead, the manager will promote the employee and risk losing him or her to another group. A good manager will never transfer a "problem child" to someone else without full warning.

## SANITY MAINTENANCE

Many managers get into tons of trouble because they cannot say *no*. The word is negative, after all, and what eager young manager wants to sound negative? Anything the boss (or the customer) wants must be done. Since all the books on "positive thinking" and "thinking big" say you can do anything, shouldn't you strike the word "no" from your vocabulary? Baloney! There are many things that *are* impossible and many more that are unreasonable. The true positive thinker is the person who can sort things out and distinguish between the reasonable and the unreasonable. Many disasters in the programming business are the result of someone allowing himself or herself to be pressured into committing to something he or she feels is impossible. There are many types of pressure situations. Sometimes your manager is in a tough position and needs a certain commitment from you to save himself. Sometimes the pressure is applied by erosion—you're asked to give in a little at a time, in easy installments, and when you finally realize what you've done, it's too late. Other times you are fast-talked and lulled into playing RAM (Repeat After Me)—the manager tells you what he wants to hear and your only job is to say it. And in still other cases, you are made to feel your job is in jeopardy.

There are many situations in which people use these tactics. Perhaps what is at issue is an estimate you have submitted that's too high for the boss to swallow. Or maybe you're asked to accept some added work you don't feel you can handle, like the situation my boss found himself in some time ago. He sat behind a desk piled high with papers; his shirt was rumpled, his tie askew, his whole appearance disheveled. He looked numb. His manager and the customer had heaped on him so many demands that he was bewildered. He could not even make a start. (I offered to pour gasoline on his desk and light it, but he didn't think that was funny.) He had simply gotten overcommitted. He was incapable of saying no. Not by coincidence, he had many personnel problems at the time, all demanding his attention.

IBM's Bill Weimer has been responsible for innovative training courses for both management and technical people. In choosing the approach and content for one set of courses, he said, "We found that technical people, in general, were actually very good at estimating project requirements and schedules. The problem they had was defending their decisions; they needed to learn how to hold their ground."

Charles P. Lecht (1967) has this to say about refusing the impossible:

> Equally responsible for the initiation of a project with predefined failure . . . is management that insists upon having fixed commitments from programming personnel prior to the latter's understanding what the commitments are for. Too frequently management does not realize that in asking the staff for the "impossible," the staff will feel the obligation to respond out of respect, fear, or misguided loyalty. Saying "no" to the boss frequently requires courage, political and psychological wisdom, and business maturity that comes with much experience.

There is another way to help maintain balance in the hectic business of programming management. An artist knows it well. Faced with a canvas that's a mess, he stands back, squints to shut out details, and tries to see the "big picture." Force yourself periodically to take a few steps back and look at the total job, not the details. Simplify. Try to get things in perspective. Get away from the job physically—no phone, no in-basket. List the things you have to do and decide which items on the list are really important. If there is more there than you can do, pass some of it on to someone else. Look for those items that you could cross off the list and never do (there are always some of these). If you take frequent enough looks, you'll begin to look at the job more rationally. You'll have a constant awareness of how much you have to do, and, therefore, how much more you can take on. Always remember your career will be enhanced by a few jobs well done, but damaged by a lot of jobs that fail.

When you assign priorities to the tasks you have to do, the "people problems" come first. Don't let your people feel that they come second to anything. If you lose their loyalty and respect, you're dead.

## FIRST-LEVEL VERSUS UPPER-LEVEL MANAGEMENT

So far I have not made much distinction between the various levels of management. The basic job is the same, whatever the level. What really varies is the ratio of technical to nontechnical involvement. This ratio decreases as you go up in the management chain. A first-level manager is normally directly involved in the technical work his people are doing. A second-level manager's technical involvement is broader; this position requires more time to be spent in such areas as finance, proposals, planning, and personnel. And so it goes until at some level the manager is concerned much more with general business decisions than with detailed technical decisions.

A difficult problem arises from all this: How does the upper-level manager have any feel for what is going on technically? How does the manager fight technical obsolescence and have any confidence that things are going well?

There are some partial answers. First, devote significant time to technical updating by reading specifications and hearing briefings by your subordinates. But resist the urge to bit-fiddle; leave detailed technical work to those best qualified to do it. One third-level manager I know could not resist the urge to get into the programmers' code. While he was messing with bits, his project fell apart and was eventually canceled.

Second, set up technical checks and balances to help assure that the technical work is getting done properly. One such check is continued involvement by the analysis and design team. Another is the presence of a separate test group. Still another is the extensive use of inspections to provide for detailed scrutiny of all the items developed on the project.

A third way to keep afloat technically is to return periodically to technical work. Some organizations discourage switching between management and technical jobs, but if you can accomplish it, it can do wonders for your technical competence and greatly enhance your confidence in being able to manage the next job.

Finally, you must read the literature in the field and attend classes whenever possible. Often this will be done on your own time.

---

### The Manager's Bookshelf

Now that you're in the middle of the development process, you should be taking the time to look as objectively as possible at your own performance. A book that can help you do this is Stephen A. Maguire's *Debugging the Development Process: Practical Strategies for Staying Focused, Hitting Ship Dates, and Building Solid Teams* (1994). Even though I've been managing teams for over twenty years, this book showed me some different ways of looking at the problems I wrestle with from project to project.

# PART V

# SYSTEM TEST

Testing is the manager's most valuable source of information about the project. It allows the manager to apply standards to the work produced under her direction. There are all kinds of tests. The Problem Specification is tested during presentations to the customer. The initial analysis is tested by submitting it to the Design Process. The designers' work is tested by both feedback from the programmers and by the performance of the final product. The programmers' work is tested through examinations and execution. Each test has the role of validating that the work being tested satisfies the requirements that it was based upon.

As the project draws toward its conclusion, testing grows to be a greater part of the overall work effort. In part, this is because there is more material to test. In part, it is because system components that were built independently are now being brought together for the first time. In part, it is because the range of each test is becoming broader—it's no longer enough to verify that the reformatting module works correctly; it's now necessary to show that the data gathered by the order entry system is accurately reflected in the picking list displayed at the warehouse and in the shipping manifest printed at the loading dock.

Testing—planning the tests, executing them correctly, determining the criteria for success or failure, recording the results, analyzing the progress—none of this sounds very glamorous. In all too many circumstances, excuses are found to cut corners on the testing process or to assign junior people to the job. As a manager, you can't afford to let this happen.

If you ask your programmers how they're doing, they'll tell you everything's great. Ask your designers how their work is progressing and you'll hear that every-thing is on schedule. You're the manager and nobody is going to go out of their way to bring you bad news.

If you are involved with the testing, you will *know* what shape your project is in. You will see that the entry screen blows up when someone puts an alphabetic character in the ZIP Code field. You will see that the Design Specification doesn't contain the audit trail called for in the Problem Specification. You will see that Chapters 4, 5, and 6 are still missing from the User's Reference Manual. Seeing all these things might not make you feel any better, but you will be on solid ground when your customer or your executives ask how the project is going.

You are the Project Manager. You have a responsibility to understand the state of the work you are directing and you have a responsibility to communicate accurately and objectively with the customer who wants to know how things are going. If you're not involved in the testing process, how can you answer the cus-tomer's questions?

**FIGURE 9–1** The System Test Process (From *Backs to the Wall: London Under Fire,* by Leonard Mosely, Weidenfeld and Nicholson, London, 1971.)

# 9

# The System Test Process

The programmers are done (they think) and are ready for the next job. They've tested their elegant modules thoroughly and intelligently. But you know something they seem to have forgotten: programmers almost never deliver a defect-free program. In fact, many are *far* from perfect. So, being a smart manager interested in delivering a high-quality product, you insist on postprogrammer testing. Before you face the customer with your product you subject it to tests neither designed nor executed by the programmers, in as nearly a live environment as possible. You enter the System Test Process hoping it will be uneventful, but it won't be.

## SYSTEM TESTING

Just before I sat down to write this section, I wrote a letter to my aunt. Then I clicked on the screen "button" that says PRINT ENVELOPE. I should have known better. Every time you try that with this package, if you have just finished editing the "addressee" portion, the system has a heart attack. Everything stops and there is no getting back in control, no matter how many times you punch "Escape" or click the mouse over various portions of the screen. This is version 6.0 of this program, and one would think people had tried editing and printing envelopes before releasing it. If the word-processing software I'm using to write this had been rigorously system tested, there's a good chance this stupid bug would have been noticed and squashed.

Managers resist system testing because it seems redundant and wasteful. Programmers resist it because it's insulting. But the errors you don't find because you skip system testing will show up later, either during acceptance testing or after the programs are operational. The cost of a problem found that late is very high; you measure it in terms of customer dissatisfaction or disgust (*yes!*), lost opportunities for follow-on work, a tarnished reputation, and a patched-up product, as well as manpower, time, and money.

System testing won't guarantee perfection, but it will bring you a large step closer than reliance on the programmers' own tests. Programmers are not stupid or uncaring, of course, but they are *too close* to their products. They cannot be expected to test with the objectivity of users. They know how they intended the programs to behave, and they test accordingly.

Be ready for system testing when the programmers deliver their product. Have System Test Specifications written, computer time scheduled, library facilities set up, and people ready.

## Test Early and Often

System testing was once left until everything else had been done. At that time, all the programs and data were brought together and everyone held their breath to see if the conglomeration actually worked. After a while, it started dawning on managers that the only process that actually works well when performed this way is the staging of a demolition derby.

Just as we go through design and programming by getting a little part right and then adding to that little part, system testing should start early and be cumulative. Both the system being tested and the breadth and depth of the test criteria should expand as modules finish unit testing and are brought into the mainstream.

You should start system testing once the first skeletal subsystem is ready to stand on its own. I mentioned my approach of starting with the Log-In and Security Check functions for a system. Once these are working to the satisfaction of the programmers, move them into system testing. Once they pass their tests, they become Version 0.0 of the final system. From that point, it's simply a matter of adding enough functionality to get to Version 0.1 and so forth. The tests you developed for Version 0.0 should work just as well with Version 0.1 and you can keep building on this base.

The collection of tests that you accumulate makes it easy to perform what's called "regression testing," where you test the newest version of the system to ensure that the functions that worked in previous versions still work. If your customer is participating in the system test process (and there are some good arguments why this should happen), a regular program of regression testing will help convince the customer that the project is moving steadily forward.

## System Test Specification

If you don't have Test Specifications, you aren't testing. Test Specification layouts are included in the Documentation Plan in the Appendix. A Test Specification describes test objectives and approach. It also contains a *requirements coverage matrix* showing every requirement the software system is to meet versus specific, numbered test cases designed to validate that the system meets those requirements. For any given system requirement, or function, it should be easy to locate in this matrix all relevant test cases. If you have trouble writing this matrix, you may have a fuzzy set of tests.

The foundation for your Test Specification is the combination of the Problem Specification and the Design Specification. From the Problem Specification, you should be able to envision tests that will demonstrate that the system does what it was supposed to. From the Design Specification, you should be able to identify the more complex areas of the programs—and this is where defects are most likely to be found.

How many test cases you need is entirely up to you. The idea is to make one test case cover a specific functional area—for example, "startup," "input message error processing," "single target detection," "target tracking," "tax computation," "single matrix conversion." Choose chunks of function big enough to be meaningful to a user, small enough that you may easily assimilate and understand test results. As a starting point, I'd guess that any software system big enough to employ your forty-member group for over twelve months would probably require a set of at least forty test cases. It's impossible to offer a more solid guideline without knowing the specific system being tested.

As outlined in the Appendix, each test case consists of a script, data, and checklists.

**Script.**    A script is a set of step-by-step instructions intended to lead test personnel almost mechanically through the tests. The script lists all actions required of human operators at each piece of equipment involved in the test. It not only tells the testers what to do and when to do it but also what to look for and what to write down for later analysis. Testers must understand the background and objectives of each test, so that you need to include little explanatory information in the script. Figure 9–2 illustrates a sample page from a script. Note that the right-hand portion of the page is left blank for jotting down notes during the test.

**Data.**    The data portion of a test case includes simulated input data, live input data, and predicted output data. Simulated input data are prepared beforehand to exercise the system during a given test. For example, if your system is a payroll processing system, these inputs may include employee data, hours worked, tax information, and deductions.

Live inputs are those that cannot be prepared ahead of time, such as telemetry data from a satellite. This kind of input provides advantages difficult to get from simulated input data: (a) randomness, and (b) normal "garbage" that your system must handle properly.

Predicted outputs are written forecasts of the exact data that should result from a given test case, where such forecasting is possible. If you determine results

---

**TEST SCRIPT**

Project:        Service Order
Test Suite:          A                    Test Number:  4                    Page 13 / 24
Test:          House Number Entry
Tester Initials:_____    Date / Time: _____

---

| Procedure | Notes |
|---|---|
| 1. Start address screen (ADR01) from top menu. | |
| 2. Verify Tab Sequence Forward and Backward. | |
| 3. Verify mouse selection for all fields. | |
| 4. Verify protected fields (Telephone Number, Customer Account Number, Customer Account Status). | |
| 5. Enter the following house numbers. Note message code returned for each rejected entry. X = Expect reject | |

|  |  |
|---|---|
| 123 1/2 | |
| 1231/2 | |
| 123Sycamore | X |
| 123S Main | X |
| A123 | X |
| A-123 | |
| A 123 | X |
| 123-A | |
| 123-45 | |
| 123-45 1/2 | |
| 123-45-67 | |
| 123-45-67 1/2 | X |
| *123 | X |
| 2nd | X |
| 1/2 | |
| A-123 1/5 | |
| 123A24 | |
| 12345678 | X |
| 22-1234567-A | X |

**FIGURE 9–2**    Sample Page from a System Test Script

in advance, it is only necessary to compare actual with predicted test outputs in order to know the effectiveness of the test. Predicting outputs in advance offers advantages other than simplifying posttest analysis. It saves calendar time because the prediction can be done in parallel with other activities, before the actual tests are run. Also, using predicted outputs can be more accurate than on-the-spot posttest analysis because the latter often gives rise to hasty decisions (Oh, it looks all right!).

**Checklists.**    Checklists prepared in advance help during posttest analysis. Checklists are powerful analysis aids when they are thoughtfully constructed. An example of a partial checklist is shown in Figure 9–3.

Each test case should be self-contained, with specific objectives and test data. Within each test there should be built-in restart points, convenient places for resuming in the event of unexpected aborts during the test. Every test should be planned so that in posttest analysis it can be clearly shown what the inputs were, what the results were predicted to be, and what the results actually were.

---

**CHECKLIST—ENTRY SCREENS**

Project:        Service Order
Test Suite:_____        Test Number:_____        Page 1 / 2
Tester Initials:_____        Date / Time: _____

| Number | Item | OK | Defect |
|--------|------|----|--------|
| 1 | Window Name Display | | |
| 2 | Close Box / Sizing Box | | |
| 3 | Protected Fields Grayed Out | | |
| 4 | Radio Button Positions—Out is Off | | |
| 5 | Protected Buttons Grayed | | |
| 6 | I-Beam Cursor Positioning in Entry Fields | | |
| 7 | Mouse / Tab / Arrow Navigation | | |
| 8 | Drop Down Menus | | |
| 9 | Protected Menu Items Grayed | | |
| 10 | Standard Controls—Standard Positions (Accept / Cancel / Next / Prev / Help) | | |
| 11 | HELP Available | | |
| ..... | ....... | | |
| nn | Standard Colors / Position on Error Indication | | |

**FIGURE 9–3**   Part of a System Test Checklist

## The Testers

Those who plan, execute, and analyze the system tests belong to the Test Group. These people must be technically competent, analytically inclined, and *user-oriented*. They must thoroughly understand the customer and the Problem Specification. Some should have participated in the original problem analysis. In addition to your own people, try to include some experienced users in this group.

Try to instill an air of competition between the testers and the programmers. The system testers are out to unearth problems. If they find none, either your programmers are heroes or your testers are sloppy or your system was extremely simple to build. You should expect problems. Some of them may be due to errors, but many will be matters of interpreting the Problem Specification or problems in ease of use of the system. Some in the latter category may be the result of faulty user documents rather than programming defects. Any problem is fair game. The system testers must "think customer" and constantly approach the system from the customer's point of view.

Don't choose as system testers people who are bland, easily intimidated, or technically dull. Testers should be demonic in their attempts to beat hell out of the system. A system failure is their "success." Look for people like prizefighter Sugar Ray Leonard, who told an audience of Harvard students: "We're all blessed with God-given talents. Mine just happens to be beatin' people up" (Augustine, 1986). Encourage testers to poke into all the dark corners of the system. Never suggest to them that they might go easy in a particular area; remember, what they don't find, the customer eventually will.

Your testers should be encouraged to build their esprit de corps just as you want your programmers to do. If you can get your testers to do this, you will have established an asset with a value that may reach well beyond your current project. Lockheed was able to do this with their renowned "black team" and the performance and value of the group grew over the years.

Testers and programmers have an adversarial relationship and some managers have difficulty in dealing with it. As a manager, you need to take care to see that

---

### A Place for Your Sociopaths

Around the fringes of any software development house are those people who are technically sharp but socially dull. No, "dull" is too tame—maybe "evil" is better. I'm thinking of the people who as children pulled wings off butterflies. Here's a place where they can earn a living without having to hide their mean and malicious tendencies. Put them into system testing.

competition between programmers and testers doesn't extend to a personal level. It really does make a difference when your testers choose between saying, "Module D failed tests 1 and 3. The scan terminated prematurely," and "When are you going to learn to initialize your pointers?"

## Timing

Don't enter system test (or any testing activity) until you have satisfied certain criteria. Entry criteria vary, depending on the product being tested, but generally they include the following:

➤ The product to be tested (program or document) must be considered complete by its developers; any exceptions must have explicit management approval. This does not mean that the system as a whole must be complete, but it does mean that any intermediate level of the system must have complete functionality in the areas being tested.

➤ The written Test Specification for that product must be finished, approved, and ready for execution.

➤ All supporting test data must be ready.

➤ Both the developers and the testing people must be present, or on call.

➤ Computer time, if needed, must be available.

➤ Any special resources (for example, remote equipment, temporary living facilities at a remote site, transportation) must be ready.

It's not enough, of course, to plan for system testing—you also have to *do* the testing. On a project I know of, managers included system test in their plans, but as time went by and they began missing deadlines they decided something had to be done in parallel with something else to speed things up. So they combined (no, attempted to combine) system testing and module testing in parallel during the late months of the Programming Process. Worse, they attempted to do even more in parallel by conducting system test at several locations at once, some of them halfway around the world! The result was disaster. Within a few days, testers found so many defects that they sent many modules back to module test. Coordination among the sites was a nightmare. Imagine debugging six versions of a system consisting of hundreds of modules at six separate sites! The people on this project were able and competent, but they were frantically looking for a way out of a problem that was project-congenital: at the outset, the calendar time scheduled for the project was inadequate, and everyone knew it. The misery was compounded when very early in the project it changed from a single-site to a multiple-site job, with no substantive change in funding or schedules. When political or economic pressures mount, even the ablest of people are tempted to throw out everything they know about good management. This buys them time for a breather, but there's always a reckoning later.

We can learn some lessons about system test from past disasters. First, no amount of luck, political acumen, or clean living will allow you to skip system testing and get away with it. In a system of any complexity at all, those hotshot programmers are going to make mistakes—and some of them will be beauts! I feel sure you'll want to find them before your customer does.

Second, in order to start effective system testing as early as possible, your subsystems must be nearly independent of one another and the interfaces between them must be clean and simple. Remember this when you start the Design Process!

Third, don't spread system testing geographically until you've reached the point at which the system looks clean and only needs testing against unique site conditions. These conditions may include modified static data bases, geographic location coordinates, varying input and output devices, and varying input loads. Remember that each time you introduce another copy of your system into the test environment, you've magnified your change management problems. Because you must include and test every change in one version in all the others, coordination becomes extremely difficult.

## Conducting the Tests

System test begins when the programmers release to the Test Group their "finished" product: a cohesive part of the final system and clean draft documentation. The Test Group manager formally accepts, signs for, and locks up the system that he receives.

A test conductor is assigned responsibility for the preparation, execution, and analysis of a set of test cases. The conductor schedules the people, the computer time, physical facilities, and any other resources required for these test cases. Before beginning a test, the conductor assures that all participants and observers are on hand and that they have all required materials, such as scripts, checklists, and predicted outputs.

The conductor initiates the test. Those taking part follow their scripts precisely, noting discrepancies or unusual conditions. The conductor makes all decisions concerning aborts or restarts unless the script already provides for these. Observers, who also have copies of scripts, should be encouraged to write down ideas and questions as the test proceeds. Observers may be programmers, other project members, and customer representatives. If you choose to invite the customer, be certain he understands it is a test of an incomplete system, not a demonstration of a finished product. The customer should know you expect problems. If he gets the idea that system test is no more than a dress rehearsal for acceptance test, there will be uneasiness, or even suspicion, every time you hit a snag.

After completing a test or series of tests, the conductor calls together the participants to analyze the results. Sometimes they complete analysis and assess success or failure immediately. In other cases, outputs require study and the conductor sets up another analysis meeting. Whatever the case, the conductor is responsible for declaring a test a success or a failure (which may mean a partial success) and reporting the result to management. A simple form should document the results. It includes the test case identification number, the test date, and the result. If the result was unqualified success, no elaboration is required. If there were problems, these are described and the test conductor follows up to be sure programmers are assigned to correct them. The test conductor also takes the lead in deciding what further testing must be done after programmers make fixes. After a repair there are several testing options from which to choose:

1. The fix may involve a documentation change only, so that no retesting need be done.

2. The change may require a major overhaul in one or more program modules because the Problem Specification was misinterpreted. Sometimes, consultation with the customer will enable you to negotiate around making a change.

3. An analysis, design, or coding change may be required that affects portions of the system already tested. You should *assume* that all changes have that effect. Now the test conductor, with the programmers' help, decides how much regression testing is necessary. Regression testing means retesting previously finished portions of the system to insure that a late change does not ripple back through the system causing new problems. Regression-test decisions are tough to make. Simple changes have a way of churning up the very bowels of the system. Always lean toward more regression testing than the programmers advise.

4. Descriptive documentation (Coding Specifications) may be in error. These descriptions must agree exactly with the programs and with the Design Specification. Insist that every module submitted for system test be cleanly compiled—no patches or undocumented "stub" programs allowed.

When a system or subsystem has passed cleanly through the final system test, lock the programs and their documentation in the library to await acceptance demonstration.

## BETA TESTING

Some commercial software houses deliver early copies of software to users to test under normal conditions before formal release. This is called beta testing. You may add this form of testing to your arsenal, but don't substitute it for system test. Beta testers don't necessarily focus on making the system fail—often they simply use the product and report results. There is usually nothing structured about their "tests." Beta testers are often normal, decent people like you and me. They're not the fiends you need for a thorough system test.

## CUSTOMER TRAINING

In parallel with system testing, you train the customer to take over the new system. There are at least two areas requiring customer training: using the system and maintaining the system.

### Using the System

Usually, you are either replacing a previous system with a new one, or introducing a new system that will need to work with existing manual and automated procedures. In either case, customer personnel must learn to operate what you're turning over to them. You should consider all the usual means of training: formal classroom sessions, seminars, on-the job training, and computer-assisted instruction. Some training will be unique to your project; other forms may be available through your company's regular education program.

You will need to write and deliver user manuals for use both in training and in future operation of the system, and here is an opportunity to shine. Many good software systems are delivered with poor user guides. Bad writing reflects adversely on your whole system. Often the user information is the only tangible part of your product for the customer, who'll judge you by the kind of writing job you do, so take pains to do it well. Find people among your analysts who have a facility with words and can get a point across clearly and briefly. Then give their output to a professional technical writer. Use an outside firm if you have to. If you want professional user documentation, get some professionals to help you develop it! And start early. Get this job under way when you complete the design, not three days before acceptance.

### Maintaining the System

Often the customer has the job of making future changes to the system, and therefore must understand in detail the product you're delivering. You may need to train a nucleus of the customer's technical people who in turn will train others. Whatever the method of training used, you will need accurate and usable documentation. Two sets of descriptive documents, the Design Specification and the Coding Specifications, should completely and accurately describe your software system. In addition, you may write special troubleshooting manuals to enable others to understand special quirks of the system or to show them short cuts for probing difficult areas of code.

Sometimes customer training is a huge task because of the complexity of the system, the numbers of people to be trained, or the costs involved in training exercises (perhaps missiles must be launched or armed forces units deployed). In these situations, provide training under a separate contract that pays you for whatever effort you expend. Essentially, you keep on training until the customer says "enough."

If your customer is a government agency, there are appropriate kinds of contracts available, including "labor hour" and "time and material" contracts.

## BUGS AND DEFECTS

Some people refer to "bugs" in the system. There's historical precedent for this since one of the first recorded computer malfunctions was caused by a moth in the circuitry. I don't use the term any more. I call these things what they are: defects. There are things you need to remember about defects:

➤ Any defects in the design are the result of mistakes by the designers

➤ Any defects in the code are the result of mistakes by the programmers

➤ Any recurring mistakes in the design or the code are the result of mistakes by the manager

Every branch of engineering makes it a point to study mistakes and learn from them. If system testing detects a problem in a program, the nature of the problem needs to be communicated so that similar problems can be detected in future code inspections. Other code produced by the programmer who introduced the defect should be checked to ensure that the defect isn't present there as well.

There are a lot of people who scoff at the idea of producing "zero-defect" software. You shouldn't be one of them. I have led two projects that have never shown evidence of a defect, even after years of operation. Two projects is only a small fraction of the total number of projects I've managed, but the feeling of pride and accomplishment that came from these projects, not just for me but for everyone on the team, has not diminished.

---

### The Manager's Bookshelf

Although Glenford Myers's book *The Art of Software Testing* has been widely accepted as the standard reference on the subject of system testing, I recommend that you try instead to obtain a copy of *Software Testing Techniques* by Boris Beizer (1990). Dr. Beizer's thoughts about the relationship between testing and quality are required reading for anyone seriously interested in producing high-quality software systems.

**FIGURE 10–1**  The Tester   (Gerome, "Thumbs Down," Phoenix Art Museum, Museum Purchase.)

# 10

# The Tester

A newspaper article in 1985 reported the troubles taxpayers were having because the IRS had installed a new computer system and was experiencing difficulties with it. Nothing new there. Then the article went on: "As part of the conversion, experts rewrote 1,500 programs—a process that normally requires some debugging." Imagine that.

## WHO'S A TESTER?

Practically everybody gets involved in testing—analysts, designers, programmers, managers, customers, and, of course, testers. Throughout the project, people should always be preparing for the next round of testing. Rather than make a product and then figure out how to test it, which is wasteful serial thinking, do your test planning *in parallel* with other work. The day integration testing is to begin, know exactly the methodology you will use and have all test cases, procedures, and test data ready. The same goes for system test, acceptance test, and site test. All debate about the conduct of a test should be settled long before the test.

Lots more people should be involved in testing than is often the case. It's folly to leave all testing to the programmers. In some ways, they are the least qualified to test their products. That's no reflection on them. Even assuming the best of intentions, we can't expect the builder to be the most objective person in the world when it comes to testing the product—he or she will have dangerous blind

> "The relative simplicity of (the testing) functions does *not* imply that the persons performing them need not have much understanding of software reliability measurement. On the contrary! The data that the test team members and debuggers collect is the ultimate source of information generated as input to decision making. The quality of this data is vitally dependent on the intelligence and understanding that they apply in interpreting the real world conditions and complexities that they encounter."
>
> John D. Musa, Anthony Iannino, Kazuhira Okumoto,
> *Software Reliability* (1987; reproduced by permission)

spots. Any poor assumptions that went into the building of the product will carry over to the testing of that product by the builder. Would you want the builder of your house to be the one to pass it through building code inspection? Surely it's safer to rely on a licensed inspector (and hope he's not on the builder's payroll!).

There are distinct types of test activity during the project, and managers must make sensible choices of people who participate in each activity. Here are some thoughts about what should be done, by whom, when, and why.

## Module Test: The Programmer

This is the programmer's domain. The individual programmer tests his or her module, with the advice and assistance of coworkers and his or her manager or supervisor. (The manager is—that is, *should* be—involved in all levels of testing, so I won't keep repeating his or her involvement in succeeding paragraphs.)

In "the old days" programmers were left pretty much alone to conduct module tests. There was little guidance and often problems that should have been uncovered during module test showed up glaringly during higher-level tests. The most economical time to find and fix a problem is at the lowest level, where its repair generally involves one programmer and consumes only one programmer's time. A defect not found until later levels of test usually involves more people and wastes much more time—and, of course, one not found until acceptance test time is a real bummer.

There is growing emphasis on controlling module testing by setting standards and providing advice, either through a "teammate" system or involvement by the manager or supervisor. A first-level manager can save enormous amounts of lost time and all-around grief by getting involved with module testing. If you manage programmers, set a policy of reviewing (or at least appointing a senior programmer to do so) the module test plan each programmer has for each module. Module test plans need not be formal documents like the other test specifications, but simple explanations of how the programmer plans to test this module. The module test plan should be created when the programmer does the detailed design for the module—before the start of coding. The manager or another programmer can spot a lot and save plenty of wasted test time by looking over such a document. Probably the biggest benefit is that the programmer, knowing somebody is going to go over the test plan, will do a better job thinking it through.

## Integration Test: The Designer

Execution of integration tests is supervised by the designers during the Programming Process. *Planning* for integration testing should be done during the Design Process and early Programming Process and the designers are the ones who should develop these plans. Even earlier than the Design Process you should make basic decisions that directly affect integration: Are you integrating top-down, bottom-up, or some combination of the two? The best of all situations would be to *start* a project with all your analysis, design, programming, and test methodologies selected, rather than test on the fly. Don't let Dullard Designer lull you into bad planning:

"Gee, boss, it's only the design part of the project. We can't be planning integration tests yet—we don't even know what the programs will look like!"

"But, Dullard, we do know we're going top-down on this one, and we already have a good pass at the design. So why can't we be looking, for instance, at the set of stubs we'll need at different stages, and the test data we'll need?"

"Well, we could, but some of that will change by the time design is finished. . . ."

"True, but we'll have a start. In fact, some of our integration planning may have an impact on the design. If you find something awkward or almost impossible to test, sometimes a bit of redesign can eliminate the problem."

"Guess so . . ." muses Dullard.

"What we want, Dullard, is for integration to be as smooth as we can make it. I'm hoping, for a change, that you guys won't be down at the computer room all hours of the day and night. If we can plan this one right, everybody else in Super Software will take notice."

Dullard is weakening. That last job *was* a nightmare. And he has been wishing he could bring up his salary, but needs a good performance under his belt first.

"Okay, boss, you've got it!" He salutes, clicks his heels, and marches out.

A few days later Dullard brings in his rough integration test plan for you to look over.

"Hey, Dullard, this is looking pretty good." You resist the temptation to say this is what you wanted in the first place. "I especially like the way you've outlined how the tests and the test data and procedures are to be packaged. Nice neat bundles!"

"Yeah, the more I got into it, the more I liked it. *I'd* like a smooth integration this time, myself!"

"Okay, you guys go ahead and carry this to the next stage and let me see what you've got, say, the end of the week. Be sure to keep in close touch with the analysis crew so that they don't sandbag you by making some last-minute radical changes you don't know about."

"Will do. Now, there's something I need to talk to you about. Mind if I close the door?"

## System Test: The Analyst

Perform system test on the completed system after the designers have finished integration test. System test is planned and supervised by people other than the programmers and designers who decided how the system would be built. Since the analysts had a key role in defining what the system was to do, they have the responsibility to oversee the work of the system testers. The idea is to test the system against the requirements stated in the Problem Specification—to test, that is, from the customer's point of view. The designers and programmers may have produced an excellent, thoroughly debugged system, but it may not deliver quite what the customer really wanted.

Your system testers should be nasty. They must "think customer" and take special delight in making the programmers' product fail. Grade them on their cunning. They must exercise the system in ways the programmers, narrow-minded individuals that they are, never thought of but in ways that the customer might. The objective is to make the system fail before the acceptance phase, if it's going to fail at all.

As a practical matter, the programmers cannot be kept completely in the dark about the system testers' plans. The more information the programming team has, the better for everyone. But the data the system testers plan to use should not be available to the programmers, nor should the programmers in any way devise or execute the test procedures. The testers should not know the programmed innards of the system and should therefore be incapable of manipulating the system in secret and devious ways to get desired results. The system testers must act the part of the eventual user, who normally will not be someone conversant with programming. A good system test team is your final guarantee (well, almost) that you won't be embarrassed during the acceptance demonstration.

Your system testers should include members of the analysis team. They are in the best position to get inside the customer's head and devise tests to assure that the customer's requirements are met. But if your analysts all go on to become designers on this job, they are not suitable as the *sole* system testers. You need to supplement them with other people who can study the customer's requirements but not know the system structure. If there is a good salesman handy, he might be useful in system testing.

## Acceptance Test and Site Test: The Manager

And now for the unveiling. Here, Mr. Customer, is what you ordered!

Acceptance testing ought to be a boring demonstration of the system. The customer should be a key participant in executing the tests and in devising them in the first place. The customer will sometimes insist on introducing data to the system that you don't get to see beforehand. You should not balk at this, but you need to determine whether the data are legitimate—that is, whether they fall within the bounds specified in the Problem Specification.

The people who conduct, or assist the customer to conduct, acceptance test are the same people who conducted system test, with one notable addition—the manager must play an active role. The customer will be reacting to the system that he sees, and you, as the person with overall responsibility for creating the system, must be right there so that you see what the customer does. You should have observed the tests prior to acceptance, and you should be ready to point out the ways in which the system meets or even exceeds the original requirements. The manager also needs to be present to ensure that the demeanor of the testing team has changed from what it was in the previous tests. Rather than a pack of wild animals making life miserable for the programmers, when they participate in the acceptance tests their primary focus is to be of assistance to the customer.

Site testing, if necessary at all, is usually a rerunning of the acceptance tests at each geographical site where the system is installed. It generally requires the same people as acceptance testing, but some site tests (particularly on military projects) can be extensive and complex and might involve whole new cadres of testers.

When it comes to testing at any level, be a skeptic. No manager can afford to take too much on faith. First-level managers or supervisors must be involved in the test planning. *Know* what's in those test specifications. Question everything. It's not an insult to ask an employee to explain to you how he is doing something. Programming managers often hesitate to interject themselves into the work their people are doing, as though that would somehow show lack of trust. It's not lack of trust at all—it's a matter of giving guidance and understanding status, two things managers are supposed to be good at.

## WHAT GETS TESTED?

Everything. The first thing to remember is that you are testing a system, not an isolated program, and the system includes documents and procedures that make the programs usable. The major items are.

### Programs

This, of course, is the focus of most testing. Programs undergo module testing, integration, system testing, acceptance demonstration, maybe site testing, parboiling, wind tunnel testing, and chemical analysis.

### Documents

This, unfortunately, is where there is too little focus. Documents are considered evils of doubtful necessity and they are usually not subjected to rigorous testing. I'll give you a for-instance that may ring your bell. I'm sitting here pecking away at a personal computer keyboard, without which I believe I would never again write a sentence. This thing and its text-processing programs are wonderful (except for a few bizarre happenings now and then). But the manuals try one's patience. If you'll pardon a terrible paraphrase: When a programmer is good, he's very good, but when he writes, he's horrid!

But if a programmer's writing is horrid, and if that horrid writing becomes part of a product people pay good money for, then the programmer's management is horrid. Come on, now, stop letting that junk get by. I know all the excuses: We ran out of time; the customer cut our funding; tech pubs screwed up; my wife had a baby. . . . It's all rubbish. The reason for bad writing getting out is the same as the reason for bad programs getting out: things are not planned well enough in the first place, and not executed well enough in the second place, and not tested well enough in the third place. All that boils down to managers who let trash get by.

You can do lots better than the general track record. First, identify the documents that are *really* important. The list might look like this:

➤ Proposal
➤ Problem Specification
➤ Design Specification
➤ Coding Specifications
➤ User manuals

Concentrate on them. There is plenty more paper around, but these are part of the final product and they all usually go to the customer, so sharpen them first.

Next, schedule the writing and editing and rewriting of these documents as carefully as you schedule design time or programming time or test time. Don't treat documents as leftovers. Have them written by people who like to write and are good at it, rather than automatically assign the writing to the programmers who wrote the programs. Talk to the people in tech pubs, if they are to produce your finished documents. Understand their needs and schedule with them in mind.

Finally, *test* your documents. We've made real improvement in testing some of them, especially the design and program descriptions, by means of formal inspections. But such critical writings as the user manuals lag behind everything else. That's insane, because they represent your work to the customer.

Question: How would you test something like a user manual?

Answer: Have people who did not write the thing carefully read every word and try to follow the operations described. This can be *very* enlightening.

Enlist the customer's own people early to help with this chore. Don't rely on your own people—get the user involved.

How about the documents that describe the actual program code? First, you never deliver a code listing that has not been cleanly compiled. That doesn't assure that the *code* is correct in the first place, but that's another subject. Second, have the people who are to be the maintenance programmers (often the customer's people) spot-check the code listings for organization, commenting, and general readability.

## Procedures

You need to test the procedures for using the system. While the testers follow scripts intended to simulate the eventual customer use of the system, they need to pay attention not only to whether something works as specified, but whether it was specified intelligently in the first place. Is the system in any way awkward to use? Are instructions or outputs ambiguous? Does the system do all it can to reduce manual operations? Are menus clear and concise? Does a given set of actions always produce the same response, or are there differing, confusing responses?

There is a whole branch of testing, called "usability testing," that concentrates on whether a system can be used effectively by the people who are supposed to use it. This is not the same thing as determining whether the system is logically correct. A system can have no technical or logical defects and still be a failure. This is because the system, which was built to help people do their jobs better, actually makes the job more difficult by requiring (for example) extensive screen navigation during data entry or by presenting inquiry results in a poorly organized format.

Get your "usability testing" underway early, and involve your users.

## WARRANTIES: A DISTANT GOAL

I dream of a time when programs might carry warranties at least as good as washing machine warranties. Here's how the "warranty" for one of my personal computer programs reads:

> The program is provided "as is" without warranty of any kind, either expressed or implied, including, but not limited to the implied warranties of merchantability and fitness for a particular purpose. The entire risk as to the quality and performance of the program is with you.

Is there another product anywhere that gets away with such an incredible copout? We can do better. I may never see a real program warranty, but I do expect to see better programs and better manuals (in fact, the most recent ones I've used *are* better than their predecessors). Improvement comes with better management.

## IS THE BUG REALLY GONE?

In the early eighties I owned an old house that I planned to renovate. Soon after I moved in I discovered a lot of cotenants: mice. I bought a "live" trap and set it every night and every night I caught a mouse. Each morning I carried the trap back to the edge of some woods about a hundred yards away and let the mouse loose. This went on for weeks. I lost count somewhere, but by the time I had ferried more than thirty mice to their new home in the great outdoors, I began to think they all looked suspiciously alike. Could it be? . . . Nah! But still I had visions of those mice following me to the house and sneaking back in (an easy way to get a nightly snack and then take a nice trip in the morning).

I felt pretty silly about this. I didn't think they were smart enough to get back home, but I figured I'd better be sure. I dabbed some paint on the ears of the next few and watched for them to show up again. How else to be really sure? Well, I caught another ten or so, and then no more. None of them had paint on their ears.

You need to track the defects during system test the way I tracked the mice. Tag them. Pay special attention to record-keeping. Every time your testers find a problem not caught during integration, log and track it until a correction has been made and retesting and regression testing have been completed. There are some simple rules that, if really honored, will keep you out of trouble during system test:

➤ When the testers uncover a problem and turn it over to the programmers for resolution, log it, give it a unique identifier (paint its ears), and assign it to a specific tester for follow-up.

➤ When a solution is found and tested by the programmers, they should submit to the system testers a newly compiled module or modules with a fresh listing and no patches.

➤ The system tester and the programmer should jointly decide how much regression testing is necessary to assure that the repair job to the carburetor did not mess with the ignition. The system tester has the final say, and he or she should err on the conservative side: When in doubt, retest. Your schedule for system testing must allow for plenty of backing up and retesting (regression testing). Give a polygraph test to the programmer who insists the fix he made affects only his module.

➤ Keep an accurate record of the modules making up any given version of the system being tested. *Never* allow two modules to exist having the same identifier.

➤ Resist any pressure or temptation to release versions of your system prematurely to different geographical locations. If the system is not yet through system test, it must remain at the "home" test site.

Some of your programmers will dislike the logging and tracking business, but the good ones, the experienced ones, will not. Don't tolerate the others. Train them, make them understand the importance of control during testing.

Here's one example.

> "But, boss, I did everything we were taught in that class we took. My module is
> loose as a goose, hardly any coupling at all . . . and there are *no* pathological connec-
> tions. I tell you, the bug was entirely confined to my module!"
>
> "Hmmmm! My understanding is that in fixing the bug you had to change a flag
> setting?"
>
> Sure, but the only other module that uses the flag is one I wrote!"
>
> "That so?"
>
> "Sure!" A moment's silence. "Except maybe PRINTX . . . wonder if it uses it
> now?"

Looks like more than one problem here, going all the way back to your basic
design. You begin to rethink your opposition to capital punishment.

Here's another example.

> Your manager pressured you and you gave in and sent your system out to four
> different sites for continued system testing. There were not enough testers to go
> around, of course, so programmers were pressed into service as system testers. You
> started everybody off with the same version of the system and with the same instruc-
> tions for logging problems.
>
> Now it's two weeks later and you have a mess on your hands. Each day's logs and
> problem reports are relayed back to your central office by fax and one of your system
> testers has the job of coordinating the reports from the four sites. There are now at least
> four different versions of the system in operation. A bug fixed at one site gets relayed to
> the others to keep all four systems current, but some get installed slightly differently
> from one site to the next and some don't get installed at all because the people at the
> other sites are busy fixing other bugs. Sometimes the same bug shows up simultaneously
> at all the sites and it ends up being fixed differently at each site. Sometimes the same bug
> gets fixed four times at one site in four different ways. You hire a statistician to make
> some sense out of the pile of reports, but he soon loses contact with reality and has to be
> locked up. Another couple of weeks and the foul-up is so bad you convince your man-
> ager (and the customer who pressured him to pressure you to do this parallel work in the
> first place) that the only thing to do is retreat, start back at the home base with the origi-
> nal "clean" version of the system, and repeat system test from the beginning.

What I've related has actually happened any number of times, except the last
part. I don't know of a case where management called everyone home for a
restart. You can't afford to lose control of testing. If you don't paint their ears,
you'll never be sure those bugs are not returning.

## AVOIDING PANIC

The project's managers sit around a conference table for the weekly system test report. Floyd Hotshot stands at the easel pointing to a chart and sums up the week's
activities:

". . . In the B-series of tests we ran 135 consecutive test cases without an error. . . ."

A smattering of applause and smiles all around. Peter Projectmanager rubs his hands. "Good going, Floyd!"

Floyd continues, "In the C-series we successfully cycled the system for fourteen hours before the first problem. . . ."

PROBLEM! WHAT PROBLEM! cry all the managers in unison. Two of them pass out and need smelling salts. Sixteen minutes later the company president arrives. He announces he has mobilized all the company's forces, and the National Guard is on alert. He is quite sure he can get the governor to declare Super Software a disaster area.

Okay, so I'm overdoing it a little bit. But only a little. Our entire upbringing urges us to pounce on problems and make them the center of our activity. Newspapers and TV news shows depend on problems—ever read a whole page or hear a whole half-hour of *good* news? Bad kids get lots of attention and good ones quietly do things well without fanfare. We come under the influence of Barbara Tuchman's Law: *The fact of being reported multiplies the apparent extent of any deplorable development by five- to tenfold.* Her book, *A Distant Mirror,* describes the calamitous fourteenth century, a time filled with chaos, crisis, and bad news, but she could just as well have been describing everyday life on a twentieth-century programming project. Rational people do irrational things when confronted by an apparent project problem. How can you avoid overreacting when problems strike?

1. Put the same emphasis on reporting smooth progress as on reporting failures. That way, a problem is kept in perspective.

2. *Plan* to have problems. Never manage under the assumption that all will go smoothly.

3. Plan to replan. Nobody is smart enough or farseeing enough to plan any sizable project fully at the outset and never need to make any changes.

4. Don't be talked out of ignoring your good sense and experience. If you have a truly tough problem and it's clear you need more resources, make your stand *now*, get the resources, and go on with the job. You'll have to take a stand sooner or later—either when the problem first arises and you see the need for help, or later, after you go ahead with nothing but hope and things get even worse.

5. When you need more resources, don't make foolish tradeoffs. The most common situation is that you need more calendar time, but your management and the customer offer you everything *except* calendar time. Adding people or even computer time rarely solves programming problems. Most often, what is needed is more time spent in analysis or design or system test or all three. Time means calendar time, not people-hours. You cannot make up for incomplete analysis or design by throwing more people into programming or testing. What's frustrating about offering this kind of advice is that everybody

already knows it. There is only the question of the will and the guts and the integrity to admit what you need and to act on that knowledge wisely rather than hope that on *this* project, throwing in eighty-six more programmers will solve the problem.

6. Plan your panic. There may be a time or two on a project when you need a short period of intense activity to get back on track and make up for a missed milestone. These drills should be rare, and of short duration, if they are to succeed. People who are routinely treated well will rally and push hard to get things back on track, but they won't do it every other week, nor should you ask them to. Testers, in particular, should be expected to put in some extra hours to do some regression testing and get the project back on schedule. Once they accomplish that, they should return to normal hours. In testing, 'normal' is hectic enough.

---

*You know your testers are doing a good job if*

    They want to spend more time with the users.
    They take pride in finding defects.
    They want to attend code inspections.
    They retest the things that weren't changed in the latest revision.
    They take the quality of the system personally.

# ACCEPTANCE

Up to now, we have been concerned with work done by teams of people. Acceptance is more of a two-person game. You, as the manager, will meet with your customer. You will have the Contract and the Problem Specification and the System Test report with you. You will jointly verify that the system does what the customer asked that it do.

All of this should be easy, but often it isn't. Acceptance, like every other facet of the project, needs to be planned and managed. The criteria for acceptance must be clear. The demonstrations of required functionality must be relevant to the Contract and the Problem Specification. There must be clear understanding between you and the customer on all issues that affect acceptance.

Acceptance isn't automatic. You need to work for it.

**FIGURE 11–1**  Acceptance  (The Union Pacific and Central Pacific Railroads at Promontory Point, Utah, May 10, 1869.)

# 11

# The Acceptance Process

At last it's time to deliver. All your work up till now aimed at making this process entirely predictable. There should be no surprises. The objective of this process is to show the customer that the system you are ready to deliver satisfies the contract you both signed. If you have worked closely with the customer (especially the user) during all the preceding processes, this one *should* be the easiest one of all.

## ACCEPTANCE TEST SPECIFICATION

The Acceptance Test Specification (see Appendix) is the guide to acceptance testing. Its test cases are similar to—and often the *same* as—those used in system test.

You write the Acceptance Test Specification in concert with the customer. You draft, he approves. In some cases there is a role reversal: The customer prepares the tests and you help. Such switched roles are an important exception to the norm and the contract should define these roles carefully.

There is no point presenting your first version of an acceptance document near the end of the project. The customer won't agree to it, and you'll be in trouble. Instead, produce this specification in stages. First, during the Definition Process, write the section called "Acceptance Criteria" (or "Success Criteria"). This is a critical document; it states the specific conditions under which the customer will formally accept your product. Then write the remaining sections of the Acceptance Test Specification and construct the test cases. Do this as you develop the system.

The Acceptance Test Specification should be finished at the same time as the System Test Specification so that the two may share test cases.

## ACCEPTANCE CRITERIA

Acceptance criteria are the conditions your system must satisfy before the customer will formally accept the system and agree that it satisfies the contract. Writing acceptance criteria is one of your most difficult chores. Your customer will be tough about this, and should be. Whoever signs an acceptance agreement knows that his or her job is on the line. Any chummy agreements you and the customer may have had in the past are out the window.

You *should* settle acceptance criteria before a contract is signed. Sometimes, however, you can only agree on general criteria that early. The least that the contract should state are a schedule for writing the final criteria and time restrictions on the customer for reviewing your drafts. The customer must agree to accept or reject your acceptance specifications within defined times. Without this clause, you may use up all your calendar time and budget and still have no agreement about acceptance terms. In setting up times for review and revision of documents, allow for more than a single iteration. Assume that the customer will want you to make changes and allow time for a second draft.

Base acceptance criteria on quantitative, measurable conditions. Your goal should be to remove subjectivity from assessment of test results (this applies to any test). If you can include in your criteria a statement that "report ABC shall be printed within three minutes after push-button request," that's far better than saying, "report ABC shall be printed within a reasonable time after push-button request." You and your customer can time three minutes with a stopwatch, but you may never agree on what is a "reasonable" time.

Acceptance criteria cover not only system performance, but delivery of the system as well. When and where should copies of the system be delivered? How many copies? In what form? How should materials be packaged? One deliverable should be the set of test cases used during acceptance demonstration.

To understand what would be good acceptance criteria, let's consider examples of bad ones. Here are some taken from actual acceptance documents:

➤ *The contractor will have priority in using the customer's computers for program acceptance checkout.*
What priority? Highest? Lowest? This statement means nothing.

➤ *An appropriate number of messages shall be included to test the system exhaustively.*
What's appropriate? Ten messages or ten thousand? What does "exhaustively" mean?

➤ *The contractor shall, with the customer's assistance, prepare test messages to exercise all options listed in the scope of work.*
How much customer assistance? Who does the analysis? Who actually types the messages? This job could take one person a week or a year.

➤ *The visual display of target tracking data shall take place in a timely manner consistent with the existing threat conditions.*
What does that mean? Whooooie!

➤ *The contractor shall make such changes as the customer directs within thirty days following formal acceptance demonstration.*
This statement within proper context might not be bad, but it was not in proper context. It amounted to an open-ended commitment by the contractor.

The strange thing about all these goofs is that they are part of acceptance agreements written by contractors, not by customers!

## EXECUTION

You conduct acceptance testing much the same as system testing, but with these differences. First, the customer plays an active role in acceptance testing. He supplies people to do some or all of the manual operations. The customer figures heavily in posttest analysis and is required, of course, to approve a test before it can be considered complete or successful. Second, the customer may insist on introducing into the system data you have never seen or used before. Third, acceptance may be conditional. For example, you may need to run later tests at scattered geographic locations ("site test") to achieve full acceptance. Fourth, you should be a full-time participant. Discussions with customers about what did or didn't happen during acceptance testing will be far more positive and productive if you were "in the trenches" when the acceptance test was performed.

## DOCUMENTATION

As acceptance testing proceeds, you may find minor flaws in both the user documentation and the system's descriptive documentation. You must make corrections, of course, before delivering the final documents to the customer. For this reason, plan to deliver final documentation at the end of the Acceptance Process or even later, so that corrections may be included cleanly. The alternative is to deliver documents earlier and then bear the expense and inconvenience of issuing errata sheets. As a buyer of many products yourself, you'll probably agree that correction pages are a nuisance and they cheapen the product. If you are using a professional technical writer to create and modify the user documentation, you'll find that he will probably insist on handling documentation properly, no matter how many corners you're tempted to cut.


## TESTING AND TIMELINESS

Many companies insist on lengthy and involved testing processes. In some cases, the time required for mandatory testing doesn't leave enough time for the careful analysis and programming that prevents bugs from getting into the system. It's a vicious circle.

As a manager, you need to work with the customer to ensure that testing does the job it is intended to do and that it doesn't become an exercise performed simply for the sake of performing it.

An approach that's worked for me in reducing the time required for testing without reducing testing effectiveness is to work with the user in designing and administering both the system test and the acceptance test. As I said at the beginning of this chapter, the acceptance test can be expected to repeat many of the scripts that

---

➤ Today is December fifteenth.

➤ The business needs the new system by the first of May.

➤ The testing cycle requires ninety days, finishing with ten days of acceptance testing.

➤ This means that you must start System Testing by February first. You estimate that it will take sixty days to build the system and this means you won't be complete until February fifteenth.

➤ If you turn over the system on February first, you will have lost fifteen days that you could have used for design and code inspections.

➤ The system you turn over to the testers will have more defects than it would have if you had the extra fifteen days.

➤ Bowing to management pressure, you turn over the system on February first and hope for the best.

➤ The testers find a bunch of errors.

➤ The testers go to corporate management and show that the testing cycle needs to be lengthened because of all the errors that aren't caught during module testing by the developers.

➤ It's now December fifteenth of the following year.

➤ The business needs a new system by the first of May.

➤ The testing cycle now requires 100 days, including twenty days of acceptance testing.

➤ Good luck.

were executed during the system test. If you can work with the customer to eliminate testing that is redundant, you will be able to save time and the customer can
start getting the benefits of the new system faster.

## SITE TESTING

This testing may amount to simply repeating earlier acceptance tests in a new environment. In some cases, site testing may be a huge job requiring a great deal of
training and expense. In this category are monster defense projects that require independently tested data processing, weapons, guidance, and communications subsystems to be merged and tested together at an operational site.

If your project requires site testing, you should take care to plan for it. Write a
Site Test Specification similar to the Integration, System, and Acceptance Test
Specifications described earlier.

There are several areas of difference between the testing we have discussed
thus far and site testing. First, the computer equipment at the operational site may
not be identical to that used during the preceding processes. There may be differences in input-output devices, versions of operating systems, storage sizes, and even
different models of a family of computers that could affect the speed of execution
and the instruction repertoire available.

Second, at an operational site your system may run for the first time without
simulation. Until site test time, you may have had to rely on simulation as a source
of inputs to your system or as a receiver of outputs, or both. Strange things happen
when you replace simulators with the real thing, no matter how brilliantly you
planned and built the simulators.

Third, the data base your system uses at the operational site may be different
from that used previously. For example, some data may be site identifiers or geographic location coordinates. Data base changes can drive you bonkers. You must
thoroughly test the tiniest adjustments.

---

It's generally accepted that defects that are found during site testing
arise in four primary areas. In ascending order of impact to the schedule, they are:

1. Areas where you thought you might find a problem, if any problems existed.
2. Areas where you didn't think you'd have any problems.
3. Areas where you *knew* there weren't any problems.
4. Areas where the idea of a problem was so remote that you never
   gave it any thought at all.

Fourth, your system may be only one of several components that must work together to yield the required result. You'll need to meet with the other groups that are involved to set up joint problem isolation and analysis procedures. As you go through the test, resist any temptation to indulge in finger-pointing when problems surface. Your job is to get your system accepted and you won't be able to do that without cooperation from people and organizations that you do not control. I'll have more to say about this in Chapter 12.

If you are to install and test your system at several sites simultaneously, make sure that the system is really *ready* to be sent out. The communication problems among several teams operating in the field at different locations will be difficult enough without the irritant of a buggy system that you should never have released.

---

*The Manager's Bookshelf*

If you only buy one of the books that I am recommending to you at various places throughout this volume, it ought to be *In the Age of the Smart Machine: The Future of Work and Power* by Shoshanna Zuboff (1988.) This is a book about users and what happens to users when computers become part of the working landscape. You are building systems that manage information for users and Ms. Zuboff's book helps you understand how you are affecting those who are supposed to benefit from your work.

---

**FIGURE 12–1**  The Customer  (Munch, "The Cry," Museum of Fine Arts, Boston. William Francis Warren Fund.)

# 12

# The Customer

"Do you, Super Software, Inc., take this fellow to be your lawfully contracted customer, till death do you part?"

"Well . . . I don't know about this death bit. . . ."

"How about 'till product is delivered'?"

"Yeah, okay, I'll buy that. I mean, I do!"

"And do you, Mr. Customer, take Super Software, Inc., to be your lawfully contracted contractor?"

"Well . . ."

"Come on, now, I've got other things to do! Yes or no?"

"Well, okay, I guess, but I've got to like the product!"

"That okay with you, Super Software, Inc.?"

"I think so, but what if he doesn't like anything I do?"

"Yes or no?"

"Ummmm, well, I guess, sure, but . . ."

"By God, make a decision!"

"Yes! Okay! I will! I do!"

"About time! I now pronounce you contractor and customer. You may embrace."

"Now, wait a minute!"

> One of the best customers I ever had was Dan Ryan, the founder of Ryan Homes. The project I managed was going well and I was constantly trying to arrange for him to come over to see how nicely his new system was coming to life. He never came. When I asked him about this, he told me that there was no point to his showing up. He couldn't make the project go any more smoothly and he thought that he would simply interrupt progress. "If you want me to come over," he said, "you'll have to screw something up that I can help fix."

## THE HONEYMOON

Courtship has ended and it's time to get serious. Depending on how new the customer people are to you—you may have flirted with them on a prior contract and certainly during the proposal stage—you may have to spend considerable time getting to know them. You'll need to find out who is responsible for what, who speaks with authority, who is likely to be a weak link, who plays politics, whom you can rely on for accurate data. Meanwhile, the customer is learning the same things about you.

Project managers often enter a contract in a negative frame of mind, ready for an adversary relationship rather than a partnership. That's totally crazy, since both of you want the same thing: a smooth project and an excellent product. Managers need to be careful how they speak about the customer. Wry comments or nasty customer jokes are likely to be picked up by your project people and translated into a generally negative view of the customer. If you go about referring to one of the customer's people as a fool, that's how your subordinates are going to view him. Don't forget, like it or not, managers are role models and their behavior will be aped by others in subtle ways.

Your dealings with your customer must be honest (it makes me wince even to have to say that). You don't have to love your customer, although it would help, but you must be straight with each other. A difficult job I worked on became more difficult because our management and the customer's management both understood early that the contract job definition was seriously flawed, yet neither could admit this publicly. It was a strain that negatively affected the entire job. Neither side had the guts or the sense to admit errors, set things right, and go from there. If you find yourself spending lots of time in meetings discussing stratagems for sidestepping the customer, take that as a warning that you need to refocus on your relationship with him. I'm not talking about ordinary disagreements that arise between any two groups of people, but about deeper problems that keep you awake at night.

## FIDELITY

Well, where do things stand this week, Mr. Contractor? Oh? But I thought you reported those modules done last week! Ah, I see. Somebody found one more little bug. Well, those things happen . . . guess you'll have to revise your bar charts, eh? I mean, since you showed this module 100 percent done last week. What's that you say? Now they're 110 percent? Ha! Ha! That's a good one, by golly! What? You're serious? Listen, what is this—a football game? You know, I'm beginning to worry about you.

Unfaithfulness begins with small things and pretty soon the marriage is ruined. Once you lose the customer's trust, it's hard to rebuild. Obviously, you need to prevent erosion by concentrating on accurate status reporting.

*Inaccurate* reporting occurs through (a) dishonesty, and (b) actual confusion about where things stand. Although dishonesty gets the headlines, it's not the more common scenario. Most often confusion is the culprit because understanding the exact status of programming jobs is tough. We know the near-impossibility of testing every path, for example, in even a simple program.

The most important requirement for accurate reporting of status is defining a realistic and sensible base against which to report. You can get much closer to Truth by scrapping all "percent complete" reporting. Describing the completion of program modules in terms of "percent complete" is a foolish exercise. There is no telling when you are 50 percent done, since the next test may expose a bug that will set the progress clock way back. Yet it's not enough to say "it's done when it's done." You and the customer need better information than that.

---

Actually heard at a status meeting:

"The system is 90 percent complete, and we expect to finish the remaining 40 percent in the next sixty days."

---

A better way is to track and report only on the status of two kinds of items: (1) *tangibles*, such as technical reports, analysis documents, design documents, test plans, user manuals, and even "completed" code; and (2) specific *events*, such as the execution of test cases.

When you developed your Project Plan back at the beginning of the job, each item on the plan should have been associated with a clear deliverable so that you could demonstrate conclusively (if only to yourself) that the plan item had been completed.

The items in your original plan provide the basis for reporting progress to your customer. Naturally, there are some items that you will use *within* the project to make sure that you are making forward progress. There are other items that you will use to demonstrate to the customer that the project is proceeding according to plan.

For *internal* purposes, you might develop a list of the reporting items for each program module. Your list might look like this:

➤ Detailed module design reviewed
➤ Code review completed

➤  Test cases defined and documented

➤  Test case #1 executed successfully

➤  Test case #2 executed successfully

➤  Test case #3 executed successfully

➤  Test case #n . . .

➤  Module documentation corrected

➤  Module submitted for integration


There are some "ifs" and "buts" even about this approach. If test case #3 fails and results in a program change, then you must do appropriate regression testing (clean compilation of the module, followed by rerunning test case #3, and maybe rerunning #1 and #2). What is important is that you have the most stable items possible to report on—and the items must be meaningful. It would be self-defeating, for example, if test cases 1 to n-1 were trivial and test case n were seismic. The approach is not foolproof and you can still get into trouble if you do not construct your list of items thoughtfully, but this method is a great deal more accurate and helpful than the thoroughly discredited percent complete method.

You can use your lists to define *milestone events* that can be used by both you and your customer to determine if the project is proceeding as planned. As an example, there may be a group of modules that enable the system to accept a customer order. Your plan should show when your system will be able to demonstrate the order-taking function and you can invite your customer to see part of the system in action when that occurs.

Milestone events that show the system performing a task that is important to the customer are the foundation of a good status reporting process. They provide a point of focus not only for the customer, but for the project team as well.

As important as constructing a sensible reporting method is the advertising of that method. Describe to the customer just what each milestone event means and what a report of "complete" for any item means. Describe how regression testing can influence the report from one week to the next. Point out the amount of detail that supports each milestone event. Having done all that in your most honest and earnest way, you can now expect the customer to be, week by week, no more confused than you.


## THE BAD NEWS BEARER

One of the toughest things you will have to do as a manager is to give the customer bad news. You *will* have to do this at some point in your career. It is not a pleasant task and if you don't handle it well, it can become downright awful. Here are some rules I have learned that help me when I am faced with a bad situation and need to inform the customer.

➤ Determine how bad the news is. If you have a good Project Plan and have been following that plan and tracking your team's progress, you should be able to gauge the impact of a design error, a key person leaving the project, late delivery of needed components, or other events that threaten the timely delivery of the system that the customer expects.

➤ Decide how you will address the problem. Identify resources that can help you recover lost time. Determine if you can meet your original schedule with reduced functionality, adding the missing parts as a second release. Estimate the additional time and cost to fix the problem. Figure out how to prevent it from recurring.

➤ Give your customer an objective appraisal of the situation, including your recommended approach to dealing with the problem. Don't minimize the problem, but don't overstate it either. The solution to a project problem usually requires action by both you and your customer. Be prepared to spend time exploring alternatives with your customer and arrive at a joint decision on how to proceed. Modify your Project Plan to reflect this decision.

Many managers, particularly those who are managing one of their first projects, will try to minimize problems when reporting them to the customer. "It's no big deal. We'll work over the weekend to get back on schedule," they'll tell the customer. This approach doesn't work. If your project starts slipping by a day here or there in the early stages, it will almost always slip by weeks or months as it gets nearer to completion.

Some managers panic when this happens and request an additional three months for work that could be completed in an additional three weeks.

Whether she's minimizing the problem or overstating it, the manager has stopped managing. She is simply thrashing about, trying to find a way out of a difficult situation. In the first case (no big deal), she is looking for words that will minimize criticism from the customer. In the second case (another year and another million dollars), she is asking for more than is needed in order not to have to announce a second round of bad news.

When bad news shows up, it's your job to *manage* it. Use your Project Plan and existing experience with your project team to give your customer an honest appraisal of what happened, how serious it is, and the course of action you recommend to recover from it. Customers don't like receiving bad news any more than you like to present it. About the only thing they dislike more is not getting the truth about the bad news when it happens.

## CHANGE MANAGEMENT (AGAIN)

Chapter 6 offers a simple mechanism for managing change. Here I want to emphasize that any change management procedures you employ will work better if you educate your customer. If he knows exactly how to make a change request and how you intend to handle each request, you'll minimize strife over proposed changes.

Don't forget: You can't even have a meaningful discussion about a change if you and the customer don't agree that what is being proposed *is* a change. He may feel that what he is proposing fits within the original work scope. There is only one way to avoid that problem: the job must be accurately defined in the contract and in the Problem Specification written early in the project by your analysts.

As a practical matter, be prepared to accommodate changes if you can without jeopardizing your schedule or your budget. When you have to say no, it can help if you have previously been able to say yes a few times.


## STEPCHILDREN

You may have to live with some customer people joining your own staff to work to-gether on the project. Make sure you have control over them if your success de-pends on their work, and be wary when assigning them tasks on your critical path.

The first place they will show up is generally in the initial processes of speci-fication and analysis. A customer representative who is knowledgeable, interested, and energetic can provide substantial assistance in helping you and your analysts understand what the customer's needs and wants really are.

However, you may find that you have been saddled with a customer represen-tative who is more a hindrance than a help. These come in several shapes and sizes:

➤ The fellow who thinks that he, not you, is actually running the project and tries to show it by dominating meetings and giving direction to your staff.

➤ The young lady who will try to use your project to grind her own political ax by steering you away from contacts and information that will later turn out to be vital. She does this because she feels that the manager of the widget de-partment (who will be a heavy user of your system) got the promotion that she should have had.

➤ The person who believes that only the part of the project that affects his work is important and who can't be bothered to consider the broader impacts for his company.

➤ The person who was assigned to the project because everyone else was too busy with important stuff.

➤ . . . and others equally helpful.

Telling your customer that you aren't satisfied with the help that has been of-fered to you is always a touchy matter. Your best chance of doing this without caus-ing hard feelings that will poison the project over the longer term is to make up a job description for each representative provided by the customer before the representative joins the project team. The job description should spell out in detail the contribution that the representative is to make to the project and should identify tasks that the representative is expected to perform. It should be explicit in describing the time that the representative is expected to contribute. Go over the job description jointly with the representative and the customer and get common agreement on what the representative's activities and schedule will be.

If experience shows that the representative isn't doing her job, you will have specifics to point to when the time comes to ask for someone new.

Even when your customer representatives are everything you could have hoped for, you may still run into problems. The "borrowed" customer people might like what they see in your organization and want to leave home and join you. You must avoid even the appearance of pirating. When customer employees make overtures, the only reasonable thing to do is tell them straightforwardly that, under the circumstances, you cannot even consider bringing them into your group until the contract has ended or unless they first openly inform their management that they want to join you. Even so, you may not be interested in them, and if so you need to persuade them, gently but firmly, that there can be no further discussion of the matter until the project ends. There are all kinds of possibilities here; the best advice is to be sensitive to what's happening and avoid encouraging anyone to jump ship.

## Other Offspring

Jake Customer answers his phone: "Hello! Jake here!"

"Hello, Jake! This is Pete Projectmanager. How are you?"

"Fine, Pete. What's up?"

"Well, now that we're under way on the project—and doing nicely, I might add—I'd like to touch base with you about how we might work together in the future."

"Oh? What future work do you have in mind?" Jake's fingers begin tapping his desktop.

"I hear you're thinking about automating your gum machines."

Jake sits upright. "Where did you hear that?"

"It's pretty common knowledge. . . ."

"Well, that's something! I'm gonna have to plug these leaks somehow!"

"I won't spread the word, Jake. Trust me." Jake shudders. He trusts no one. "Anyway, do you think we might have some informal talks about it . . . by the time you're ready to roll we might have some decent ideas to offer."

Jake pauses. "Peter," he begins slowly, "it's a little early. We're barely into the current project. And by the way, I understand we missed the first milestone. . . ."

"The problem spec . . . yes, it's a little late, but . . ."

"When we do the gum machines, I want to be sure we go with the right contractor. It'll be a sticky job."

"Sure, sure, Jake. Well, listen, we'll talk more. Just wanted you to know Super Software is ready to serve you!" He manages a hearty but hollow laugh and ends the conversation.

Conceiving follow-on work only makes sense if the marriage is going smoothly. Don't talk about follow-on jobs before showing you can handle the current one. I state the obvious because I've witnessed the dilution of effort on contracts by expending effort too soon on follow-on. In each case the result was negative. One customer, an important one, finally put his foot down and told the project manager: Don't talk to me about XYZ; let's see if you can do ABC first!

## SOMETHING YOU ALREADY KNOW, BUT RARELY THINK ABOUT

Some managers seem to spend all their time trying to manage the customer relationship. Others spend most of their time managing the technical work. Successful managers understand that both of these are important and that each project demands its own balance between them. The balance is defined by the nature of the technical task, the behavior of the customer, the maturity of the project team, and the business context of the project.

As a project manager, you need to periodically take the time to evaluate where you are putting your emphasis and why. It is a worthwhile exercise to get to the office fifteen minutes early so you will have time to think about the question "Out of the things I could do today, which ones will make the most difference to project success?"

## HAPPILY EVER AFTER

Break your vows and expect divorce. Be caring and honest and hardworking, and look for a happy relationship.

If you treat your customer as a nuisance or a "necessary evil," you're in for trouble. Think of the people you've dealt with in life when *you* were the customer. There are incredible numbers of people out there who have no business facing a customer—people who are surly, unsmiling, or just don't give a damn. Those who make you feel welcome stand out because they are so rare. They are the people you're most likely to do more business with.

Back to the idea of service. If you can be happy providing excellent service, you have a shot at a successful relationship with your customer. If you give service grudgingly, you have an unhappy time ahead of you.

*You know you have a good customer if*

He insists that your analysts, designers, and programmers talk to his users.

He wants to hear any bad news as early as possible.

He wants proof of getting high quality.

He wants you to suggest ways to make the system more valuable.

He gives you plenty of advance notice before changing any requirements.

# PART VII

# MIGRATION

You have completed the analysis, design, programming and testing. Your customer has looked at the system that was built for him and has stated his satisfaction with your work. Now comes the tricky part.

When you place your new system in production, you will be moving out another system that the customer uses on a regular basis to run her business. You need to be sure that none of the existing data is corrupted and that you don't lose any transactions. You need to be sure that the users are aware of the changes and you need to be prepared to deal with occasional misunderstandings and questions. "Why did you move the account number over here? I'm not used to seeing it on the left. I've already messed up twice by using the part number, which is where the account number used to be. Get this #@!**! system out of here and put me back on something that works!"

For really big systems, the time and cost required for migrating from the old system to the new system can be greater than the cost and time needed for the development of either one. Even with small systems, the potential for extensive disruption of the data processing workflow can be substantial.

To get through migration successfully, you'll come to appreciate the skills of the support staff that has been laboring in relative obscurity while your programmers and analysts occupied center stage. Migration requires the work of many hands and a healthy respect for Murphy's Law.

**FIGURE 13–1** Migration (Breugel: "Parable of the Blind" The National Museum, Naples.)

# 13

# The Migration Process

The odds are better than four to one that the system you are building will replace a system that is now in place. It probably won't be a one-for-one replacement. Your system may have new technology. It may consolidate functions currently performed by several other systems. It may split out some functionality that has been buried in an enormous mainframe program that can no longer be modified safely. In some cases, such as a shift from mainframe to distributed client-server technology, the migration process may be more complex, time-consuming, and expensive than development of the new system.

No matter what the situation is, you are still going to be faced with replacing a system that is used on a regular basis to support the company's business. Relax. This is no more difficult than performing a liver transplant on a professional athlete while he's competing.

## THE MIGRATION SPECIFICATION

At every step of the development cycle, I have emphasized the need to have a clear and documented specification of the work to be done. The Migration Process is no exception.

The Migration Specification grows directly from the Problem Specification and the Design Specification. It includes the following sections:

1. A description of the production environment, focused on the physical characteristics:
   ➤ Identification of the computers where the system will run
   ➤ Identification of the databases used by the system and their physical characteristics (location, size, access rates, table structures)
   ➤ Identification of system interfaces—on-line terminals, other systems, specialized devices
2. A detailed description of existing data to be used by the new system, including all conversion rules.
3. A description of the operational constraints (If you can only move from the current system to the new one on the third Sunday of the month, you need to document that in the Migration Specification.)
4. Identification of all of affected organizations (may include some of your customer's customers) and contacts within those organizations (if you are going to migrate to a new system, keep track of the people who must know what you're doing and when).
5. A detailed plan clearly identifying each step to be taken, who is responsible, the steps that precede it, and the steps that follow it. (This plan is part of the more inclusive Installation and Operation Plan described in Section 9 of the Appendix.)

The Migration Specification is not a document that you keep in your drawer, unfolding it only to prepare your status reports. It is first and foremost a communications document for everyone involved in the migration process. Since this may be your first time actually to meet some of the people who will be affected by your new system, you should spend some time with them going over the Migration Specification. Make sure they understand that you are going to be referring to it throughout the Migration Process and that you expect them to do the same.

A significant difference between the Migration Specification and the other specifications used in the development cycle is that the Migration Specification is a *process* specification as opposed to a *statement of objectives*. In the Problem Specification, the functionality objectives were described; in the Design Specification, the structure and components of the system were described; in the System Test Specification, the objectives of each test were described. In the Migration Specification, you need to describe not only the steps to be taken, but the sequence in which they are taken, the decisions to be made at key points in the process, and the contingency plans that allow you to deal with potential problems.

## CUTOVER

Cutover is the moment when the customer stops relying on the old system. Cutover is like Chinese cooking. In Chinese cooking, the ingredients are actually heating in the wok for a very short time, often only a couple of minutes. However, the preparation that occurs before the cooking takes much longer. Preparation is also the heart of all conversions. You need to account for all the details. Start by considering the major questions:

*Cutover criteria.* What are the conditions for cutover? When is the magic moment? Will it be done by gut feel or only after thorough inspection of system outputs?

*Cutover responsibility.* Who makes the decision? Normally it will be the customer, but not always. The two of you must decide this in advance.

*Operating responsibility.* Who operates the system up to the point of cutover? You or the customer, or both?

*Recovery options.* Almost all systems should have explicit procedures for recovering in case of equipment failure, human error, and so on. You should have addressed recovery, of course, way back in the Definition and Design Processes. What's important now is that the people operating the system understand how to use recovery features.

*Rehearsals.* If you were told that your raise depended on your ability to successfully shoot five consecutive foul shots on the basketball court tomorrow morning, what would you do? You'd leave the office, go to the court, and practice your foul shots. Michael Jordan would do the same thing. If you are going to do a flash cut—turning the old system off, turning the new one on, and never looking back—wouldn't you take some practice runs through all the steps to verify that everything works? Make sure you and your customer have allowed time for rehearsals and make sure that the necessary people, both your team and the users, are prepared to put in the time to rehearse.

## DATA CONVERSION

As a memento of his data conversion experiences when AT&T was split into local and long-distance phone companies, one of my friends keeps a little plaque in his office. It reads:

☞ If you add a cup of champagne to a barrel of sewage,
     you'll have a barrel of sewage.

☞ If you add a cup of sewage to a barrel of champagne,
     you'll have a barrel of sewage.

Data conversion, like writing report programs in COBOL, gets little notice or respect in the data processing community. If you do a good job, nobody thanks you, but if you mess up . . .

As a manager, you need to recognize the importance of data conversion and put good people on it. The data you are dealing with is probably worth far more to your customer than is your system (or your salary) and you need to respect that fact. You might be putting some wonderful point-and-click interfaces in front of the customer service representatives, but if the customer data base has been messed up, those interfaces will be no help at all.

Here are some data conversion areas that should concern you:

- ➤ *Data Sources.* Where are the databases that now hold the data you're going to convert? Are they likely to change while you're trying to convert the data that's in them? How accurate is the data that's now in those data bases? How do you know how accurate it is? Can you improve the quality of the data as you're converting it? Are there constraints on your access to the data? Is this classified or highly sensitive data?

- ➤ *Process Controls.* Are you going to convert all the data at once, or through selected extracts? What controls will you use to ensure that data has not been lost during conversion? What controls will you use to ensure that data has been translated correctly? At what points will you apply the controls? Will you use control totals, sampling, or a combination of both?

- ➤ *Completion.* How will you decide if the data conversion was successful? Is there a way to handle exception cases? Are you going to perform incremental backups during the conversion? Can you restart conversion without going back to the beginning?

You need to talk through all of this with the conversion team and with your customer and you'll find that your discussions will be more effective if you use a picture. I've found that the best communication and documentation tool for data conversion is a flowchart. I believe that the flowchart's effectiveness comes from the fact that everyone already knows how to read one. Armed with a flowchart and table layouts for the databases that are affected, you should be able to verify that every data element is moving from its source to its destination correctly and that any verifications or translations are occurring at the correct point in the process.

If there are points in the data conversion process where operations staff or user representatives must perform quality audits, don't forget these points when you create your flowchart.

## MIGRATION STRATEGIES

You and your customer are faced with two migration options. You can choose the "flash cut" approach where you abruptly stop using the old system and start using the new one. Or if that seems too risky, you can take what one of my managers called "the Wells-Fargo approach" where you get to your final configuration in stages. Either approach can work, but only if you understand the risks and only if you and your customer are in complete agreement not only on the choice of approach, but also on the reasons why you chose it.

The choice of a migration strategy is one of the most subjective tasks in the entire development cycle. You and your customer need to consider the following questions as you discuss which strategy to use:

➤ What level of business disruption is acceptable? There will be some degree of business disruption no matter how smoothly the migration is handled. Faced with the new system, users will make some mistakes. In addition, if there are any defects remaining in the system, their impact will be magnified.

➤ How much latitude is there to adjust the "in production" date? Extending the migration period isn't an option if the new system is required in order to satisfy new government regulations or if your company ran a thirty-second ad just before the opening kickoff at the Super Bowl announcing the availability of a service that requires your system.

➤ How much internal opposition to the new system is there? Users are human and humans resent having things shoved down their throats. There may be a payoff for an approach that allows users to get comfortable with the new system, but this needs to be balanced against the cost.

➤ How comfortable are you with the quality of the system? You have guided the system from its initial requirements through the acceptance test. You know how it's been put together and you know the people who built it. You know in painful detail all of the things that you would do a little better if you had another chance. Well, you don't have another chance on this system. You have to decide if the risks the customer doesn't see need to be brought into the open.

Migration might seem to be a strange time to bring up these questions. In truth, both you and your customer probably have discussed them before. However, this is the point where you must move from discussion to decisions. It's not always easy.

Up to this point, the system has lived in an incubator. It has processed test data rather than real data. The role of the user has been played by your programmers, analysts, and testers. The other systems that it interfaces with have been using test data in an artificially constrained environment—in fact, you may have been interfacing with simulators. Migration brings the system out of the incubator and exposes it to erroneous data, inept users, and other systems that have idiosyncrasies of their own. You are doing things with the system that it has not done before. No wonder you're nervous.

## FLASH CUT

If you're going to adopt a strategy of completely replacing an existing system in a single step, there are two ways to proceed: immediate replacement and parallel operation.

## Immediate Replacement

This is the software version of what happens when your computer is replaced. A time is scheduled and everyone except the migration team stops using the old system. Backups are made, the old software is removed, data is converted, the new software is loaded, the new system is started, and there's no turning back.

Many software project managers and their customers are frightened by this approach. It seems so, well—*absolute*. If you are tempted to avoid immediate replacement, consider the following:

> ➤ If you have done a good management job up to this point, you *know* that the new system does the job that it's supposed to. The chances that you have overlooked anything of major importance are nil.
> ➤ You will have tested the system and demonstrated that it works under conditions that are as real as you can make them.
> ➤ For the customer to get any benefit from the new system, he must use it. If the users think that they can go back to what they were used to on a moment's notice, there will be less incentive for them to learn about the new system.

When I started out as a manager, I was scared to death of the immediate replacement approach. As I've gained more experience and confidence in my ability to ensure the quality of the systems that my teams build, I've become much more comfortable with it.

## Parallel Operation

Parallel operation is what you do if you and your customer feel that immediate replacement is simply too risky. Parallel operation means that you don't throw out the old system until you're sure the new one is working. Here's what Robert Townsend (1970) has to say about parallel operation:

> No matter what the experts say, never, never automate a manual function without a long enough period of dual operation. When in doubt discontinue the automation. And don't stop the manual system until the *non-experts* in the organization think that automation is working. I've never known a company seriously injured by automating too slowly but there are some classic cases of companies bankrupted by computerizing prematurely.

Townsend's point can also be applied when you're replacing an automated function. When the parallel operation approach is used, the customer has maximum flexibility. Your customer can use outputs from the new system immediately, with the possibility of reverting back to the old system at any time. He can have the users check regularly to see that the new system is producing the same results that the previous one did and use this to build their confidence and familiarity with the new system.

In order to manage parallel operation, you will need to develop operational procedures and automated links that keep data in the two systems synchronized. When you do this, you'll need to be very careful to ensure that errors in the new system can't corrupt data in the old one.

## STAGED CONVERSIONS

Many software projects are undertaken to replace so-called "legacy" systems that have grown over the years to the point where they can no longer be economically extended or maintained. Many of these legacy systems are large mainframe systems that use hierarchical data bases—hardly a fashion statement for the start of the twenty-first century. However, many of these systems are so large that developing complete replacements for them isn't practical. Instead, their functionality is re-placed in phases. For example, the part of the order management system that main-tains customer records may be moved to a data server that can be accessed by other systems as well. The data server is a project in its own right and should provide ben-efits to the company beyond its role in simply replacing a piece of the old order management system.

Continuing to use the example of the data server, when you develop your Mi-gration Plan, you'll need to be aware of the following:

➤ There are going to be changes to the legacy system in addition to those that are made to allow the customer records to be moved to the data server. Some of these changes may be made to support other legacy projects that are run-ning in parallel with your new development. Assuming that you want to avoid surprises, you should make sure that your migration process is linked to the change management process that is used for the legacy system.

➤ There are likely to be systems that already receive data from the legacy sys-tem as part of their normal input stream. Just like the legacy system, these systems will also be changing as you develop your system and go through the migration process. And just as you did with the legacy system, you need to make sure your project is linked to their change management processes.

➤ Your customer data server project may rely on the completion of a previous project—in our example, this is the credit check system. This means that your migration plans can be affected by the migration plans of your predecessor.

➤ Other systems will be relying on the successful migration of your system and you need to make sure that the project leaders for those systems have input into your migration plans.

➤ In order to deploy your customer data server, you may need to develop soft-ware that synchronizes your customer data and copies of the customer data that are kept in the legacy system to produce the shipping manifests. This synchronizing software will need to stay in place until the shipping functions are moved to their own server during a later phase of the overall legacy system replacement project.

This is a lot of stuff to keep track of. It takes a lot of thought, a lot of correspondence, a lot of meetings, and a lot of patience to get everything under control. In large projects, you should encourage your customer to treat phased migration as an independent project. This approach provides the opportunity to establish clear lines of authority during the migration period, and for multistage projects this period may extend over several years.

## Rollout

The employee records system you just developed is going to bring together data from several other systems. The plan that you and your customer have agreed on calls for you to start by moving all the employee data for the headquarters staff to the new system and to follow that by adding the data for the plant employees and then finish up by adding the sales offices and the regional service centers. The practice of introducing a system to an enterprise as a series of cutovers is called "rollout." The idea is to reduce disruption by providing substantial training and support for the users at the time that the new system will be introduced to them, and, at the same time, to control the cost of this training and support.

Each rollout involves at least one cutover, and the data conversion requirements may differ from one cutover to the next. Each set of users will have its own idiosyncrasies in terms of expectations about the new system. Each new step in the rollout gives you another chance to mess up. The only practical advice is to treat each step as if it is the only step.

## Keep Talking

Throughout the migration process, you are going to attend meetings, generate E-mail, put in longer hours than you planned on, and get to be very good at explaining what is going on. You need to be tireless in locating people who are to participate in the migration process or be affected by it. Over and over again, I've seen migration held up because someone didn't issue user ID's or because nobody had told the security guard that the new terminals were going to be installed over the weekend.

You are going to be personally involved in the process to a greater extent than you were in the programming process because you are the one who has the ability to cut through the red tape most quickly. You are the one who authorizes the purchase of the five modem cards that were missed on the PC order and have someone drive over to Computers R Us to pick them up right now. To be an effective participant in the migration process, you need to be sure that you can always be reached when someone needs your help and you also need to go out of your way to ask people what you can do to help them. Most people won't ask for help until they really, really need it and by the time they ask, the problem has often grown to several times its original magnitude. To make sure that your help is timely, you need to offer it early and often.

---

## The Manager's Bookshelf

What you need at this point is something that talks about how to *manage* the software that you and others have built. The book you are looking for is the *Software Management Technology Reference Guide*. It gives you information about tools and techniques for integrating your new software into old environments. It has chapters on configuration management, reverse engineering, software administration, and other nonglamorous aspects of the software world. It was put together by Nicholas Zvegintzov and members of the Software Maintenance Association. These are people who provide advice and information that you can put directly into practice. You can order the *Software Management Technology Reference Guide* from:

Software Maintenance News, Inc.
B10-Suite 237
4546 El Camino Real
Los Altos, CA 94022
Email: 73670,2227@compuserve.com

**FIGURE 14–1**   The Support Staff   (Daumier, "Rue Transnonain," Courtesy of the Art Institute of Chicago.)

# 14

# The Support Staff

Once upon a time the supporters stopped supporting. They all went on strike, and stillness fell over the office. Phones rang and nobody answered. Daily report runs were scheduled but nobody ran them. Memos went untyped and paper went unfiled. Backup tapes sat idle in their little plastic cases. No progress reports got written. The coffee pot grew cold—the managers and programmers and designers and analysts and testers did not know how to turn it on. The cream curdled and mice ate the sugar.

Finally one day the head manager, looking wan and resigned, opened the door of his dark office, swept aside some cobwebs, and called to the strikers marching silently around the reception room.

"Okay!" said the head manager, "Okay! I give up! Everybody gets a 20 percent raise!"

The marchers marched and none smiled.

"And an extra week's vacation!"

The marchers marched and none smiled.

"More sick leave!"

The march continued.

In frustration, the manager, tie askew, hollow-eyed, palms out, pleaded: "For God's sake, don't you all know we need you?"

"Ahhhhhh!" chorused the strikers. The strike was over.

## RECOGNITION

Arthur came into my office and settled comfortably in a chair. He looked as though he planned to stay a while.

"Where would this project be without me?" he sighed. I had enough presence not to be flip. The words *"probably on schedule"* formed somewhere in my brain, but I replied slyly:

"Huh?"

Arthur folded his hands across his belly and continued: "The programmers get all the credit but they'd be pretty bad off if I hadn't made sure that the backups were done on a regular basis. I don't think support people get much notice around here. In fact, none of those people even thanked me for getting them back up after the server crash."

As I leaned forward to give an earnest impression of listening intently, Arthur quickly covered all the jobs done on the project by people who rarely got recognition. Although the hour was late and I was tired, I had to grudgingly agree he had a point, and in a moment of managerial weakness, I told him so.

"Any ideas what to do about it, Arthur?" He did indeed.

"A raise would help," he suggested cheerfully. I decided he was so devious that I promoted(?) him to salesman.

Arthur was right. Without people to do the unglamorous jobs, it might be impossible for anybody to do the glamorous ones. Still, it's all too common to find that an excellent secretary is being paid less than a mediocre programmer.

Most companies consider secretaries easier to replace than programmers; these companies don't require secretaries to have a college education, but they expect their programmers to have a degree. Administrative people are historically paid less than technicians yet if you really consider the worth to the project of Ellie Efficient, the effective secretary, and Wally Whiner, the journeyman programmer, Ellie Efficient's contribution to the project's success may be much more substantial than Wally's.

Before we can properly deal with the needs of support people, we need to identify who they are and what their jobs are. On our hypothetical project, support people are secretaries, librarians, administrative assistants, instructors, computer operators, and technical publications people—anyone who is not a manager, analyst, designer, programmer, or tester.

Write a one-page job description for each of your support people (you have no doubt done this for each of your other employees, no?). If you cannot write anything more meaningful than "responsible for assisting management in reporting progress" or "responsible for secretarial assistance to project manager," then you are operating much too loosely, or you don't know what your people are doing, or you have people on the payroll who have no real jobs.

After identifying and defining every support job on your project, pay attention to the titles you hang on those jobs. My neighbor Hilda proudly announced to me one day back in the late fifties that she had been hired by IBM. She said she was a documentation logistics specialist. Her job was to distribute updated manuals. Although IBM sometimes went to goofy extremes, I applaud the idea of defining jobs in a way that gives them dignity. But what's more important than fancy labels is to promote the importance of the jobs in the first place.

Don't take for granted the routine chores that support people do. Let the people know that you know the value of what they do. Tell them during routine appraisals of their work and during daily casual conversations with them—those are private times. Also acknowledge their importance *in public*. Get in the habit of specifically recognizing good work done by the support staff in the progress reports that you send to the executives who are sponsoring your project. Make sure everyone who works for you has a chance to see these reports. If you were doing a support job, wouldn't you feel great if you saw that your name and a description of the good work you were doing was put in front of the company's Executive Vice-President?

When awards are being considered, don't just think about manager-of-the-year or programmer-extraordinaire; consider librarian-of-the-century. Not many things are accomplished solely by the one who ends up getting the credit. DeeDee Divine may be up for an academy award, but where would she have been without her acting coaches, costars, supporting actors, her director, her orthodontist, her Mommy? When your project finishes successfully and the company throws a shindig for the whole crew, everybody gets invited. But the speeches of praise mention the managers and a few lead technical people by name, while the support cast is left chewing their creamed chicken and wishing *they* were up in lights. Recognizing the value of people's service makes them feel good about themselves and about their jobs and about you. Everybody wins.

## BEING OF SERVICE

Earlier I touched briefly on the idea of service: anyone doing any job is ultimately providing a service for someone else. The work of support people is usually more obviously of a service nature, so it's important that support people feel comfortable with the notion of providing service.

Consider Arthur, who gathers and packages and transports tapes, diskettes, and listings between programmers and the data center. He is an important link in the chain of events connecting the design of a program with a working program. If he delivers late, many programmers may lose a day's test runs. If he is sloppy about packaging listings he can cause unnecessary loss of efficiency among all the people he is serving. Clearly, he is important to the project—but does he know it? Does anyone tell Arthur he's important?

How about the people who type your correspondence and file your paperwork? Do you realize how important it is to have paper (and "electronic paper") filed in an intelligent way so that you can retrieve it without wasting valuable time? Is it important to you to have your letters and memos and reports done expertly, with style and accuracy? Your written work says a lot about you to the people who read it. I remember a simple comment made by Russ Washburne one day to my secretary, who had prepared a letter for him: "Shirley, you sure make my letters look great! Thanks!" Shirley blushed with pleasure and I took note: When was the last time *I* had complimented her on her work?

## NO DUMPING ALLOWED

Support areas are often a dumping ground, or at least a holding area, for people with no real assignment. There are several categories of people-nobody-knows-what-to-do-with: Manny Manager, who did not quite hack it on his last assignment and nobody wants to take a chance having him manage again; Sally Seller, who is bright as can be, but lacks the personality to get along with "those dumb-ass customers"; Eugene Engineer, whose training was in the field during the good old days of card punches and abacuses, who has seen technology pass him by; Paranoid Programmer, who doesn't want anyone else to look at his code.

You can put all these people into two categories: (1) those who are incompetent, lazy, obnoxious, disruptive, and refuse to do anything except what they are accustomed to doing, and (2) those who may be in the wrong niche, but obviously are of value to the company. I've seen very few in the first category; the ones in this group generally deserve to be fired; a company's responsibility toward salvage operations has a limit somewhere. Most are in the second category and organizations generally deal with them in two ways: retraining or dumping.

*Retraining*, whether through formal classes or on the job, is nearly always good for the company. It's the smart (and loving) thing to do. You end up with someone newly trained in B who also has experience in A, and that's a plus. Not only is the retrained person more versatile, but he or she is likely to be more loyal, as well. That translates to a happier person and better productivity.

*Dumping* means assigning someone to a project and trying to keep him or her busy. If the project needs help, and this person can fill a real need, fine. But often the project has neither the need nor the budget for another body, and the dumpee hangs around trying to be either useful or invisible. The dumpee is assigned to some manager who really has enough to do already, and now must work at finding something for the dumpee to do.

I have vivid recollections of dumpees. Some tried not to be noticed. Some found meaningful work to do and became useful. Some dreamed up unnecessary work and made life miserable for other project members by involving them. Many wandered the halls grumbling and complaining and being generally disruptive— they became the proverbial rotten apples in the barrel. An unbusy person among busy people can cost you a whole lot more than just his or her wasted salary; he or she wastes a terrific amount of other people's time. These dumpees spend their time complaining about management, the company, and the world in general. They cost the company a great deal in terms of the lost productivity of the people whose ears they fill daily with their grumbling.

In the IBM division I called home, it was common for people to be without meaningful work for periods of weeks or even months—ours was the young and iffy Federal Systems Division trying to work our way into Uncle's wallet. I remember a particular time when a group of four or five dumpees spent an entire day compiling a list of clichés, for no particular reason. I still have it. It's four hundred entries long, and cost the company about a thousand dollars. Need a cliché? Call me.

In this same division there was a group of dumpees assigned to write quality assurance regulations. They measured their success the way proposal writers do: by tonnage. The heavier the pile got, the more certain no one would ever use it. As they wrote their rules and drew their charts and checkoff lists, they wasted the time of other people (such as I) who had to read and comment on their work.

What's the alternative to having the company assign spare people to your programming project? The company should train them for other jobs, *but keep them in a training pool* until legitimate jobs are available and not assign them to projects where they are not needed. If people are to consume company funds while being retrained and awaiting assignments, have them do so in a group or department set up specifically to handle them, rather than siphoning off the energies of projects that have no current need for more bodies.

## QUALITY OF LIFE

The veal on the dinner table last week came from an animal whose entire life was spent in a tiny, filthy enclosure, practically unable to move and fed on a diet deliberately lacking in iron so that its meat would be pale and tender. Zero quality of life. Lots of secretaries, typists, librarians, and other support people spend the working part of their days the same way. They occupy mental cubbyholes where they do their work almost mechanically. They could do the same work, but better, and with more enjoyment—all they need is some understanding of how their work relates to the project.

Consider Terry Typist, who sits all day typing memos or technical documents with little notion of what the documents mean. Theoretically, a good typist can type anything perfectly without understanding content, but think how mind-dulling that has to be! Wouldn't most of us have more fun typing a draft of *The Joy of Sex* than a treatise on laser beam theory? If your reaction is "Since when should a job be fun!" I fear you have been born into the wrong era and might be more comfortable managing a nineteenth-century sweatshop. I have tried to make the point in as many ways as possible in this book that a good manager will consciously seek ways to make people's work enjoyable.

If your typist has even a rudimentary understanding of programming, typing the programmers' technical jargon will be easier and the results more accurate. Consider this conversation between Terry Typist and Pancho Programmer:

"Terry, I'm afraid this will have to be retyped."

"What's wrong, Pancho?"

"Well, first of all, you've changed the indentation here where I've written these program instructions."

"Well, gee, when I type a memo I use the rules of indentation I've been taught. What you wrote was a mess!"

"Ummmm, well, you see, when you write program language instructions the indenting is meaningful. It's not the same as with ordinary text."

"Sorry, Pancho, I didn't realize. . . ."

"And another thing, you changed some lower case to upper case and vice versa—they all need to be typed just as I wrote them."

"Mmmmm! I'm real sorry, Pancho. I'm so used to typing nontechnical stuff on my last job . . . well, let me fix this. . . ."

Fortunately, Terry uses a word processor, so the fixing is not a big deal. Were Terry working with a plain typewriter, the story would be different. Still, time has been lost and feelings bruised. If Terry had had a short course in "programming for nonprogrammers," both the lost time and the bruises could have been avoided. *Even a rudimentary understanding by all project members of what the project is about will pay off every single day.* Training Terry in programming is *not* a waste of time.

Training your nontechnical people in technical subjects is not expensive. You don't expect Terry to write programs, only to have a feel for the jargon, so the training need not get into coding anything. You can give Terry and others a good start with the expenditure of only two hours a day for a week or so; spread the time to fit people's workloads. Topics covered might include an understanding of computers, programs, and programming languages, with some simple examples of programs coded in the project's languages, and a description of what they mean.

Such training can be carried further for those whose support work involves more interaction with the programmers than typing their technical materials and

---

### No Support at All

Support people should *support*, not *thwart*. My racquetball partner, Chuck (who works for the federal government), tells of a facilities manager who is good for nothing but getting in the way. With a move to a new building going on, the facilities guy refuses to let people take an early look at the new quarters. He doesn't answer questions about file space, office arrangement, telephones. Trust me, he tells Chuck. What he's really saying is, this is my turf and it's none of your business.

*That's* a guy who needs straightening out. Or firing. (I forgot—this is the government—you don't fire people, you transfer them.)

correspondence. Librarians and computer operators, for example, would benefit from more extensive training than that given typists.


## CREDIBLE SUPPORT

I was sitting across the desk from Danny, a programming manager on a large defense project. The mail boy breezed in, deposited a thick envelope, and left. Danny put aside his coffee cup, peeked inside the envelope, and commented colorfully on the ancestry of someone named Barney.

"What's the fuss?" I asked.

"Barney! He's cranking out paper again!" Danny spread out the contents of the envelope. The impressive-looking page headings read something like this:

Project 599L

Office of Standards and Procedures

Date

Standard: STD-100-A/6

Application: All Programming Managers

New Pages: xxx.1 and xxx.2

Replacement Pages: aaa.4 - aaa.9

Deletion Pages: aaa.10,11

Summary of Standard: . . .


and attached were the new pages to be inserted into the Standards and Procedures Manual. Danny leaned back and snatched his copy of the S and P Manual from his bookshelf. There were two volumes, each in a two-inch thick binder.

"Dammit! The standards are thicker than the program listings!" He swore a little more and then, feeling cleansed, leaned back with his hands clasped behind his head.

"What do they get for scrap paper these days?" he wondered.

"About a nickel a hundred pounds."

"Let's see . . . at that rate we could sell all these damned manuals and get the project back in the black!"

We traded wry comments about the standards manual until we tired of the sport. Then Danny, now sober, got to the nub of things:

"There are two things wrong with this manual," he began.

"I know," I broke in, "volume one and volume two!"

"No," he grinned, "volume and Barney."

"I don't follow."

"Well, the sheer volume is way out of line . . . there's so much in here that nobody bothers using any of it. It's full of needless crap. It tries to tell you how to do everything but tie your shoes!"

"Page ninety-three," I said.

Undeterred, Danny continued: "But the other thing that's wrong is Barney. Barney is a *very* nice guy, but the people around here won't listen to him."

"Why not?"

"No credibility. He has no technical background, so every time he puts out a standard, it's suspect—no matter who originated it. You've got to have a guy in that job who has enough technical background that the people on the project respect his judgment and listen to what he puts out."

"But he doesn't just pick these things out of the air. Management signs off on them all."

"Not good enough! Managers get too busy and rubber-stamp things they shouldn't. No, you've got to start with somebody who knows programming to begin with. That guy will get listened to."

"Okay!" I laughed, "I'm convinced!"

"Good!" Danny grinned. "I've recommended you for the job!"

"I'll kill you!" I said, and left his office.

Two days later I had a new assignment.

## THE RIGHT TOOLS

There's no reason your support people should labor with old tools while your programmers are playing with the latest computers, languages, compilers, and test and documentation aids. In particular, your secretaries, typists, and program librarians ought to be using PCs to do all kinds of chores:

➤ Secretaries and typists can originate, edit, duplicate, and retrieve documents quickly and easily.

➤ Librarians can file and catalog documents and retrieve them on demand; lists of available documents can be sorted, updated, and produced at will.

➤ Managers and administrative aides can bring together project status data from multiple sources and combine them to produce status reports without the need for cutting and pasting. All kinds of charts can be maintained, modified, and printed without the laborious business of drawing and redrawing.

➤ Conference room schedulers can keep track of available space and how the time is distributed.

There are a number of "groupware" products available for networked PCs that can make life easier for your support staff. The development of general applications that use underlying "groupware" such as Lotus Notes© is too promising to overlook.

## QUALITY ASSURANCE

Cal Quality brings the meeting to order by rapping his brass knuckles on the Formica table.

"Okay, you guys . . ." he begins, in a vain attempt at a Jimmy Cagney impersonation, "you dirty rats, let's see what quality work you're putting out. . . ."

The programming managers try desperately not to make eye contact with one another. The slightest smirk and they'll all break up before the meeting even gets under way. They tolerate goofy Cal and try to keep these meetings as painless as possible.

"Jerry," says Cal, "let's look at your programs first. Now, my list says you've completed and turned over to the library CPCIs (for those of you who don't speak governmentese, these are Computer Program Configuration Items) numbered twelve through seventeen. . . ."

"Ummmm, yeah, Cal, except that their real IDs are different. . . ."

"Jerry, couldn't you number your programs the way we do so we don't get all confused? The Air Force insists we use CPCI nomenclature."

Jerry mutters something obscene and then says aloud: "Cal, halfway through the project you come along and want us to throw out our entire way of doing things just to conform to an idiotic configuration management scheme originally meant for hardware. The system is unnatural and uncomfortable. It's force-fitting software into molds made for hardware!"

"Jerry, what's the difference what you call something? The product is still the same."

"Exactly! So let's use our standard names and forget this CPCI bull!"

"Can't, Jerry. Customer insists."

Jerry sighs. The meeting drones on. Cal calls out identifications of deliverable items and Jerry and the other programming managers point to appropriate piles of listings and disks neatly stacked on the table. They testify that such-and-such disk and listing do make up the item that Cal has called out from his checklist. So help them God.

When the meeting is over everyone agrees that the stack of programs on the table matches Cal's list of items promised the Air Force at this stage of the project.

So lists are made to agree. Cosmetics are attended to. But deep in the stack of disks is one that replaced its original just before the meeting to correct a very minor, late-found bug. The printed listing does not agree with the changed disk. Further down in the pile are several listings whose identifiers have been altered because someone had found several pairs of programs with the same identification symbols.

This is a project in trouble. Change management isn't working, among other things, but compounding the other problems is the imposition of a separate "quality assurance" function armed with good intentions but fighting a losing battle.

Quality assurance is the job of the managers responsible for the product. A separate group can't "assure" much if the responsible managers have not done their jobs properly. A separate group is a layer of bureaucracy that costs a lot and does not necessarily produce much. Managers should be held responsible for quality and not be allowed to slough off part of their responsibility to a group whose name sounds right but that cannot be expected to guarantee quality if the responsible managers failed to do so.

If your project *does* include a separate quality assurance group (whether you like it or not) there are some sensible things you can do to make the scheme work better:

1. Make sure the quality assurance function is planned at the beginning of the project, not after you are already well along. Settle all matters of responsibility, procedures, and nomenclature early.

2. Don't make the quality assurance group dumpee-heaven. Look for people not only knowledgeable in the quality assurance procedures your customer requires, but in the programming business. Don't assume that a network quality assurance person can automatically do a competent job in software.

3. Don't let quality assurance become a sort of pseudo-management. Have quality assurance people *support* management, not replace it.

## MANAGING SUPPORT PEOPLE

There is no trick to managing support people. Just remember they *are* people and need the same caring and understanding as the programmers and analysts. Don't be absurd and tell every person he or she is so critical to the project that the project would die without him or her. Don't use puffery. Just honestly let each person know he or she counts. Here are some kinds of things to pay attention to.

Understand that almost every secretary can type, but not everyone who can type is a secretary. Respect the secretary's status and make the position one to which a clerk might aspire. Don't make the title "secretary" meaningless by giving him or her nothing but typing and filing jobs; make the job more responsible. Your secretary can help you manage your time, usually a manager's scarcest resource. A good secretary can organize your files in an intelligent, orderly way—something my first secretary tackled immediately. He or she should be your assistant, not your flunky. On larger projects, it's a good idea to make clear which secretary handles whose work—perhaps the senior secretary handles the managers' calendar and one of the junior secretaries schedules the conference rooms. Try for enough harmony and flexibility that when one person is overloaded, it's natural for another to come to the rescue. That's not so easy if you allow too much concern about turf. A secretary who looks down on doing a task normally assigned to a clerk, for example, is someone who has been allowed more insulation than is good for your project.

Encourage support people to help define their own jobs and to offer ways of doing those jobs better. Arthur, who shuttles between programmers and computers, will suggest refinements to the procedures for submitting and retrieving test runs if he knows his suggestions will get a thoughtful response (something other than, "Oh, that's just Arthur's idea—what does he know?"). Keep your ears and mind open to what these people have to say. Their working lives *are* the support services they offer; if they are good workers, they are bound to come up with better ways of fitting their jobs to the needs of the project.

Decide that support people will not replace management. There are at least two areas where this might happen. The first is where you give administrative assistants so much apparent authority that people think they always speak for management and are tantamount to management. The second is when the roles of quality assurance (or sometimes system test) people become so strong that programmers and others begin taking direction from them, to the exclusion of management. There are other examples: strong-willed secretaries replacing introverted bosses; salary administrators playing God by jerking purse-strings; computer operators deciding they know better than management how to assign computer time priorities. This may sound as though I think managers should have godly status, never to be challenged, but that's not my point. Managers exist to plan and direct and control the project. Part of the way they control is to listen to and weigh advice. Once they make a decision, that's the way things should proceed until a new decision overrides the old. Erosion of management decisions by people who always "know better" undermines managers' credibility and can bring a project to grief.

---

*You know your support staff is doing a good job if*

> They keep more records than they really need to, but not *too* many more.
>
> They talk to programmers, testers, and users to find out what's needed *before* it's needed.
>
> They develop their own contacts in the customer's organization.
>
> They look for ways to simplify *your* job.
>
> They don't let you forget their value.

# PART VIII

# OPERATION

"It ain't over until the fat lady sings." This may be a crude way to think about opera, but it's a useful reminder that your project is not complete until your system is actually operating, dealing with real transactions and providing real data to the people who need it.

No amount of testing and no amount of care in migration can fully prepare you for what will happen when your system is exposed to real users and real data. To prove it, I offer an instructive incident from my own experience:

➤ I once worked on the development of a system designed to minimize errors when taking orders over the phone. The screens were designed after careful study of the latest ergonomic studies and standards. The care even extended to modification of the cubicles where the users would work so that there would be fewer distractions. The screens themselves made excellent use of color to guide the operator through the order sequence and on-line HELP was automatically invoked when errors were detected.

➤ Unknown to any of us, two of the users on the second shift were color-blind.

**FIGURE 15–1** Operational Process (Photograph from New York Bureau of Public Roads.)

# 15

# The Operational Process

Many small projects end when the Acceptance Process ends. Perhaps you conduct acceptance demonstrations on the customer's equipment, and at the successful end of the demonstrations the system is already installed and operational. The customer accepts responsibility for all future changes to the system, thanks you and tells you she'll be in touch when another project comes along. In other cases, however, delivery of the system is followed by continuing responsibility for maintenance and tuning. I'll briefly cover these tasks in this chapter.

## MAINTENANCE AND TUNING

Many contracts call for the contractor to provide maintenance and tuning assistance for a specified period after delivery of the system. Maintenance means *fixing problems* that show up late, including bugs or documentation errors uncovered during the Acceptance Process. Tuning is the *adjustment or refinement* of parameters somewhere in the system. It can be done only after observing the system in operation for some time. All of this work is best done under a separate "labor hours" contract under which you supply people to fix whatever the customer wants fixed and the customer pays you for the expense incurred. Operating under other kinds of contracts, such as "fixed-price" contracts, can be costly because the customer may want an endless stream of "repairs" that are really new wrinkles or improvements.

However you choose to operate, follow change management procedures. Those procedures are at least as important now as they were during the Programming Process. The system is on the air, and an ill-considered change could do real damage.

There is a tendency to treat maintenance as an afterthought, but many studies of the lives of projects have found maintenance to be the tail that wags the dog. Most systems last many years, often *decades*. Many programs are older than the programmers assigned to maintain them! Companies don't simply toss out all that effort because it's time to trade it in on a new model. If a system keeps chugging along for ten or fifteen years with here a change, there a change, everywhere a change, the cost of those changes can *easily* eclipse the cost of the original system. This argues, of course, for the cleanest, clearest possible design and documentation. It also means that there is a paying (although not particularly exciting) business out there for someone.

Once a project is finished, wouldn't you love to keep intact the crew you've worked so hard to put together? They know you, they know the business, and they've gotten great training under your direction, but now they may get scattered and you and your company lose the benefit of the teamwork you've developed. Sadly, this happens a lot because new jobs don't always line themselves up neatly. It also happens because people want to move on to do something new. You can't always begin a new project the day after you end an old one. Taking on maintenance contracts is one way you can keep your programmers (and others) busy during between-contract lulls.

## PROJECT EVALUATION

You're finally finished with your project—almost. There's one more job to do. Take time out to think about how it all went and write an evaluation report. Use it yourself as a reminder on future jobs, and give it to your management. Make use of the Project History you've been keeping (haven't you?) and include in your evaluation the following items:

---

### Project Games

If you play chess or checkers or even tic-tac-toe, you learn enough each time you play to make your odds for success better the next time. Treat your job the same way. Consciously track data and events in your current project and use that information to plan and execute better the next time. As you get more projects under your belt, write guidelines for other people to use in playing their project games.

➤ *Project overview.* A few brief paragraphs describing what the problem was and how it was solved.

➤ *Major successes.* Blow your horn. Point out major deadlines met, profitability, customer satisfaction, whatever was happy about the outcome.

➤ *Major problems.* There were some, weren't there? You might place the problems in these categories: missed schedules, budget overruns, technical performance, personnel, customer relations, management support (or lack of).

➤ *Manpower estimates versus actual.* Get these data from your Project History and present them as guidelines for estimating the next job.

➤ *Machine time estimates versus actual.* Get this also from the Project History and tabulate the data for future use.

➤ *In retrospect.* What would you do differently if you were to repeat this job?

There is another kind of evaluation that can help steer you on the next job. Conduct a post-implementation review with the customer after his system has been operational for a few months. Not only can you learn a lot about how you did—you'll look like a caring contractor to the customer.

---

## The Manager's Bookshelf

At the end of the project, you have an opportunity to look at how well you did and also (and this is more difficult) at how you know how well you did. When you look back at the controls and techniques you used, you will probably see room for improvement.

Before you leap into action, I'd advise you to buy a copy of Watts Humphrey's book *A Discipline for Software Engineering* (1995) and read it from front to back. In this book, Mr. Humphrey extends the principles behind his development of the Process Maturity Model (which applies to organizations) so that they focus on improving the performance of the individual software practitioner. As a manager, one of the most important improvements you can make in your performance is to improve the performance of the people who work for you. This book is the best one I have found on this vital subject.

You might also get a copy of Robert B. Grady's book *Practical Software Metrics for Project Management and Process Improvement* (1992). One of the best parts of this book is the study data showing the benefits of code inspections and application of structured analysis and design. This is data you can use to initiate change at your company and make yourself a better manager.

**FIGURE IX–1** Special Considerations (*David Prepares to Battle Goliath,* W.S. Webb, 1893.)

# PART IX

# SPECIAL CONSIDERATIONS

So far we've looked primarily at a medium-sized project, which I arbitrarily defined as forty people. Here are some thoughts about bigger and smaller projects, along with a few other ideas I felt should be treated separately.

## BIG PROJECTS

First, do you *need* a big project? Do you really need a hundred, six hundred, a thousand people on a programming job? You can accomplish a lot with a handful of really good, well-managed people. There is absolutely no question that your forty-person group working as a real team can accomplish more than a fractured, tough-to-manage mass of hundreds. And it may be that even your forty people are too many, and that a group of six really sharp people could handle this job beautifully. It's never so obvious as on a massive, overstaffed job that 10 percent of the people do 90 percent of the work. So think about it: do you need a big project?

There are some galling arguments that lead to last-minute hiking of initial manpower estimates. One of them is this: If you propose a significantly smaller number of people for a job than your competitors propose, your people obviously don't understand the problem. Another goes this way: Since the customer expects big numbers, you 'd better propose them.

I've seen manpower estimates arbitrarily *tripled* because they didn't fall in line with the manpower being used by the same company on a "similar" project.

The trouble is that no matter how many people are put on the job they all end up apparently doing something to justify their presence. It's a self-fulfilling prophecy. If you propose six hundred people to write a program, by gosh, you use six hundred. Each is busy writing thirty lines of code and two hundred status reports.

Those arguments aside, some projects are legitimately big, and big projects have problems all their own. Let's look at a few.

## The Processes

In Figure I and throughout this book I've described a project in terms of seven processes: Definition, Design, Programming, System Test, Acceptance, Migration, and Operational. In a big system your programs may be only one of several major subsystems that all must be integrated. One or more additional processes may be added to the development cycle in Figure I, resulting in something like Figure IX–2.

The first four processes are the same as those in Figure I, except that now the system your team builds is a subsystem of a larger system. In parallel with the work on your subsystem, there is work on other subsystems, such as real-time data collection, perhaps by other companies. These parallel activities are not independent of one another. During the Definition Process, or even earlier, great amounts of analysis and consultation are necessary to write specifications outlining the individual subsystems. During that time, besides the normal pushing and shoving among companies vying for an attractive piece of the total job, there is plain, honest confusion. For example, in some mammoth military systems the technical problems alone are staggering, let alone questions of logistics, personnel, contract administration, and so on. These factors all contribute to project growth.

Your work will be easier if you do a good job writing the Problem Specification. (It may be called by another name, such as "Software Subsystem Requirements.") Make sure it describes (1) the general problem, (2) the specific problem your program subsystem must address, and (3) how your subsystem is to interface with the others. This difficult job demands your best people. They will usually work as part of a team representing all the contractors and chaired by the customer or his representative.

Once you have an acceptable Problem Specification, you can operate in roughly the same way described in the preceding chapters until you reach the System Acceptance Process. You should insist on acceptance testing of your software, even though acceptance this early will be conditional. Expect a lot to go haywire later as you integrate your subsystem with the others. When the inevitable problems arise, it will be invaluable to you to be able to use those conditional acceptance tests as a baseline. If you leave them out, every problem that pops up is likely to produce a long wrangle going all the way back to who said what during the Definition Process.

The Total System Test Process in Figure IX–2 may be subdivided into a "laboratory" or "controlled" phase and a "live" or "field" phase. During laboratory system test, all subsystems are tied together at a special test facility before they are sent

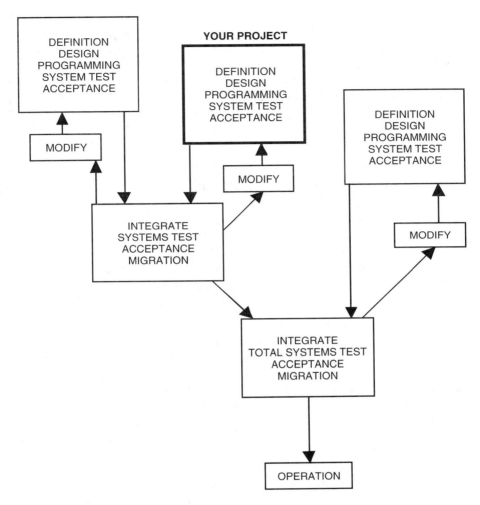

**FIGURE IX–2**   Extended Development Cycle

to a testing site where live conditions can be more closely approximated. As an example, if the system being developed is a ground-to-air missile weapon system, the program, computer, communications, radar, and missile subsystems may be integrated at the laboratory site and tested under partially simulated conditions. It will be necessary to move to a remote live site to actually fire missiles at targets. Theoretically, all testing could be done at the live site, but this is usually not economically feasible because it would require large numbers of people and extra equipment to be moved far away for long periods. By the time laboratory tests are completed, remaining problems should be lessened and fewer people required at the live test site.

The Operational Process acknowledges that even the live test site just mentioned may not be the last stop. You may send copies of the system to each of several geographic locations where they are finally to become operational. At operational sites you'll run more tests, once contractors adjust subsystems for conditions peculiar to individual sites. All this testing may, of course, take many months or even years, especially in an area as delicate as defense systems. During this time, effective procedures for change management are especially important to prevent urgent field changes from contaminating the master copy of the system.

## Organization

The basic organization in Figure 6–3b is a good starting point, no matter how big the job is. As the number of people grows, however, you may add more levels of management. The positive side to this is that you maintain an adequate ratio of managers to programmers (or other workers). The negative side is that you now have more communication problems and more fragmenting of the job.

Besides the size or complexity of the job, there are other causes of project growth. One common requirement is to build programming support tools. You may not be programming a computer for which satisfactory support programs exist, so you may need to write input simulators, trace programs, test aids, or even a complete network emulator. Since all this may easily be as big as the main job, you may need to add a big new box under the project manager called "support programming." (You must add a major new section to your Project Plan to cover this effort.)

You may also have to account for hardware diagnostics—programs that exercise the hardware and the network methodically to locate existing faults or attempt to predict imminent failures. Hardware manufacturers often supply test programs with their hardware, but you may need to supplement them, particularly if you are integrating hardware from several manufacturers. You may even need to build an entire system of such diagnostic programs and tie them to the operational system so that they can be automatically invoked. Another box under the project manager!

All the other boxes in Figure 6–3b are likely to undergo a population explosion as you move from a medium-sized to a large project. The Staff Group will include more control functions—for example, Configuration Management—and will be beefed up to handle more and bigger status reports and a great heap of other documentation. The Analysis and Design Group may grow to conduct studies and to control the definition of several different versions of the evolving system; it may also do simulation modeling. The Test Group's functions will become more critical in a big system because it will be necessary to test interfaces with other subsystems.

## Customer Controls

Big projects mean big money and big money means people breathing down your neck. The customer will insist on far more control over a multimillion dollar project than over one with a modest price tag. That's understandable, but what's distressing is the mountain of paper accompanying these controls. For example, the United States government applies to many of its contracts a control scheme called "Configuration Management," which I'll define in the next section. It's a conceptually simple system: you write a baseline definition of something to be built and control all changes to those baselines. Unfortunately, the mass of manuals, regulations, specifications, and reports built around that straightforward idea scares people to death. When programmers hear "Configuration Management, " they hide behind the water cooler. Having seen the piles of manuals and forms, they want no part of them.

It's not that difficult. You can use Configuration Management on your job without trauma if you can find someone who understands programming and programming management and who can write well. Make this person a translator. Have him or her spend a month or so learning the particular Configuration Management version your customer requires you to use. There are different schemes, depending on which military branch (or NASA) you're dealing with. They're alike conceptually, but different in implementation (naturally). Then have the translator do a translation for your project. The existing manuals and other descriptive materials cover all cases. What you need is something tailored to *your* project. If your writer has the knack of boiling things down to their essence, the result will be a guide that will be about 10 percent the size of existing manuals.

There are other areas where the customer may impose controls beyond those applied to a smaller project. For instance, he may insist on seeding some of your groups with his own people to influence design, programming, and testing, as well as train a cadre of people eventually to take over maintenance of the system. You may think all this a pain, but it need not be if you consider the following:

1. Try to have some veto power over the individuals the customer "lends" you. He may try to leave you with a few problem children.

2. Negotiate a clear understanding of your control over the customer's people— how long they are on loan to you, who manages them, and who appraises their work. On several jobs I know of, the people on loan were military men, some of whom left the job at critical times when their service hitches expired or when they were rotated to other areas.

3. Don't count one customer employee equal to one of your own and, therefore, reduce your manpower estimate accordingly. If your customer's employee turns out to be a dud, you're in trouble.

4. Control the assignment of customer people to a task on your "critical path."

Probably the best places to use customer personnel are in the analysis and testing areas, and in preparing user manuals. In analysis they should add their unique understanding of the requirements of the job. In testing they may help you avoid later acceptance problems. And they obviously have an interest in writing good user documents.

Another kind of "customer control" is the customer's insistence that you use his terminology, definition of the development cycle, review schedule, and so on. We're not talking trifles here. If you agree to be bound by the customer's way of operating, then operate that way from the start of the project. Don't use your own system and then attempt a mass conversion at the end of the project. Every time that's done, the result is great confusion, misunderstanding, and unnecessary expense.

## Configuration Management

The Department of Defense (DoD) has issued a series of documents, such as DoD-STD-2167A, that establish ground rules for contractors proposing to do work for the DoD. These regulations attempt to make software development as "visible" and traceable as possible. They are based on a development cycle like the one in this book. At the heart of these standards is Configuration Management.

The underlying idea of Configuration Management for programming is this: define a program to be produced, control all changes to that original definition, and show that the final product is completely consistent with the original definition as modified by accepted changes.

The basic unit of work to control is called a Computer Program Configuration Item (CPCI). A CPCI is a major piece of work, probably on the order of a subsystem or package in Figure 4–2.

For each CPCI, you establish certain baselines. A baseline is anything you can use as a departure point; it is what you and the customer agree will describe or constitute a product. Anything that later departs from a baseline is a change, and the customer must approve a change in advance. There are three baselines: (1) the *functional baseline,* which is a description of the CPCI at a gross level, established at or before the beginning of the project; (2) the *allocated baseline,* a more detailed description of the CPCI established during the Definition Process; and (3) the *product baseline,* describing the CPCI after it has been built and tested. Each successive baseline becomes the new standard against which changes for that CPCI are judged.

Your staff keeps track of the status of each change for each version of the programs. The staff ensures that all necessary documentation changes are made and that the documentation and programs are kept in step. At specified times the staff arranges for audits during which you show the customer that programs and documents agree.

## Multiple Releases

We talked about this earlier in the Migration Process chapter, but it's useful to restate some of the points as they apply to large systems. On a big project there will usually be a need for more than a single version of the system. Three or more major versions, or "releases," are not uncommon for a project that spans several years. It's common to find a high-level plan, often refered to as the "Strategic Systems Plan" that defines the functionality in each release of the system in broad terms. Some systems are so technically difficult and so enormous in scope that they cannot be finished in a single development cycle. They require iteration, some trial and error, a careful building toward an ultimate system. Multiple releases are an important safeguard against the danger of having "all the eggs in one basket"—that basket being a single system delivered at the end of a long project.

Multiple releases pose new management problems. How do you avoid confusion among the releases? Start by scheduling the beginning of work on each new release to coincide with the publication of a new Problem Specification. If you plan three releases, plan three Problem Specifications, each building on the preceding. Figure IX–3 shows a typical multiple-release schedule. Each black wedge represents publication of a new, more complete version of the Strategic Systems Plan. Each release bar represents a more or less complete program development cycle. The first release cycle may be abbreviated because the programs developed during that cycle may not be complete enough to subject to the final process (full system testing and installation at an operational site).

Key the beginning of each new release cycle to the issuing of a new Problem Specification—major changes in that specification on a weekly or monthly basis would make it nearly impossible to produce *any* working version of the system. The

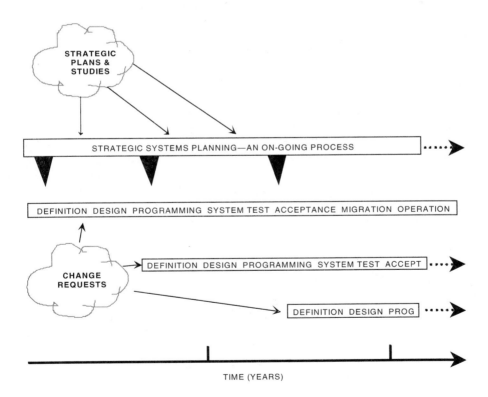

**FIGURE IX–3**   Scheduling Multiple Releases

idea is to accumulate changes and issue them in batches, that is, as part of the next Problem Specification.

It can be difficult to keep track of the many modules in an evolving multiple-release system. There are tools available that can help you manage your releases and distributions. Such tools are often called "configuration management" tools. Although the term has a meaning similar to the federal government's Configuration Management procedures, these tools are more general and you can apply them to any job. You should consider them for use on any medium-to-large project involved in multiple releases.

Working on more than a single release at any given time makes manpower scheduling difficult. If there are three releases under way, it hardly seems reasonable to set up three complete organizations to produce them. Probably the best approach is to have a single Analysis and Design Group writing Problem and Design Specifications and to segment the Programming Groups.

## Some Big Project Benefits

If you are assigned to work on part of a big project, you'll find that there are some good things to balance the complexity that you're faced with. First and foremost, there are likely to be experienced project managers assigned at the higher levels of the project and they can be a source of guidance and encouragement. You'll probably need both from time to time. I'd advise you to find a senior manager who is willing to serve as your mentor and that you set up a regular schedule to meet with her.

Another benefit is that you're likely to have some powerful management tools at your disposal. Managers working on small projects in small companies aren't likely to have more than a PC-based project management system. Most small companies I've worked with haven't invested in CASE or automated estimating tools. If you're working on big projects, you'll have a chance to be exposed to the cutting edge of management support technology and you ought to take advantage of every opportunity you have to learn more about it.

## SMALL PROJECTS

Small projects provide wonderful opportunities for you to focus on refining your management skills. Take advantage of the chance to do everything the right way. Unlike larger, more visible projects, you will have more time to yourself on the small jobs. This means that you can use this time to look carefully at the quality of the documents and the underlying analysis and design that goes into them. In a small project, you will be closer to your programmers and you can get a better feel for the problems they face (and whether you are causing some of them.)

Don't rush small projects. Take the time to do them right. The planning recipe provided in this book applies to any project, even one with only a handful of people.

A small project needs a Project Plan, although it may be but six pages long; it needs Problem, Design, and Coding Specifications; it needs a plan for testing the system. You need to do all the things we've discussed if you are to produce something of excellence. The difference lies in the amount of effort required. On a small project one person handles more than one job. Some tasks that consume great amounts of energy on big projects, such as integration test, can be done in a breeze on small projects. And, of course, all that extra management and staff help needed on the big project just to handle the "bigness" and the interactions simply does not exist on the small job.

There is one danger on small projects to watch for. The manager may get sloppy in the control of a small task that requires perhaps six or eight people. He or she is on top of everything and nothing could possibly go wrong. A Design Specification doesn't get written, let alone a Problem Specification. Programs are not documented thoroughly because, after all, Charlie Programmer has the whole system in his head. Why insult Charlie by making him write it down? A Project Plan is obviously unnecessary—why write down a plan for an eight-person job? The manager who lets things go this way is begging for trouble, and when trouble comes, he or she will look far worse than the manager with the forty-person job who gets in trouble. It's *expected* that a competent manager can run a little job without bankrupting the company.

So tailor the advice given in earlier chapters to fit your job. If you eventually want to manage a bigger project, take advantage of the time you spend on smaller ones to demonstrate that you understand how to bring excellence to the work that you're responsible for.

## PROPOSALS

Managers are commonly pressed into service to assist in writing proposals. As I write this, I'm finishing up a project that keeps customer address data bases synchronized in two very different computing environments. I'm also helping to write a proposal for a different project to keep invoice data bases synchronized in a similar pair of environments.

A proposal is an offer to do a job. Make sure the ones you work on are based on conservative assumptions. Many proposals promise things that can't possibly be accomplished. Most of the time (but not always) such proposals are written by competent people who have good intentions. All too often, these proposals wind up derailing the careers of the people who have to deliver on them.

You know the arguments about how tough it is to write proposals. There's never enough time; the job description is vague and volatile; the RFP (Request for Proposals) is poorly written; adequate manpower is not available. Writing proposals *is* tough, but there are guidelines to ease the task considerably:

**1.** Be selective. Don't write a proposal for every job in sight. Concentrate on the ones you really want and do a first-rate job on them. One proposal guide (McDonald, 1968) observes:

Many companies work on the basis that the number of contracts received will be in some ratio to the number of proposals generated. This is wrong. The number of successful proposals will be in direct relationship to careful proposal selection and preparation. A bad proposal is worse than none. First, it will not win. Second, it destroys the company's reputation and chances for the future. Third, it takes up the time of expensive talent and interferes with other work.

**2.** Cut the baloney. You're not kidding anybody by encasing three pages of good proposal work in a crust of garbage. Do you think proposal reviewers enjoy reading all that junk? Aim for a pithy piece of writing. Decide what you want to say, say it, and stop!

**3.** Assign a proposal manager who has authority. He or she should be able to make decisions fast and make them stick. There's no time for monkeying with a management chain a mile long.

**4.** Make specific work assignments. Assemble your people in a kickoff meeting, clearly state the objectives of the proposal task, and pass out the work. Some assignments will be investigatory; some will involve writing sections of the proposal. After people have had a chance to dig in for a couple of days, call another meeting and adjust the assignments.

**5.** Outline the proposal early. You'll waste countless hours of work if nobody bothers outlining the proposal document. Each participant will write in his or her own way, only to find that his or her writing doesn't mesh with anyone else's. Result: massive, wasteful rewrites. Settle the outline and writing guidelines first and avoid the waste. The Project Plan outline in the Appendix may provide you with a good start at outlining the proposal document.

**6.** Schedule the work. Developing a proposal is, after all, a project. This project has objectives, deadlines, and limited resources. Schedule what must be done, when, and by whom. Schedule time for reviewing drafts and rewriting. Leave enough time for sign-off and possible revision by upper management, and don't forget to allow sufficient time for technical editing, proofreading, final typing, reproduction, collating, and distribution of the finished copies.

**7.** Don't be fast-talked into changing your estimates because they "won't sell." If upper management decides to take a business risk by lowering your estimates, make your position clear. Don't, by your silence, give anyone the idea that you agree to the cut if you're actually opposed to it.

**8.** State your assumptions. When you submit to your management a finished proposal and a set of estimates, include in writing all assumptions you made along the way and your opinion of risks inherent in the estimates. State your assumptions prominently, and don't be afraid to repeat them. You cannot presume that the customer (or your own executives, for that matter) can see into your mind and understand what you were thinking when you wrote the section on your technical approach.

**9.** Don't overcommit. In most contracts the written proposal, unless amended by the contract, is considered a commitment. The proposal, warts and all, is often incorporated in the contract. If you promise more than you can deliver, you're likely to be stuck with that commitment.

**10.** Play it straight. Proposals are big business. They are life and death ventures for many companies. The temptation to bend the truth, to use weasel words, to gloss over problems is sometimes overpowering. Many times I've heard an associate moan, "If we're completely honest about this estimate, well lose, because you know Company X isn't going to be honest about its estimate." Nuts! Resist that kind of thinking. Keep your integrity intact.

## EVALUATING NEW TECHNOLOGIES: OBJECT-ORIENTED DEVELOPMENT AS AN EXAMPLE

By the early 1990s a new set of buzzwords was on the lips of programming gurus: "object-oriented analysis (OOA)", "object-oriented design (OOD)", and "object-oriented programming (OOP)." All of these fall under the umbrella term "object-oriented development," or simply "object orientation (OO)."

Like any new software development methodology, OO has its champions and its critics. Among its champions are dozens of people offering varying definitions of OO, with differences in definitions of terms, notations, and so on. There is little doubt that OO will become a major player in software development until we reach the next, as yet unknown, plateau. According to Ed Yourdon, whose book *Object-Oriented Systems Design* (1994) is a good place to start learning about OO, object-oriented technology at that time was "being used in a serious fashion by only 3–5 percent of the software engineering community." It's instructive to look at OO as an example of what managers must face when they consider using new technology.

If you skim a few of the many books on OO, you're struck by the difficulty people have in *defining* OO. One of the definitions is from Yourdon's book:

> A system built with object-oriented methods is one whose components are encapsulated chunks of data and function, which can inherit attributes and behavior from other such components, and whose components communicate via messages with one another.

Alan Fisher (1991) likens object-oriented designs to a client-server system, where

> . . . a set of servers [objects] sit waiting to provide some service or function for clients. Clients appear periodically, request a service from a particular server, the server performs the function, and the client is satisfied.

---

# The *Real* Leading Edge of Technology

In 1804 French inventor Joseph Marie Jacquard invented a loom for weaving intricate patterns, guided by stacks of cards with holes punched in them. Almost two centuries later, modern Jacquard looms were used to make two of my nicer ties.

In 1834 British mathematician Charles Babbage used Jacquard's idea in planning his device called the Analytical Engine, which was intended to do a variety of calculations according to "instructions" and data entered on punched cards. His plans called for mechanically storing information in the machine, an early form of "memory." Babbage's machine attracted the attention of an amateur mathematician named Augusta Ada Byron, Countess of Lovelace. Often called the first computer programmer, she introduced extensions to Babbage's ideas, including the processing sequence we now call a "loop." The Ada programming language is named after her.

Babbage's 1834 Analytical Engine was never built, but later an American named Herman Hollerith used the idea of punched cards in an electromechanical machine that tabulated the results of the 1890 census. He built a successful business selling these tabulators. That business eventually became International Business Machines (*Understanding Computers: Computer Basics,* 1989).

---

In an article in *PC Computing* magazine Michael Kolowich (1991) describes object-oriented software this way:

> Traditional software design regards a program as a sequence of actions or procedures. Do this, and then do that—Object-oriented software design treats a program not as a sequence of steps but rather as a collection of interacting software components—each with its own characteristics and capabilities. At its simplest, object-oriented programming represents a sophisticated modular approach to software design—one whose components are reusable in many different contexts within a program and, conceivably, across different programs.

With all the talk of OO being a paradigm shift in software methods, you need to consider whether the techniques of object-oriented analysis, design, and programming will fit comfortably with the practices and procedures you and your development team are used to. In the case of OO, you might find a closer fit than you'd initially expect. Object-oriented analysis and design might suggest a more iterative cycle, as "objects" are defined and redefined until a set of classes evolves that satisfies the user's needs, but this has several parallels with the process of successive refinement in a procedural programming environment. As more software developers become comfortable with OO technology, variations on traditional development cycles may emerge. They will be driven by more widespread use of class libraries and greater emphasis on software reuse than we have today. Although you can build a high-quality system using the tried-and-true techniques we've discussed in this book so far, I think you have a responsibility to begin learning about OO with an eye to making a reasoned, informed decision at some point whether to adopt OO technology for work under your direction. When the time comes, you'll probably want to manage a pilot project before tackling a mission-critical system.

Pilot projects are critical in evaluating new technology, but only when they're approached objectively. If you've already made up your mind that you're going to adopt the Superlanguage of the Month, the chances are good that you will set up your pilot project so that it supports your conclusion. You won't be helping your customer, your company, your programmers, or yourself if you do a "rigged" pilot project and then announce your "findings" that prove you were right about Superlanguage.

Until you try a new technology on a realistic project, neither you nor the people who developed the technology can say if it's the right technology to apply to your customer's problems or if it's a technology that your programmers and analysts will be able to use effectively. The pilot project is the place to find out.

If this is your first pilot project with OO, don't expect that your project will show the gains in productivity and quality that have been claimed in some of the books and articles you have read. You are going to spend the pilot project firmly encamped on the learning curve and you will make enough mistakes and false starts to put any hopes of productivity gains right into the wastebasket. The pilot project is a place to *learn* about the problems and benefits of OO; it's not a contest to see if you can get written up in *Datamation*.

Pick a real project for the pilot. Find a system that needs to be built to meet a real customer's needs, but not one that will put the company into bankruptcy if the project fails to deliver on time or under budget. Pick good people for your team; it's important to understand how effective OO is in the hands of skilled technicians. Don't try to save money on training. You want an objective look at the technology and no technology, be it OO or mail-enabled applications, is going to look good in the hands of people who don't have the faintest idea how to use it.

On your pilot project, *track everything!* Record the successes, missteps, confusion, defects, unexpected costs—everything. After the pilot project is completed, you are going to need to look at your records and produce a real evaluation. You might conclude that your company needs to do more pilot projects, or that you should just forget about OO, or that you should press the accelerator all the way down and commit to OO as your core technology. No matter what you conclude, you will have the records from your pilot project to back up the conclusions.

The most common mistake in setting up pilot projects is to try to rush them in order to minimize the expense. You need to to allow extra time so that you can do the detailed project tracking and so that you can accommodate the mistakes you are surely going to make. I used to inject a 40 percent adjustment to my function point results if I was going to use new technology on a project. Today, I'd be more likely to use 60 percent.

As a manager, you should be constantly on the lookout for technology that improves software quality and increases the productivity of your staff. If someone who works for you tells you about something they read about on the INTERNET, pay attention. You want to encourage people who work for you to get better, and if they come across something that *they* believe would help, the chances are pretty good that it has some potential for doing so. Your job, when you look at new technology, is to make sure that decisions are based on fact rather than fad, and to make sure that the people who are going to be most directly affected by the new stuff understand what it is supposed to do and also understand the problem you're trying to solve.

Do not, do not, do not fall into the trap of trying out new technology just because it's new. Before you invest your time, figure out what problem the technology is supposed to solve and then make sure that it's a problem with which you're faced.

**FIGURE X–1**  Impact  (Miller, "Jude", Courtesy of the artist.)

# PART X

# IMPACT

In July 1985 sixty or so people staged an illegal sit-in and takeover of offices at the National Institutes of Health (NIH) in Bethesda, Maryland, just outside Washington. The goal was to shut down the University of Pennsylvania's head-injury clinic. This was a place where, thanks to tax-supported funding by NIH, various primates for years had been subjected to the most brutal treatment imaginable. The clinic, seeking to discover the effects of traumatic injury to the head such as people might sustain in a football game or an automobile accident, used various ingenious devices to inflict damage on the skulls of helpless primates. A baboon, for example, would be confined in a harness and its head would be rammed by a jackhammerlike contrivance. Then it would be examined to determine the effect of the blows.

The story is long and involved. The happy ending is that the four-day civil demonstration succeeded in a dramatic way. Health and Human Services Director Margaret Heckler, the cabinet official who had jurisdiction over NIH, agreed over the vehement objections of NIH officials to suspend funding to the head-injury clinic, pending an investigation. Shortly after, NIH cut off funding completely and the clinic was out of business. Hundreds of defenseless animals from among the millions mutilated and savaged each year in laboratories around the world were saved from lives of extreme pain and helplessness.

You may disagree with the actions of the people who took part in this civil disobedience, but here's my point: almost all of us involved were ordinary, quiet citizens. None were foaming-at-the-mouth radicals. But each one, simply by his or her presence, made a real difference.

I am not a born activist. I get nervous when a waiter looks at me with disdain. I'd like it if everyone would just "be nice." But, much later in my life than I like to admit, I've begun to learn about standing up for things that I think matter.

Some writers about management claim that a manager doesn't matter much in the lives of the people who work for him or her. I'm in foaming-at-the-mouth disagreement! Almost everything any worker has to say about his or her job, whether good or bad, is the result of what some manager does (or fails to do). As a manager, every move you make will influence dozens, hundreds, perhaps thousands of people. That's not a thought for the faint of heart. Your influence can be positive or negative, major or minor. I believe that if you go about your job in a caring way, with real concern for the people around you, you will successfully reach or exceed your business goals—and everyone will enjoy the trip.

You really can make a difference.

# A MODEL PROJECT PLAN OUTLINE

## INTRODUCTION

This appendix suggests a format for a Project Plan. The plan is divided into eleven sections. All sections except the last (the Index) follow the same outline:

> Section n
> n.1   Objective
> n.2   Discussion
> n.3   Detail

The first subsection (Objective) states in a single sentence the intent of that section of the plan. I have included in this outline *in italics* my concept of the objective of each section.

The second subsection (Discussion) is a short tutorial passage. The outline suggests *in italics* the kind of information appropriate to each section.

The third subsection (Detail) contains the specifics. This subsection defines terms, tools, procedures, functions, responsibilities, schedules, and so on. Again, some suggestions are included *in italics*.

The sections of the Project Plan are:

Section 1:      Overview
Section 2:      Process Plan
Section 3:      Organization Plan
Section 4:      Test Plan
Section 5:      Change Management Plan
Section 6:      Documentation Plan
Section 7:      Training Plan
Section 8:      Review and Reporting Plan
Section 9:      Installation and Operation Plan
Section 10:     Resources and Deliverables Plan
Section 11:     Index

## SECTION 1:   OVERVIEW

### 1.1 Objective

*The objective of this section is to summarize the entire Project Plan.*

### 1.2 Discussion

*Set the stage. Identify the customer and his experience in this field. Describe briefly the job to be done. Give any background necessary for an understanding of the job environment. Then state your project's objectives under the contract.*

*Next, explain how the plan is organized. Promise that the reader can gain a good understanding of the plan by reading each section's Objective and Discussion, and then keep your promise.*

*Now list the assumptions and restrictions on which the plan is based. They're important. State them honestly and simply.*

### 1.3 Detail

*Show a gross schedule for the project. Include all major efforts bearing on this project, whether under your control or not. For example, if other contractors are responsible for such tasks as writing specifications, developing hardware, or system testing, show all these efforts along with your own on a single diagram. If you're planning multiple releases, show how they are scheduled.*

## SECTION 2:   PROCESS PLAN

## 2.1 Objective

*The objective of this section is to define the development effort in terms of a series of time-slices called "processes."*

## 2.2 Discussion

*Define your development cycle and, briefly, each process making up the cycle. Include an illustration such as Figure I (inside the front cover). Establish basic definitions and point out that the remaining sections of the plan are tied to these definitions.*

## 2.3 Detail

*For each process list primary and secondary objectives and define each objective as rigorously as possible.*

2.3.1  Definition Process
    2.3.1.1  Primary Objectives
        (a)  Analyze problem
        (b)  Write Project Plan
        (c)  Define acceptance criteria
        (d)  Choose project tools
    2.3.1.2  Secondary Objectives
        (a)  Find people
        (b)  Understand customer
        (c)  Form tentative design ideas
2.3.2  Design Process
    2.3.2.1  Primary Objectives
        (a)  Design operational programs
        (b)  Design support programs
        (c)  Refine Project Plan
        (d)  Conduct project review
    2.3.2.2  Secondary Objectives
        (a)  Prepare for integration testing
        (b)  Set up change management
        (c)  Construct simulation models
        (d)  Find people for subsequent processes
        (e)  Prepare for programmer training
        (f)  Publish Programmer's Handbook

          (g)  Do initial preparation for system test

          (h)  Do initial preparation for acceptance test

          (i)  Do initial preparation for site test

          (j)  Set up project libraries

2.3.3  Programming Process

    2.3.3.1  Primary Objectives

          (a)  Do detailed design, coding, and module test

          (b)  Integrate modules

          (c)  Document

    2.3.3.2  Secondary Objectives

          (a)  Prepare in detail for system test

          (b)  Prepare in detail for acceptance test

          (c)  Prepare in detail for site test

          (d)  Prepare for customer training

          (e)  Prepare for migration

2.3.4  System Test Process

    2.3.4.1  Primary Objectives

          (a)  Test system against Problem Specification

          (b)  Test as "live" as possible

          (c)  Test by nonprogrammers

    2.3.4.2  Secondary Objectives

          (a)  Complete acceptance test preparations

          (b)  Train customer

          (c)  Correct descriptive documentation

          (d)  Complete user documentation

          (e)  Reassign people

2.3.5  Acceptance Process

    2.3.5.1  Primary Objectives

          (a)  Execute and analyze acceptance tests

          (b)  Sign formal acceptance agreement

    2.3.5.2  Secondary Objectives

          (a)  Complete customer training

          (b)  Clean up documentation

2.3.6  Migration Process

    2.3.6.1  Primary Objectives

          (a)  Assist in data conversion

          (b)  Establish cutover criteria

          (c)  Establish fall-back plans

          (d)  Define migration sequence

          (e)  Assist in cutover

    2.3.6.2  Secondary Objectives

          (a)  Establish liaison with affected groups

          (b)  Support audit procedures

2.3.7  Operational Process
    2.3.7.1  Primary Objectives
        (a)  Assist in beginning operation
    2.3.7.2  Secondary Objectives
        (a)  Test on-site
        (b)  Continue maintenance and tuning
        (c)  Evaluate project

# SECTION 3:   ORGANIZATION PLAN

## 3.1 Objective

*The objective of this section is to define the organization of the project and the assignment of responsibilities.*

## 3.2 Discussion

*State the basic reasons for establishing an organization: clarity of job assignment, minimizing interactions, controlling change, establishing points of responsibility and focus. Sketch the main flow of work within the organization, starting with problem analysis and design and running through programming, testing, documentation, and delivery.*

## 3.3 Detail

*In the first subsection list the groups found on the organization charts and the responsibilities of each group. Then show an organization chart for each process (the organization will generally not be the same for all processes; for example, during the Definition Process there may not yet exist a Programming Group).*

3.3.1 Groups and Their Responsibilities
    3.3.1.1 Analysis and Design Group
        (a) Writing Problem Specification
        (b) Writing Design Specification
        (c) Change management
        (d) Data control
        (e) Simulation modeling
        (f) Writing user documentation
        (g) Assist in Integration test
    3.3.1.2 Programming Group
        (a) Detailed design
        (b) Coding
        (c) Module test
        (d) Integration test
        (e) Descriptive documentation
    3.3.1.3 Test Group
        (a) Writing System Test Specifications (including test cases)
        (b) Writing Acceptance and Site Test Specifications
        (c) Gathering and generating test data
        (d) Choosing and obtaining test tools
        (e) Setting up test libraries

       (f)  Scheduling test resources
       (g)  Executing tests
       (h)  Analyzing test results
       (i)  Documenting test results

3.3.1.4  Staff Group

       (a)  Library services
       (b)  Computer time control
       (c)  Planning and installing terminals and PCs
       (d)  Issuing Programmer's Handbook
       (e)  Training
       (f)  Special technical assignments
       (g)  Technical liaison
       (h)  Document control
       (i)  Report control
       (j)  Contract change management
       (k)  Supplying clerical support
       (l)  Maintaining Project History

3.3.2  Organization chart: Definition Process

3.3.3  Organization chart: Design Process

3.3.4  Organization chart: Programming Process

3.3.5  Organization chart: System Test Process

3.3.6  Organization chart: Acceptance Process

3.3.7  Organization chart: Migration Process

3.3.8  Organization chart: Operational Process

## SECTION 4:  TEST PLAN

### 4.1 Objective

*The objective of this section is to define the tools, procedures, and responsibilities for conducting all levels of test of the software system.*

### 4.2 Discussion

*Briefly define each test level (module, integration, system, acceptance, site) and show how the different levels fit together in a test hierarchy.*

### 4.3 Detail

4.3.1 Module Test
*Testing done on the individual program modules before they are integrated with other modules.*
    4.3.1.1  Module Test Objectives
    4.3.1.2  Module Test Responsibility
    4.3.1.3  Module Test Procedures
    4.3.1.4  Module Test Tools

4.3.2 Integration Test
*Combining tested modules into progressively more complex groupings (specify either top-down or bottom-up or some combination) and testing these groupings until the entire software system has been put together and tested.*
    4.3.2.1  Integration Test Objectives
    4.3.2.2  Integration Test Responsibility
    4.3.2.3  Integration Test Procedures
    4.3.2.4  Integration Test Tools

4.3.3 System Test
*Retesting the completed software system in as nearly live an environment as possible by personnel other than those who produced the programs.*
    4.3.3.1  System Test Objectives
    4.3.3.2  System Test Responsibility
    4.3.3.3  System Test Procedures
    4.3.3.4  System Test Tools

4.3.4 Acceptance Test
*Exercising the software system under conditions agreed to by the customer in order to demonstrate that the system satisfies the customer's requirements.*

4.3.4.1  Acceptance Test Objectives
4.3.4.2  Acceptance Test Responsibility
4.3.4.3  Acceptance Test Procedures
4.3.4.4  Acceptance Test Tools

4.3.5  Site Test

*Testing the software system in its ultimate operating environment to assure readiness for operation. This will not be necessary for all projects.*

4.3.5.1  Site Test Objectives
4.3.5.2  Site Test Responsibility
4.3.5.3  Site Test Procedures
4.3.5.4  Site Test Tools

4.3.6  Common Test Facilities

*Describe the facilities and tools common to several or all levels of test.*

4.3.6.1  System Library
4.3.6.2  Computer Facilities
4.3.6.3  Desktop Systems
4.3.6.4  Operating Systems
4.3.6.5  Special Languages
4.3.6.6  Test Run Pickup and Drop Areas
4.3.6.7  CASE Tools
4.3.6.8  Simulators

4.3.7  Testing Support Programs

*Describe anything unique about the testing of the test tools themselves.*

## SECTION 5:   CHANGE MANAGEMENT PLAN

## 5.1 Objective

*The objective of this section is to define the procedures for controlling change in the evolving software system.*

## 5.2 Discussion

*Describe the need to establish critical baseline documents acceptable to both customer and you, and to control events always relative to those baselines. Whenever a question is raised, the baseline documents are the reference point. Anything anyone wants that is not covered in the baselines is a change, and must be negotiated. When a change is deemed necessary, its cost and impact, if any, must be assessed, and the change must be written into the baseline document(s). A revised baseline document becomes the new baseline.*

## 5.3 Detail

5.3.1  Baselines
  *Define which documents are to be baselines on your project.*
  5.3.1.1  Problem Specification
  5.3.1.2  Design Specification
5.3.2  Proposing a Change
  5.3.2.1  Who May Propose a Change
      (a)  Project members
      (b)  Customer
      (c)  Other contractors
  5.3.2.2  Change Proposal Document
5.3.3  Investigating a Proposed Change
  5.3.3.1  Who, How, When
  5.3.3.2  The Investigator's Report
      (a)  Summary of proposed change
      (b)  Originator's name and organization
      (c)  Classification of the change
      (d)  Impact on costs, schedules, other programs
      (e)  Recommendations
5.3.4  Types of Changes
  5.3.4.1  Type 1
  *The change affects a baseline or would cause a cost, schedule, or other impact.*
  5.3.4.2  Type 2
  *The change affects no baseline and has negligible cost, schedule, or other impact.*

## SECTION 6:   DOCUMENTATION PLAN

### 6.1 Objective

*The objectives of this section are to define the procedures and resources required for the publication cycle AND to outline a basic set of project documents.*

### 6.2 Discussion

*Emphasize that all project documents are outlined in this section and no new kinds of documents are to be written unless management is shown why those included here are inadequate. Include a chart such as that shown at the end of this section (Figure A-1) summarizing the Documentation Plan, complete with details peculiar to your job.*

### 6.3 Detail

6.3.1 Publication Procedures and Responsibilities
     6.3.1.1  Preparation and Approval
     6.3.1.2  Typing
     6.3.1.3  Proofing and Editing
     6.3.1.4  Reproduction
         (a)  Routine
         (b)  Bulk
     6.3.1.5  Distribution
         (a)  Within the project
         (b)  To the customer
         (c)  Other contractors
         (d)  Company management
         (e)  Vital records storage
     6.3.1.6  Electronic Storage
         (a)  What gets stored electronically
         (b)  Who controls
         (c)  Who has access

6.3.2 Project Document Outlines
     *Include here the standard outline for each project document. An outline might look something like this:*

| | |
|---|---|
| PROJECT LOGO | Any standard you wish to use to identify the project's documents. |
| DOCUMENT NAME | Identifies the subject—for example, *Problem Specification, Design Specification, Coding Specification, Change Proposal, Test Case, Test Report.* |
| DOCUMENT NUMBER | The unique identifier assigned the document by the project librarian. |

| | |
|---|---|
| APPROVALS | Names of anyone required to approve this document before it may be issued. Not all kinds of documents require approval. |
| DATE OF ISSUE | Self-explanatory. Make sure this appears on each page along with the document number. |
| BODY OF DOCUMENT | What this document is about. |

### 6.3.3  Document Contents

*Here are suggested outlines for the bodies of each of your documents. You may choose quite different arrangements, depending on the nature of your project and your own tastes. Whatever you choose should appear here in your Documentation Plan so that anyone writing a given document can refer to this plan and know what's expected to be in the document.*

## PROBLEM SPECIFICATION

*The Problem Specification describes the "why" of the project and the requirements of the software system, that is, the job to be done by the programs. It is a baseline document and its most recent edition is to be adhered to strictly by all project personnel. It is written using the documentation tools chosen during the Definition Process—DFDs, decision tables, and so on.*

*The Problem Specification spells out the functions required of the software system, performance constraints (such as transaction times), data requirements, and human performance requirements.*

## PROJECT PLAN

*The Project Plan is the "road map" that describes the path your team is going to take in order to accomplish its goal of delivering a system that satisfies your customer's requirements.*

## DESIGN SPECIFICATION

*This document defines a solution to the problem described in the Problem Specification. The Design Specification is the foundation for all program implementation. The design logic described here is detailed enough that all required functions are satisfied and all interfaces, system files, and the logic connecting all program modules are defined. The lowest level of program module is specified in terms of the functions it must perform and the interfaces it must have with other modules, but the actual internal design of these lowest-level modules is left to the implementing programmers.*

*If the project is to produce more than one software system (for example, sup-*

*port programs in addition to operational programs) there will be more than one Design Specification.*

*The Design Specification includes:*

### Design Standards and Conventions

*Definition of all standards and conventions adopted for use in this design document and to be observed during later detailed design. Included here is identification of (a) documenting tools (e.g., DFD, Object Maps), (b) standards for naming entities within the system, such as file names, (c) interfacing standards, (d) message formats.*

### Software System Design

*Definition and description of the software system and all system files.*

### Coding Standards and Conventions

*Definition of all standards and conventions to be observed during coding, including (a) languages, (b) prohibited coding practices, such as no GOTOs, and (c) required coding practices, such as structured programming conventions.*

## CODING SPECIFICATION

*Begin with a standard statement linking this document to the Design Specification, such as: "This document contains the detailed description of program module ID _____."*

### Program Structure

*Describes the logic of the program module according to the standards and conventions adopted and stated in the Design Specification.*

### Local File Structures

*A complete, detailed description of all local files. Local files are unique to this program module. They are not accessed by other modules.*

### Program Listing

*The machine-produced instruction listing showing the complete set of source code for this module, including any local files.*

## CHANGE PROPOSAL

### Proposed Change

### Reason for Change

### Impact

*A discussion of the cost of making the change, as far as the originator can determine. This section is optional.*

**Attachments**
*Papers, listings, and so on that help explain the problem and the proposed solution.*

---

## PROBLEM SPECIFICATION CHANGE NOTICE

*Any change to the current Problem Specification; distributed to all holders of the Problem Specification. This should be issued in the form of replacement pages.*

---

## DESIGN SPECIFICATION CHANGE NOTICE

*Any change to the current Design Specification; distributed to all holders of the Design Specification. This should be issued in the form of replacement pages.*

---

## TEST SPECIFICATION

*There are four separate sets of test specifications: Integration, System, Acceptance, and Site Test Specifications. The outlines for all four are identical, except that the appropriate qualifier ("integration," "system," "acceptance," or "site") must be inserted. The content of the specifications may, of course, vary considerably, although two of them (acceptance and site) will often be identical.*

**Testing Philosophy**

**General Objectives**

**General Procedures**

**Success Criteria**

**Coverage Matrix**
*A chart listing all areas to be tested versus test case number(s) covering each area.*

---

## TEST CASE

**Objectives**

**Assumptions**

**References**

**Success Criteria**

**Data**
*Identification and description of the data to be used in the test.*

**Simulated Input Data**

**Live Input Data**

**Predicted Output Data**

**Script**

*Step-by-step instructions for conducting the test. The script lists procedures (actions to be taken by the testers) down the left half-page and leaves space for comments to be written down the right half-page. The script addresses the following:*

1. What is to be done?
2. By whom ?
3. When to do it?
4. What to look for?
5. What to record?

**Checklists**
*Checklists appropriate to this test case to aid in posttest analysis.*

---

## TEST REPORT

*The test report may refer to either an integration, system, acceptance, or site test; the report title should be filled in accordingly. No matter which type of test is involved, the report is keyed to a unique test case number.*

**Name of Test Conductor**

**Test Case Number**

**Problems Encountered**

*If no problems, so state. Otherwise, each identifiable problem is listed on a separate sheet attached to this cover sheet. For each problem, the following information is to be given:*

1. A unique problem identification using the test case number as a base.
2. Identification of the program module(s) in which the problem occurred, if known.
3. A description of the problem, with all available supporting data.
4. Recommendations, if any, for solutions to the problem.

---

## MIGRATION SPECIFICATION

*The Migration Specification describes the way in which the new system will be introduced into its operating environment. It includes descriptions of data conversion and fall-back practices. The Migration Specification is used as a communications document by the many organizations that must work together to make sure the introduction of the new system goes smoothly.*

## TECHNICAL NOTE

*These are documents such as working papers and technical ideas—anything of a technical nature not explicitly covered by another document. They may be generated by anyone. The only control over them is that each is assigned a unique number, as is any other document, and each is filed in the project library.*

## ADMINISTRATIVE NOTE

*These are documents conveying nontechnical information—for example, announcements, minutes of meetings, organizational changes. Some Administrative Notes are simply cover sheets for such documents as contract changes. Each note is assigned a unique document number and is filed in the project library.*

## PROGRAMMER'S HANDBOOK

*The Handbook a collection of basic technical information required by all programmers on the project. It is important that the Technical Staff (responsible for issuing and updating the Handbook) not allow additional materials to be added randomly. Otherwise, the Handbook will grow large and unwieldy and its usefulness will be destroyed. Here are topics to be included:*

### The Problem
*An overview of the Problem Specification. Includes a tutorial description of the customer, the environment, and the job to be done. This should start from scratch and be written so that a new project member can easily know what the job is all about. The limit should be about two pages.*

### Testing
*The entire Test Plan is included here.*

### Support Programs
*Descriptions of the programming tools (including documentation aids) available to the programmer, and how to use them. Each main category of tools should be separately tabbed within this section.*

### The Design Specification
The entire Design Specification is included here. This document contains several main subsections that should be given separate tabs in the Handbook—e.g., *Design Standards and Conventions; Coding Standards and Conventions.*

## Documentation
*A summary chart similar to that at the end of this section.*

## Equipment
*A description of the operational and support hardware to be used on the project, complete to the level of detail required by the programmers. The kinds of information included are:*

1. *Gross diagrams showing main elements of the hardware and their interconnections.*
2. *More detailed diagrams describing individual hardware subsystems.*
3. *Tabular data needed by the programmer, such as input-output timing characteristics, data transfer rates, storage capacities, character sets.*

## Glossary
*Definitions of project terms, including the names of program levels and testing levels, customer jargon, equipment nomenclature.*

---

## TECHNICAL STATUS REPORT

### Description of Task
*A single descriptive sentence.*

### End Date
*When the task is scheduled to be finished.*

### Status
*Both a qualitative and quantitative assessment.*

### Problems

---

## PROJECT HISTORY
*A general statement telling the reader the intent of this document. It is a historical record of important events and data on the project for use in planning and estimating later processes of this or future projects. It is should be a crisp summary, not a huge collection of paper.*

### Significant Events
*A chronological listing and brief summary of important events during the life of the contract, including missed milestones, new estimates, contract changes, project reviews, equipment installation dates, important agreements, important disagreements, meetings with the customer, and meetings with subcontractors, team members, or vendors.*

## Manpower History

*Charts showing two major items:*

1. *Total estimated manpower (in man-months) at the beginning of the contract in each of the categories listed in Figure 1–10.*
2. *Total manpower actually used during the contract in each category above, and notations explaining deviations from what was originally estimated.*

## Machine Resource History

*A series of charts similar to the manpower history. Keep one chart for each type of machine used. Each chart shows:*

1. *Total resources (time, storage, media) estimated for this machine at the beginning of the contract in these categories:*

   *module/integration test*
   *system test*
   *acceptance test*
   *other*

2. *Total machine resources actually used during the contract in each category listed, and notations explaining deviations from what was estimated.*

---

## DOCUMENTATION INDEX

*An index of all current project documents. It is maintained in computer storage for quick updating and frequent printing. This index is a chart with the following column headings:*

1. *Document number*
2. *Document title*
3. *Date of issue*
4. *Author (if appropriate)*

| NAME OF DOCUMENT | CONTENTS | PREPARATION | | | APPROVAL | | DISTRIBUTION | |
|---|---|---|---|---|---|---|---|---|
| | | Who Writes | When Finished | Formal Edit by Tech Pubs | Who Approves | Approval Window (Days) | Who Gets | Number of Copies |
| Problem Specification | Description of the requirements of the problem to be addressed by the system | Analysts | End of Definition Process | Yes | Customer | | Managers, Analysts, Designers, Testers | |
| Project Plan | Description, often in chart form, of the activities to be performed to complete the project | Manager, Analysts, Admin. Staff | End of Definition Process | No | Manager, Customer | | Project Staff | |
| Design Specification | Description of the design to be used by the programmers when building the system | Designers | End of Design Process | Yes | Analysts, Customer | | Manager, Analysts, Designers, Programmers, Customer | |
| Coding Specification | Detailed description of the modules produced by the programmers | Programmers | End of Acceptance Test | Yes | Designers, Analysts, Customer | | Designers, Analysts, Programmers, Customer | |
| Change Proposal | Description of a proposed change to the Problem Specification or Design Specification | Anyone | Anytime | No | Nobody—this is just the request | | Change Review Team | |

**FIGURE A–1** Documentation Summary

| NAME OF DOCUMENT | CONTENTS | PREPARATION | | | APPROVAL | | DISTRIBUTION | |
|---|---|---|---|---|---|---|---|---|
| | | Who Writes | When Finished | Formal Edit by Tech Pubs | Who Approves | Approval Window (Days) | Who Gets | Number of Copies |
| Problem Specification Change Notice | Description of adopted changes to the current Problem Specification | Analysts, Designers | Anytime | Yes | Customer, Manager | | Customer, Manager, Analysts, Designers, Programmers | |
| Design Specification Change Notic | Description of adopted changes to the current Design Specification | Analysts, Designers | Anytime | Yes | Customer, Manager | | Manager, Analysts, Designers, Programmers | |
| Integration Test Specification | Description of the objectives and procedures involved in integration test; includes matrix of test cases | Programmers, Designers, Testers | End of Design Process | No | Analysts, Designers | | Manager, Analysts, Designers, Programmers | |
| System Test Specification | Description of the objectives and procedures involved in system test; includes matrix of test cases | Analysts, Designers, Testers | End of Programming Process | No | Analysts, Users | | Manager, Analysts, Designers, Users, Customer | |

**FIGURE A–1**  Documentation Summary (Continued)

|  |  | PREPARATION | | | APPROVAL | | DISTRIBUTION | |
| NAME OF DOCUMENT | CONTENTS | Who Writes | When Finished | Formal Edit by Tech Pubs | Who Approves | Approval Window (Days) | Who Gets | Number of Copies |
| --- | --- | --- | --- | --- | --- | --- | --- | --- |
| Acceptance Test Specification | Description of the objectives and procedures involved in customer acceptance test; includes matrix of test cases and formal acceptance criteria | Manager, Analysts, Designers, Testers | Preliminary at end of Definition Process; Final at end of Programming Process | Yes | Customer | | Manager, Analysts, Designers, Customer | |
| Site Test Specification | Description of the objectives and procedures involved in site test; includes matrix of test cases | Analysts, Designers, Testers | End of Programming Process | Yes | Customer | | Manager, Analysts, Designers, Customer | |
| Test Case | Individual test script and data | Testers | Prior to test execution | No | Analysts | | Testers | |
| Test Report | Report of testing outcome; includes descriptions of problems encountered | Testers | Following test case execution | No | Nobody | | Customer, Manager Analysts, Designers, Programmers, as appropriate to level of test | |

**FIGURE A–1**   Documentation Summary (Continued)

| NAME OF DOCUMENT | CONTENTS | PREPARATION | | | APPROVAL | | DISTRIBUTION | |
| --- | --- | --- | --- | --- | --- | --- | --- | --- |
| | | Who Writes | When Finished | Formal Edit by Tech Pubs | Who Approves | Approval Window (Days) | Who Gets | Number of Copies |
| Migration Specification | Description of the steps to be taken to introduce the system into the current environment; includes data conversion requirements. | Analysts, Designers, Customers Analysts | End of Programming Process | Yes | Customer, Manager | | Customer, Manager, Analysts, Designers | |
| Technical Note | Miscellaneous technical correspondence | Anyone | Anytime | Yes, for collection | Depends on content | | Depends on content | |
| Administrative Note | Miscellaneous administrative correspondence | Anyone | Anytime | Yes, for collection | Depends on content | | Depends on content | |
| Programmer's Handbook | Collection of information needed by programmers | Analysts, Designers, Manager | End of Design Process | Yes | Manager | | Programmers, Designers | |

**FIGURE A–1**  Documentation Summary (Continued)

| NAME OF DOCUMENT | CONTENTS | PREPARATION | | | APPROVAL | | DISTRIBUTION | |
| | | Who Writes | When Finished | Formal Edit by Tech Pubs | Who Approves | Approval Window (Days) | Who Gets | Number of Copies |
|---|---|---|---|---|---|---|---|---|
| Status Report | Standard form used to report progress and problems to higher levels of the project management and to customer | Managers at all levels | Periodically | No | Nobody | | Managers, Customer | |
| Project History | Set of charts showing: significant events manpower (est. vs. actual) cost (est. vs. actual) | Administrative Staff | End of project | No | Manager | | Manager, Executive Management | |
| Documentation Index | Listing of all current project documents including revision levels and locations | Administrative Staff | End of project, but published periodically | No | Nobody | | On request | |

**FIGURE A–1**   Documentation Summary (Continued)

## SECTION 7:   TRAINING PLAN

## 7.1 Objective

*The objective of this section is to define the project's training responsibilities.*

## 7.2 Discussion

*There are two categories of training: internal (training your own people) and external (training the customer, the system contractor, and others).*

## 7.3 Detail

7.3.1  Internal Training
      7.3.1.1  Technical
            (a)  coding languages
            (b)  use of test tools
            (c)  desktop resources
            (d)  data-processing hardware
            (e)  interfacing with other subsystems
            (f)  the problem
            (g)  baseline design
      7.3.1.2  Nontechnical
            (a)  management techniques
            (b)  change management procedures
            (c)  documentation control
            (d)  reporting requirements
            (e)  clerical procedures
7.3.2  External Training
      7.3.2.1  Installing the software
      7.3.2.2  Using the system
      7.3.2.3  Modifying the system
7.3.3  Resources
      *For each type of training identified show:*
      7.3.3.1  Training schedules
      7.3.3.2  Instructors required
      7.3.3.3  Training materials
      7.3.3.4  Facilities (classrooms, computers, etc. )
      7.3.3.5  Numbers of trainees
      7.3.3.6  Special computer programs for training

## SECTION 8:   REVIEW AND REPORTING PLAN

## 8.1 Objective

*The objective of this section is to describe the means of reviewing and reporting progress.*

## 8.2 Discussion

*There is informal review and reporting going on at all levels more or less continuously. This plan addresses not the informal, but rather the formal reviewing and reporting. The Discussion subsection should describe in a general way the reporting structure. It should stress the importance of making financial and technical reports consistent with one another.*

## 8.3 Detail

8.3.1 Reviews

    8.3.1.1  Internal Reviews

        *Participants in each internal review include project members and outside reviewers.*

        (a)  Definition Process Review

            *When: End of Definition Process*

            *Objectives: To review the Problem Specification and determine readiness for the Design Process; to review and assess the Project Plan; to review acceptance criteria.*

        (b)  Preliminary Design Review

            *When: Midway in the Design Process*

            *Objective: To review the baseline design, as far as it has been developed, in order to assure the validity of the design approach.*

        (c)  Design Process Review

            *When: End of Design Process.*

            *Objectives: To review the completed Design Specification to determine whether or not it satisfies the Problem Specification and is reasonable and programmable; to review the Project Plan.* ***Include outside reviewers.***

        (d)  Programming Process Review

            *When: End of Programming Process.*

            *Objectives: To review program integration results and determine readiness for the System Test Process; to review program documentation.*

(e)  System Test Process Review

*When: End of System Test Process.*

*Objectives: To review system test results and determine readiness for the Acceptance Process; to review program documentation.*

(f)  Postmortem Review

*When: End of Acceptance Process or Operational Process.*

*Objective: To review and approve the Project History document.*

8.3.1.2  External Reviews

*Participants in each of these reviews include representatives of the contractor and the customer.*

(a)  Preliminary Design Review

*When: Midway in Design Process, after internal review.*

*Objective: To review the validity of the design approach.*

(b)  Design Review

*When: At the end of the Design Process, after internal review.*

*Objectives: To review in detail and concur on the Design Specification; to review the contractor's Project Plan in preparation for entering the Programming Process.*

(c)  Acceptance Review

*When: End of Acceptance Process.*

*Objective: To review the results of the completed acceptance tests and determine any remaining problems that must be corrected before the customer will formally accept the programs.*

8.3.1.3  Formal Inspections

*A formal inspection is held whenever there is a product (a design, code, test plan, user manual, anything) ready for a close look by other project members. It is directed by someone who has been trained in inspection techniques and it uses a checklist of commonly encountered defects. The objective is to find errors, not to report status.*

8.3.2  Reports

8.3.2.1  Generated by Nonmanagers

(a)  Frequency: *biweekly.*

(b)  To: *immediate manager.*

(c)  Format: *Technical Status Report (see Documentation Plan).*

(d)  Scope: *one report for each task assigned.*

8.3.2.2  Generated by Managers

(a)  Frequency: *biweekly.*

(b)  To: *immediate manager.*

(c)  Format: *Technical Status Report.*

(d)  Scope: *one report for each milestone task.*

8.3.2.3  Generated by Project Manager

    (a)  Frequency: *monthly and quarterly. A quarterly report should replace the monthly report normally due at that time.*

    (b)  To*: company management and customer.*

    (c)  Format: *depends on company and customer requirements, but should include these types of information:*

        ➤ technical status of major tasks

        ➤ milestones met

        ➤ milestones missed; why; remedial action

        ➤ significant problems

        ➤ financial status, expenditures vs. budget

8.3.2.4  Generated by Company Staff

*Describe reports fed back to project management by the company. These reports are usually financial and might include actual cost information for the current week, actual vs. budget data for the current month, and a picture of the project's overall financial status thus far.*

## SECTION 9:    INSTALLATION AND OPERATION PLAN

## 9.1 Objective

*The objective of this section is to define the contractor's responsibilities for installing and operating the accepted software system. The Installation and Operation Plan includes the migration plan.*

## 9.2 Discussion

*The amount of participation by a contractor in installing and operating a system he has delivered is a variable from one project to the next. In this subsection, describe the degree of this involvement for your project.*

## 9.3 Detail

9.3.1  Installation
    9.3.1.1  Responsibility
    9.3.1.2  Schedule
    9.3.1.3  Migration
       (a)  Strategy
          *Phased introduction of functionality. Phased introduction by business units. Schedule drivers, etc.*
       (b)  Method
          *Parallel operation, immediate replacement, etc.*
       (c)  Cutover criteria
          *How to decide to cut off the old system and rely on the new.*
       (d)  Who makes cutover decision
       (e)  Fallback positions if system fails
    9.3.1.4  Introduction of Data
       (a)  Who gathers data
       (b)  Who validates data
       (c)  Who manages the data conversion process
    9.3.1.5  Multiple-Site Considerations
       (a)  Site installation teams
       (b)  Site-to-site coordination
9.3.2 Operation
    9.3.2.1  Responsibility for Operation
    9.3.2.2  Responsibility for Maintenance and Tuning
       (a)  Change Management procedures
       (b)  Work location
       (c)  Funding
    9.3.2.3  Duration of Responsibilities

## SECTION 10: RESOURCES AND DELIVERABLES PLAN

### 10.1 Objective

*The objective of this section is to gather in one place a summary of all resource estimates and a schedule for all deliverables.*

### 10.2 Discussion

*Various resources, schedules, and deliverable items are mentioned or implied in other sections of the Project Plan. Here they are all tied together and made explicit.*

### 10.3 Detail

10.3.1   Manpower
*A chart showing total manpower planned for the project on a monthly basis. A main chart should show two broad categories: programming and nonprogramming manpower. Included in the first are programmers and their first-level managers; in the second are all other kinds of manpower. Supporting charts should break down the two categories into more detail.*

*If the project is large and if there are a number of major program subsystems, show separate manpower charts for each. Examples of major subsystems might be an operating system; tactical programs; support programs; maintenance and diagnostic programs.*

*If the Project Plan calls for a number of releases of the complete software system, show manpower for each release separately.*

10.3.2   Computer Resources
*Show monthly computer resource requirements (dedicated processor time, storage, terminals and other peripherals, supplies) broken down by program release, by major program subsystem within release, and by use category: module/integration test, system test, acceptance test, site test. If more than one type of computer installation is used (for example, contractor's facility, customer's facility) show separate estimates. Show computer resources separately for other categories, such as project administrative uses.*

10.3.3   Other Resources
10.3.3.1 Publications Costs
  (a)  Reports
  (b)  Problem Specification
  (c)  Design Specification
  (d)  Coding Specifications
  (e)  User documents
  (f)  Test documents

10.3.3.2  Travel Costs
  (a)  To contractor's own facilities
  (b)  To customer facilities
  (c)  To other contractors' facilities
  (d)  To test sites
10.3.3.3  Relocation of Employees and Equipment
10.3.3.4  Equipment and Supplies
10.3.3.5  Special Purchases or Rentals
  *Such items as extra office space or temporary quarters in trailers.*

10.3.4 Delivery Schedules
 *Chart(s) showing dates for all deliverables called for in the contract or in any subsequent agreements; accompanying the chart should be a set of narrative capsule descriptions of each item shown on the chart.*

10.3.5 Milestones Chart
 *A chart showing all milestones against which reports to the customer are to be made. A good base for this chart would be a variation of Figure I (inside front cover). It's helpful to show milestones overlaid on a development cycle, so that one can better relate each milestone to the planned major activities, that is, the processes. Include a separate sheet giving a capsule description of each milestone indicated on the chart.*

10.3.6 Budget
 *A copy of the financial budget showing how funds are allocated to each of the cost categories shown in preceding sections. As estimates are reconsidered and changed, the budget must change. When that happens, this subsection must be updated to reflect the change.*

## SECTION 11: PROJECT PLAN INDEX

*A conventional index of major subjects to help the reader find topics within the Project Plan. A few hours' attention to an index will render the entire plan more useful.*

# References and Selected Bibliography

Albrecht, A. J. "Measuring Application Development Productivity." *Proceedings of the Joint IBM/SHARE/GUIDE Application Development Symposium*, October 1979, pp. 83–92.

Aron, J. D. "The Superprogrammer Project." In *Software Engineering Techniques*, ed. J. N. Buxton and B. Randell (Brussels: NATO SCIENTIFIC Affairs Division, 1970), pp. 50–52.

Augustine, Norman R. *Augustine's Laws* (New York: Viking Penguin, 1986).

Autry, James. *Love and Profit* (New York: Avon, 1992).

Baker, F. T. "Chief Programmer Team Management of Production Programming." *IBM Systems Journal* 11, no. 1 (1972): pp. 56–73.

———. "Structured Programming in a Production Programming Environment." *IEEE Transactions on Software Engineering*, no. 2 (June 1975): SE-1.

———. "System Quality Through Structured Programming." *Proceedings, AFIPS 1972 FJCC*, 41 (1972): 339–43.

Beizer, Boris. *Software Testing Techniques* (New York: Van Nostrand and Reinhold, 1990).

Boehm, B.W. *Software Engineering Economics* (Englewood Cliffs, NJ: Prentice-Hall, 1981).

———. "Software Engineering." *IEEE Transactions on Software Engineering*, December 1976.

Bohm, Corrado, and Guiseppe Jacopini. "Flow Diagrams, Turing Machines, and Languages with Only Two Formation Rules." *Communications of the ACM* 9 (May 1966): 366–71.

Booch, Grady. *Object-Oriented Analysis and Design* (Redwood City, CA: Benjamin/Cummings,1994), pp. 39, 137.

Brooks, Frederick P., Jr. *The Mythical Man-Month: Essays on Software Engineering* (Reading, MA: Addison-Wesley, 1975). Timeless observation and advice on the software business, delivered with wit and clarity—the book all writers in this field wish they had written.

————. "No Silver Bullet: Essence and Accidents of Software Engineering." *IEEE Computer*, 20, no. 4 (April 1987): 10–19.

Coad, Peter, and Edward Yourdon. *Object-Oriented Analysis.* (Englewood Cliffs, NJ: Prentice-Hall, 1990).

————. *Object-Oriented Systems Design* (Englewood Cliffs, NJ: Prentice-Hall/Yourdon Press, 1994).

Churchman, Charles W., Russell L. Ackoff, and E. Leonard Arnoff, *Introduction to Operations Research* (New York: Wiley, 1957), pp. 411–14.

*Communications of the ACM* 36, no. 10 (October 1993). This issue has a special section called "Project Organization and Management" containing nine thoughtful articles that explore many facets of software development, including team approaches.

Currid, Cheryl. *The Electronic Invasion* (New York: Brady Publishing, 1993). A good introduction to office electronics—E-mail, LAN, etc.

Davis, Alan M. *Software Requirements: Objects, Functions, and States* (Englewood Cliffs, NJ: Prentice-Hall, 1993). An excellent, highly readable coverage of all aspects of software requirements specification. Presents many analysis techniques without an axe to grind for any one of them.

DeBono, Edward. *The Five-Day Course in Thinking* (New York: Basic Books, 1967).

DeMarco, Tom. *Controlling Software Projects: Management, Measurement and Estimation* (New York: Yourdon Press, 1982).

————. *Structured Analysis and System Specification* (Englewood Cliffs, NJ: Prentice-Hall, 1979), p. 41. Along with Edward Yourdon, DeMarco was responsible for early and continuing work on some of the more popular and widely used structured techniques. Like Yourdon, he writes about complex subjects in a straightforward and enjoyable way.

DeMarco, Tom, and Timothy Lister. *Peopleware: Productive Projects and Teams* (New York: Dorset House, 1987). *Must* reading for every programming manager. Valuable insight into the people who populate programming projects, told with humor and warmth.

Dreger, J. Brian. *Function Point Analysis* (Englewood Cliffs, NJ, Prentice-Hall, 1989), p. 5. An excellent introduction to Function Point Analysis with good examples you can use for self-training.

East, E. William, and Jeffrey G. Kirby. *A Guide to Computerized Project Scheduling* (New York: Van Nostrand Reinhold, 1990). A good introduction to CPM, PERT, bar charts, and milestones, but slanted toward construction projects, not software projects.

Fellows, Lawrence. "Never Too Late," *Evening Star* (Washington, DC), July 12, 1971.

Fisher, Alan S., *CASE: Using Software Development Tools, Second Edition* (New York: John Wiley & Sons, 1991), p. 153. A good introduction to CASE tools. Covers their beginnings, where they fit in, and current, specific packages. Describes CASE current dependence on underlying structured methodologies and discusses emerging technologies, such as object-oriented programs and their relation to CASE.

Gane, Chris, and Trish Sarson. *Structured Systems Analysis: Tools and Techniques* (New York: Improved Systems Technologies, 1977).

Garment, Suzanne. "Give Them the Papers." *Washington Post*, January 9, 1994, p. C7.

Grady, Robert B. *Practical Software Metrics for Project Management and Process Improvement* (Englewood Cliffs, NJ: Prentice-Hall, 1992).

Gunning, Robert. *The Technique of Clear Writing* (New York: McGraw-Hill, 1968).

Hughes, Joan, and Jay Michton. *A Structured Approach to Programming* (Englewood Cliffs, NJ: Prentice-Hall, 1977).

Humphrey, Watts. *A Discipline for Software Engineering* (New York: Addison-Wesley, 1995).

Hyman, Risa. "Creative Chaos in High-Performance Teams: An Experience Report." *Communications of the ACM*, 36 (October 1993): 57ff

International Function Point Users Group (IFPUG), Blendonview Office Park, 5008-28 Pine Creek Drive, Westerville, OH 43081-4899; Fax (614) 895–3466

Jackson, Michael. *Principles of Program Design* (New York: Academic Press, 1975).

———. *System Development* (Englewood Cliffs, NJ: Prentice-Hall, 1983).

Jones, Capers. *Programming Productivity* (New York: McGraw-Hill, 1986). An excellent discussion of the status of attempts to measure and quantify software productivity. Covers the impact of dozens of factors on productivity and estimates, and discusses bases for estimates other than lines of code.

Kepner, Charles H., and Benjamin Tregoe. *The Rational Manager* (New York: McGraw-Hill, 1965).

Kolowich, Michael. "Is the Business World Ready for Object-Oriented Software?" *PC Computing,* November 1991, p. 72.

Kreitzberg, C., and B. Schneiderman. *The Elements of FORTRAN Style* (New York: Harcourt Brace Jovanovitch, 1971).

Lecht, Charles. P. *The Management of Computer Programming Projects* (New York: American Management Association, 1967).

Linger, Richard C., Harlan D. Mills, and Bernard I. Witt. *Structured Programming: Theory and Practice* (Reading, MA: Addison-Wesley, 1979), p. 1.

McConnell, Steven C. *Code Complete: A Practical Handbook of Software Construction* (Redmond, WA: Microsoft Press, 1993).

McDonald, Paul R. *Proposal Preparation Manual* (Covina, CA: Procurement Associates, 1968).

McGowan, Clement, and John Kelly. *Top-Down Structured Programming Techniques* (New York: Petrocelli/Charter, 1975), pp. 97, 125–32, 148.

McMenamin, Stephen M., and John F. Palmer. *Essential Systems Analysis* (New York: Yourdon Press, 1984).

Maguire, Stephen A. *Debugging the Development Process: Practical Strategies for Staying Focused, Hitting Ship Dates, and Building Solid Teams* (Redmond, WA: Microsoft Press, 1994).

Maltz, Maxwell. *Psycho-Cybernetics* (New York: Pocket Books, 1969), pp. 19–20.

Martin, James. *An Information Systems Manifesto* (Englewood Cliffs, NJ: Prentice-Hall, 1984).

Martin, James, and Carma McClure. *Structured Techniques: The Basis for CASE* (Englewood Cliffs, NJ: Prentice-Hall, 1988). An assessment of the need for structured techniques as the foundation for CASE tools. Includes an excellent account of the evolution of programming techniques.

Metzger, Philip W. *Programming Project Management Guide* (Gaithersburg, MD: International Business Machines Corporation, 1970).

Mills, Harlan D. "Human Productivity in Software Development," unpublished paper, 1976.

————. "Software Transactions." *IEEE Transactions on Software Engineering*, no. 4 (December 1976): SE-2.

Musa, John D., Anthony Iannino, and Kazuhira Okumoto. *Software Reliability.* (New York: McGraw-Hill, 1987), p. 72

Nelson, E. A. *Management Handbook for the Estimation of Computer Programming Costs* (Santa Monica, CA: System Development Corporation, 1967). An ancient book with some still-valuable advice; the source for much of the information in Figure 1–14.

Orlicky, Joseph. *The Successful Computer System* (New York: McGraw-Hill, 1969), pp. 111, 113.

Pietrasanta, A. M., "Managing the Economics of Computer Programming." *Proceedings of the 23rd National Conference, Association for Computing Machinery*, 1968, pp. 341–46.

Pirsig, Robert M. *Lila: An Inquiry into Morals* (New York: Bantam Books, 1991), p. 336.

Plauger, P. J. *Programming on Purpose* (Englewood Cliffs, NJ: Prentice-Hall, 1993), p. 65. A compilation of twenty-six essays ranging all over the software business. Witty, delightful, informative. A second volume is also available.

Rettig, Marc, and Gary Simons. "A Project Planning and Development Process for Small Teams." *Communications of the ACM* 36, no. 10 (October 1993): 54.

Ruhl, Janet. *The Programmer's Survival Guide* (Englewood Cliffs, NJ: Prentice-Hall/ Yourdon Press, 1989), p. 213

Schneiderman, Ben. *Software Psychology* (Cambridge, MA: Winthrop Publishers, 1980), p. 62.

Stevens, W. P., G. J. Meyers, and L. L. Constantine. "Structured Design." *IBM Systems Journal* 13, no. 2 (1974).

Strunk, William, Jr., and E. B. White. *The Elements of Style* (New York: Macmillan Publishing, 1979). You can pick up this paperback gem for about two bucks. It's a tiny book (85 small pages) but it contains a big bookful of writing help.

Thomsett, Rob. *Third Wave Project Management* (Englewood Cliffs, NJ: Prentice-Hall/Yourdon Press, 1993).

Townsend, Robert A. *Up the Organization* (New York: Alfred A. Knopf, 1970), pp. 11, 36, 37.

*Understanding Computers* (Alexandria, VA: Time-Life Books, 1989). The volumes entitled *Software* and *Computer Basics* present a fascinating history of computers and software.

*USA Today*, June 27, 1986.

Watson, Thomas J., Jr., and Peter Petre. *Father, Son, & Co: My Life at IBM and Beyond* (New York: Bantam Books), pp. 316, 322.

Weinberg, Gerald M. *The Psychology of Computer Programming* (New York: Van Nostrand Reinhold, 1971).

————. *Understanding the Professional Programmer* (Boston: Little Brown & Co., Boston, 1982), p. 11.

Will, George F. *Washington Post*, October 4, 1992.

Wood, Jane, and Denise Silver. *Joint Application Design* (New York: John Wiley, 1989).

Yourdon, Edward. *Managing the Structured Techniques,* 4th ed. (Englewood Cliffs, NJ: Prentice-Hall, 1989). An eminently readable description of structured techniques by one of the founders of these techniques. Covers structured analysis, design, and programming; top-down design and testing; walkthroughs; and more. Must reading for any programming manager.

———— *Techniques of Program Structure and Design.* (Englewood Cliffs, NJ: Prentice-Hall, 1975).

Zuboff, Shoshanna. *In the Age of the Smart Machine: The Future of Work and Power* (New York: Basic Books, 1988).

# Index